THE AUTISM *of* GXD

THE AUTISM *of* GXD

An Atheological Love Story

RUTH M. DUNSTER

Foreword by David Jasper

PICKWICK Publications • Eugene, Oregon

THE AUTISM OF GXD
An Atheological Love Story

Copyright © 2022 Ruth M. Dunster. All rights reserved. Except for brief quotations in critical publications or reviews, no part of this book may be reproduced in any manner without prior written permission from the publisher. Write: Permissions, Wipf and Stock Publishers, 199 W. 8th Ave., Suite 3, Eugene, OR 97401.

Pickwick Publications
An Imprint of Wipf and Stock Publishers
199 W. 8th Ave., Suite 3
Eugene, OR 97401

www.wipfandstock.com

PAPERBACK ISBN: 978-1-7252-6835-7
HARDCOVER ISBN: 978-1-7252-6833-3
EBOOK ISBN: 978-1-7252-6834-0

Cataloguing-in-Publication data:

Names: Dunster, Ruth, author. | Jasper, David, foreword.

Title: The autism of Gxd : an atheological love story / Ruth Dunster ; foreword by David Jasper.

Description: Eugene, OR : Pickwick Publications, 2022 | Includes bibliographical references and index.

Identifiers: ISBN 978-1-7252-6835-7 (paperback) | ISBN 978-1-7252-6833-3 (hardcover) | ISBN 978-1-7252-6834-0 (ebook)

Subjects: LCSH: Autism—Religious aspects—Christianity. | Autism—Religious life. | Religion—Philosophy. | Church and social problems. | Theology. | Christianity and the arts. | Arts and religion. | Christianity and literature. | Religion and literature.

Classification: RC553.A88 D84 2022 (paperback) | RC553.A88 D84 (ebook)

VERSION NUMBER 111022

"Little Gidding" by T S Eliot reproduced with kind permission of Faber & Faber.

"At Our House" by William Stafford reproduced with kind permission of the Estate of William Stafford.

"St Francis, Jongleur de Dieu" (illustration) by r. Lentz, reproduced by kind permission of Trinity Stores 10200 Park Meadows Drive, #2324 Lone Tree, CO 80124, 720–344–9212

"Chop Suey!" Words and Music by Daron Malakian, John Dolmayan, Shavo Odadjian and Serj Tankian (System of a Down). Copyright (c) 2001 Sony Music Publishing (US) LLC, Ddevil Music and ilovecoffee Administered by Sony Music. Reprinted by Permission of Hal Leonard LLC.

Cover Art: "Solitude" ©Kit Dunster

For David Jasper and Paul Dunster

R Dunster
3/2/23

To Paul & Ena with love and gratitude for your support.

Contents

Images | ix
Foreword by David Jasper | xi
Acknowledgments | xv
Read Me | xvii

Where to Begin? | 1
By My-self | 3
Our Theology: A Beginner's Guide | 5
Our Approach to Autism: A Beginner's Guide | 28
Introduction: What Does This Book Do? | 45

CHAPTER ONE
The Autistic Trinity | 60

CHAPTER TWO
Literal Metaphor and Incarnational Metaphor | 95

CHAPTER THREE
The Autism of Apophatic Fiction | 144

CHAPTER FOUR
The Autism of Gxd | 209

CHAPTER FIVE
The Autism of Poetry | 268

CHAPTER SIX
The Autism of Nothing | 299

By One-Self: In the End, One Is by One's Self | 350

A Last Word from Paul | 360

Glossary | 363

Bibliography | 391

Index | 409

Images

DIAGRAMS

Figure i. The Trinity of Autistic Attributes | 74

Figure ii. The Trinity of Mythical Autism | 85

Figure iii. Neurotypical and Autistic Horizons | 105

Figure iv. Absolute Mindblindness: Zero Sharing of Horizons | 106

ILLUSTRATIONS

Illustration i. St Francis, Jongleur de Dieu by r. Lentz, Trinity Stores | 70

Illustration ii. Piety and Divinity by Paul Douglas Dunster | 359

Foreword
by David Jasper

This is an extraordinary book that "works" on a number of different levels. It is at once deeply personal, learned, theologically radical, interdisciplinary, and highly original. It covers an enormous field, making considerable demands on the reader, yet at the same time it is highly readable, indeed, absorbing. It begins with two beginner's guides—the first to theology and the second to autism, guides that are already rooted in an initial, startling statement by Ruth Dunster: "Autism and the indissoluble, intuitive search for God have been my curse . . . [and] also my deepest blessing." These guides are offered as optional, but in fact they set the scene for the book at the very heart of its two preoccupations—Gxd and autism. (I leave Ruth to explain the spelling.)

    All good theology and religious reflection begin with provocation. Can Gxd be autistic? It is a shocking question. But even more: can Gxd be somehow impaired, ab-normal or disordered? Or is this question a deliberate displacement, another example of the gospel formula, "you have always thought, but I say to you"; a radical shifting of the ground beneath our feet so that we might begin to see more clearly? Another way to see it is as a new hermeneutic, a new way of reading things. If what *we* see as metaphors are simply read *literally*, is this an example of abnormality or at best eccentricity, or the beginning of another powerful way of seeing and knowing. And it may not just be "another way" but the beginning of radically new insights about language, the world, and our theology. Our narrow band of social normality and comprehension is suddenly expanded and we are called to be attentive to new ways of seeing and knowing that enliven and are enlivened by the great theologians of the apophatic (Ruth will explain that word too), above all St. Teresa of Avila and St. John of the Cross.

Ruth Dunster knows her Christian theology and more, and she confidently establishes her narrative in the traditions of Thomas Aquinas and Duns Scotus, Karl Barth and Paul Tillich, Kierkegaard and Wittgenstein. There is no cutting of corners. But above all, and most significantly, she celebrates the extraordinary and radical a-theology of Thomas Altizer, who wrote and spoke his theology of the death of God on the far edge of language, syntax almost shattered by vision of the *coincidentia oppositorum*—the coincidence of opposites. Altizer was a God-haunted man of searing honesty, and he would have understood the poetic profundity of this book perfectly.

For indeed this book, and the autism of Gxd, can only be finally understood as a theological poetics. That is, this is not a poetics that serves as a handmaid to theology, but a poetics that *is* theological in its own mysterious heart and being, its *haecceitas*. It was such a poetics that drove Gerard Manley Hopkins to write and finally, as poet and priest, tore him apart. Ruth Dunster knows well that the heart of her book is not the theologian, in the end, but the poet and writer—Blake, Hopkins, Pirandello—visionaries who are doomed to be misunderstood, as were Teresa and John of the Cross in their own time.

This book is not a comfortable read, but it offers a genuinely radical and necessary vision of the autism of Gxd, a vision that those who feel comfortable and supported at the center of worldly norms and the establishments of churches will find it hard to accept but difficult to dismiss, if they are honest. The Jesus of the gospels was ultimately a lonely and eccentric figure, but one whom we ignore at our peril and can only accept in faith. I commend this courageous book to the attentive reader who is prepared to read it as a love story that expands our boundaries of the normal.

We read here of the Ascent of Mount Carmel by St. John of the Cross. Many years ago, I gave this poem to a group of theology students, not telling what it was or who wrote it. They read it as a love poem, which it is, but they were puzzled why we were reading it in a class dedicated to theological studies. It is a small illustration of how we live within boundaries that need to be expanded and sometimes demolished if we are to perceive the truth of the matter. You will find that this is what this book does, so be prepared to follow.

David Jasper

Acknowledgments

If they were here, I would thank my late mother, Marnie Jack, and the courageous, late atheologian Thomas J. J. Altizer, for both asking such probing questions and then encouraging me to keep going. I have a huge debt of gratitude also to Canon Professor David Jasper who has helped so much over the years to guide me toward making this book possible, and for his incisive comments during the writing of this book. His work, along with that of others at the Centre for Literature, Theology, and the Arts at the University of Glasgow, supported me on my journey toward this book. Patricia Durham has also wonderfully supported and encouraged me with her friendship and helpful comments while engaging with my work. I owe a debt of gratitude to my friend Alastair Clarkson for introducing me to his concept of The Sensory Connoisseur.

    Thanks to those also who have commented, helped, and discussed along the way: Dr. Iida Saarinen, Annita Macdonald, my daughter Dr. Joanna Dunster, Eva Spivak, and Mike Dunster. I am particularly grateful to Dr. Jonathan Birch, whose insightful theological dialogue with this work has been so generously given.

    Thanks to "Bean's Daddy" for permission to quote from the Autistic Bean blog.

Many, profuse thanks to my offspring, Kit Dunster, for diagrams and for cover art, and huge thanks to Trudy Lynn for proofreading and editorial conversations. Lastly, my thanks to my son, Paul Dunster, for his honest, atheist, autistic response to my thinking, and, not least, for his faithfully engaging and interrogating my work with the right, searching questions—which has been a beautiful experience.

Read Me

"You must finish this book—it's what your whole life has led up to," my mother, Marnie Jack, told me, a matter of weeks before she passed away. "I could see this having a real impact," the atheologian Tom Altizer emailed me, a matter of months before he also passed away.

    Why did these two very different people sense why this book needed to be written? My mum belonged to the generation where women of her social class were expected to become the secretary of a man, and then to give up their work to marry a man. She did not have a university education or, in fact, anything like as much education as her keen mind wanted. But she knew me. She had watched me wrestle with Gxd over a lifetime, struggling both for an adequate personal relationship and for an adequate intellectual apparatus. After all, women of my generation had been told to leave theology to the men, and it was only later in my life when it became acceptable for women like me to become theologians. She had also watched my clumsy attempts at life in general. She had seen the distress it caused until, during my graduate theology studies (I was by then in my forties), I was diagnosed with Asperger's Syndrome—a high-functioning form of autism. Mum understood that this book could be written by someone who had lived with Gxd, with autism, and with a struggle to find theological moorings.

Tom Altizer became central to my theological project when I grasped that his death of Gxd theology was a profound metaphor for exile, and the exile of our times from much that has been stable and familiar, at the end of Western Christendom. My lifelong experience had been exile from the world of "normal" people, with autism diagnosed and undiagnosed, and I sensed that this exile, as the Quakers say, "spoke to my condition."

Therefore, this book, *The Autism of Gxd,* took shape with their encouragement. However, as well as encouragement, I also needed to be taught, and specifically, to be taught to read. Delayed skills are common in children with autism, and I remember my mother patiently going over the shapes of letters and words until I both knew and loved them. Rudolf Bultmann writes that without the experience of a range of emotions—love, jealousy, rage—it is impossible to understand a novel. So, post-diagnosis, as I gained the confidence of self-understanding, I learned to interact with other human beings, however imperfectly. I learned to experience and, equally importantly, to identify and name the range of human emotions. Novels, plays, and poems came to life for me! But there was still one piece of the jigsaw to be found and that was how to read as a theologian. Unsurprisingly, perhaps, I had been drawn, early in my dealings with Gxd, to a fairly literalist Evangelicalism. For reasons that will become apparent in this book, it appeared the perfect fit. And yet, as my cognitive and emotional life developed, I realized I had too narrow an intellectual and emotional bandwidth. I was hungry to explore other ways to "play with Gxd." My teacher, David Jasper of the University of Glasgow, was Professor of Literature, Theology, and the Arts. How perfect for someone whose love of the word and the Word was growing exponentially. David patiently taught me to read both, and their glorious interaction one with the other.

Both autism and the indissoluble, intuitive search for a Gxd have been my curse, as life has been complicated and painful. It has also been my deepest blessing, as my autistic attentiveness to the world and all therein has been fulfilled with a beauty beyond all I dared to hope.

I hope this book will convey how unique this autistic searching after Gxd truly is. I hope it will also convey how valuable these insights might be for the wider world, who do not possess this curse and this blessing.

Please note—readers unfamiliar with theology can turn to "Our Theology: A Beginner's Guide"; readers unfamiliar with autism can look at "Our Approach to Autism: A Beginner's Guide"; or, of course, both, or neither! I hope these sections will be useful to refer to, along with the glossary at the back of the book. I have put these Beginner's Guides before the main body of the Introduction so you can approach it with an idea of what the technical terms mean.

Perhaps, although I hesitate, I will give a "spoiler alert." This book is likely to offend; it will offend some people's intellectual sensibilities; it will offend many people's theological convictions. If you read on, I will come to the (non)conclusion that "this is all nonsense" in chapter 5; but I do drop hints along the way that we are in a strange territory that makes sense only when it "makes no sense." Perhaps it helps if I say that, in the end, this book is really a poem, or even a strange hymn. The question is whether or not you sing along.

First, however, the question: where to begin?

Where to Begin?

Why do I write not "God" but Gxd? This is the question of Gxd's "x." Really, I would prefer that you think this through as a polysemic riddle; in other words, there are a number of ways to interpret this word, and it is for you to ponder which one, or ones, might be valid. Chapter 4 will reveal at least one of these answers. X marks the spot . . . of hidden treasure, of a kiss, a multiplication, a crossing out, a non-gender . . . ? You must decide for yourself. Now we can begin.

What is the autism of Gxd? Doesn't this make Gxd some kind of impaired being?

> People with ASD tend to have communication deficits, such as responding inappropriately in conversations, misreading nonverbal interactions, or having difficulty building friendships appropriate to their age. In addition, people with ASD may be overly dependent on routines, highly sensitive to changes in their environment, or intensely focused on inappropriate items.[1]

ASD (Autistic Spectrum Disorder), for sure, is a dis-ability.

Carers (but perhaps not so often autists themselves) have been known to claim that Gxd "heals" autism, or that

---

1. American Psychiatric Association, "Autism Spectrum Disorder," 1.

Gxd can be known "in spite of" autism; autism remains an impairment which needs to be managed, or even, if possible, removed (with a (covert) sigh of relief, all too often) in the faith community. The faith community, and by implication, "God," are the "safe," normative world of non-autism.

So, is the idea of Gxd's autism absurd? This absurdity is irreverently depicted with cruel but undeniable humor in the satirical animation series, *Family Guy,* when the characters Peter, Quagmire, Cleveland, and Joe go to heaven to meet Gxd. Gxd, here, is the archetypal old man with a beard, mild, doddery, and an ineffectual meddler. As they leave, Peter goes to give Gxd a hug, and Quagmire tells him, "I wouldn't do that. God doesn't like people touching him—he's mildly autistic."[2] An "autistic God" is everything Christian theology wouldn't want "him" to be. *Family Guy*'s Gxd is funny, and part of an all too incisive commentary on the ineffectiveness of much contemporary religion. And obviously (few things are off-limits in *Family Guy)* autism is the butt of humor here as well.

So we have two concepts here—both an autism and a (stereotypical) God who are all too worthy of satire. Turning both these perceptions upside down is the different, holy blasphemy which this book is intended to express. This means arguing that an autistic theological perspective is a privileged one, speaking from the margins but with a truth which the neurotypical ("normal") world misses to its cost. To suggest the autism of Gxd might also be to offer praise to a Gxd who is known in ways the World misses to its cost. If it is perceived as heresy, it is a divergent heretical view which has the honor of integrity, and is, in fact, like much heresy, profoundly Christian.

---

2. "Acts of God," *Family Guy.*

By My-self

Alternatively:

Firstly, this book challenges, interrogates and celebrates different modes of theological thinking, in a radically counter-cultural way. In this sense, it is a deeply theological project, leading the reader into demanding intellectual questions.

Secondly, it also, however, begins and ends with lived experience: the experience of living with, and observing, autism; and the lifelong experience of wrestling with Gxd. As befits autism's atypicalities, this lived experience leads into the counter-cultural questions which challenge theological norms.

Thirdly, this book embraces art, music, and the poetic. Indeed, autism is cast in the form of a story, and a sacred story at that. This is a radical departure from the stereotype of autism as a positivistic or pedantic condition, and its premise leads to some surprising results.

This particular story, then, (because, be aware, this is a study of myth, personal and theological) arises from the lived experience of autism. Like all stories, it is unique; like all stories, it aims to reach something of the universal. It works by means of myth, and at its core, the myth of the absence of Gxd; autism coming into dialogue, ultimately, with what the atheologian Thomas J. J. Altizer terms *The Gospel of Christian Atheism*.[1]

Lest this seem too much the eccentric preoccupation of one autistic person, let me relate the following story. In 2012, under the auspices of the University of Glasgow and *ASPARRG* (the UK Autistic Spectrum People and Religion Research Group), I co-organized, with the autistic writer and advocate Christopher Barbour, a seminar on Autism and Religion. Christopher and I wondered, with some trepidation, whether anyone would attend, and if so, who. To our surprise, a call for papers produced a fascinating array, including a number of papers written by autists whose "special interest" was in some way religious. We were delighted on the day to find that the seminar was not only so full as to be "standing room only," attended by academics and pastoral/carer specialists, but there were also a fair number of autists themselves (interestingly, largely female autists). It seems that an autistic quest after Gxd is perhaps less incredible than it might seem.

Lastly, the chapters of this book chart a journey of theological discovery, so it is best to read them in the sequence in which they are presented. Here are the Beginner's Guides: feel free to use them, or skip them and go straight to the Introduction (entitled: What does this book do?) which follows them.

---

1. Altizer, *Gospel of Christian Atheism*.

Our Theology
A Beginner's Guide

WHAT IS THEOLOGY?

It might sound strange but, on my journey of wrestling with the Gxd of my autistic understanding, I had a shock of joy upon discovering theology. And I mean that fundamentally—discovering that theology existed, what it is, and is for. My options had been severely limited before studying theology; I hadn't known the most basic ideas of theological debate—for example, that the doctrine of the Trinity (Father, Son and Holy Spirit) hadn't been finally formulated until the fourth century, or that during the early Church's history there had been fierce controversy about whether Jesus was divine, human, or, as the Nicene Council finally decreed, mysteriously both. I had everything to learn. I would love to include my dialogue with other faiths, from many of which I have learned much, but the scope of this book is limited to the Christian tradition. I hope people from all faiths and none could write similar accounts; it would be fascinating to find our points of divergence and agreement.

The word theology comes from two Greek words—*Theos* and *Logos*. *Theos* is god or Gxd, and *Logos* is word, but "word" also in a deeper meaning than how we normally use it—as meaning, as rationale, as truth. In the Beginning, Gxd *said* let there be light—and there was light[1]; the Word, then, is also creative and generative. Jesus, in the Prologue to John's Gospel, is called "the Word"[2]: the Cosmic *Logos*.

My revelation was that it is possible to search for the meaning and significance of that opaque word, Gxd; and to explore different people's searches for that meaning. My church had presented one fixed meaning, which was taken more or less from a literal meaning of the whole of the Bible, with little or no room for questioning or exploring different ways of reading that book and its contents. So I am, however strange it sounds, excited about theology, and I am all too aware that this short introduction cannot even scratch the surface-of-the-surface of an incredible tradition, or traditions, of theological thinking and its dazzling array of thinkers.

Instead, I am going to briefly outline the thinking of the theologians who feature in this book. In following chapters, it will become apparent, if you don't already catch a glimmer, of why they have been chosen. Central to the Autism of Gxd is the twentieth/twenty-first-century American "death of Gxd" theologian, Thomas J. J. Altizer. First, however, in chapter 1, we need to establish our parameters

---

1. Gen 1:3–26.

2. "In the beginning was the Word, and the Word was with God, and the Word was God. He was with God in the beginning. Through him all things were made; without him nothing was made that has been made" (John 1:1); "The Word became flesh and made his dwelling among us. We have seen his glory, the glory of the one and only Son, who came from the Father, full of grace and truth" (John 1:14).

and lay a foundation. What can an autism of Gxd mean? Chapter 2 then explores why this might be approached as poem and story, in terms of myth's use of language. Then, to begin approaching toward Altizer's atheological breakthrough, chapter 3 will turn to mystical theologians before turning to Altizer's "atheology" in chapter 4, along with some of his theological forebears.[3] Each one, like all good theologians, "shook things up," and encouraged Christians to consider new possibilities for approaching *Theos-Logos.* It seems to me that there is a particular resonance for our concept of autism with Altizer. There could be many paths for this book to take, but this, from my own, particular autistic point of view, is the strongest and truest. For this reason, because of the importance of Altizer's twentieth and twenty-first-century writing, there is a focus on the Christian theologians of the twentieth century, with one or two exceptions.

HERMENEUTICS

Before we start, I should say that another amazing concept was explained to me as I studied theology. This concept was *hermeneutics.* Hermeneutics is the study of *how* we examine the messages we receive, and discern them. It means becoming aware of different individual hermeneutics (plural). For example, a historical-critical hermeneutic reads the Bible as a book written in different styles by different, historical authors; an allegorical hermeneutic reads the Bible as a symbolic story from which we can learn, and so on. A large part of the purpose of this book is to develop an *autistic* hermeneutic.

---

3. Chapters 5 and 6 will be "case studies" for how our autistic Gxd might be thought of.

8 THE AUTISM OF GXD

But as you read on, you will be aware (as I had not been) of the fascinating, creative range of hermeneutics each of our theologians develops.

The theologian Werner Jeanrond defines hermeneutics as the theory of interpretation, adding that:

> The word contains a reference to Hermes, the messenger of the gods in Greek mythology. Hermes' task was to explain to humans the decisions and plans of their gods. Thus, he bridged the gap between the divine and the human realm [so that] hermeneutics is concerned with examining the relationship between the two realms, the realms of a text or a work of art on the one hand, and the people who wish to understand it on the other.[4]

He then provides a useful way to think about becoming hermeneutically self-aware:

> The hermeneutical problem may become clearer to us when we recall the odd experience of reading a book for the second time. Such a re-reading often opens up a new reception of the text. We may discover something new, something different in the text, and we may say now that we see the book with different eyes. . . . our perspective has changed. . . . This experience teaches us that understanding is in fact not an automatic and unproblematic exercise of deciphering a set of consistently identical signs on paper . . . it demands that we lend of our reality to the text so that it can become real for us.[5]

If we can "see the text through new eyes," by re-reading it, the implicit logic is that some particular set of "eyes" is always required, as we create our own response and understanding. If different eyes bring different realities

---

4. Jeanrond, *Theological Hermeneutics*, 1.
5. Jeanrond, *Theological Hermeneutics*, 1.

to the text, different hermeneutics create different textual worlds. This is a question not only of technical approach but also of epistemology (how we can know things). For example, the purpose of a historical-critical hermeneutic of the Bible is to bring out the stylistic differences between different parts of Scripture, which make it possible to construct a redaction history.[6] However, underlying this is an (implicit or explicit) set of philosophical, theological, and epistemological assumptions. In this case, it might be that the reader might believe, for example, that the Word of Gxd is divinely and literally inspired; or that the word of Gxd is a human construct; that the Bible contains the Word of Gxd but is not itself the Word; or that we cannot postulate any divine authorship, but only what can be demonstrated in empirical historical terms. The science of hermeneutics establishes that "we never read a text 'objectively' or 'neutrally' . . . no human reader has an unlimited perspective."[7] Consciously or unconsciously, we adopt our own hermeneutic. One could well say that hermeneutics are inescapable; all reading, whether we are aware of it or not, is *interpretive*.

DEISM, NATURAL THEOLOGY, AND LIBERAL THEOLOGY

The Church as an institution no longer has the central place it once had in public life; we have lived through a long period of secularization. In the Enlightenment of the seventeenth and eighteenth centuries in the West, two related forms of belief gained traction. Firstly, Natural

---

6. For example, a redaction historian will see a sudden change of style and content midway through the book of Isaiah, and conclude that the two halves were written by different authors: "Isaiah" and "Deutero-Isaiah."

7. Jeanrond, *Theological Hermeneutics*, 2.

Theology was the belief that we could prove the existence of Gxd without needing Scripture to reveal Gxd—William Paley's famous analogy of the watch and the watchmaker[8] encapsulated this. If a man found a watch on the seashore, he would look at its complexity and workmanship and conclude that there must exist a watchmaker; similarly, looking at the complexity and "workmanship" of a vast and beautiful cosmos should, according to this analogy, lead people to believe that there must be a Creator. Natural theology had a long and venerable history in Christianity, complementing Scriptural authority. However, secondly, in the Enlightenment and related to Natural Theology, was a theological stance known as Deism, from Latin *Deus* (Gxd). *Deus,* unlike *theos,* did not demand particular Christian belief in a personal Gxd, but could have a sense of the divine without needing these clear parameters. This was more a philosophical than a theological Gxd. As Natural Theology and Deism eroded biblical ways of doing theology, the Church began, largely in Protestant countries but also in the French Revolution, to lose its authority. A new form of theology called Liberal Theology attempted to accommodate these belief systems which no longer saw the Bible as completely, historically and literally true. We could perhaps say, rather crudely, that Liberal Theology tried to avoid throwing the baby out with the bathwater. So, for example, a tireless nineteenth-century Scottish Church reformer named Hugh Miller, fighting for social justice and Christian morality, was also a geologist who comfortably explained to his audiences at public lectures that the "days" in which Gxd created the cosmos

---

8. Paley was an eighteenth-century English clergyman and philosopher; this "watchmaker" argument is an example of a teleological argument for the existence of Gxd. (Telos meaning end, or purpose; the world must be created with some design and purpose in mind, and this is also known as the "argument from design").

in the book of Genesis were symbolic representations of vast geological eras. In a sense, this was nothing new—analogy and symbol had had important roles in Medieval theology—but now, in the nineteenth century, there was a sense that the truth of the Bible was altogether more slippery than we might believe.

HEGEL

Georg Wilhelm Friedrich Hegel was a major nineteenth-century German philosopher who conceptualized Gxd as *Geist* (Spirit), as human consciousness evolving. *Geist* is the World-Spirit which develops through history. Hegel's concept of progress was that of dialectic—namely, that when opposing intellectual or spiritual phenomena meet, they cancel each other out through a process of synthesis which results in a new phenomenon, and this is repeated as consciousness develops teleologically[9] throughout history.

HEIDEGGER

Martin Heidegger was a twentieth-century philosopher. Although not a theologian, he is relevant to our theological thinking because of his understanding of phenomenology which, put very simply, is a state of simply being and observing, in the first person, without thoughts or judgements which take us away from the essential experience of "being there," which is an approximate rendition of his most famous term, *Dasein*.

---

9. Teleology means the end or purpose toward which phenomena tend, or for which they exist.

EXISTENTIALISM

We need to explain briefly what Existentialism was (and is). For intellectuals in the early twentieth century, a Gxd-less world meant experiencing both an emancipation and a certain sense of dread and emptiness. By taking charge of our own existence, we face existential questions with new force. The nineteenth-century Christian philosopher-poet Søren Kierkegaard approached the Bible and morality in existential terms, and this was a powerful way for an early Existentialism to view the world. Existentialism then was able to move into altogether non-theistic approaches. Twentieth-century writers such as Jean Paul Sartre, Albert Camus, and (earlier, in the nineteenth century) Fyodor Dostoyevsky explored these questions in philosophical writing which also had a poetic or novelistic form. Dostoyevsky, although not overtly religious except in rare moments, nonetheless could be seen wrestling deeply with questions of faith and in particular, the problem of evil.

KARL BARTH

Into this context of Liberal Theology and Existentialism, a Swiss pastor named Karl Barth emerged in the early twentieth century. Barth came from a family of fairly conservative religious beliefs in the Swiss Reformed Church, but as he was led more and more deeply into theological thinking, he became more and more aware of Liberal Theology. Barth was also profoundly influenced by Existentialism. The two Existentialist thinkers who feature most significantly in Barth's work are Dostoevsky and Kierkegaard, and both of these writers articulate something of the human situation as flawed and uncertain.

In Barth's famous biblical commentary, *The Epistle to the Romans*, he reveals something of his own poetic sensibilities through his use of striking metaphors. *The Epistle to the Romans* was written in 1918—precisely the end of the carnage of the First World War where he had served in the midst of the trauma. A number of his metaphors are taken from the world of war and catastrophe; for example, his metaphors for the cosmic Christ event include "crater," "exploding shell," and "flood."[10] This expresses two separate but undoubtedly related realities. First, Barth's traumatic service in the trench warfare of the First World War clearly influenced his thought. Secondly, however, there is a related but not identical sense that Liberal Theology is not enough to carry us through a world of trauma and uncertainty. Barth termed this trauma and uncertainty *Krisis* and, in his theology, *Krisis* becomes the meeting point where human fallenness, imperfection, and uncertainty are met in Gxd's (and our) own "crisis," with the Incarnation and saving Crucifixion of Christ.

The saving power of the Crucifixion as Christ dying to absolve or annul human sinfulness and guilt was not new in theology. It is a powerful theme in Paul's Epistles, and Medieval Christianity developed various different models for this soteriology (study of Christ as savior). What was new in Barth was that he saw Christ as the answer to Existentialist anxiety, but also as an Existentialist phenomenon. *Krisis* as the meeting point between Gxd and humanity could be where the extremes of guilt in Dostoevsky and uncertainty in Kierkegaard could be thought on a cosmic level. So, Christ as Atonement could be an answer to the Existentialist crisis of the twentieth century.

10. E.g., "the effulgence, or, rather, the crater made at the percussion point of an exploding shell, the void by which the point on the line of intersection makes itself known" (Barth, *Epistle to the Romans*, 29).

DIETRICH BONHOEFFER

Barth survived World War One; however, famously, the German theologian Dietrich Bonhoeffer did not survive World War Two. Unlike many German church leaders, Bonhoeffer preached against National Socialism, and after being found guilty of a failed assassination attempt on Adolf Hitler, was executed by the Nazis—just weeks before the Camps were liberated at the end of the War. Bonhoeffer's theology, it might be surmised, was a very practical one, and two key themes were discipleship and community. There was nothing sentimental about his understanding of these realities of Christian practice, as will be seen. Like Barth, Bonhoeffer's thinking has a flavor of Existentialism. In his letters from prison, he writes in truly opposite terms to any pious platitudes: "The same God who is with us is the one who forsakes us (Mark 15:34)!"[11]

This idea of the absence of Gxd, as we will see later, is not a new one by any means—the Medieval mystics had formulated what the theologian and Church historian Denys Turner calls "The Darkness of God."[12] But in Bonhoeffer, it takes on a particularly urgent quality, where faith is an existential choice demanding action in the face of that apparent desolation; even as the desolation itself is a vital part of his Christology (understanding of Christ) and soteriology (understanding of Christ as Savior):

> Before God, and with God, we live without God. God consents to be pushed out of the world and onto the cross; God is weak and powerless in the world and in precisely this way, and only so, is at our side and

---

11. Bonhoeffer, *Cost of Discipleship*, 478–79. In the Crucifixion: "And at the ninth hour Jesus cried with a loud voice, saying, Eloi, Eloi, lama sabachthani? which is, being interpreted, My God, my God, why hast thou forsaken me?" (Mark 15:34).

12. The title of Turner's historical study of mystical theology.

helps us. Matt. 8:17 makes it quite clear that Christ helps us not by virtue of his omnipotence but rather by virtue of his weakness and suffering! This is the crucial distinction between Christianity and all religions. Human religiosity directs people in need to the power of God in the world, God as *deus ex machina*.[13] The Bible directs people toward the powerlessness and the suffering of God; only the suffering God can help.[14]

This is a powerful narrative from a man who is facing his execution in a Concentration Camp, and it is easy to see that his understanding of what it means to follow Christ would be radical. However, his radical commitment is evident even before this, in his 1937 book *The Cost of Discipleship.* In this theological study, which is also a very practical theology, Bonhoeffer argues that Christianity must mean much more than a formula assented to but not lived through. He calls this cheap grace:

> Cheap grace is the deadly enemy of our Church . . . [it] means grace as a doctrine, a principle, a system . . . an intellectual assent to that idea is held to be of itself sufficient to secure remission of sins . . . no contrition is required, still less any real desire to be delivered from sin. Cheap grace therefore amounts to a denial of the Incarnation of the Word of Gxd.[15]

Bonhoeffer also came to see community-building in very practical ways. He was influenced deeply by time in New York where he saw the depth of both very practical discipleship and community in the black Charismatic churches of Harlem. He also describes the aim of a

---

13. Literally "god from a machine"; in theatre, literally the device of bringing down a god onto the stage by means of pulleys, so that the god can resolve the tensions of the plot and conclude the play; figuratively, a plot element that is inserted into a play to (rather artificially) do the same.
14. Bonhoeffer, *Cost of Discipleship*, 479.
15. Bonhoeffer, *Cost of Discipleship*, 43.

"religion-free" Christianity—the Church freed from oppressive traditions.

PAUL TILLICH

A "good autist" would approach a literal reading of Scripture and say, "but this is nonsense; Gxd didn't make the world in seven days—the earth formed over billions of years." A "good autist" would most likely resemble what Paul Tillich calls the "honest atheist,"[16] and this is, as will be seen, a key to our furnishing of the room which is mythical autism. The German theologian Paul Tillich fled World War II Germany but his conscience called him back; eventually he was persuaded by friends to leave again, and emigrate to the USA. A radical transcendence of Gxd is central to his theology, in order to preserve its integrity. Atheism can be an alluring response to theology when, as Tillich writes,

> In making Gxd an object beside other objects, the existence and nature of which are matters of argument, theology supports the escape to atheism . . . the first step to atheism is always a theology which drags Gxd down to the level of doubtful things. The game of the atheist is then very easy. For he is perfectly justified in destroying such a phantom and all its ghostly qualities.[17]

If Bonhoeffer writes a "religion-less Christianity" from the shock of the existential threat of Nazism, Tillich, like Barth, also writes from the existential threat of the World

---

16. Honest atheism is a fundamental starting point for each chapter, and how they work as a whole; see Mindfulness of Separation in the glossary. Chapters 1 and 3 discuss Christian atheism, and chapter 3 discusses the absence of Gxd encountered in mystical theology. Chapters 4 and 5 see poetic presence as a freedom to absent itself from propositional narrative.

17. Tillich, *Shaking of the Foundations*, 52–53.

OUR THEOLOGY

Wars, so that he can write of *The Shaking of the Foundations*.[18] He is also writing within a theological context where Existentialist thought has raised questions of what he terms "threatenedness." He has read Dostoevsky, Kierkegaard, Nietzsche and other Existentialists, and his theology responds to the weight of their challenge to a traditional Christendom. Tillich's theology of culture is a response to threatenedness which listens to Existentialist thought and argues that

> the human condition always raises fundamental questions which human cultures express in various ways in the dominant styles of their works of art, and to which religious traditions offer answers expressed in religious symbols.[19]

The correlation between art as fundamental question and religion as symbolic answer moves religious discourse into an existential tension where the arts are taken very seriously as an expression of meaning, and religion must answer authentically. This agenda which lifts art beyond a mimetic (representative) function, into something to which religion must answer, is a secularizing one, but by no means a dilution of religious thought. Tillich has been called an atheist, but his "atheism" is not the rejection of powerful Gxd-language, in fact the very opposite. Tillich's atheism is the expression of the majesty of Gxd conceived beyond theism. The theologian David Kelsey comments that for Tillich, Gxd cannot "be a 'supreme being' for, by definition, *any* entity, *any* being, is finite. Hence, Tillich

---

18. The title of the 1949 collection of Tillich's sermons. The (in)famous English John Robinson, bishop of Durham, published *Honest to God* in the 1960s, as Thomas Altizer was writing similarly in the USA. *Honest to God* picked up on Tillich's "a-theist" thinking of Gxd, and, widely misunderstood as a simple atheism, scandalized his British readership.

19. Kelsey, *Fabric of Paul Tillich's Theology*, 64.

refuses to speak of the 'existence' of Gxd."[20] To do so would only make Gxd an object among other objects.

David H. Kelsey expresses Tillich's thinking of the personal authenticity of faith as "the question about our 'ultimate concern.' Whatever concerns us ultimately, says Tillich, is our 'God.'"[21] Religion can easily displace our Ultimate Concern—Gxd—so that

> ... religious ritual, myth or institutions are ambiguous, "functioning religiously" to express the unconditioned ... [but] they invite for themselves the ultimate concern appropriate only to the unconditioned. Thereby they become "demonic," powerfully destructive of the life trying to "transcend" itself.[22]

Tillich provides a thinking of theology as "a/theist" Existentialist authenticity, also in the light of the artistic revolution of Modernism. The death of Gxd movement (which we will consider imminently) can be seen, in a very real way, to rely on this.

THOMAS MERTON

Thomas Merton was an American twentieth-century Trappist monk who converted to Christianity after what the official Merton.org website calls "a rambunctious adolescence and youth."[23] Merton was concerned with social and political issues, particularly the peace and civil rights movements of the American 1960s. He also went on to become deeply engaged with Buddhism, and Eastern religions more generally, establishing dialogue and what

---

20. Kelsey, *Fabric of Paul Tillich's Theology*, 66.
21. Kelsey, *Fabric of Paul Tillich's Theology*, 65.
22. Kelsey, *Fabric of Paul Tillich's Theology*, 70–71.
23. http://merton.org/chrono.aspx.

we might call a Christian-Buddhist (and more generally Eastern) syncretism (fusion).

Merton was a prolific writer on these issues; he is, however, probably best remembered for his writing on contemplative practice, which is poetic and thought-provoking. He issued a caveat about how to read his work:

> One of the things that was misleading about the earlier version of (*New Seeds of Contemplation*) is that it seemed to teach the reader "How to become a contemplative." This was not the author's intention, because it is impossible for one man to teach another "how to become a contemplative." One might as well write a book: "how to be an angel."[24]

Merton is best known for his spiritual autobiography, *The Seven Storey Mountain,* and his contemplative practice as he explains it in his writing has inspired countless readers within and beyond his own Catholicism.

APOPHATIC THEOLOGY: DIONYSIUS AND JOHN OF THE CROSS

We will be focusing a great deal on apophatic theology, but a good place to start is by distinguishing it from its opposite, kataphatic theology. In both cases, the Greek term *phasis* means speech, but *apo-* and *kata-* are opposites.

Translations of the Greek preposition *kata* include "Down from, through, out, according to, toward, along."[25] These are all prepositions of material, spatial or conceptual relation. "According to" is a prepositional phrase which functions as a metaphor of physical connection, to indicate the object partaking in the quality of its subject.

---

24. Merton, *New Seeds of Contemplation*, author's preface, x.
25. Strong's Lexicon of New Testament Greek, "Kata."

So kataphatic discourse expresses a direct connection between subject and object which we can affirm; "Tom is a boy," for example. It can be used to develop systematic theology, which is constructed by using these kinds of predicative statements

The Greek preposition *apo* is translated as follows: "Of separation, distance physical, of distance of place; temporal, of distance of time or origin of the place whence anything is, comes, befalls, is taken of origin or cause."[26] Again, the metaphor is of spatial relation, but a relation which is interrupted. Apophatic theology, then, is discourse which acknowledges the distance of language from Gxd; speaking of that which cannot be spoken. So apophatic theology is also termed negative theology.

Two famous apophatic theologians will be discussed in this book; Dionysius the Areopagite and Saint John of the Cross. (We will also see elements of apophatic theology in the work of Saint Teresa of Àvila, in a slightly different way). Dionysius is thought to have written his works around the sixth century, and John in sixteenth-century Spain. Both share a conviction that in all their language, they can only speak of Gxd as an absence; and yet, paradoxically, absence is the only place where presence ultimately can be found. In his introduction to Dionysius, the Areopagite's *The Mystical Theology and The Divine Names,* C E Rolt encapsulates the need for apophatic discourse very simply; apophatic discourse arises as "merely a bold way of stating the orthodox truism that the Ultimate Godhead is incomprehensible: a truism which Theology accepts as an axiom and then is prone to ignore."[27] This is so in Christian theology because "the various Names

---

26. Strong's Lexicon of New Testament Greek, 14, 40.
27. Dionysius the Areopagite, *Mystical Theology*, 7.

of God are . . . mere inadequate symbols of That Which transcends all thought and existence."[28] This means that, far from annulling or contradicting orthodox theology, apophatic theology expresses what is implicit in orthodox theology. Therefore, negative theology is best understood not as the negation of theology, but the theology of negation.[29]

TERESA OF ÀVILA

Saint Teresa of Àvila was a sixteenth-century Spanish reformer and writer within the Carmelite order of nuns. She is most famous for her inspirational book, *The Interior Castle*. In it, and in the *Life of Saint Teresa by Herself*, are accounts of mystical union with Gxd, the Beloved. These are often read as supernatural events, but it is impossible to verify this. Our approach is to disregard the question of the reality or otherwise of these phenomena, and concentrate on her writing strategies as poetry and theology.

JOHN DUNS SCOTUS

In the Western civilization of the Middle Ages, a huge event occurred which would lay the foundations for the following period, the Renaissance. Most of the ancient Greek philosophers' writing had been lost in the West. However, a number of their works had been preserved in the Islamic world, translated from ancient Greek into Arabic. When these works of philosophy were translated from Arabic into Latin in the thirteenth century, their influence created a shock in the Latin-speaking Western world of Christian philosopher-theologians.

---

28. Dionysius the Areopagite, *Mystical Theology*, 7.
29. See Turner, *Darkness of God*, 22.

Although these Greek philosophers, particularly Plato and Aristotle, were seen as a threat to Christian belief, two theologians, Thomas Aquinas and Duns Scotus did engage with them in fruitful ways. Their work is complex and profound. To some extent, their debate about how to speak about Gxd hinges on two concepts—analogy and univocity. In analogical language, we speak figuratively of something as *like* something else; in univocal language, we are straightforwardly saying that something *is* something else. For example, analogy would say "the sun is like a dazzling ball in the sky," while univocal language might say "the sun is a dazzling ball of burning gases." This matters when speaking about Gxd, as this language corresponds to the very different philosophies of Aristotle and Plato.

Aristotle, although he did not have access to the kind of experimental techniques we have today, used scientific reasoning to classify different concepts and modes of being which he termed categories; primarily, the category of substance, but also general realities such as quality, quantity, and relation. However, he recognized that there were places where the physical properties he had classified did not work; how can we speak of the color of Gxd, the Universal Being and Prime Mover of the universe? Aristotle reasoned that the Universal was present in the physical world, but was not the physical world itself.

By contrast, Plato taught that the Universal, or the spiritual, was totally different to the physical world; the physical world was merely an illusion. In his famous myth of the cave, people chained inside a cave see shadows projected onto the wall. Because the shadows are all that they can see, they assume that those shadows are reality. In this way, Plato taught a form of dualism (two opposing levels or phenomena) where the physical world is only a shadow of the real, and meditation would lead to the ultimate reality.

The Christian thinker Aquinas responded to these issues by stating that language about Gxd was only ever analogy. Duns Scotus responded by insisting that our language about Gxd is true just as it is; when we say "Gxd is love," we mean exactly what our purest love means in our actual existence, although Gxd's love is infinite and perfect, as ours is not. In contrast, Aquinas would teach that our human version of love was a poor imitation of a spiritual property of Love, which existed beyond and could only be spoken of by analogy.

In keeping with his teaching about this "univocity," Scotus develops the concept he terms *haecceitas.* This is in direct contrast to Aquinas' thinking. Following Aristotle, Aquinas develops a "natural philosophy"—what we could now call the science of physics. Aristotle has specified the properties of physical objects according to their properties—form, material, potential, and other ways of considering matter. Underlying all is Being, the Prime Mover, who (as we have seen) can only be described by analogy.

Aquinas, following Aristotle, names these properties by the Latin term *quidditas,* which can be translated as "that-ness." However, Scotus looks at the qualities of physical objects and describes them as them as possessing *haecceitas,* a Latin word which can be translated as "this-ness." "This" instead of "that" might seem simply a matter of grammar, but to these Medieval logicians it meant much more. "That" is a physical quality of this-worldly matter, but "this" is something more immediate—a non-categorical individuation which means that, although this pear belongs to the category of pears along with other ones, its non-categorical individuation (*haecceitas*) makes it its own self, distinct from any other. For Scotus, as a Christian thinker, this is something, in fact, imbued with Spirit. This might seem a huge leap for us, but for Scotus, Gxd within us is an immediacy, a "this," a Gxd-given identity, and to apply the same *haec*—this—to matter in our material world is to assert that a very real identity, Gxd-given, could apply also to the material world. Scotus was developing a doctrine of immanence (the existence of the Spirit present in matter). He was a Franciscan monk, and in this he was not far away from the Founder of his order, Francis of Assisi, whose love of nature, preaching to the animals, and famous *Hymn to Brother Sun and Sister Moon,* all suggest that Francis, in some way, was alert to spiritual qualities within the material world. He was reveling in the divine *Logos* of Creation, which is also the divine *Logos* of Christ.

ATHEOLOGY: THOMAS J. J. ALTIZER

The American theological thinker Thomas J. J. Altizer began his writing career in the early 1960s and continued writing right up to his death in 2018. Altizer very much followed through on Tillich's a-theist theology, in a radical way, to establish the "death of Gxd" school of theology. He attracted controversy and hostility which is perhaps undeserved when his thought is examined more closely. Altizer had been influenced greatly by Paul Tillich, but also by the anthropologist Mircea Eliade, and so his hermeneutic is a literary/mythical one, where Gxd dies on Golgotha in the death of Jesus, and this is a parable for the end of Christendom. This is a shocking proposition—we could see it as a daring return to a Primitive Christianity which seeks to overturn the Church's traditions and doctrines.

Also, more fundamentally, as we shall see, this parable of the end encapsulated in the beginning has a cosmic, existential significance.

Altizer writes that his "three prophets" are William Blake, G.W.F. Hegel, and Friedrich Nietzsche. All three of these men, in different ways, point to a decay of Christianity toward the kind of god-less world which emerges in the twentieth century.

A brief word also needs to be said here about Mircea Eliade, who will feature later. Altizer studied under Eliade and learned an approach which was then (early in his writing, in the 1960s) unusual, and would now be termed as part of Religious Studies. Eliade's work was among primal societies (which were then termed "primitive") and he theorized that sacred story and ritual were not, as was usually thought, primitive attempts at scientific explanations for the natural world. Eliade argued instead that sacred story (i.e., myth) and ritual were expressions of a worldview, not a scientific one but a moral, social and spiritual one.

Therefore, perhaps the important thing to note about Altizer, which is often overlooked and causes confusion, is his very particular hermeneutic. He is consciously using a mythical hermeneutic in reading the Bible. This is not to say that other hermeneutics are invalid; it is merely to say that when the Bible is read as a myth, it can work well as a telling of our particular time in history—a time when Gxd is dead and we have an anonymous Jesus. For Altizer, this can genuinely bring in a new age where, as Bonhoeffer, Tillich and in some ways even Nietzsche also argue, we can know a "religionless Christianity." Except Altizer goes much further, arguing that, in this post-Christendom world, we can only know a crucified Gxd; a Gxd whose death has left us bereft and, in that sense, radically and constantly living in Barth's *Krisis.*

RUDOLF BULTMANN

The last of the theological thinkers in this very brief survey is the twentieth-century German biblical scholar Rudolf Bultmann, because he leads us straight into the particular method for constructing the Autism of Gxd.

A generation after Barth, Bultmann was conceptualizing what he termed demythologization. If Barth had sought to pull theology back from Liberal tendencies, Bultmann, in a sense, argued that Liberal Theology had not gone far enough. According to Bultmann, this means rejecting the miraculous as mere myth or legend, but also preserving a core of truth. Bultmann writes:

> The whole conception of the world which is presupposed in the preaching of Jesus as in the New Testament generally is mythological. . . . This conception of the world we call mythical because it is different from the conception of the world which has been formed and developed by science since its inception in ancient Greece and which has been accepted by all modern men (sic). . . .[30]
>
> We must ask whether the eschatological preaching and the mythological sayings as a whole contain a still deeper meaning which is concealed under the cover of mythology . . . this method . . . I call *de-mythologising.* . . . Its aim is not to eliminate the mythological statements but to interpret them. It is a method of hermeneutics.[31]

---

30. Bultmann, *Jesus Christ and Mythology*, 15.
31. Bultmann, *Jesus Christ and Mythology*, 18.

Bultmann is influenced by nineteenth-century German theology, particularly David Friedrich Strauss' infamous *Life of Jesus,* which casts the Gospel stories as mythology formulated by the Evangelists.[32] Bultmann took this thinking into a reading of the Gospels, stripping away the miraculous to reveal Jesus' core message. As we shall see, where Bultmann has *de*mythologized the New Testament, we are now embarking on a journey to *re*mythologize both autism and theology—in an enterprise which will lead us to an Autism of Gxd.

---

32. Jonathan Birch discusses the links between Strauss and Bultmann in Birch, "Gospel Narratives," 61–93.

Our Approach to Autism
A Beginner's Guide

A SHORT HISTORY

The first known reference to autism as a condition came from the psychiatrist Eugene Bleuler in 1910, describing a type of child he observed in his clinics as having a quality of *autos* (self) meaning the way in which they were withdrawn from others. Similarly, in 1938, the clinician Hans Asperger observed a particular type of child in his clinical work and described them as "autists," with a condition he termed "autistic psychopathy" (a term with which we will certainly take issue), describing a set of phenomena for high-functioning autistic children (and later, also adults) which would come to be known as Asperger's Syndrome.

Asperger makes explicit the gap which excludes the autist from the non-autistic world and indeed from all others:

> Human beings normally live in constant interaction with their environment, and react to it continually. However, "autists" have severely disturbed and

considerably limited interaction. The autist is only himself (cf. the Greek word autos) and is not an active member of a greater organism by which he is influenced and which he influences constantly.[1]

Ten years after Asperger published his findings, there was mention of autism as a clinical condition in 1949, by the psychiatrist Leo Kanner. Kanner described an autistic child in this way:

> He seems almost to withdraw into his shell and live within himself . . . (he) never looked up at people's faces. When he had any dealings with persons at all, he treated them, or rather parts of them, as if they were objects.[2]

As more attention began to be paid to autism in children, clinicians Lorna Wing and Judith Gould drew up a systematization of their observations of autistic children, which they termed the triad of impairments. They described an autism where:

> The abnormalities of social interaction, verbal and nonverbal communication, and imaginative activities so consistently occurred together (Wing & Gould, 1979) that they could be referred to as "the triad of social and language impairment."[3]

In the twenty-first century, at the time of writing this book, the international benchmark for defining autistic phenomena (although not without controversy) is the American Psychiatric Association's *Diagnostic and Statistical Manual of Mental Disorders*, Fifth Edition (DSM-5). DSM-5's definition of autism is a dyad of impairments:

---

1. Asperger, "'Autistic Psychopathy' in Childhood," 38.
2. Kanner, "Autistic Disturbances," quoted in Baron-Cohen, *Mindblindness*, 161.
3. Wing, "Language, Social, and Cognitive Impairments," 17.

- social communication and interaction;
- restricted, repetitive patterns of behavior, interests or activities.[4]

This triad or, according to DSM's definition, dyad of attributes is a complex set of parameters. The clinician Judith Gould writes:

> The concept of a spectrum of autistic disorders fitted the findings better than the categorical approach. This does not imply a smooth continuum from the most to the least severe. All kinds of combinations of features are possible.[5]

The psychiatrist and autism expert Simon Baron-Cohen has also argued that the autistic spectrum is a universal human category, with the general population existing on a normal distribution between autistic and neurotypical ("normal") extremes.[6]

MINDBLINDNESS

Asperger and Kanner both focused on autism in terms of *autos* (self); namely a separated self, disconnected from the world of others. The autistic adult Leneh Buckle, describing her childhood, actually (and very significantly) writes "I was happier when I couldn't communicate."[7] Psychological testing and theorizing have clarified more of the mechanism she is describing; it is more subtle than being unable physically to talk or listen. One famous experiment is the Sally Anne test.

---

4. American Psychiatric Association. *Autism Spectrum Disorder*, 1.
5. Gould, "Triad of Impairments."
6. Baron-Cohen et al., "Autism Spectrum Quotient"; see also Baron-Cohen, "Current Perspectives."
7. Buckle, "Is Increasing Functionality Always Good?"

Clinicians Uta Frith, Alan Leslie and Simon Baron-Cohen devised this test, which involved moving a toy marble while one child has left the room, but the other stays in the room. When the absent child returns, the still present child is asked where the previously absent child will *think* the marble is hidden. The autistic child points to the new location, being unable to enter the mind-state of the absent child who doesn't know it has been moved. Children with a different cognitive impairment, of the same age and development, pass the test; but something about understanding another child's *belief* is compromised in autism.

Baron-Cohen coined the term *mindblindness* to explain this core feature of autism. This is an impairment of what evolutionary biologists call Theory of Mind Mechanism (TOMM). TOMM is what humans use intuitively to discern the beliefs and feelings of others; Baron-Cohen also draws on the idea of Nicholas Humphrey[8] that the use of TOMM is a kind of "social chess" where one can theorize, or mentalize, another person's most likely next move, by understanding their previous one. Humphrey writes:

> In evolutionary terms it must have been a breakthrough. . . . Imagine the biological benefits to the first of our ancestors who developed the ability to make realistic guesses about the inner life of his rivals; to be able to picture what another was thinking about and planning to do next; to be able to read the minds of others by reading his own.[9]

In mindblindness, it is difficult or impossible to discern what is happening in the mind of another person.

---

8. Baron-Cohen, *Mindblindness*, 18.

9. Humphrey, *Consciousness Regained* (page no. not given), in Baron-Cohen, *Mindblindness*, 21.

Sarcasm, implied criticism, body language, and unspoken signs of emotion are all hard to pick up as the beliefs of others cannot be guessed.

This leads to a particular isolation; if I can't figure out what is happening in the multiplicity of human indirect cues, how can I form a meaningful relationship with you? This is a painful reality, and it takes a particular skill and compassion to reach out to someone whose degree of mindblindness is severe. This creates a very particular kind of solitude.

LITERAL-MINDEDNESS

"For autistic people, the literal meaning of words does not change in different settings . . . autistic individuals need to make an intense effort to learn to recognize subtle or shifting meanings that depend on the speaker's attitudes and intentions."[10]

This definition, by the clinician Uta Frith, is borne out by countless anecdotes, often amusing but just as often frustrating or upsetting. The clinician Tony Attwood gives examples such as a child being asked to "put her work right," and the child then moving her workbooks to the righthand side of the desk. Similarly, another girl, being asked if she could count to ten, said yes and then silently continued playing. More distressingly, a child became upset when told that "she had her father's eyes," taking it literally.[11]

Attwood comments:

> The person is not being deliberately annoying, or stupid. Rather, they are less aware of the hidden, implied,

---

10. Frith, *Autism: Explaining the Enigma*, 127–28.
11. See Attwood, *Asperger's Syndrome*, 76.

or multiple meanings. This characteristic also affects the understanding of common phrases, idioms or metaphors.[12]

The autistic writer Donna Williams gives an example of how she took things literally as a child (she has learned coping strategies as an adult):

> When I once received a serious lecture about writing graffiti on Parliament House during an excursion, I agreed that I'd never do it again and then . . . was caught outside writing different graffiti on the school wall. To me, I was not ignoring what they said, nor was I trying to be funny: I had not done *exactly* the same thing as I had done before.[13]

It is not difficult to see how Mindblindness and literal-mindedness feed into each other; if I am mindblind to your intentions in speaking, I will fail to interpret your use of figurative language. Similarly, if I am unfamiliar with how figurative language works, I will be blind to what your intentions are.

Baron-Cohen argues for a "systemizing versus empathy" phenomenon whereby autistic people who are poor at cognitive empathy have a high score at systemizing (being drawn to, and extremely good at understanding systems).[14] Effectively, this means understanding "things" better than people.

This is something which we are only outlining now, but will merit an entire chapter in its own right (chapter 2).

---

12. Attwood, *Asperger's Syndrome*, 76.
13. Williams, 1995, as cited by Attwood, *Asperger's Syndrome*, 78.
14. See also Baron-Cohen, "Attenuation of Typical Sex Differences." Baron-Cohen identifies brain differences between males and females and plots an empathy/systematizing/graph for males and females, both with and without autism. The results suggest that people with autism, male and female, are largely skewed toward the "systematizing" part of the graph, supporting his thesis of an "autistic male brain."

AUTISTIC FASCINATION

Heightened sensory sensitivities are a feature of autism which can cause pleasure or distress. Loud noises, bright lights or crowded places can create an overwhelming sensation which can be almost unbearable for autists. For example, one autist is deeply uncomfortable and distressed by the noise of electric hand driers—even when heard through a wall! And for a description of the effects of noise, crowd, light, and over-stimulation, one only need read Mark Haddon's masterly description of the fictional autist Christopher in Haddon's novel *The Curious Incident of the Dog in the Night-Time.* As Christopher takes a train journey to London, he reaches the Underground station where the overwhelming barrage of sight and sound is almost unbearable—he completes it only through an act of extraordinary courage and determination.

The canonical twentieth-century clinical narrative from, for example, Lorna Wing and Uta Frith, records numerous sensory sensitivities. Frith describes "sharply uncomfortable sensory and strong emotional experiences . . . out of the ordinary";[15] and Wing also describes sensory abnormalities, using the language of both fascination and distress as signs of intense reaction to the sensory:

> [an autistic] child may be fascinated by some sounds such as that made by friction drive toys or the ringing of a bell. They may find some sounds intensely distressing and will cover their ears and cringe away from, for example, the roar of a motor bike . . . or even some comparatively quiet sounds . . . odd responses to sounds, especially . . . oversensitivity.[16]

---

15. Frith, *Autism*, 14.
16. Wing, *Autistic Spectrum*, 50.

She makes the same observation about visual stimuli as either fascinating or distressing. In particular, she describes the fascination with bright lights which is the "most common."[17] Joel Bregman records the same features, and also uses the word fascination:

> Among those with a more classic form of autism, a great deal of sensory exploration may occur, often involving minor details of parts of toys or objects. Often there is a fascination with subtle physical characteristics of toys and objects, such as texture, shading and hue.[18]

The key word is fascination. He gives the example of "the intense visual scrutiny of light diffraction patterns when a prism-like stone is twirled in the sunlight."[19] So sensory sensitivities can bring real distress at times, and deep joy at others.

The other form of what I am terming fascination is "narrow, circumscribed interests." This is fascination which is not sensory but cognitive, an intellectual focus of an extreme nature. Uta Frith describes the behavior of autistic people with a narrow, intense, particular interest as follows:

> [Autistic people's] special interest is often their sole topic of conversation . . . autistic repetitions and obsessions appear to be different from compulsions as the autistic person does not try to resist them, but apparently greatly enjoys enacting them . . . [which] can lead to outstanding achievements.[20]

---

17. Wing, *Autistic Spectrum*, 51.
18. Bregman, "Definitions and Characteristics," 13.
19. Bregman, "Definitions and Characteristics," 13.
20. Frith, *Autism*, 14.

Tony Attwood records some examples of Autistic Fascination he encounters in his clinical work: "the young child may develop an interest in collecting specific items . . . the lids of tubes of Smarties . . . the labels from bottles of beer . . . butterflies or keyrings . . . yellow pencils, vacuum cleaners or toilet brushes."[21]

The next stage of development is "fascination with a topic rather than an object. Common topics are transport . . . dinosaurs, electronics and science. The person develops an encyclopedic knowledge . . . a common feature is a fascination with statistics, order and symmetry."[22]

An autistic adult explains how this continues in adult life:

> If you put two or more people together who have Asperger's syndrome, the question is bound to come up. Translated, it means, "So, what one single thing have you been focusing on all your life?"
>
> Not everyone with Asperger's syndrome will be able to relate to such a question, but when you take the repetitive nature of this unique group, along with their narrow, restricted interests, and mix that together with an intense curiosity or profound devotion to whatever strikes their fancy, a lifelong interest in one particular subject is often the result. Even more amazing, this special interest typically begins at a very early age. Without a doubt, my focus has been on all things futuristic. Robots are a big deal for me, along with architectural designs of a futuristic nature. I could sit and stare at a drawing of a futuristic city all day long. Come to think of it, I have.[23]

Another autistic blogger, Sunfell, relates on the same website that:

21. Attwood, *Asperger's Syndrome*, 89.
22. Attwood, *Asperger's Syndrome*, 90.
23. Bridges, "Special Interests."

> My Special Subject is systems—any kind of system . . . I have many other deep interests, too. . . . Life for me is one vast puzzle-box, a huge system to explore and exploit and I have found a place of contentment in this world.[24]

Hans Asperger's original description of autists includes the observation that they display "egocentric" preoccupation with unusual or circumscribed interests. Uta Frith gives even more apparently bizarre examples:

> railroad telegraph pole line insulators, personal information about all the members of Congress, and knowledge of the passenger list of the Titanic, weather information, and various models of deep fat fryers.[25]

Uta Frith has theorized an explanation for this phenomenon of RRBIs (Repetitive and Restricted Behaviors and Interests) as a brain abnormality, which she terms Weak Central Coherence (WCC) where attention to detail is phenomenal, but it is hard to grasp "the bigger picture"; and FMRI brain scans examining neural connections in autistic versus neurotypical brains suggest that she is right. (WCC is a "pathology," but holy Autistic Fascination will recast it as a gift).

The clinician Joel Bregman's language is dismissive of these phenomena:

> [with] Intense preoccupying interests . . . such individuals literally can become world experts on such topics, yet resist suggestions to transform this interest and knowledge into functional, meaningful or marketable skills.[26]

---

24. Bridges, "Special Interests."
25. Frith, *Autism and Asperger's Syndrome*, 37.
26. Bregman, "Definitions and Characteristics," 14.

RESTRICTED AND REPETITIVE BEHAVIORS AND INTERESTS (RRBIS)

Restricted and repetitive behaviors (RRBIs) will be important in our mythical autism. They are, firstly, the phenomenon of stimming; patterns of repeated body movements such as rocking or hand flapping, as a way of relieving stress (most people also stim, unconsciously, e.g. scratching your head or drumming your fingers on the desk—only that, in autism, it is more pronounced). RRBIs also involve unusual attachment to, and pleasure in, specific sensory and motor activities, e.g., stroking a piece of velvet or watching spinning shiny objects in a hanging mobile. Secondly, special interests (the obsessive, often all-consuming interest in a topic) are also considered as RRBIs.

SAVANTISM

The autistic savant is a person with an incredible talent, often with numbers or memory, but this can also be within the realms of art. This is exemplified in the "Rain Man" archetype.[27] In Barry Levinson's 1988 film *Rain Man,* Dustin Hoffman superbly portrays how challenging autism can be, in his character Raymond ("Rain Man"). The plot, however, also includes the discovery of his phenomenal powers of memory which seem to defy explanation (and are exploited); but this is a recognized phenomenon. Some autistic people, including those apparently quite "impaired," possess exceptional talents. In the past, the term "idiot savant" was used, but now people with savant talent are described as possessing an "islet of ability."[28]

---

27. Levinson, *Rain Man*.
28. See Treffert, "Savant Syndrome" in Happé and Frith, *Autism and Talent,* 1–12.

SENSORY CONNOISSEUR

Happé and Frith's Introduction to their 2010 book *Autism and Talent* describes "the beautiful otherness of the autistic mind," and this otherness is suggested by their interpretation of RRBIs as something potentially wonderful. They write:

> Repetition is not repetition, for example, if you have expert levels of discrimination . . . a connoisseur, seeing minute differences between events that others regard as pure repetition.[29]

I am grateful to my friend, the autism advocate and writer Alastair Clarkson, for sharing with me his concept of autistic people as "sensory connoisseurs," whose appreciation of the sensory world exceeds that of the normal, so that they (we) are indeed connoisseurs in ways incomprehensible to others. We will discuss the Sensory Connoisseur later, in ways which will emerge as highly significant.

NEUROTYPICALITY

Neurotypicality, in contrast to the culture of the autistic neurotribe, means being "neurally typical." Neurotypicals are cognitively "normal" people.

INTENSE WORLD SYNDROME

The psychologists Makram, Rinaldi and Makram propose an "intense world syndrome" model as an alternative theory of autism, addressing the sensory sensitivities which we have subsumed into Autistic Fascination. They write:

---

29. Happé and Frith, *Autism and Talent*, xvii.

the world may become painfully intense for autistics and we, therefore, propose autism as an *Intense World Syndrome*. . . .

We, therefore, propose that the autistic person may perceive its surroundings not only as overwhelmingly intense due to hyper-reactivity of primary sensory areas, but also as aversive and highly stressful due to a hyper-reactive amygdala, which also makes quick and powerful fear associations with usually neutral stimuli. The autistic person may well try to cope with the intense and aversive world by avoidance. Thus, impaired social interactions and withdrawal may not be the result of a lack of compassion, incapability to put oneself into some else's position or lack of emotionality, but quite to the contrary a result of an intensely if not painfully aversively perceived environment.[30]

They conclude that:

the *Intense World Syndrome* suggests that the autistic person is an individual with remarkable and far above average capabilities due to greatly enhanced perception, attention and memory. In fact, it is this hyper-functionality which could render the individual debilitated.[31]

The psychologist Olga Bogdashina tests out intense world syndrome in the light of earlier clinical narratives and finds a great deal of supporting evidence from the psychologists Bregman and Escalona, who record that "variations in sensory impression that made no difference to the average child made a great difference to (autistic spectrum) children."[32]

---

30. Markram, Rinaldi, and Markram, "Intense World Syndrome," 87, 90.

31. Markram, Rinaldi, and Markram, "Intense World Syndrome," 92.

32. Bergman and Escalona, "Unusual Sensitivities," 333, quoted in Bogdashina, *Autism and Spirituality,* 55; see also Bregman, "Definitions and Characteristics of the Spectrum," 13, where they are also using the language of sensory fascination.

In summary, the model I am proposing combines sensory sensitivities and "narrow, circumscribed interests," and subsumes both of these phenomena under the umbrella of what we will call Autistic Fascination. This is not a scientific construct,[33] but one constructed in order to create a mythical archetype. Here, we have spent some time discussing it, to clarify what (and how, and why) our Autistic Fascination is.

AUTISTIC EMPATHY

Autistic love manifests itself differently to non-autistic ("neurotypical") love. Lorna Wing, the "founding mother" clinician who did much in the 1960s to establish a more nuanced understanding of autism, describes an autistic boy as not uncaring, but simply unaware of the suffering of others. He is

> unable to acquire the skills necessary for social interaction. Nevertheless, he is kind and gentle and, if he realizes someone is ill or unhappy, he will be most sympathetic and do his best to help.[34]

Regarding this, the disability theologian John Swinton has argued that autists are not emotionally "thin" people lacking depth, but rather, expressing love in a different but equally valid way.[35]

I also am basing this on the neuroscientist Simon Baron-Cohen's *Zero Degrees of Empathy: A New Theory of Human Cruelty and Kindness,* but also on accounts of

---

33. Although I would be delighted if I were proved right in psychological, scientific terms!
34. Wing, "Asperger Syndrome."
35. See Swinton, *Reflections on Autistic Love*.

clinical observations and indeed, my own experience of autistic people among my family and friends.

Using an "Empathy Quotient" questionnaire, Baron-Cohen measures tests subjects' scores and finds empathy to be distributed as a bell curve where there is a normal distribution—a few at either end, but most in the middle. He explains Wing's observations by postulating two different kinds of empathy. His argument is that people with Asperger's Syndrome have a "zero degree" of severely reduced cognitive empathy but unimpaired affective empathy.[36] His theory is that two similarly appearing behaviors can in fact be polar opposites; that there are two kinds of empathy: cognitive empathy and affective empathy. Cognitive empathy is the ability to read another person intuitively; to be an expert mind-reader. Affective empathy is the kind of empathy which feels for the other person at an emotional level. His hypothesis is that there are two types of "zero empathy" which he calls "zero negative" and "zero positive." Zero negative, he argues, is the state of having psychopathic tendencies. The zero negative type is described thus:

> The psychopath *is* aware that they are hurting someone because the "cognitive" (recognition) element of empathy is intact in their case, even if the "affective" element (the emotional response to someone else's feelings) is not.[37]

The opposite kind of impaired empathy, zero positive is, in contrast, manifested in autistic spectrum disorders:

> People with Asperger Syndrome have zero degrees of empathy, but they are Zero-Positive for two reasons. First, their empathy difficulties are largely restricted

36. Baron-Cohen, *Zero Degrees of Empathy*, 65.
37. Baron-Cohen, *Zero Degrees of Empathy*, 85.

to the "cognitive" component (also called "theory of mind"). Their "affective" empathy is frequently intact. We know this because—when it is pointed out to them that someone is upset—it often upsets them. Unlike people who are type P (psychopath), someone with Asperger Syndrome is very unlikely to hurt their pet. Indeed, the opposite is true. Many people with Asperger Syndrome rescue stray dogs or cats because they feel sorry for them and want to look after them.[38]

So, when a person has very good cognitive empathy coupled with very poor affective empathy—they understand the other but don't care—this is a "zero negative." This is the profile of the manipulative psychopath who misuses their cognitive ability to harm others because they lack the affective empathy in order to care about the other's wellbeing. At the opposing end are the autistic people with impaired cognitive empathy but enhanced affective empathy; someone who clumsily tries and fails to read other people, but even in the face of this failure cares deeply.

Baron-Cohen lists examples from his clinical work, and among my circle of autistic friends I have seen examples of extreme affective empathy: giving large amounts of hard-earned cash to a beggar, adopting stray cats, devoting hours to listen to a distressed friend. However, impaired cognitive empathy means getting it wrong; an ill-judged joke, a gift the other person "obviously" won't like, an inability to let the other person speak when I am too excited about my own idea. Or turning away in frustration when I find another person's conversation boring; most of all, social behaviors simply lacking in "good manners" or tact. (My mother, when I was a teenager, once told me that

---

38. Baron-Cohen, *Zero Degrees of Empathy*, 73.

I would never have a career as a diplomat—of course, I had no idea what she meant!)

Baron-Cohen's argument is that these two "zero degrees" of empathy explain two kinds of cruelty, deliberate and undeliberate. One is a triumph of evil, and the other is love which fails in its object. Because both can look alike, people, sadly, often misjudge autistic people as cold and unfeeling. So autistic empathy, if this is the case, is a tragic combination of love and inability. Its failure to mind-read blocks its fascination which would love "better" if it could.

Baron-Cohen sums this up:

> In an imaginative study, Berlin neuroscientist Isabel Dziobek and colleagues found that people with Asperger Syndrome did not differ in how much concern they felt for people who were suffering, compared to typical individuals, even though they struggled to identify what others were feeling or thinking . . . people with Asperger Syndrome do care about others, whilst struggling to "read" them. Those with type P don't care about others, whilst "reading" them with ease; the mirror image is the profile of psychopathy. So the early clinical labels of "autistic psychopathy" are both cruel and inaccurate.[39]

So autistic empathy could be termed "love against the odds," and this is an important idea which can now be developed, with some other key autistic traits, in our search for the Autism of Gxd.

---

39. Baron-Cohen, *Zero Degrees of Empathy*, 81.

Introduction: What Does This Book Do?

THE TITLE OF THIS WORK IS "THE AUTISM OF GXD"

Is it blasphemous to describe Gxd as autistic?

Is it blasphemous, alternatively, to trace the *imago dei* (image of Gxd) only in the able-bodied (or "able-minded")?

These are good questions which underlie the myth at the heart of this book, which is an atheological love story of autism. A colleague reading this manuscript accused it of being political; I don't believe it is, but a political view might be taken from some of its consequences. Certainly, I must candidly state that I am inferring a radical, speculative and challenging view of autism from my own life with autism; and not merely that, but also the observations of my autistic friends, those known personally and those known in their written testimonies. I will explore scientific and clinical concepts of autism methodically, to test my instincts; and something new will emerge to challenge not merely our current understanding of autism, but of theology too.

> More importantly, I am developing a mythical autism which has its own agency and is able to validate marginal theologies, where it stands in solidarity. And crucially, I will claim that this autistic support is not a narrow, "disabled" one, but a radically counter-cultural one; which challenges norms of being and belief for every reader.

This matters because I have found that there are some marginal but profound theologies which seem almost to be crying out for an autistic hermeneutic—strictly as myth—to come and play, and to find something as remarkable as we do. We find a new validation, mutually, between autism and the theologies the Church's agenda has possibly had to forget.

"I am Autism," an infamous campaign in the 1990s by the US research charity *Autism Speaks,* scandalized autistic people, their friends and their carers by speaking of autism as an "invader," as an evil which sneaks in and destroys happy homes.[1] This reflected *Autism Speaks'* agenda of research for a "cure" for autism.

This book reclaims those words *"Autism Speaks"* so that when this mythologized autism speaks to theology, it is not only valid, but a powerful voice which itself validates profound theological ways of thinking. Being on the margins can be a powerful place, seeing things which might not be visible from the center. Autism speaks to theology, by means of its mythologized tropes, and challenges theological thinkers to listen.

What is at stake is a mythical autism of Gxd.

---

1. Autism Speaks, "I Am Autism."

INTRODUCTION: WHAT DOES THIS BOOK DO? 47

THE SUBTITLE OF THIS WORK IS "AN ATHEOLOGICAL LOVE STORY"

First, the love story. Like all good love stories, its course never runs smoothly (of course, this is particularly true of the gospel story) and thus, it is not devoid of sorrow and pain. The approach to love here, undergirding the atheological love story, comes from the work of the autism expert Simon Baron-Cohen. It is the "Zero Degree Positive" which we discussed in "Our Approach to Autism: A Beginner's Guide," where a "zero positive" is low cognitive empathy coupled with high affective empathy; whereas "zero degree negative," diametrically opposed, with high cognitive empathy and low affective empathy, would be people with psychopathic conditions.

Most of us are somewhere in between both types of empathy, but there is an intuitive logic to Baron-Cohen's findings: the psychopath understands you perfectly well (all too well, perhaps, in order to manipulate you) but doesn't care; while the autist doesn't understand you, can't *read* you, but does, deep down, care about you. Like Baron-Cohen, I have witnessed the extreme, often unwise, generosity of autistic people—the girl who takes in umpteen stray animals, the young man who, despite his own poverty, hands a £20 note to the beggar in the street.

This way of seeing autism is at the heart of this book, although there are other aspects too, which will be discussed later. As we shall see, we will take these qualities, including this extraordinary and strange form of empathy, and weave them into a mythology. So in this case, this absolute autistic empathy, in terms of the Jesus myth, is Love, and ultimately (as we shall see) Crucifixion; a narrative of struggle and suffering founded in total love because

"God is Love."[2] A lifelong wrestling with Gxd, undergone by this autistic author, finds a real resonance with this Autistic Gxd. And yet also, as we shall see, when an autistic mythology of delight is examined theologically, Gxd is everywhere—the world is filled with the glory of Gxd, and the story of ultimate love, Christ Crucified, is affective empathy personified (we will see this in extended form in chapter 5, although every chapter really incorporates autistic empathy as divine Love; particularly discussing Crucifixion in chapter 4).

THIS IS ALSO AN ATHEOLOGICAL STORY

What is atheology? *A-theology, (a)theology, atheist theology, a/theology*? All these terms are used to describe a theology of the death of Gxd, not cynical or hostile, but offering a path for a real and deep faith. The journey into atheology comes from, and finally embodies, the lifelong struggle with a Gxd who *is not* and yet *is*. The autistic theological thinker is blessed/cursed with the relentlessly logical mind of autistic questing after truth (rather in the same sense as Mark Taylor's homonymic (punning) title *After God*).[3] Where is Gxd? So many theological dogmas and forms of worship are, for this relentlessly logical mind, all too absurd—and yet—and yet—my sense of the sacred imbuing all the world with wonder, and my inescapable pull toward the richness of Scripture mean I am unable to forsake Gxd. I search *After Gxd*.

But why atheological? This quarrel with the absurdities of religion, while still longing "After Gxd," has found a deeply meaningful (non)resolution in the late Thomas

---

2. 1 John 4:8.
3. Taylor, *After God*.

J. J. Altizer's *Gospel of Christian Atheism.* For Altizer, the crucifixion of Jesus is also the death of Gxd. It is a misapprehension to condemn Altizer too readily. He revels in the label of heretic, in the sense that the prophet is rejected in his own land;[4] and that has certainly been the case. It is also, deeply, a misapprehension to believe that Altizer is an enemy of true Christian faith. Like his "prophet," William Blake, Altizer sees in Christendom an abusive power structure which has distorted the primitive Christianity of Jesus.

More importantly, Altizer is approaching Bible as myth, following the studies of myth which his teacher Mircea Eliade examined in Comparative Religion. It is, perhaps, almost possible to say that the truth or falsehood of theological dogma is irrelevant to Altizer's work—his project is altogether different to propositional theology. In his writing, he follows what he has learned from Paul Tillich, a theology of culture. Where he departs from Tillich, however, is that Altizer approaches Bible as myth, not as the kind of relatively straightforward answer to Existentialist questions which Tillich developed. Altizer, for much of his career, in fact, taught literature, not theology.

He is approaching Bible in terms of a myth-source which he correlates to a world where, in the early twentieth century, Modernism has "made everything new." This phrase, "make everything new," was used by the novelist Henry James to express Modernism's project for radical change, not only in *what* is made, but equally, especially in the Arts, in *how* it is made. Altizer approaches theology in the light of Modernism (which leads to the ever-*Post* [one could even say, ironically, *ever after*] of Postmodernism).

---

4. Jesus says, "Truly I tell you." He continued, "No prophet is accepted in his hometown" (Luke 4:24); also, the death threats that we will discuss in chapter 4.

He inverts Karl Barth's existential *Krisis*, so that instead of the moment of despair being the moment of redemption, the moment of redemption paradoxically also remains the moment of despair. This is to take Barth's (non-literal) interpretation of the cataclysm of the First World War, and resolutely refuse to sanitize it into a redemptive moment. There is no such theodicy.[5]

This is why Satan and Hell feature in Altizer's work;[6] faith operates in a world of suffering and evil, not in a transcendent experience. In this sense, the transcendent Gxdhead dies in the Crucifixion. Faith in Jesus is faith in the darkness, and critics of Altizer's work might ponder not only the discourses of darkness, absence, and abandonment in the Christian mystical tradition. (In fact, Denys Turner's excellent study of mystical theology is entitled *The Darkness of God*). They might also meditate on Jesus' words of abandonment on the Cross *(why hast thou forsaken me?)*[7] and Paul's reminder that *"we walk by faith, and not sight."*[8]

"DEEP CALLS TO DEEP": ECHOING METAPHORS

The locus for listening to autism in this book is the interdisciplinary area of literature and theology. Before exploring the contours of this territory, it needs to be stated at the outset that the origin of this book lies a sense of being where Psalm 42 says "deep calls to deep."[9] A "depth"

---

5. Theodicy: a theological argument to justify the coexistence of evil and suffering alongside a loving God.

6. Although Satan is also the transcendent God in which, in Nietzsche's terms, "we have killed" our enemy.

7. Matt 27:46; Mark 15:34.

8. 2 Cor 5:7.

9. "Deep calls to deep in the roar of your waterfalls; all your waves and breakers have swept over me" (Ps 42:7); this is also a sense of overwhelming, which will be considered in terms of art/theology/disability.

of the thinking where literature and theology have met in the twentieth/twenty-first centuries, meets a "depth" of autism. Both are conceived in the double metaphoric meaning of depth; a place of descent ("I'm in at the *deep* end") and a place of value ("*deep*ly meaningful").[10]

Another metaphor, akin to this depth and overwhelming ("all your waves and breakers have swept over me"), is darkness, but it is also dually conceived, being a paradoxical darkness which is also dazzling light.[11] Autism will be represented as this "darkness," which is paradoxically also dazzling light, but it meets with depth and darkness, primarily, at least, not within the discourses of practical theology or theology of disability.[12] The particular understandings of depth and darkness that are invited into conversation are drawn from the interdisciplinarity of literature and theology, because it is the thesis of this author that autism calls out to them, illumining them and perhaps also being illumined by them, but always, in this paradox.

A third metaphor for the common ground in this conversation is liminality (being on the edge); furthermore, the paradox that the marginal might be the true center. This means that ex-centricity is in fact the true center, and consequently, the "eccentric" perception will be validated as both deep-end meaning and dazzling darkness. To contextualize this, the territory of literature and theology needs to be explored briefly, and then possible reasons for

---

10. This also echoes Tillich's existentialist sermon "The Depth of Existence," where his texts are 1 Cor 2:10 ("But God hath revealed them unto us by his Spirit: for the Spirit searches all things, yea, the deep things of God") and Ps 130:1 ("Out of the depths have I cried to thee, O Lord"). Tillich, *Shaking of the Foundations*, 59.

11. This is the "self-consuming" metaphorical language of Dionysius the Areopagite's mystical theology, which will be explored in chapter 2.

12. Practical theology and theology of disability are relevant, especially in the light of the "Autism Speaks" controversy (see note 1). They will be discussed in the next section, but our real territory is not within these disciplinary fields.

listening to autism can be explained. The aim is that each of all three—autism, literature and theology—should be honored and validated in the light of each other.

LITERATURE AND THEOLOGY—AN INTERDISCIPLINARY SPACE

If autism knows, *par excellance*, how to live "on the margins,"[13] perhaps it is no accident that it can enter conversation with literature-and-theology, as another discourse of marginality. David Jasper writes, perhaps not entirely humorously:

> In recent times the study of "literature and theology" or "literature and religion" has been granted, if often somewhat grudgingly, its place in the curriculum of the academy, often uncomfortably suspended between academic departments of literature and theology.[14]

Being "uncomfortably suspended" is not an accident which should be too hastily dealt with by the administrative policies of the academy, at least in terms of how it is thought—although, of course, at that level, being given a place is very important. Glasgow University's Centre for Literature, Theology and the Arts (CLTA) has been an important and extremely fruitful development in the late twentieth and early twenty-first century, as was the emergence of the journal *Literature and Theology*. Without this hospitable, creative academic environment, this book would never have been written.[15]

---

13. In the sense that autists, with divergent thinking styles and difficulties in the social and communicative domains, are frequently "on the outside," as will be discussed.
14. Jasper, *Study of Literature and Theology*, 15.
15. University of Glasgow, Centre for Literature, Theology, and the Arts.

INTRODUCTION: WHAT DOES THIS BOOK DO? 53

However, the creativity of this research space perhaps depends on the fact of being "uncomfortably suspended." The depth of the twentieth/twenty-first century "Literature, Theology and the Arts" (LTA) conversation could be seen to stem from its conscious existence within the depth of an abyss of a post-Christian, paradoxical theological thinking. The American a-theological thinker of LTA, Mark C. Taylor, uses two powerful images which express the nature of this abyss. Barry Moser's untitled lithograph,[16] as the frontispiece to Taylor's 1984 book *Erring: A Postmodern A/theology*, shows a huge, underground, rugged crevasse, with widening fissures splintering out from it. The landscape above conceals this crevasse from view, if it were seen from the surface, but that landscape itself is being struck by a lightning bolt. The abyss, in theological terms, has always been there, as the mystics' apophatic writings indicate. However, it is the ebbing of the sea of faith which might burst the landscape open to reveal it; and it is art which discloses it.[17] The abyss figures also in Taylor's second frontispiece art work, this time in his 1989 book *Tears*. This image is a black and white photo of Enrique Espinoza's art installation "The Silence of Jesus."[18]

Espinoza's installation is of two jagged black shapes which, when seen from a certain angle, as in the photo, reveal a profile where the empty space between them is the shape of the crucifix. The statue could be called an anti-statue, since its object, the image of Christ, is a non-object: it is an absence and a void. Christ is "not there," and in fact *is* the not-there. The moment you move, to walk around or walk away, "he's gone." The abyss is of Christ

16. See frontispiece artwork, Taylor, *Tears*.

17. The role of art is also the "disaster" of the "unpresentable before," which Taylor also sees in *Paysage Foudroyé* (Taylor, *Tears*, 7).

18. See frontispiece art, Taylor, *Erring*.

emptied into nothingness, but embodied as art—and, as Taylor writes, "in the postmodern world, the Disaster takes place (without taking place) *in* art *as* art."[19] It is understood as an absence, where Christ is "not there," yet the "not there" is Christ, if seen from a certain viewpoint. This is a "two-fold" abyss, as an abyss of theology and an abyss of literature and the arts; and this abyss offers an honoring (post-holocaust) space for their meeting.

When theodicy (the theology of justifying evil) becomes obscene in post-holocaust thought, and the demise of Christendom silences theological discourse, the bottomless claims of metaphor can become the powerful poetry of the cry of dereliction.[20] Heather Walton discusses this possibility in *When Love Is Not True*, writing: "My own journey into interdisciplinarity was largely provoked by the inadequacy of theological responses to the age-old problem of evil."[21] Walton continues, quoting David Jenkins:

> The dreadful thing about so much theology is that, in relation to so much of the human situation, it is so superficial. . . . Theologians need to stand under the judgements of the insights of literature before they can speak with true theological force of and to the world this literature reflects and illuminates.[22]

---

19. Taylor, *Tears*, 10.

20. Maurice Blanchot writes, "The poem is the answer's absence." *Space of Literature*, 247.

21. Walton, *Literature and Theology*, 45.

22. David Jenkins, quoted in Jasper, *Sacred Desert*, 4, quoted in Walton, *Literature and Theology*, 44; Jenkins, the scandalously radical bishop of Durham, gained infamy by stating publicly that he did not believe in the Virgin Birth or the Resurrection. The Bible was literature, not history, to Jenkins, and the gospel was at heart the compassion resulting in the concern for social justice. Uncannily, days after Jenkins' scandalously "heretical" public remarks in 1984, Durham Cathedral was struck by lightning. Perhaps this was the backdrop (or the zeitgeist hand of God) when in 1990, Mark C. Taylor similarly wrote about radical theology in the figure of the *Paysage Foudroyé* (see note 55).

INTRODUCTION: WHAT DOES THIS BOOK DO? 55

This is a real, kenotic and vulnerable "disabled" theology; Walton writes elsewhere that "literature resists being assimilated by theology in order to communicate the insights of faith . . . it cannot be simply and effectively appropriated in this way and is as likely to confound our understandings of faith as to confirm them."[23] This is a vulnerability involving "wrestling long and hard with intractable problems and (recognizing) that there is spiritual value in facing ambivalence without denying religious and political obligations . . . through discomforting processes of radical critique."[24] This is a discourse of a searching for authenticity, and the territory it leads to in this book is the a-theological and the apophatic, as will become clear. When theology becomes a-theology, the abyss of the a-theological text can be thought as a reading of this poetic abyss.[25] In this sense, a theology of disability is shifted to a disability of theology, and a deeply theological disability, of the kenotic Christ. In all of this, authenticity in the face of the abyss is brought under the scrutiny of a particular autistic integrity, which will be developed as a paradoxical (dis)ability.

In the light of LTA's liminality, abyss, and darkness, the conversation with autism can now be framed. This will be developed in the following chapters, once our terms for understanding autism have been established.

TAKING THINGS LITERALLY

"Walking by faith, and not by sight," is not far removed, in a certain sense, from Samuel Taylor Coleridge's concept of

23. Walton, "Introduction," in *Literature and Theology*, 2.
24. Walton, "Introduction," in *Literature and Theology*, 2.
25. Mark C. Taylor performs these readings in *Erring* and *Tears*, and Taylor's thought will provide a vital narrative, which will appear in chapter 2.

the act of reading as a "willing suspension of disbelief," as discussed by David Jasper in his influential development of the field of Literature, Theology and the Arts.[26] In much of his work, Jasper places the faith the reader brings to the work of literature by suspending disbelief, alongside a similar suspension of disbelief which is commonly termed religious faith.

So, bringing this double "suspension of disbelief" into dialogue with a mythical autism, another strand of this book emerges: the game of "let's pretend" which goes by the name of metaphor. Bringing together the two kinds of suspensions of disbelief Jasper discusses is a challenge for the mainstream clinical narrative of autism, as well of popular perceptions of autism. The autism specialist Uta Frith characterizes autistic thinking as "taking metaphor literally."[27]

Where this book aims to develop its journey toward the autism of Gxd is not least in questioning what Frith's statement means; in a Postmodern understanding of language, as we shall argue, all language is ultimately grounded in metaphor, dead or otherwise.[28] In other words, we are all in the business, for the most part unconsciously, of "taking metaphor literally." To think of dissecting the metaphorical language unconsciously used in everyday use, ask any cryptic crossword aficionado! Furthermore, this book argues that taking poetic language "literally" might, more accurately, mean taking it seriously; engaging with it in a more vital and interrogative way, so that autism

---

26. Jasper co-founded the Oxford University Press journal *Literature and Theology* in 1987, and established the interdisciplinary Centre for Literature, Theology and the Arts (CLTA) at the University of Glasgow.

27. See Frith, *Autism*, 127.

28. Derrida's view of language as defaced coinage will be an important way into this in subsequent chapters.

might, in fact, in its tenacious way, respond more deeply to poetic language. Of course, this is paradoxical—many, if not most, autists, recoil from poetry precisely because it leads into a territory where "believing what is not true" requires a faith which does not compute; as we shall see, this is precisely the point. But hanging on to this strange counter-intuitive leap, crucially, if this is the case, then this deep and counter-cultural engagement with the poetic might extend to the poetry of mythical language.

ABSENCE AND PRESENCE

The autism of Gxd, as we will see, hinges on the death of Gxd, which in Altizer's rich mythologizing of Scripture is the paradoxical meeting of absence and presence. In this, he is drawing on mystical theologies, Buddhist and Christian, although this writer is not qualified to explore Buddhist philosophy and so I am approaching this paradox from within the Christian tradition. *Where her heart is, there also will her treasure be.*[29]

How does this absent presence play out in an autistic mythology? Absence, for the mythical hero, lies in the distance which her people feel from the neurotypical ("normal") majority who are paradoxically both more and less "prosaic," able to discern with ease what is and is not literal. Her absence is, for us, equally profoundly, from the socially and intellectually shared discourse of propositional theology, as much as from the everyday conventions of neurotypical conversation.

However, a word also needs to be said about the co-existing presence which accompanies absence, as its inverse face. This is an understanding of presence which

29. See Matt 6:21.

draws on the mythologizing of another aspect of autism. This is a mythologizing of the RRBIs which we explained in "Our Approach to Autism: A Beginner's Guide." To recap, the clinical literature tends to pathologize (view as illness or disability) the autistic trait of narrow interests, which can appear obsessive or boring to the onlooker. From an autistic point of view, the reverse is true; these are a source of deep and fulfilling delight. The autism specialist Francesca Happé also has the wonderful insight of viewing the peculiar sensory sensitivities of autistic people as similarly of value to the autistic person. These sensitivities can be unpleasant, when sound or light can be distressingly intense, but they can also be beautiful, when the touch of a fabric or the sparkling colors of Christmas tree lights can give comfort, communion and pleasure.

> **My view, as developed in this book, is that both narrow interests and sensory delight might be termed, taken together, as Autistic Fascination. Thinking theologically, the words of the poet Gerard Manley Hopkins when he writes that *The Earth is charged with God's grandeur* would make sense in terms of this Autistic Fascination. This fascination is an opening into a rich understanding of the legends we call Scripture.**

In the theologies we will visit, there is a paradoxical *coincidentia oppositorum* (co-existence of opposites), of absence and presence. As we will see in chapter 1, in autism also, presence happens only within absence.

To anyone who knows autism, this is going to seem completely counter-intuitive. To be blunt (I am thinking of myself) autism can seem brilliant but pedantic—sometimes, also prosaic. So how can I associate autism with poetry? Simply because we are not looking at autism from the outside, but inhabiting it on the inside. There, what might seem (frankly) boring or obscure to the outsider is a thing of great beauty to the autist within her own world. *I am not saying that autistic people are poets* (although some are—and fine painters, too, to think of the Glasgow autist Peter Howson).[30]

Absence, presence, metaphor, myth, fascination, love—these, then, are the themes which make possible the concept of a beautiful autism of Gxd (chapter 1). This will then be established, through metaphor (chapter 2), mystical theology (chapter 3), and atheology (chapter 4). From there, it will remain only to add two working examples/embodiments/excursi and a coda. Focusing on presence as fascination (chapter 5), we will read the nineteenth-century English poet/priest Gerard Manley Hopkins in company with mythical autism; and lastly, focusing on absence as Mindblindness (chapter 6), we will focus on two all-too-unrecognized novels by the nineteenth/twentieth-century Italian playwright Luigi Pirandello.[31] The coda which concludes this work will then be in a position to assert its full counter-cultural force—not merely that pastoral theology can reach out to validate autism, but the converse; that autism is a force which, if heard, can validate radical kinds of theological thinking, which in our current climate are surely, sorely needed.

---

30. See ScottishAutism, "Peter Howson."

31. Pirandello's genius largely paved the way for the twentieth-century Theatre of the Absurd, and his understanding of absence is a profoundly challenging one.

Chapter One

The Autistic Trinity

STORIES OF SEPARATION

> Perhaps they were the reason for the ancient legends of "fairy changeling" children, in which the fairies were believed to steal away a human baby and leave a fairy child in its place. In some versions of the story the changeling was remarkably beautiful but strange and remote from human kind.[1]

> The hedge of thorns or the glass coffin are perfect for representing the impossibility of reaching the child. In the case of autism, however much the child's appearance seems to indicate that it is normal and healthy ("awake"), the child's social isolation shows after all that it is not ("asleep").[2]

Can we think of clinical characteristics in poetic or mythical terms? Perhaps these examples already give us a clue. The first, drawing on fairy stories which talk of the changeling (the substitute, alien baby given by the fairies when they steal the human baby), portrays the idea of the *autos* as "strange and remote," as envisioned by the autism clinician Lorna Wing. Similarly, in the second, the

---

1. Wing, *Autistic Spectrum*, 17.
2. Frith, *Autism*, 17.

psychologist Uta Frith sees in the fairy tale *The Sleeping Beauty* a way of representing autism's separateness—the sleeping beauty is enclosed in a glass coffin, sleeping behind a hedge of thorns.

These archetypes hold all the universal power of which fairy stories are made, voicing our hopes and fears in fictional form. Wing and Frith are speculating on whether autism could be represented in the stories too. To extrapolate from this power, we will speculate on *autism itself* as something archetypal, and this is, at its heart, this book's journey. In a sense, this is the reverse of what Wing and Frith are doing in these fairy story examples.

> **In their examples, *the story yields a way to talk about autism*. In our journey, conversely, *autism yields a way to construct a story*, which can be told as the myth of a cosmic, universal autism.**

Not only this, but this cosmic autism will radically validate and revive sacred, marginal, theological discourses; it can search out the places where an archetype of autistic separation asks demanding and important questions. Mindfulness of Separation is the conscious awareness that this radical separation exists in this theological universe, and that a (mythical) universal autism discerns degrees of separation present to some degree everywhere. This idea of autism as omnipresent gains traction from the autism expert Simon Baron-Cohen's concept of the autistic spectrum, where autism, to some degree, is part of humanity in a spectrum of varying degrees. An autistic separation from others, like the changeling and Sleeping Beauty, has a pathos, but also, as we shall see, an unexpected theological power. It co-exists with the other parts of an "autistic trinity," operating together and always connected to its heart of love.

Stories and conceptions of solitude could, of course, be found in a thousand places, but another two examples will be enough to illustrate the point that a universal separation is not an uncommon idea in our poetic and intellectual universe.

The Punjabi poet Batalvi's love poem, *Separation, You are King*, begins and ends with the quatrain:

> Let us speak of separation,
> Separation is king.
> A body that does not feel separation,
> Is dead body.[3]

The critic Robert Scharlemann writes:

> The very universality of being is appropriable only not in the form of something common or general but in the form of the singular: inevitably, everyone asks the question of the meaning of being, but everyone must ask it as an "I."[4]

Scharlemann's essay expresses solitude, distance and difference as essential to individuation, while Batalvi's love poem (it is a love poem) goes further, to suggest that, without separation, we cannot even have relationship. This is a universal separation. This particular theological thinking of universal separation takes on a new power when it comes into dialogue with autism. Autism can be seen as the radical experience of separation; when "separation is king," in theological terms, an autistic mythical power can envision this universal reign within an autistic perspective.

---

3. Batalvi, *Separation, You Are King*.
4. Scharlemann, *Inscriptions and Reflections*, 33.

A NEUROTRIBAL APPROACH: STEVE SILBERMAN

How can we justify this claim that autism, for all its disabilities (or even, also, because of them), has a legitimate and distinctive voice? One starting point might be the philosophy set out in Steve Silberman's 2015 *Neurotribes: The Legacy of Autism, and How to Think Smarter about People Who Think Differently.* Silberman defines neurodiversity as

> the notion that conditions like autism, dyslexia, and attention-deficit/hyperactivity disorder (ADHD) should be regarded as naturally occurring cognitive variations with distinctive strengths that have contributed to the evolution of technology and culture rather than mere checklists of deficits and dysfunctions.[5]

Thinking about autistic people as a "tribe" who think differently with a "distinctive strength" would offer the possibility of moving autism out of a narrative of pathology (i.e., seeing autism as a mal-function) into celebration of its contribution to a plurality of world views. Silberman adds that "the idea of neurodiversity has inspired the creation of a rapidly growing civil rights movement."[6] In accord with this recognition that being different is not being inferior, an important term is "validation," affirmation of validity.

A PASTORAL APPROACH: JOHN SWINTON

Could this be an "inter-faith" exercise in celebrating diversity? Could it even be, as this book will argue, that the divergent perception style of autism offers a valuable theological insight?

---

5. Silberman, *Neurotribes*, 16.
6. Silberman, *Neurotribes*, 16.

A theology of love, approaching the lived experience of autists, would seek to honor neurodiversity, and this approach is put forward in the disability theologian John Swinton's 2012 *Reflections on Autistic Love: What Does Love Look Like?* Swinton defines disability theology as a seeking "to give theological voice to people and experiences that have not been taken seriously in the construction of theology."[7] In the case of autism, this voice, for Swinton, "may be counter-cultural and perhaps counter-intuitive, but . . . nonetheless authentic."[8] The scope and aim of Swinton's research here is "listening to the stories of people with autism," so that this "may actually be the beginning of opening up a new discourse about the nature of love."[9]

Swinton puts this listening into practice, and as a result is able to challenge the perception that autists are "thin" people, lacking in emotional depth and incapable of meaningful forms of love. Instead, in listening to autistic people, he discerns radically different ways of experiencing and expressing love. This is a powerful "antidote" to the hateful rhetoric of attempts to silence and discount autism's very being. (As voiced, notably, in the "I am Autism" campaign of *Autism Speaks* which we discussed earlier). Swinton's emphasis on inclusivity and acceptance is deeply theological, as the thinking of the gospel in action in the loving act of listening to autistic people, founded in an understanding of what the *keygma* (gospel message) truly entails. It is also, perhaps, even more deeply theological in its open-ness to new modes of theological thinking which consider autistic love as a valid mode of human

---

7. Swinton, "Reflections on Autistic Love," 275.
8. Swinton, "Reflections on Autistic Love," 275.
9. Swinton, "Reflections on Autistic Love," 275.

experience. This is a powerful statement, seeing autistic being as a valued part of creation and not, as in *Autism Speaks,* an "enemy."

Similarly, although Nancy Eiesland's *The Disabled God: Towards a Liberatory Theology of Disability* focuses more on physical disabilities and adopts a more sociological approach, her narrative also validates disability within the Church. For example, she criticizes elements in Christian attitudes which "have treated people with disabilities as objects of pity and paternalism."[10] She writes that "the dissonance raised by the nonacceptance of persons with disabilities and the acceptance of grace through Christ's broken body necessitates that the church finds new ways of interpreting disability."[11] Crucially, "In presenting his impaired hands and feet to his startled friends[12] the resurrected Jesus is revealed as the disabled God."[13] Can we take up this challenge?

THE AUTISM OF GXD: A HERMENEUTICAL APPROACH

The awareness offered by Silberman and Swinton opens up the possibility of allowing, and celebrating, diverse hermeneutical approaches to the text. Theologically, interfaith conversations work to nurture a sense of reverence for the other whose approach to the text, or Gxd, or the world, is different from our own.

A neurotribal autistic hermeneutic could function as a legitimate strategy, resting on a legitimate epistemology. This will be autism giving itself permission to see the world

10. Eiesland, *Disabled God*, 20.
11. Eiesland, *Disabled God*, 23.
12. Luke 24:36–39.
13. Eiesland, *Disabled God*, 100.

autistically, with the ability to discern a mythical autism of the text.

This book's journey, however, as a way of constructing a mythic hermeneutic, is not to ask about autistic people's individual religious experience, or even theological perspectives as such. Instead, it starts, as it were, from the other end. That is to say, although it begins with an intuitive sense of autistic perception, for the purposes of this myth it is not specifically person-centered (although person-infused) but universal, as we shall see. *This hermeneutic can then illuminate a kind of innate autism poetically inherent in poetic, atheological and mystical discourses.*

This does draw on autistic people's constructions of experience, as a starting point for thinking about what autism is. However, the point here is for theology to consider autistic modes of seeing as a radically different *mythical* lens. An autistic hermeneutic might be taken by theological thinking as another strategy in its own array of hermeneutical possibilities. This could be expressed as an elucidation of a "hidden autism," not of the reader *per se*, but in the world of the text. *Adopting this autistic hermeneutic would be a conscious strategy to discern that inner autism (where we find it) in theology.* The following points explain how this works:

- This strategy works by seeking out hospitable narratives where mythical autism might have its strongest potential to amplify and elucidate. That is deliberately worded; these theological narratives are not intended to *validate* autism, so much as to be validated *by* autism.
- It's compelling to see a strange, divergent, mythical autistic perception when it becomes an embodiment

of the radical and marginal spaces of mystical theology and atheology.

- Put differently, a theoretical/theological autism *of the text* could be called a mythology of autism. This sees autistic traits as archetypes, present in the text, which can be discerned by entering into the text via an autistic hermeneutic.

This autistic perspective will be celebrated as a strength, and a legitimate, and even privileged, hermeneutic, of real value to theology. We are looking for a language in which an autistic-theological hermeneutic can express its authenticity. This is an authenticity that, as the Quakers say, "speaks to our condition" as we, *as readers, autistic or not*, enter into the workings of an autistic mode of being.

To do this, our autistic mythology will create a radical, mythical hermeneutic. This will elucidate (and validate) the discourses of absence, or more accurately and paradoxically, an absent presence, within mystical theology and atheology.

We will have a conversation between mythical autism and its conversation partners of firstly, mystical theology and secondly, atheology. There, on that meeting-point, they will be able to read each other hospitably in hermeneutical sympathy.

THE HOLY FOOL

We have seen how writers such as Steve Silberman and John Swinton see autism as a different ability, which may seem odd to the world. This different ability has been conceptualized by a number of writers who compare the autist to the "holy fool." First, then, what does the tradition of the holy fool involve?

The critic Philip Gorski writes about examples from the Russian Holy Fool tradition[14] through his reading of the Russian novelist and playwright Nikolai Leskov. Leskov recounts the story of Alexander Afenasevich Ryzhov, the police chief who refuses to take bribes and is described as *"having gone as far as Christ"* in his literal-minded honesty, and therefore receives the verdict from the archpriest that *"it's all up with him."*

Church historian Christine Trevett comments that:

> The Russian traditions of the fourteenth through sixteenth centuries in turn owed much to the Byzantine traditions. Those texts used holy folly with its ascetic pretense of foolishness as explanation for gullibility, oddity, and shocking unconventionality. . . . St. Basil's cathedral in Moscow has as its patron one such "blessed" person—a practitioner of *yorodstvo*, i.e., he was a fool of the holy kind.[15]

Thinking of the Holy Fool as an archetype for autistic "oddness," Trevett surveys both the Russian tradition[16] and the Western Church's use of the idea and goes further, tracing back the holy fool archetype to late antiquity and the early Christianity of the Desert Fathers:

> With their rags and narrow food preferences, they had been concerned with simplicity, regardless of whether those who encountered them were disconcerted by their non-communication and did not want to be left alone with them. The earliest references to holy folly came out of the setting of such desert monasticism.[17]

---

14. See Gorski, "Holy Fools."
15. Trevett, "Asperger's Syndrome," 145.
16. See also Frith, *Autism*, 22–23.
17. Trevett, "Asperger's Syndrome," 142.

Coming forward to the twenty-first century, Trinity Stores comment about the "holy fool" tradition:

> St. Paul speaks of foolishness for Christ's sake in his letters to the first Christian churches. Holy foolishness, at its heart, is a prophetic path. It names the lifeless idols we worship in place of the living God—things like our possessions, our social status, and anything else we use to prop up our egos.[18]

and places St Francis within this tradition:

> Francis of Assisi embraced holy foolishness when he began his life of penance. Having once admired the elegant troubadours of southern France, he now called the motley band of his first followers jongleurs, instead. The jongleur did somersaults, stood on his head, and juggled assorted objects to entertain royal folk in between the troubadour's songs. Francis and his followers were to be jongleurs for God's people and the heavenly court.[19]

---

18. Lentz, "St. Francis."
19. Lentz, "St. Francis."

Le Jongleur de Dieu

St. Francis, Jongleur de Dieu, by r. Lentz.

The twentieth-century novelist G. K. Chesterton also shows the power of the "holy fool" nature of St. Francis, and how an (autistic?) holy fool can have great influence on the world:

> . . . the coming of St Francis was like the birth of a child in a dark house, lifting its gloom; a child that grows up unconscious of the tragedy and triumphs over it by his innocence. In him it is not only innocence but ignorance . . . it was such an amnesty and reconciliation that the freshness of the Franciscan spirit brought to the world.[20]

Christine Trevett speculates on the similarity between Francis' early follower Brother Juniper and autistic traits, while cautioning against too readily equating the two. Trevett is developing the autism expert Uta Frith's idea of Brother Juniper as an autistic holy fool,[21] to consider the role of autists in the Church. Trevett writes:

> Holy Fools afflicted the comfortable and the AS-ish[22] Juniper did the same. His person and his actions challenged fear-driven choices. He made manifest everyone's horror of being labelled "abnormal" and the stories about him were a question mark over excessive regard for the regard of others. Juniper challenged people's desire to see themselves reflected back when they engaged with someone. He offered no such reflection and in his peculiarity he was iconic. So just as the Franciscans' message implied that there should and could be no grounding for the Christian in humanly-based security, so the Juniper stories implied, in addition, that there should and could be no grounding in the security of others being predictable and conformist.[23]

Trevett explores Brother Juniper's abnormalities and sees many features with potential similarities to autism. Like Trinity Stores, she points out that the "foolishness" of

---

20. Chesterton, *Saint Francis of Assisi*, 178.
21. See Frith, *Autism*, 18–21.
22. Asperger's Syndrome-ish.
23. Trevett, "Asperger's Syndrome."

divergence might in fact be spiritual wisdom. If this is so, then there might be also the quality of innocence, which Francesca Happé suggests: "fools are innocent, and as such they are embodiments of divine grace."[24]

So, is one form of holy foolishness innocence? The above examples seem to suggest a naïveté which defies conformity, not caring about normal expectations. On the subject of innocence in autism, there are numerous accounts. For example, on the autism community website wrongplanet.net, the blogger JustElliot—Snowy Owl writes:

> So I've been told most of my life that I am naïve in a lot of ways . . . I've also been told that I come across as so innocent, like someone who would never hurt a fly.[25]

The parent of one autistic child gives this explanation:

> Bean isn't cunning, he has little or no guile and he does not manipulate others because he simply does not have the necessary theory of mind to do so. . . . But Bean has never even attempted (being manipulative) because his autism prevents him from making that very basic inference about how his action will affect another person's behavior. So when Bean cries it is because he is hurt and that's all there is to it. This applies to other forms of manipulation as well, crying for attention is perhaps the most basic manipulation possible; other more sophisticated types are completely beyond our boy. This purity of purpose and intent is actually quite beautiful if you think about it![26]

In fact, for an autistic hermeneutic, something similar and yet very different is happening. Bean, as a small child,

---

24. Happé, "Staging Folly," 165.
25. http://www.wrongplanet.net/postt166182.html.
26. "Beautiful and Dangerous Innocence."

"As for me, I can only fall on my knees and pray that the Lord Christ, who has died for me, might have his own way with me- that it might be worth His while to have done what He did and what He is doing now for me. To my Elder Brother, my Lord and my God, I give myself yet again, confidently, because He cares to have me and because my very breath is His. I will be what He wants, who knows all about it and has done everything that I might be His own — a living glory of gladness."
George Macdonald.

lacks the theory of mind to develop the skill of manipulativeness; in other words, he has Mindblindness. However, as an autistic adult, I feel I am capable of choosing (or at least trying) to learn whether or not to develop strategies to overcome this naïveté.

> **Our autistic hermeneutic is a conscious autism, a strategy adopted consciously, to enter into the spiritual nature of this "innocence."**

This is in order to explore, in a new way, the words and nature of Jesus regarding innocence and childlikeness when he says that "unless you become like little children you cannot enter the Kingdom of God."[27] This is what we might call an "acquired naivete"—where the reader knows perfectly well that she is unlearning (or relearning what she knows perfectly well to have already once known); this is the gift of innocence, akin to what the critic Paul Ricœur terms a "second naïveté"; *a rediscovered naïveté of awe and wonder*. This awe is similar to T S Eliot's poetic moment where:

> the end of all our exploring
> Will be to arrive where we started
> And know the place for the first time."[28]

Could autism, in fact, already be there?

THE AUTISTIC TRINITY: A CLINICAL MODEL

In the "Our Approach to Autism: A Beginner's Guide" section in the introduction and the general introduction, we looked at Mindblindness, literal-mindedness, autistic empathy and lastly, the Autistic Fascination of what Alastair

---

27. Matt 18:3.
28. Eliot, "Little Gidding," in "The Four Quartets," *Complete Poems and Plays*, 197.

Clarkson calls the Sensory Connoisseur.[29] (Following his logic, and that of DSM-5's RRBIs categorization, we will take sensory sensitivities and "narrow, circumscribed interests" (obsessions/special interests) together as forms of fascination.)

So how can we mythologize these key facets of autism? We need a skeleton, which we can then "enflesh." We start by thinking of key, clinically observed autistic traits as a kind of trinity, [see fig. i] with a *perichoresis* (mystical unity) at its heart, shown in the center. Each part of this triangle shares in some way with the others so that, seen in the fullness of this mythology, they become interactive and part of one reality. Before exploring these terms, here is a simple diagram of this trinity. (Of course, this trinity is not to be compared with the doctrine of the Trinity of God, Father, Son and Holy Spirit—except that in both, love at the center fills each, and that each is joined indissolubly to the other).

```
                  Mindblindness
                       /\
                      /  \
                     /    \
                    / Autistic \
                   /  Empathy   \
                  /_____\
         Fascination        Literal-mindedness
         and obsession
```

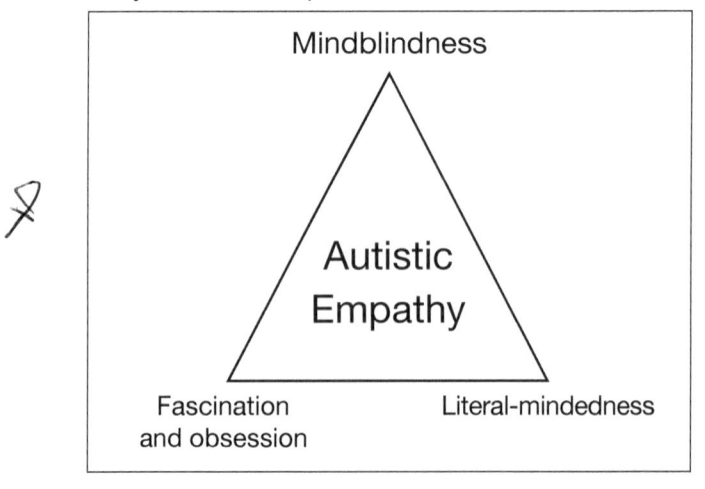

Figure i: The Trinity of Autistic Attributes © Ruth Dunster.

---

29. See the "Sensory Connoisseur" section in "Our Approach to Autism: A Beginner's Guide."

Because this author (*my self*) is on the autistic spectrum, and so are a number of my friends and family, when studying the clinical terms, I am also experiencing for myself just how they look and feel. I can *be* the protagonist who experiences this mythical world, as I now explore the clinical characteristics which form a rigorous basis from which to distill the tropes of mythical autism. A short recap will perhaps be useful.

Therefore, to begin, perhaps the best-known thing about autism is the difficulty connecting with other people and understanding them; what the Autism Introduction termed **Mindblindness**. This can be painful or liberating, depending on the situation and the person. For example, the liberating aspect is expressed when the autist Leneh Buckle tells us she was happier when (as a young child) she was unable to communicate. The painful aspect is seen a thousand times over when the autistic child in the playground is bemused by other children teasing her, or she is struggling to join in games; sometimes, she is happier not to participate.

Secondly, *literal-mindedness* is also one of the classic and best-known facets of autism, as the autism introduction explained. A neurotypical person knows that "I'm starving" colloquially means "I'm very hungry"—whereas taking it literally means "being so ill of hunger that I am about to die." Thinking it through, here there is a fundamental issue with language.

The third corner of the triangle, **Autistic Fascination**, is perhaps less well-known. Here, I am being controversial by suggesting that, as far as an autistic mythology is concerned, two separate phenomena might be different shades of the same thing, largely because this is my own experience, but also because it has a logic to it. This aspect of autism is Fascination-and-Obsession. Anyone who knows, or experiences what it is to be, an autistic person will testify to the love of shiny lights, velvety fabrics, crinkly leaves . . . and this seems to hold good for people with more profound or non-verbal autism just as much as it does for people "higher" (higher-functioning) on the spectrum. There seems to be an extreme sensory sensitivity which takes a real joy from these sights and objects, and I am terming this, as Francesca Happé does, *fascination.* Of course, this attenuated sensitivity can be very unpleasant too, in terms of texture, sound and light; some autists wear colored "Irlen glasses"[30] to filter out light frequencies which particularly stress their nervous systems (I, personally, find Irlen glasses useful).

Similarly, however, I suggest that fascination also encompasses the narrow, circumscribed interests which can seem at times also to consume an autistic person. This is where some stereotypes of autism can emerge—for example, the geek. The writer Luke Jackson describes his account of life with autism in *Geeks, Freaks and Asperger Syndrome;*[31] in other words, having obsessive, often highly intellectual interests makes the autist a geek. There is much online debate about whether Sherlock Holmes,[32] or Sheldon from *The Big Bang Theory,* or numerous other "geeks" in television, film, literature and history are autistic characters.

For our purposes here, what matters is the element of intense immersion and joy which can come from both sensory sensitivity and "restricted, repetitive behaviors and interests."[33]

30. See "Autism/Asperger Syndrome."
31. Jackson, *Geeks, Freaks and Asperger Syndrome.*
32. See also Frith, Autism, 24–25.
33. See the "RRBIs" section in "Our Approach to Autism: A Beginner's Guide."

At the center, in a mystical union with each of these mythical qualities, is the **autistic empathy** which, according to Simon Baron-Cohen, is the totally opposite mirror image of psychopathy. It is love which doesn't understand, but cares nonetheless. As the autism introduction made clear, this autistic "affective empathy" is much misunderstood, but perhaps even partly as a result, it can be a very pure love, full of self-sacrifice and perseverance. Absolute, pure autistic empathy can be read as akin to the key theological concept—Love—in perhaps surprising ways.

"AUTISM AND THEOLOGY?"

We can now explore what might happen if theology listened to autism. Would there be particular kinds of theological thinking which would answer the call and say yes, I recognize what you are saying? The answer, I think, is yes.

Autistic thinking is still all too marginal in our culture, so perhaps it is no surprise that the theologies which seem to resonate most clearly are also quite marginal theologies. My hope is that this conversation will give a strange strength and a hope to those who are devoted to marginal theologies, that they are honored by the powerful voice of autistic integrity—a strange thought perhaps, unless one is willing to believe that, as the Psalmist says, "deep calls to deep."[34]

My hope is that autistic searchers for truth, as I have been, might also find this book of value. Perhaps, equally, neurotypical people might learn from autism, too.

How can autism speak to theology? There are various approaches. One would be for autistic people to tell the Church what their needs and wants are; this is where

---

34. "Deep calls to deep, in the overwhelming of Your waters" (Ps 42:7).

pastoral theology such as the practical theologian John Swinton's enables a listening friendliness toward autism. Another would be for autistic people to describe their religious experiences; and this has been intriguingly documented and theorized by writers such as William Stillmann and Olga Bogdashina.

However, our thinking of autism as a privileged theological epistemology differs in essence from the thinking of Bogdashina and Stillmann, who view autistic being in terms of privileged spiritual experience. The two approaches are not necessarily mutually exclusive: where Bogdashina and Stillman see perceptual/sensory traits as the mystical experience of spiritual gifts, autism and mysticism are brought together for us at the level of discourse; *our territory is where autism functions at the level of story, not lived experience*; to think of autism in terms of a sacred story, to which theology can listen and from which theology can learn. In other words, this book builds a mythology of autism. A good place to start, then, is to examine why myth is important, and then how it might work as an approach for bringing an autistic voice into the world of theology. In other words, this book is about an autistic mythology which has power and truth. First, what exactly is myth?

WHAT IS MYTH?

The anthropologist Mircea Eliade studied non-Western cultures for many years, observing in them powerful forces of ritual and story. He realized that these stories, enacted by ritual, gave meaning to a culture. In this, he was performing what the founding father of Religious Studies, Edmund Husserl, termed phenomenological bracketing—namely, putting aside one's own worldview to enter into the worldview of another culture. As a friend commented to me, phenomenology means many things, but not least, at its simplest, it is a form of empathy where we "enter into" something.

In "primitive" or primal cultures Eliade discerned what he called the sacred and the profane—the ordinary, "profane," everyday things; and the holy things which give heightened meaning both to the cosmos and to humanity's place within it. (The contemporary meaning of profane as blasphemous or irreverent is not relevant here. Eliade is drawing on the literal meaning of profane from its Latin roots: *pro-fanus,* (outside from the temple)). Therefore, Eliade describes ritual and sacred story in these terms:

> In imitating the exemplary acts of a god or of a mythic hero, or simply by recounting their adventures, the man of an archaic society detaches himself from profane time and magically re-enters the Great Time, the sacred time.[35]

Eliade's insight was that these belief structures which we call myth, were perhaps not primitive attempts to answer questions in terms of physics and scientific cosmology. Instead, they were ways of expressing the meaning of qualities which invite reverence and hold together a culture's values and concerns. So, for example, Ninian Smart recounts an (unspecified) tropical African myth which tells that

> The sky, where God dwells, was once much nearer. So near was it that the sky could be touched. But one day some women took bits of the sky to cook in the soup, and God became angry and retired to his present distance.[36]

---

35. Eliade, *Myths, Dreams and Mysteries*, 23.
36. Smart, *Religious Experience of Mankind*, 60.

This story is myth, not in the present day common Western meaning of a false story, but myth as a truth-telling story. One might speculate on what sacred meanings are embodied here: respect for the environment, or perhaps principally, the transcendent nature of God, or even the (transgressive) nature of the female?

Another good example of this action of entering into the sacred is James Cameron's 2009 film *Avatar*, where the paraplegic Jake Sully becomes so immersed in a simulated "primitive" culture that he actually enters *into* that world of mythical truth; it has become more meaningful than the mechanistic, scientifically defined world from which he came. The same thing happens in a good novel or poem. For example, in George Eliot's classic novel *Middlemarch*,[37] the scholarly clergyman Edward Casaubon devotes his life to endless drafts and revisions of a book which aims to be (strangely enough) a compendium of all mythology. Ruining his health in this obsessive, hopelessly over-ambitious task, Casaubon dies of heart failure, unable to rest and take adequate care of himself. He is arrogant, insecure, and neurotic; hardly the qualities which would make a good member of the clergy. The truth of George Eliot's characterization is hard to miss; what a warning to writers (and clergy) who are unable to sacrifice the unattainably perfect in exchange for the perfectly adequate, finished good! This is the mythical power of fiction—to bring home a truth which impacts how we live our lives, and the choices and values we decide upon. At a deeper level still, good fiction changes and enhances how we perceive reality.

Another way to think of the sacred and the profane, this time in New Testament terms, is the distinction of

---

37. Eliot, *Middlemarch*.

Chronos and *Kairos*. *Chronos*, as the name suggests, is ordinary, chronological, historical time which can be measured scientifically in the normal world. In contrast, *Kairos* is a heightened, cosmic moment or dimension of spiritual significance.[38]

The "Our Theology: A Beginner's Guide" section in the introduction explained that the teaching of Jesus is interpreted by Rudolf Bultmann as an *existentialist* (as opposed to literal) truth calling the hearer to *metanoia* (turning around—i.e., repentance or change of direction) and discipleship. This is in contrast to a literal or historical reading of Scripture. Are we doing something similar, by seeing stories as, in the novelist Flannery O'Connor's phrase, "true lies?" There is a subtle difference here. Bultmann approached a text of Scripture with a demythologizing hermeneutic. When he argued that myth needed to be separated out and stripped of historical and scientific interpretation, it was to reveal myth as an existential truth, relevant to our personal choices and convictions.

> **In contrast, in our hermeneutic here (an autistic hermeneutic, a reading not *of*, but *by* autism), we are actually *creating* myth. In fact, we are developing a mythological hermeneutic which reads the clinical and lived experience *as if* it were myth. We are looking for the possibility of autistic traits as mythical archetypes.**

Actually, this is not so distant from the medical/clinical narrative as it might seem. Early on in the history of autism diagnosis, the psychiatrist Hans Asperger in the early 1940s described children with unusual traits as having a

---

38. "And do this, understanding the present time *(kairos)*: The hour has already come for you to wake up from your slumber, because our salvation is nearer now than when we first believed" (Rom 13:11); "I tell you, now is the time *(kairos)* of God's favor, now is the day of salvation" (2 Cor 6:2).

distinct syndrome which was named after him—Asperger's Syndrome. This word syndrome is interesting. Its Greek etymology is roughly *syn* meaning "together" and *dromos* meaning "course" or "path"—taken together, pathways which are grouped together in the same course; so a syndrome is a collection, in fact, of symptoms. A syndrome, as such, does not require an etiology (origin; medical explanation of its causes), it is simply an observation and classification of observed phenomena. In medical terms, then, a syndrome is a confluence of symptoms. In other words, a group of signs which together indicate a "something" called autism or (now a branch of a range of different forms) Asperger's Syndrome.

It is reasonable to see the "syndrome" as a group of clinically observed attributes and behaviors. Where we truly develop our own pathway is to see these phenomena as archetypes, in our mythology, just as, in the African myth, the sky is a collection of attributes, a "something" or *syn-drome,* an archetype of God's distance, personification, etc., embodying its mythical qualities.

The African myth does not try to be an "etiology"—although obviously, this can happen as Western physics and astronomy approach the distant sky in terms of causality. The same goes for the clinical syndrome—medical science looks for its causality, but the syndrome, as such, remains a collection of observations. Looking at these symptoms, these phenomena which simply *are*, awaiting interpretation, we will mythologize them as if an astronomer were to become a storyteller.

Our project is to take these observations as archetypes, on a mythical journey, remembering that myth embodies existential truth. We can then see which kinds of theological thinking might embody existential truths which the autistic myth articulates.

Just as importantly, we will see, in its own right, how an autistic myth takes on real validity and power as an existential truth. Theological thinking might be truly enriched by listening to its depth of insight in spiritual terms.

So, how can we write a mythological autism, which offers us possibilities of value and meaning? And could theology learn from a mythical autism? This mythological autism, as a *syn-dromos,* will work by observing the phenomena we can see, in the same way that the African tribe observe the sky. Like them, it constructs a story, which offers up a series of deeper meanings. What are the main phenomena to look at for creating this mythological autistic universe? How do we begin to think of mythological autism? What approaches to autism might lay the foundations of such a concept?

THE AUTISTIC TRINITY: A MYTHICAL MODEL

Absolute Autism

Here, it is important to explain another set of terms now moving into the territory of myth rather than clinical narrative. These are mythologized terms featuring in this book's autistic hermeneutic, as follows:

- Relative autism
- Universal autism
- Absolute autism
- Conscious autism

Relative autism is the kind of autism we see in the autistic spectrum; some people show marked autistic traits, some less so. Simon Baron-Cohen argues that every person is on the autistic spectrum to some degree, even if it's only a very slight tendency or perhaps a negligible quantity of one or two traits. This is the real, clinical autism as it is diagnosed in real, individual people, in all its complexity. It could also be called person-specific autism.

Universal autism is a mythical idea, relevant to the conversation autistic thinking might have with theological thinking. This is where we begin to think of autism in cosmic terms. A universal Mindblindness, for example, would be the idea that there exists, on a philosophical and theological level, some kind of isolation where propositional ("ordinary") language fails to reach the truth; and in mythical autism, this is a powerful archetype.

Absolute autism is **universal autism** taken to its logical conclusion, as a totality in mythical terms. So an absolute Mindblindness would be a total, absolute isolation where language fails, totally and absolutely, to make any connection with a truth or reality. This absolute will relate to the Absolute as we mythologize our autism as an atheological love story.

Conscious autism is the hermeneutical strategy of the reader who enters, knowingly, into the mythical approach of autism; or the consciousness of a fictional character who is aware of her inner, cosmic autism.

As symptoms move to signs and then to mythical archetypes in universal autism, we can now discern that they are the transmuted symptoms from our original triangle of mindblindess, fascination (RRBIs) and literal metaphor. These mythical elements now emerge, transmuted from the original triangle, as follows.

```
        Mindfulness
        of Separation
             /\
            /  \
           / Autistic \
          /   Love   \
         /_____\
Autistic Fascination   Autistic Metaphor
```

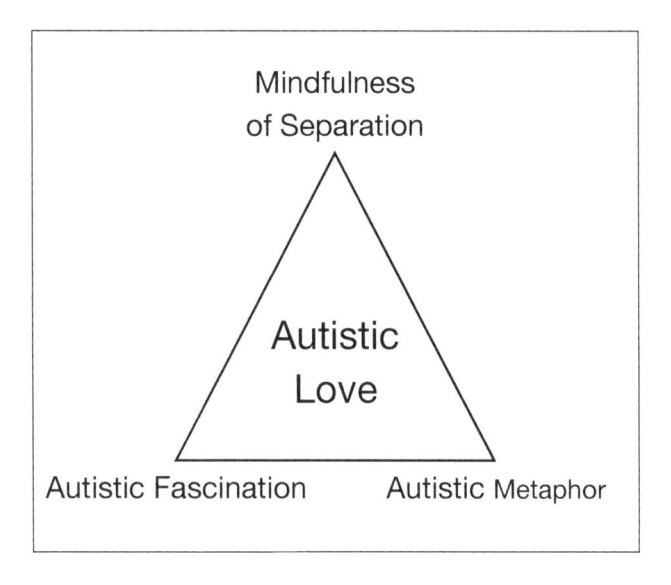

Figure ii: The Trinity of Mythical Autism © Ruth Dunster

Mindfulness of Separation

As the introduction explained, Hans Asperger and Leo Kanner both focused on autism in terms of *autos* (self); namely a separated self, disconnected from the world of others. Leneh Buckle, describing her childhood as an autistic person, writes "I was happier when I couldn't communicate."[39] What is the potential of this kind of separation, if it can possess the sacred meaning of myth?

This potential is realized when a mythical absolute Mindblindness can be thought of in terms of a message to theology. It invites theology to take heed of this place where autism speaks. Theology which listens to this voice could cultivate an awareness of a deep inner Mindblindness, which we will term *Mindfulness of Separation*. This is a mindfulness which permeates certain modes of theology

---

39. Buckle, "Is Increasing Functionality Always Good?"

with a particular intensity, if they are receptive to its voice. Mindfulness of Separation will speak of a universal autism, as a mythical quality embodying one facet of its sacred story.

Fascination

Our model of Autistic Fascination is a speculative way to form an important part of our mythology. I will spend some time, here, contextualizing it, in order to clarify. RRBIs, as "Our Approach to Autism: A Beginner's Guide" explained, are Restricted and Repetitive Behaviors and Interests; the need for sameness, stimming, and the fascination with particular topics. We saw how the model of the Sensory Connoisseur explained that repetition is not a negative, boring quality for autistic people if they are in fact discerning qualities which are invisible to the less discriminating observer. What is elegant in Happé' and Frith's "beautiful otherness of the autistic mind"[40] and Clarkson's model of the Sensory Connoisseur[41] is that we can combine sensory sensitivities with RRBIs (Restricted and Repetitive Behaviors and Interests), as a holistically thought cluster of features. Following this line of reasoning, we will take RRBIs and sensory issues together, as one component of our mythological autism. For ease of writing, I will simply call it, from here on, *fascination.*

To illustrate, there are some beautifully poetically termed examples of fascination in the autism literature. It can be seen as an intensely creative mode of being in the world. Frances Tustin gives an outstanding example of fascination:

---

40. Happé and Frith, *Autism and Talent*, xi-xx.
41. See "Our Approach to Autism: A Beginner's Guide."

> The controls of an autistic child are of an all-or-nothing variety. . . . He is either devoid of sensation, or he is flooded by it. Such floods of heightened consciousness seem to have much in common with those produced by hallucinogenic drugs in which the subject feels that colors and shapes are apprehended with ultra-vivid clarity and there is the sense of being actually inside a colour or a shape. Autistic children who have become articulate have shown me that they experience things in this way. For example, an autistic child called Peter, as he left the therapy room, pointed to a tall yellow daisy and said, "I'm inside that yellow flower—it's the yellowness I'm inside." He was at a loss to describe his experience any further. His whole body was taut with heightened responsiveness, the pupils of his eyes were dilated and his eye shone with preternatural brightness.[42]

When Peter says, "It's the yellowness I'm inside," he is in the territory of Autistic Fascination. Michael Fitzgerald writes, "Hans Asperger wrote about 'autistic intelligence' and saw it as a sort of intelligence hardly touched by tradition and culture—'unconventional, unorthodox, strangely 'pure' and original, akin to the intelligence of true creativity."[43]

This "strangely pure" way of relating to the world can give rise to intense, immersive responses which are expressed as musical, artistic and literary sensibility (subverting the narrative of autists as prosaic and pedantic; although these qualities, too, will be discussed below). The autist Temple Grandin speaks about "thinking in pictures" in her TED Talk and points out that autistic people tend to have particular fascinations and abilities with pictures (art),

---

42. Tustin, *Autistic States in Children*, 149.

43. Asperger, "'Autistic Psychopathy' in Childhood," pp. 37ff cited in Fitzgerald, *Genesis of Artistic Creativity*, 5.

words (hyperlexia and reading/writing) or mathematics, and that these can generate particularly creative interactions with the non-human world.[44] Similarly, the autistic writer Donna Williams describes a sense of oneness:

> It was this side of me that felt part of the things around me, not with them, but as them. In sensing them, yet sensing them without the selfhood of interpretation, significance and realization, I became "one" with the things I sensed.[45]

Williams continues:

> Classical music poured out of me; music spoke the force and variation of wind and rain, sunshine through clouds, the contrast and magic of dusk and dawn and flying.[46]
>
> The city lights and reflections playing upon the river . . . statues, beautiful parks, old wooden cathedrals, and marble sculptures, paintings by Renoir or scenes by Monet, captured me and brought home the beauty of "the world." . . . The frosted trees and icy fields . . . the beauty moved me so deeply I found myself crying.[47]
>
> Some things hadn't changed much since I was an infant swept up in the perception of swirling air particles, a child lost in the repetition of a pattern of sound, or a teenager staring for hours at colored billiard balls, trying to grasp the experience of the particular color I was climbing into.[48]

The autistic artist Wendy Lawson also comments about fascination:

---

44. Grandin, "World Needs."
45. Williams, *Autism—An Inside-Out Approach*, 249.
46. Williams, *Autism—An Inside-Out Approach*, 245.
47. Williams, *Autism—An Inside-Out Approach*, 59.
48. Williams, *Autism—An Inside-Out Approach*, 52.

> I find color simply fascinating and it stirs all sorts of feelings in me. The stronger and brighter the color, the more stirred up I become. My favorite colors are rich in emerald green, royal blue, purple, turquoise and all the in-between shades of these colors.[49]

How, then, does fascination function as a mythological quality? It is a sacred joy, akin to Saint Francis' "holy foolishness" which savored the uniqueness of every tree. Just as these sensory examples are forms of this joy, so, equally, are "restricted interests," which the outsider does not see as possessing the sacred joy that the fascinated, holy fool sees; and yet, possibly, as we shall consider, it is the fool who is the truly wise.

A mythical Autistic Fascination would be a sacred, heightened sense of what is; a sense of presence and immanence. As has already been noted, this can be pleasant or unpleasant—in the sphere of grace, that Presence would be Love.

Literal Metaphor

Isn't the term "literal metaphor" a complete contradiction in terms? Indeed; or perhaps a better word, as we shall see, might be paradox.

The autism introduction discussed autistic literal-mindedness as a difficulty with processing metaphor. What if this "difficulty" was thought of rather as a divergent mode? In everyday life, it is a disability to be unable to tell, for example, when someone is teasing or being serious; to watch a television drama and "take it seriously," viewing it as reality; or to read a poem and puzzle over why a large

---

49. Bogdashina, *Autism and Spirituality*, 67.

number of golden daffodils on a hillside would be called a host.

But the autistic mythology is not about everyday life. Rather, it is about a distilled or abstracted quality which provides a particular hermeneutic. This is where "taking things literally" becomes very interesting. On an everyday "real" level, taking theological language and Bible literally might mean embracing a Fundamentalism which takes the Bible "literally." Perhaps this is why many highly intelligent autists reject religion entirely, because they find the Bible as a literal document too hard to swallow. But our mythology deals with an *absolute* literal-mindedness, not an everyday, relative one. In this sense, seeing language as literal has interesting potential. Theologically, it would seem logical that taking things literally might lead to unfruitful places: do we take the Genesis Creation and Garden of Eden stories literally?

But when we inhabit *theological* language, we enter hermeneutics, and an autistic hermeneutic paradoxically engages with the text at a deeper level. Perhaps taking theology "literally" means taking it more seriously. This really requires a whole chapter (chapter 2), as it will take us into the thinking of Jacques Derrida, Ian Ramsey, Martin Heidegger, and Ludwig Wittgenstein. For now, as a foretaste, consider the simpleton Chauncey Gardener, Peter Sellers' character in Hal Ashby's 1979 film *Being There*. Chauncey stands, looking through the railings at a tree on the White House lawn. "The tree is sick," he says, before moving on from the tree and the White House. So, when is language truly literal and truly figurative? The answer might be more complicated than it seems. Is he a holy fool, uttering truths in a naïf way for the benefit of those who are not fools, and yet unaware of them himself? Is he telling us the White House (and the Government) is sick, without even knowing he is doing it?

Pathologizing this issue (conceptualizing it as a clinical problem/condition), misses how the richness of autism might actually be doing something creative with language. Again, theology might learn a lot from listening to this in terms of a mythical richness of meaning.

Autistic Love

The "Our Approach to Autism: A Beginner's Guide" and the Introduction chapter generally, explained Simon Baron-Cohen's thinking of autism as a "zero degree positive" of unimpaired affective empathy combined with impaired cognitive empathy. This is the converse of psychopathy, which is a "zero degree negative" of impaired affective empathy and unimpaired cognitive empathy.[50]

What would this autistic empathy be in a myth which approaches the sacred? It would surely be a suffering love. In an approach to the *perichoresis* (mystical unity) of the autistic trinity, taken as universal autism, it might be the co-existence of Mindfulness of Separation (absence) and fascination (presence)—a sorrowful love, its loss of cognitive connection coupled with its heightened affective desire. A Suffering Servant, perhaps, as the prophet Isaiah describes. Certainly not, as John Swinton reminds us, an archetype of "thin," unfeeling people. Absolute autistic Love will, in fact, as we shall see, partake in the *kenosis* or self-emptying of Gxd in Christ.

As fig. ii demonstrated (p. 85), the original trinity of Mindblindness, Fascination/Obsession, and Literal Mindedness can now be transmuted, and enter their mythical

---

50. Baron-Cohen, *Zero Degrees of Empathy*, 30ff.

framework, as follows. In perichoresis, or mystical unity, each interacts with the other as the story progresses, to the point of merging identity and becoming one. As we now turn to examples of this mythological hermeneutic in practice, it will be evident that they are interconnected, with costly, autistic love, at the heart of each.

What kinds of stories can these mythical figures tell, and who are their perfect, hospitable hearers? The following chapters turn to different theological worlds, to see if autism speaks in each place or if, as Jesus suggests, there are places where "no great work can be performed."[51] There will, however, be the miracle of theological spaces where a work of grace is, in all its fullness, possible; where the myth finds a meeting place and "Autism (Truly) Speaks."

AUTISM AS GIFT

It would be ridiculous to deny that some aspects of autism function as a disability in the everyday life of people with autism, causing frustration and distress. It would also be ridiculous to deny that the clinical narrative is useful in elucidating how autism manifests itself, for diagnosis and designing appropriate support. However, we have also seen the strength of the thinking of the autism advocacy movement which sees people with autism not as disabled but as differently abled.[52] Taking insights from both perspectives, a theologically minded autistic mythology views autism as both a challenge and a strength. This is not simply challenge-and-strength, but challenge-as-strength.

---

51. "And he could do no mighty work there, except that he laid his hands on a few sick people and healed them" (Matt 6:5); "And He did not many mighty works there, because of their unbelief" (Matt 13:58).

52. For example, Silberman, *Neurotribes*.

THE AUTISTIC TRINITY

Autism as a challenge (disability) is inverted by thinking the disability itself, theologically, as a gift, also as the gift of disability itself.

Firstly, this is a spiritual gift because it offers a theological understanding of "disability" as a way of envisioning the human condition in terms of creaturely status and the biblical myth of the Fall. In other words, human beings are imperfect, and the "flaw" we call autism resolutely refuses to stop reminding us of this. Recognizing this very disability as a universal truth (on the autistic spectrum) is a new form of thinking what the theologian Karl Barth terms *Krisis*. For Barth, *Krisis* is the moment where our separation from God is caused by our sinfulness, and it is the exact point where Gxd both judges and forgives us. In autistic Mindfulness of Separation, our *Krisis* is not so much the separation of human sinfulness but an existential need for grace—Gxd's help—in the face of a universal human autistic separation from Gxd. This can engender a new level of self-knowledge and humility in the outworking of faith.

Secondly, at a deeper level, however, this means also speculating on *an autism of Gxd,* seen, at least for now, as transcendence. Disability here is separation from Gxd simply because we cannot conceive of something as vast and unsearchable as Gxd. Thinking of an autistic Gxd as disabled makes sense at Calvary, where total disability becomes total ability in kenotic sacrifice [kenotic comes from the Greek word *kenosis*, which means self-emptying].[53] As Jesus "empties himself" on the Cross, he cries out: "My God, my God, why have you forsaken me?" What mysterious words! How can Gxd abandon Gxd? Ultimately, in later chapters, this will be a separation *within* and *from*

---

53. Jesus "made himself nothing" (*ekénōsen*) (Phil 2:7).

Gxd, expressed in the mythological narrative of Thomas Altizer's *Gospel of Christian Atheism* (see "Our Theology: A Beginner's Guide").

However, we will also see that, crucially, our thinking of transcendence as Mindfulness of Separation co-exists, in the paradox indicated by apophatic theology, with a thinking of immanence as Autistic Fascination. Like two sides of a coin, these two modes of thought come together at a mythical, metaphoric level. This is hard to explain without examining the mystical theologians we will meet in chapter 3; so we shall "take it as read" for now that in the extremes of what saintliness discerns, Gxd is both utter absence and utter presence.

In an important sense, this is all built on Swinton's thinking of an active listening to the voice of autistic love. The argument for a radical autistic hermeneutic rests on the conviction that honoring the modes of autistic perception can lead to the validation of a theological voice which attempts to listen to a mythology of autism.

Chapter Two

Literal Metaphor and Incarnational Metaphor

THE RABBITS AND RUTH

> The teacher divided the young children into reading groups, each group named after an animal. It so happened that Ruth was assigned to the Rabbits. The teacher called for each group in turn to sit at her desk and practice their reading. "Will the rabbits come out?" she asked. Ruth remained at her desk—because in truth, she was not a rabbit. From that day on, the teacher said "Will the rabbits and Ruth come out?"

This chapter explores what literal metaphor means, so that we can move on to an atheological understanding of it which we will term "Incarnational metaphor." To begin, let's consider what happens when someone is unable—or refuses—to pretend to be a rabbit. This is the enigma of the game which sees children as rabbits, because they have been described as rabbits; is this "pretending" an act of considerable imagination, or an act of simple conformity?

But there is a logic in resisting the game, and this is, of course, one of the features of the autistic trinity—what we have called literal metaphor (which immediately sounds self-contradictory; we will negotiate this contradiction as we go along).

> For ease of reading, we are calling this hermeneutic "literal metaphor" although it actually means, of course, *"the mythical conception of autistic abnormal processing of metaphor"*—but that's far too clumsy to repeat over and over. An autistic hermeneutic, which interprets the text "literally," will produce a "literal" metaphor.

There are as many examples of this "taking things literally" as there are incidents in the life of autistic people. The clinician Tony Attwood discusses this phenomenon in his canonical work *Asperger's Syndrome,* and to name but one of his examples, the young child who is told "you must only ride your bike downstairs" is only just prevented from taking his bike upstairs in order to ride it down the stairs.[1] A friend of this author's, when told by a big-nosed teacher that he was "getting right up her nose" (i.e., annoying her) in all simplicity replied that there was plenty room up there! And so on, again and again—this really is a major feature of how the autistic mind works. In other words, we are not pretending to misunderstand! Instead, we are dealing with autistic literal metaphor.

Listening to the Rabbits and Ruth story as a myth means developing the concept of literal metaphor, so that it can function as a radical hermeneutic (that is, a tool for reading the world and the book/Book differently). Radical, because this hermeneutic takes us on a path which, if we follow it, will take us to a truly deep and new theological understanding. This is by no means the only autistic hermeneutic: other authors will have other approaches.

---

1. Attwood, *Asperger's Syndrome*, 76.

HERMENEUTICS AND METAPHOR

When we looked at hermeneutics in the theology introduction, we learned from Werner Jeanrond that "we never read a text 'objectively' or 'neutrally' . . . no human reader has an unlimited perspective."[2] This awareness opens up the possibility of allowing, and celebrating, diverse hermeneutical approaches to the text. Theologically, as we saw earlier, interfaith conversations work to nurture a sense of reverence for the other whose approach to the text (or the world) is different from our own. In mythical autism, we are certainly looking from a very different angle to most. Ours, in this book, in our particular autistic hermeneutic, is a mythical perspective, which invites us to be a non-rabbit in our own very different way; alternatively, to see rabbits "in a most delightful (if peculiar) way."

> **However, the point is this: a neurotribal autistic hermeneutic can be a legitimate strategy, resting on a legitimate epistemology. This will be autism giving itself permission to see the world autistically, with the ability to discern an autism of the text. And there is no reason why we should be barred from the table of inter-faith dialogue.**

This, as we have seen in chapter 1, is a hermeneutic which works within a mythical framework. In fact, *ultimately it will be a mythical hermeneutic which only works theologically. We will see that, in the end, this literal metaphor is a deeply theological one, and a radical one at that*. We will be able, finally, in light of this, to most fully name it: Incarnational metaphor.

Before we start, it will be useful to define some technical terms regarding language:

---

2. Jeanrond, *Theological Hermeneutics*, 2.

- Pragmatic language: language which is simply useful, serving a clear purpose;
- Propositional/prosaic language: language which is not poetic but simply straightforward, involving truth claims/fact stating;
- Ostensive language: language which carries the speaker's intentions to convey meaning, usually by pointing to examples;
- Poetic language: language which uses imagery and devices such as metaphor and simile; rhyme; rhythm; alliteration, to create sound, texture and mood beyond simply its *meaning* (or meanings). We might call it a form of literary embodiment in its effects.

A good place to start is by considering what "metaphor" actually means. The word metaphor derives from the Greek *meta* (after; with; across), combined with *pherō* (to bear; to carry). This means that metaphor is a "carrying across" of meaning, and the Oxford Dictionary of Literary Terms defines metaphor in this way: "a figure of speech, in which one thing . . . is referred to by a word or expression normally denoting another thing, so as to suggest some common quality shared by the two."[3]

So we could say that, in normal language use, or rather a propositional, "common-sense" hermeneutic, understanding the meaning involved in the *carrying over* means decoding it by *carrying it back* into how we understand its meaning. So, for example, in a metaphor such as *the road of life*, to understand the intent, the reader brings the (imaginary) image of *road* back into the (real) meaning of *life*.

---

3. Baldick, "Metaphor."

Aristotle distinguishes metaphor from simile in a succinct way:

> When the poet says of Achilles that he leapt on the foe as a lion, this is a simile; when he says of him "the lion leapt," it is a metaphor—here, since both are courageous, he has transferred to Achilles the name of "lion."[4]

The Oxford Dictionary of Literary Terms also explains the difference between metaphor and simile:

> In metaphor . . . resemblance is assumed as an imaginary identity rather than directly stated as a comparison: referring to a man as "that pig," or saying he is a pig is metaphorical, whereas "he is like a pig" is a simile.[5]

To inhabit the metaphor is to be in the imaginary space where a man is a pig, and of course, staying within the metaphor is absurd, because a man is not a pig. What the metaphor really means is that, in some respects, by sharing pig-like attributes the man is *like* a pig.

> **Obtaining meaning from metaphor is only possible by effectively using "common-sense," reducing it to simile, and this is, we could say, to kill the metaphor.**

Reading the metaphor neurotypically, the reader is perfectly well aware that resemblance is only that—resemblance—and a literal identification is non-sense for the common-sense point of view. So, by using common-sense, metaphor is contained and sealed off from its "dangerous" potential of losing a common-sense, stable meaning. Thinking of the pigness of the man, or the

---

4. Aristotle, "Rhetoric," in *Complete Works*, book III, ch. 4.
5. Baldick, "Metaphor."

roadness of life, is rescued from an absurd confusion by thinking of pigness as *like* the man, and roadness as *like* life. This is the pragmatic avoidance of absurdity, through reducing metaphor to simile. If this is a common-sense, neurotypical response to metaphor and simile, an autistic literal metaphor offers a different response—possibly, even, a new theological possibility. Imagine a mythical world of literal metaphor, where images we use as figures of speech stay in their magical (and irrational) potential. Literal metaphor resists the neurotypical common-sense pragmatic reading; it outwits neurotypical perception. Neurotypical "pragmatic metaphor" (the non-autistic, common-sense processing of metaphor) ironically fails, because it kills metaphor's power by reducing it to simile. In fact, Aristotle saw this issue when he wrote about metaphor being "dangerous" because it poses a threat to logic.

How exactly does autism resist this? The autism expert Francesca Happé puts forward a model of this "disability" (which we call literal metaphor) by considering how autistic people process what is termed ostensive metaphor. Ostensive metaphor is a term originally used within the linguistic concept of Relevance Theory as put forward by Deirdre Wilson and Dan Sperber.[6] Relevance Theory's ostensive language is defined as communicative activity which offers a common-sense intention to communicate—in this case, using metaphor. The hearer can therefore easily decode (de-code) the pragmatic use of figurative language in everyday settings. Happé gives a clinical understanding of autism's "failure" relating to ostensive language:

> Without the principle of relevance to guide them, the transparency of intentions that allows humans to use

6. See Wilson and Sperber, *Relevance Theory*.

language in a truly flexible way is not open to autistic communicators.
In the face of the puzzle that ostensive communication must pose them, they may have no choice but to adopt a rigid interpretation—a default value of the propositional form of the utterance.[7]

I am now taking Happé's terminology of "rigid interpretation" and "default value" and subverting them. In fact, this "propositional form" of autistic processing, I want to suggest, is *really an imaginative leap into what appears to be a creative absurdity,* where lives are roads and men are pigs. We could almost say our mythology is a form of magical realism, in the same vein as Salman Rushdie's opening sequence of a magical flight from a crashing airplane in his 1988 *The Satanic Verses.* Rushdie's narrative proceeds to a story of immigrant integration and non-integration—all within the framework of this magical, angelic flight to earth, where even the protagonist wonders how he survives. In this kind of magic realism, we are invited to inhabit the metaphor and the world it offers us within the book.

Ostensive language, to recap, is pragmatic, and "ostensive metaphor" is how we define a pragmatic stance which treats metaphor as a tool for conventional, shorthand, colloquial usage.

Now, here is our mythical inversion of ostensive and autistic metaphor: it is ostensive assumptions, not autistic processing, which tend to use metaphor in a way which is essentially prosaic, lacking in poetic potential, and we can contrast it with autistic literal metaphor's gifted divergence. A mythical literal metaphor inverts the clinical narrative *by de-pathologizing literal metaphor*. In turn, it will now be able to reverse our normal expectations. It will actually,

---

7. Happé, "Communicative Competence," 103.

subversively pathologize a "normal" ostensive metaphor in theological terms, as lacking richness of theological insight. This is truly paradoxical; what seems literal is in fact poetically and theologically rich, as we shall see.

This raises the question: what happens when one responds, purely and simply, to the metaphor itself, or rather the image it presents? What if Ruth puzzles over the enigma of rabbits who are somehow five-year-old children, and mythical autism celebrates that magical ability? What if she thinks there must be rabbits hidden in the cupboard? A neurotypical child might hop and bounce to the teacher's table saying "I'm a rabbit," but Ruth will be the one who looks for real rabbits, and stays perplexed. In the end, it seems, the children must somehow *really* be rabbits, and this is non-sense. But after all, there is more to life than pragmatism!

An autistic hermeneutic's apparent "failure," then, is the cognitive inability to configure meaning by the pragmatic decoding of metaphor. But what if, in mythical autism, it is a conscious game of dancing and swerving around pragmatism to another beat?

To explore this (in/)ability, we can think of literal metaphor as a co-existing manifestation of fascination and Mindfulness of Separation—the other members of the autistic trinity. Autistic empathy, as ever, will be in the center, the Love infusing and nourishing all parts. This works as follows.

METAPHOR'S PLACE IN THE AUTISTIC TRINITY

Mindfulness of Separation: This Is Not a "Conversation"

To see how literal metaphor works as a hermeneutic, firstly we will consider it as Mindfulness of Separation. Martin Heidegger writes that "we—mankind—are a conversation. The being of man is founded in language. But this only becomes actual in conversation."[8] Here, however, the autistic hermeneutic works not as the conversation of language, but as the silence of language. Perhaps literal metaphor is a silent conversation, between silences, on the bridge of language between the human and the divine; a privileged conversation possible only for a mythical autism which, paradoxically, as we have seen, finds ordinary human conversation so very difficult. Here, we are preparing the way for the kind of paradox we will come to in chapter 3.

To distinguish between autistic and neurotypical hermeneutics in terms of a possible Mindfulness of Separation, we could similarly think of Hans-Georg Gadamer's metaphor of the "fusion" of hermeneutical horizons. Gadamer writes:

> In the process of understanding there takes place a real fusion of horizons, which means that as the historical horizon is projected, it is simultaneously removed. . . .[9] Understanding is not to be thought of so much as an action of subjectivity, but as the placing of oneself within a process of tradition, in which past and present are constantly fused.[10]

Werner Jeanrond, commenting on this, expresses this meeting of horizons as being such that "language is the

---

8. Heidegger, *Hölderlin and the Essence of Poetry*, 277.
9. Gadamer, *Truth and Method*, 27–34, quoted in Jeanrond, *Hermeneutics*, 66.
10. Gadamer, *Truth and Method*, 258, quoted in Jeanrond, *Hermeneutics,* 65.

middle ground in which understanding and agreement concerning the object take place between two people."[11]

This is precisely what does *not* happen in autism. It is the first way in which literal metaphor can be thought of as absence, because there *is* no effective conversation where metaphor is concerned. An autistic hermeneutic is not one which discerns the social context of a body of tradition so that horizons fuse. In autism *qua* autism, there *is* no "understanding and agreement."

If this is tantamount to saying that there is, then, no genuine hermeneutical fusion of horizons, attaining understanding and agreement, then

> it is in fact accurate to say that an "absolute" autistic hermeneutic is a non-hermeneutic. The words are ultimately, in the myth of (impossible) absolute autism, "only" (and utterly bafflingly) words, which do not achieve the fusion of horizons. However, the space of a non-hermeneutic becomes interesting theologically if this is thought of as the "hermeneutic of the non."

This is precisely how the autistic hermeneutic will come alive as an atheological hermeneutic, by situating itself within the non-language of mystical theology and atheology. In this sense, the pathology becomes a privileged theological strategy.

This mythical autistic hermeneutic takes the image, as it were, literally, straight out of the horizon without seeing "beyond the horizon" to the other's horizon. In that case, there is no "fusion of horizons," but only one horizon, seen through the autistic eye. To some extent, our horizons do meet, but only "up to a point." Language is not a middle ground between two people, because there is (at least to

---

11. Gadamer, *Truth and Method*, 34–56, quoted in Jeanrond, *Hermeneutics*, 66.

some extent) only the autistic eye (I) (in the sense of *autos* = self). (We could equally say that this exposes the myth of total Mindreading, because in truth, no-one is a complete Mindreader!) The figurative image is not something shared between conversation partners, resulting in a new understanding, but simply is, in solitude. We could express it like this.

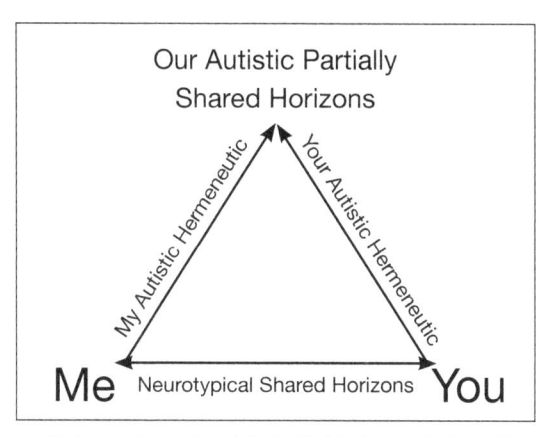

Figure iii: Neurotypical and Autistic Horizons © Ruth Dunster

The ideal neurotypical reader projects toward their respective horizons, but in autistic hermeneutics we can't see past our own horizons. The magic of meeting in the middle—the base of the triangle—is the trick which Dennett terms Theory of Mind, and Baron-Cohen terms Mindreading—the instinctive ability, intuitively, to read without the troubling apex of any degree of Mindblindness. It seems like a magic trick but we are simply collapsing each of our horizons down to a horizontal line where we can see each other's "angle," except that the angle is now zero, because we have been able to flatten down self or other into a place of mutual understanding. Perhaps autism, in its blind hermeneutic reaching up and out toward infinity, angled upwards with the potential to exceed that meeting point, has simply missed the point. In a way, of course, certainly it has, although tantalizingly, figure iii suggests the opposite. However, by now, it should be evident that this "mismatching hermeneutic" does not lack significance and value, in its own counter-intuitive way.

What if we think of a mythical Absolute Mindblindness, where there is absolutely no meeting of horizons? We could envisage it like this:

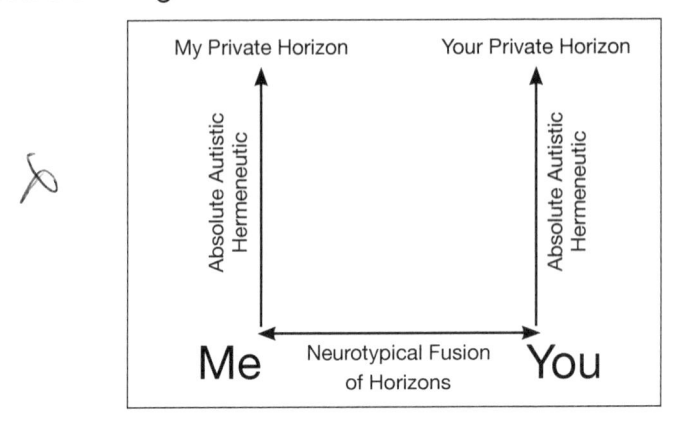

Figure iv: Absolute Mindblindness: Zero Sharing of Horizons © Ruth Dunster

This is precisely the point, in fact, if faith is in "what is not seen," requiring faith in a different seeing of the figurative itself. The eye of an ultimate, Absolute autistic faith can attain this, but, as we will see, this is actually, finally, at the expense of sanity, which however becomes an autism of saintliness.

> **The crucial point is that this insanity with the bafflement engendered by separation from the horizon of the other, is a genuine theological strategy. This strategy of bafflement might be more authentic than a systematic theology which could be too quick to contain God in a doctrinal system.**

It will lead, in subsequent chapters, to a thinking of apophatic language as Mindfulness of Separation, fascination, and an ultimately absolute Incarnational metaphor.

FASCINATION: INTUITION DIVORCED FROM CONVERSATION

The Impossible Fascination

There is no fusing of hermeneutical horizons to achieve union with the other, in the sense of a breakthrough to grasp the meaning of the other's intent. What there is, instead, is the union with the image itself, divorced from the intent "on the other horizon." This is an intuition of appreciating and inhabiting the image for its own sake. Being divorced from conversation means being separated from the fusing of horizons of meaning. It is in that space, by definition only in that space, that an exclusively intuitive and total oneness with the image takes place. (One may argue that a neurotypical reader might just as equally achieve oneness with the poetic object. What we will go on to explore in chapter 5 on the autism of poetry, is whether this could actually a streak of universal autism with which the poetic reader is blessed). This works by the kind of intense fascination which stays with its object, in the terms Uta Frith describes, and which Alastair Clarkson attributes to the autistic connoisseur, as discussed in the autism introduction.[12] This fascination, when thought theologically, is the union with the literal image.[13]

---

12. To recap, fascination is a thinking of RRBIs in terms of Alastair Clarkson's "sensory connoisseur" model. In this book, it also is pure affective empathy toward phenomena, manifest at times in intensity of sensory response as delight (or distress) and at other times as the affectivity of delight in the obsessive narrow interests common in high-functioning autistic people.
13. This paradox stands here for now, to be explored later.

There is a difference between being ignorant of the rules and deliberately breaking the rules. Ignorance of hermeneutical rules means naïvely assuming that there are no rules, and lacking awareness of the array of possible hermeneutical strategies (perhaps, even, ignorance of one's own hermeneutic).

The consciously, mythically minded autistic theologian knowingly breaks the rules, in the sense that they knowingly disrupt and exceed the boundaries of hermeneutical propriety. The text in effect is not "interpreted" at all. In this mythical, conscious, autism, there is only a one-ness of being "in the text."

This glory of metaphor can be seen in this second face of the coin: Autistic Fascination. This is, of course, impossible. How can a person *meaningfully* read a text at all, if there is no attribution of meaning? It is impossible, it would seem, to call a lack of interpretation a reading strategy. Or is it? The autistic child with echolalia (echoing and repeating words) repeats words "for no useful reason," but in her world, she is celebrating the musicality and pleasure of words at a higher level than merely *using* them pragmatically.

This is where the real nature of a mythical/theological autistic hermeneutic emerges, and why the Introduction insisted that this is not at the level of everyday usage or clinical autism. The profusion of images where God is mother, father, friend, lover, provider, lion, lamb, are anathema to the literal-minded autist who wants to settle on one image of God, or even none, because this riot of plurality and paradoxical contradiction can't be logically coded and makes no sense.[14] An autistic reader, typically, in real

---

14. This is exactly the point: do neurotypical readings pass over too lightly the phenomenal profusions and clashes of God-imagery in Scripture? How can it make sense for a loving shepherd to be a consuming fire?

life, would avoid the baffling nature of imagery as much as possible, and avoid both poetic and religious language.[15] However, for a *theological* autistic hermeneutic, the impossible task of "making sense" of this as propositional logic is not the issue, because it operates, ultimately, as an impossible ideal.

If a good, logical positivist autist steps away from this chaos, it is understandable (and common, perhaps necessarily). However, staying in this chaotic glory is the challenge of a mythical autistic theological hermeneutic. In other words, our failure to read aright is our key to a strategy of radical otherness.

Fascination as Presence: Dasein and Trees

We can also think of fascination, in literal metaphor, as love. Fascination is when the autistic child Peter says "it's the yellowness I'm in." What does it mean to be *in* a metaphor, just as he is *in* the yellow? It means staying in the image—abiding in it. It's worth taking a brief detour here to explain this, and look at an idea developed by Martin Heidegger. One of Heidegger's most famous terms is *Dasein*. Literally translated from German, *Dasein* means "the one"—but Heidegger means something much more. He means something like being the one which is truly "being there." In Heidegger's essay *What Is Called Thinking?*, he writes about what it is to gaze at a tree:

> when we think through what this is, that a tree in bloom presents itself to us so that we can come and stand face-to-face with it, the thing that matters first

---

15. Although when an autistic friend read this book in manuscript form, he found that a later chapter (chapter 5) actually *taught him* how to read poetry, aware of its conventions and intentions, and he then did so with great (autistic) delight.

> and foremost, and finally, is not to drop the tree in bloom, but for once to let it stand where it stands.
>
> Why do we say "finally?" Because to this day, thought has never let the tree stand where it stands.[16]

Heidegger's description of truly seeing the tree, beyond the constructions imposed by "thought," means an ability to outwit the thinking of Western metaphysics (our pragmatic, logical mindset), to access the tree's pure "being there" (*Dasein*).

The twentieth-century Italian novelist Italo Calvino says something similar when he writes that, blinded by signs, we are incapable of simply seeing a cloud as a cloud, because our minds go toward interpreting its shape:

> However the city may really be, beneath this thick coating of signs, whatever it may contain or conceal, you leave Tamara without having discovered it. Outside, the land stretches, empty, to the horizon; the sky opens, with speeding clouds. In the shape that chance and the wind give the clouds, you are already intent on recognizing figures: a sailing ship, a hand, an elephant.[17]

A pure Autistic Fascination would see the tree as a tree; the cloud as a cloud; and the word rabbits (impossibly) as rabbits. Of course, there is another tree we discussed earlier—the tree seen outside the White House by Chauncey Gardener, when he remarks in an unconsciousness of his own metaphor "The tree is sick." So the film carries another layer of meaning for us in this light; the title of the film is, by no accident, *Being There*—just as Heidegger's *Dasein* indicates the tree in bloom being there, which we fail to really see, through the busyness of

---

16. Heidegger, *What Is Called Thinking?*, 44.
17. Calvino, *Invisible Cities*, 14.

our minds. And in mythical autism, we can truly be there, where the White House hovers in the background, but the unconsciously metaphorical Chauncey sees only that the tree in the foreground really is a sick tree. Chauncey sets up the metaphor for us; we are "in on the joke" to interpret the White House as a sick tree, but the originator of this wisdom remains a fool. Surely Chauncey here is a holy fool, unconsciously pronouncing a deep truth.

This mythical literal metaphor can give us a really powerful hermeneutic. It indicates to us that this is a myth of being "stuck there" within the metaphor; failing to make the cloud an elephant or (as a friend told me recently) a frog in her throat be not a small amphibian but a gravelly sound to her voice (gravel: another metaphor—as we shall see, this chain of metaphors grows and grows; chain: another metaphor *et cetera*). Making a cloud be simply a glorious cloud is joyful to the autistic adult who loves to classify and gaze upon clouds. Having a small amphibian in her windpipe is terror to the woman who is told she has a frog in her throat; so literal metaphor as fascination, staying in the image, can be pleasure or pain, but either way it is, in the magical myth of literal metaphor's fascination, utterly real. Like the myth of the African story of the sky being pulled apart to cook, this fascinated literal metaphor gives meaning within this myth, but, crucially, not in the pragmatic terms of ostensive language. Something much deeper and stranger is happening. The frog is a frog which clogs up the throat; there must, perplexingly, be rabbits in the classroom; the cloud is beautifully and simply a cloud; and the tree is fully there.

MYTHICAL AUTISM: INCARNATION AND RESURRECTION

The autistic "impairment" of an epistemology of metaphor, seen in terms of a clinical narrative, is a disabling pathology; and in pragmatic, everyday terms, this is true. However, in mythical terms, we can also consider the disability itself as a radical theological possibility, which is that of a Resurrection which is at the same time Incarnation. (We will see this logic of a unity of Christ events unfolding when we explore Thomas Altizer's atheological thinking in chapter 4).

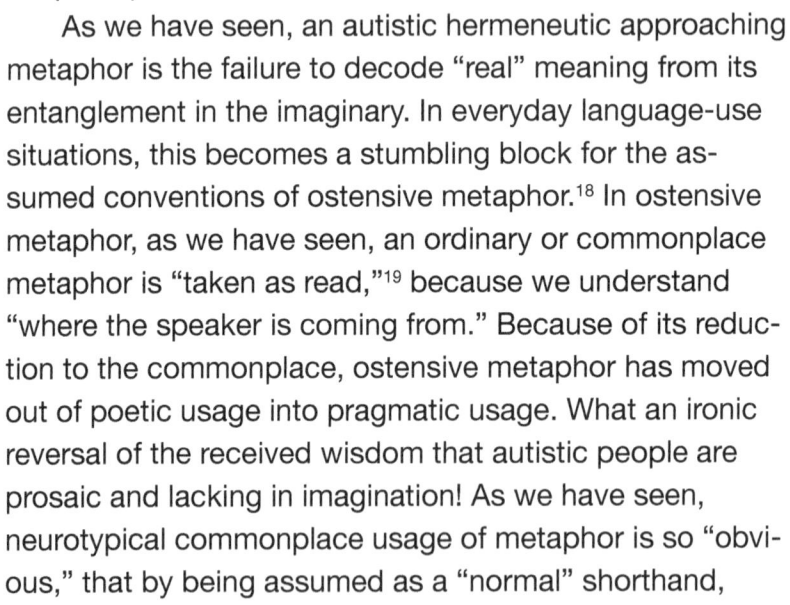

As we have seen, an autistic hermeneutic approaching metaphor is the failure to decode "real" meaning from its entanglement in the imaginary. In everyday language-use situations, this becomes a stumbling block for the assumed conventions of ostensive metaphor.[18] In ostensive metaphor, as we have seen, an ordinary or commonplace metaphor is "taken as read,"[19] because we understand "where the speaker is coming from." Because of its reduction to the commonplace, ostensive metaphor has moved out of poetic usage into pragmatic usage. What an ironic reversal of the received wisdom that autistic people are prosaic and lacking in imagination! As we have seen, neurotypical commonplace usage of metaphor is so "obvious," that by being assumed as a "normal" shorthand,

---

18. Ostensive metaphor in everyday, pragmatic use is very different to poetic metaphor. However, the argument for killing poetic metaphor by reducing it to simile is still the same in principle. Killing metaphor would be a reading that intends to extract meaning rather than enjoy the poetic space of the imaginary sharing performed by tenor (what is signified) and vehicle (what signifies it). In chapter 3's reading of Maurice Blanchot's *The Space of Literature*, the argument is developed that true poetic reading can be viewed autistically, divorced from pragmatism, as an act of inhabiting Incarnational metaphor.

19. Ironically, "taken as read" means the opposite; it means "reading something into it."

LITERAL METAPHOR AND INCARNATIONAL METAPHOR   113

it loses its status as living metaphor. The power of living metaphor slides into common-sense propositional language, effectively losing the figurative power of an imaginative space. The original metaphor has effectively ceased to be metaphoric at all, with its origins of figurative reference changed by a shift into assumed common-sense meaning. Effectively, by being "taken as read" in ordinary decoding, it has become a dead metaphor. Therefore, as the Oxford Dictionary explains, "much of our everyday language[20] is . . . made up of metaphorical words and phrases that pass unnoticed as "dead" metaphors, like (for example) the branch of an organization."[21]

Thinking through metaphor as dead or alive raises interesting possibilities for an autistic hermeneutic of literal metaphor. The dead metaphor example given here would be particularly pertinent to Happé's approach to autistic literal mindedness.[22] "The branch of an organization" is exactly the kind of figurative language where autistic literal mindedness would fail to function with an appropriate response, because the "branch" would be envisioned as part of a tree. Thinking theologically, we could say that this tree comes to life through the power of autism to rethink and regenerate the image of the branch. The tree is made incarnate, the metaphor is resurrected. One can think of the office as puzzlingly part of a living tree (as if "I am the

---

20. Paul Ricœur, as will be discussed later in this chapter, argues that all language is at base metaphoric, as *Métaphore Vive* (living metaphor). This is an excavation and resurrection of metaphor, which would interrogate dead metaphor to bring it back to life. This is another way of thinking of the resurrection power of autistic Incarnational metaphor, as will emerge.

21. Baldick, "Metaphor." Again, this anticipates Ricœur's *métaphore vive* and Derrida's *White Metaphor*, which will be discussed later.

22. See Introduction.

true vine, and you are the branches"[23]—how do we approach this image?).

In fact, for literal metaphor in its poetic and theological potential, what clinical narrative calls "literal interpretation" is actually the opposite. Literal metaphor is a withdrawal from the social convention of dead metaphor as a propositional statement and an assumption where "branch" has lost its poetic roots as imagery. It is a rehabilitation, back into figuration, however baffling—but we will see the glory of this bafflement as we proceed.

> So the autist who is thinking of the branch of a tree when the branch of an office is "really" meant, is re-entering the figurative power of metaphor, to puzzle over how an office can be part of a tree. This is more than halfway toward being a poet. In pragmatic, ostensive terms, this is absurd in the same way that the inability to "decode" metaphor into simile is absurd. It is, however, the resurrection of figurative power, from dead metaphor into living metaphor.

Staying baffled at the absurdity of a space of pure living metaphor is the ability to inhabit an autistic space where language exceeds its containment in pragmatic, connotative meaning. Consequently, we can say that *autistic "literal-mindedness" resurrects dead metaphor*. The crucial point here is that by bringing back its figurative, imaginative potential, this absurdity can become a powerful theological hermeneutic. This works, crucially, as a theological resurrection of metaphor, which chapter 4 will show to be at once Incarnation, Crucifixion, Resurrection, and (in a sense) Ascension. It is impossible except within the foolishness of the gospel; the gospel, the sheer, paradoxical

23. John 15:1.

absurdity of the Christ event, "doesn't make sense," just as metaphor, purely unresolved, doesn't "make sense." In practice, autists often turn away from poetry because of an acute sensitivity to how it doesn't make sense; the unresolved absurd leap of imaginative pairing is baffling, and too demanding. This book stays there, it must be remembered, as myth, to consider what an impossible, imaginary, absolute autism could be. For this reason, when this "odd" autistic hermeneutic is taken as a theological hermeneutic, Incarnation and Resurrection are free to be clearly baffling, taking their full power of mystery seriously. The Christ event in all its moments will be seen to occur as the baffling mysteries of Incarnation, Crucifixion, Resurrection and Ascension.

Thinking of a mythical autism, we can now explore religious language as bafflement, oddness and excess. This is to see whether a hermeneutic of mystery and reverence, which reads the Christ event as baffling, odd and exceeding the power of words, can be read equally as an autistic hermeneutic. This is because, within the text, literal metaphor can become a literal presence—which can be read theologically as Real Presence in a sacramental Incarnation of metaphor. This autistic theological language of the Christ event is one which offers an embodiment in "absurd" language of the paradox of the God-man Incarnate Christ. The Christ of paradox is present (for us, in our hermeneutic) by means of a literary-theological autistic baffled metaphor, enacting the baffling theological potential of the Christ event.

In this light, we can now theologize literal metaphor, and dare to call it Incarnational metaphor. The end point and purpose of this journey is to vindicate the autistic hermeneutic, so that its "failure" is inverted into, as one of Jesus' parables says, a "pearl of great price."[24] It might equally be buried treasure;[25] when Jesus inverts our moral and personal values in the Beatitudes,[26] we might relate to this inverted kingdom, as holy fools.

POETIC-AUTISTIC RESISTANCE TO PRAGMATIC SIMILE

This is important as we approach the Bible as story, and therefore, also, for how mythical literal metaphor approaches the golden chain of metaphors we call poetry. Not all readings of poetry are of the "common-sense" kind that wears down or denudes poetic space, by reducing it merely into the question "what does this poem mean?" If an autistic reading resists this denudation of metaphor, then so too does a certain kind of poetic response which simply revels in word, sound and image. So, for example, in the Christian poet Gerard Manley Hopkins' poem *As Kingfishers Catch Fire*, the poem is dedicated "to Christ our Lord." One reading is to say that in various ways, by various poetic techniques, the kingfisher is represented to be *like* Christ, the Fisher of Men and the King. However, it is quite another thing to say that, in the space of the poem, the kingfisher *is* Christ the King, and we revel in his kingfisher-glory. Indeed, this will be chapter 5's subject: a brief excursus/working example/embodiment looking at the rich potential offered by an autistic hermeneutic's response to Hopkins' work. We will see that in a powerful sense, true poetic response, in fact, could itself have the embodiment of autistic privilege in it. This offers mythical literal metaphor a real opening into a space which differs

24. Matt 15:25.
25. Matt 13:44.
26. Matt 5:3–12.

from a prosaic neurotypical norm. It will be seen to be a beautiful, mythical space.

The writer Maurice Blanchot describes a "space of literature"[27] where art exists—not our "interpretation" of it (like the shapes we make in the clouds) but the work of art itself. The neurotypical pragmatic norm fails to inhabit this space,[28] as it resists staying in the space of something as meaningless, pointless, and useless as the space of this radical divorce from pragmatic/mimetic function—which is actually the holiness of being (an inner *Dasein*) in the image. "Art for art's sake?"; autism for myth's sake? We can now see what is in practice, and how it works in different theological hermeneutic scenarios.

"Getting it wrong" might actually be "getting it right" when the autistic mode of reading metaphor sheds light on a theological hermeneutic. Here, where this literal-mindedness has been pathologized as a "lack of imagination,"[29] the argument for a theology of Incarnational metaphor would be the very opposite. Theologically, it would be a privileged seeing of language as a *real* embodiment, of what we will see as the body of the kenotic Incarnate Christ, in the text.

One could say that trying to see children as rabbits leads to an incredible sense of bafflement; but is there, then, in a myth of literal metaphor, a "holy bafflement?" We can now bring together two places of similar bafflement, where the autistic hermeneutic meets a theological bafflement of language.[30] This might give us a *theological*

27. See Blanchot, *Space of Literature*.

28. As neurotypicality itself—but neurotypical art lovers, as we shall see, are also partaking in the fascination we call autism.

29. E.g., Baron-Cohen and Craig, "Creativity and Imagination," where children are "tested" for creativity; see also Happé and Frith, *Autism and Talent*, where "savant skills" are viewed as repetition by rote.

30. Which also becomes an (equally coherent) language of bafflement.

autistic hermeneutic, as a particular kind of incarnation. This lack of neurotypical sense will unfold in the subsequent chapters, but the reason for highlighting it now is to explore *theologically* how utterly different it will be than "normal," propositional theology would allow.

THEOLOGICAL LANGUAGE AS BAFFLEMENT, ODDNESS, AND EXCESS

Riotous Language

Glossolalia, or speaking in tongues, is a phenomenon where the speaker, filled with the Holy Spirit, utters words they do not understand, but which are often interpreted by another person. It is seen as a gift of the Spirit in Pentecostal churches, and indeed the Book of Acts records a filling of the disciples of Christ with the Spirit so that they speak spontaneously in other languages which can be understood by onlookers who speak these languages;[31] this giving of the Spirit is celebrated in the Church calendar at what we call Pentecost; hence the name of these churches. So glossolalia is a gift from God, without human origin. The utterer of the words is content to remain in bafflement, and any interpretation will come (if at all) from another person.

The theologian Ian Ramsey discusses a similar kind of spiritual bafflement. In *Religious Language: An Empirical Placing of Theological Phrases*,[32] Ramsey describes the Christian revelation as a "disclosure situation." The word disclosure in Ramsey's argument has the meaning of an opening upon something utterly other and utterly given. It

---

31. Acts 2:4.
32. Ramsey, *Religious Language*.

is an enigma, not in the sense of a puzzle to be solved but a mystery to be inhabited.

Propositional language is language which follows logical rules and has no mystery within it, although it may allude to it. In the "disclosure situation," kerygmatic (gospel message) language operates outwith a "normal" propositional epistemology. This is not a situation where logic can reason toward assent through reasoned understanding; Ramsey writes that

> Christian doctrine . . . can only be justified on an epistemology very different from that which lay behind traditional views of metaphysics. In no sense is Christian doctrine a "super-science."[33]

Instead, "Prophetic language work(s) as disclosure language."[34] He describes this "disregard" for logic in Peter's preaching in the early Church, as recorded in the book of Acts:

> St. Peter's concern was first and foremost to evoke the distinctive Christian situation, and the logical behavior of his words did not at all interest him. Here was the kerygma, the preaching, and its whole point was to evoke an appropriate situation of challenge and response.[35]

Ramsey argues that true religious language, then, is doxological (a language of praise and worship), and the point is to inhabit divine mystery with reverence.[36] This is a (non) sense beyond (not beneath or falling short of) logic. It requires a language other than, and beyond logic. This

---

33. Ramsey, *Religious Language*, 17.
34. Ramsey, *Religious Language*, 152.
35. Ramsey, *Religious Language,* 154–55.
36. Ramsey, *Religious Language*, 185; Ramsey also sees disclosure as dependent on a quality of discernment, which could be compared to Newman's concept of assent.

is the "foolishness of the gospel"[37] which the apostle Paul describes and the *skandalon* (stumbling block)[38] he also calls the gospel. Paul also, in the same epistle, writes that the wisdom of God is foolishness to the world.[39] Ramsey comments that "neither Jews nor Greeks could formulate a credible language in which this preaching could be expressed."[40] This doxological language is a language of excess. Ramsey describes kerygmatic prophetic language as:

> a riotous mixture of phrases . . . in effect a rough and ready attempt to secure that special logical impropriety needed to express the Christian message.[41]

He describes the anomaly of the disclosure situation in the "common-sense" world as "odd," and requiring an "odd" language:

> Compared with "what's seen" and our appropriate attitude thereto, the characteristically religious situation—characterized by a "discernment-commitment"—(is) nothing if not odd . . . the currency for such an odd situation would have to be suitably odd language.[42]

Bafflement as Doxology and Literal Metaphor

Within faith, the "odd" language of the *kerygma* is not illogical but supra-logical. Encapsulating into doctrine what Charles Wesley's poetic expression could describe as "Our

---

37. 1 Cor 1:18.
38. 1 Cor 1:23.
39. 1 Cor 3:19.
40. Ramsey, *Religious Language*, 155.
41. Ramsey, *Religious Language*, 154–55.
42. Ramsey, *Religious Language*, 151.

God contracted to a span / incomprehensibly made man"[43] is, rightly thought, baffling. Ramsey discusses how in doctrinal controversies, when opposing doctrinal statements are not resolved, their co-existence, even contradiction, is valid "in order to understand, as best they can, a mystery which is bound to exceed both their attempts."[44] If "odd" disclosure in prophetic language is "riotous" and "rough and ready," and "odd" doctrinal language expresses "a mystery which is bound to exceed (its) attempt," both of these discourses are discourses of excess. Bafflement is the expression of being faced, in faith, with what cannot be contained, and the inevitable, spontaneous, response to this mystery, once it is glimpsed, is doxology (praise). Praise as reverence is an attitude which keeps mindfulness of this mystery open.

Thought through in any profound, theological way, the God-man is nothing if not baffling; and I want to suggest here that *the bafflement Ramsey describes gains support from universal autism's literal metaphor*. In an autistic hermeneutic, this necessary "oddness" of doxological language is precisely the place where mystery is incarnate (as a dwelling-place) in the bafflement of literal metaphor. *Theologically*, our mythical autistic hermeneutic keeps open the possibility of literal metaphor, this time as the mysterious discourse which is the site of a mythical, poetic Incarnation of Christ.

The next step is to take autistic doxological bafflement as a way to outwit "the wisdom of the world."[45] To achieve this, we might consider this "odd" autistic incarnation in terms of what the theologian Fergus Kerr terms

---

43. Wesley, "Let Earth and Heaven Combine" (1745), Singing the Faith no. 208.
44. Ramsey, *Religious Language*, 171.
45. 1 Cor 3:19.

post-Cartesian theology. Cartesian, of course, refers to the thinking of the Enlightenment philosopher René Descartes, whose legacy is much more than mathematical Cartesian co-ordinates. Descartes emphasizes that logic and scientific evidence must be the basis of knowledge; most famously, in the logic of *cogito, ergo sum* (I think, therefore I am). Kerr aims to challenge the sway of Cartesian rationalism, to argue, simply put, for the necessity of insoluble mystery in our world-view. One way Kerr does this is by performing a theological reading of the philosopher Ludwig Wittgenstein, to whom we now turn. (This is the next stage of the journey toward deconstructive theology, which, in turn, will work toward an autistic hermeneutic of the mystical and the atheological).

"WITTGENSTEIN'S AUTISM"

Before we begin, let me clarify that we are *not* claiming that Wittgenstein was autistic. The genre of the retrospective biographical autism diagnosis can be alluring, but is not, as by now is clear, the purpose of this book. Rather, we are seeking places where elements of Wittgenstein's thinking are *hospitable* to our autistic hermeneutic.

Wittgenstein famously writes that "whereof one cannot speak, thereof one must be silent."[46] This is more than a truism; it indicates that, put bluntly, there are things beyond language's reach. In our mythical autism, absolute Mindfulness of Separation would equally be beyond language's reach. This is strikingly brought back "down to earth" in a remark of Wittgenstein's which could be read, temptingly, almost as a definition of "actual real, everyday

---

46. Wittgenstein, *Tractatus* 7.

autism."[47] Baron-Cohen's Theory of Mind mechanism, as was discussed in the introduction, is the inability to intuit the intentionality of the other person, not least by the ability to "read" their face. Consider how this contrasts with an account of Wittgenstein's approach, as reported in his students' notes. Kerr recounts:

> Wittgenstein sought to bring out the power of "the strange illusion" which possesses us "when we seem to seek the something which a face expresses whereas, in reality, we are giving ourselves up to the features before us."[48] *It is as if, when we look at a man's face, we had to check the outward expression against "a mold made ready for it in our mind." . . . We cannot take anyone at face value; the meaning is concealed behind the phenomena.* (my italics)[49]

Wittgenstein, *for an autistic reading*, is offering us an entry into absolute, mythical autism, challenging the (absolute, mythical) neurotypical[50] assumption that there is no (innate) "autistic-ness" in the world. In the myth of autism, a perfect, absolute neurotypicality would feel that understanding the other is unproblematic, in a perfect marriage of subjectivity and objectivity. This would be the (absolute) neurotypical assumption that total Mindreading can offer a genuine objective understanding to the subjective Mindreader. "We cannot take anyone at face value; the meaning is concealed behind the phenomena" counters this mythical neurotypical Mindreading, and it reads as

---

47. Again, this is not to attribute clinical autism, as a speculative retrospective diagnosis as practiced by Fitzgerald, Baron-Cohen, and others. Instead, for our purposes, it is to credit Wittgenstein with insight that sheds light on the perspective offered by the autistic theological hermeneutic.
48. Wittgenstein, *Blue and Brown Books*, 166.
49. Kerr, *Theology After Wittgenstein*, 164.
50. See absolute autism and autistic spectrum in glossary.

a classic conscious autism in its awareness of universal Mindblindness.

Kerr also draws attention to another passage from Wittgenstein which could be read for the purposes of an autistic hermeneutic. This is, for us, an invitation to become aware of universal autism (consciously understood or strategically adopted) in another sense. This is the issue of extreme attention to detail, resonant with Autistic Fascination manifest in savant talent.

Savant talent is the phenomenon where extremely high ability in one area is combined with "low intelligence" generally, and it can be an amazing phenomenon to see in real life, such as when the autistic artist Steven Wiltshire can "draw a whole city from memory."[51] Or when Dustin Hoffman's autistic character Rain Man,[52] in the eponymous film, has a phenomenal memory which can count cards instantaneously in the casino.

As the introduction explained, Weak Central Coherence (WCC) theory sees this as a pathology where "common-sense" fails to integrate detail into a "bigger picture," but here Wittgenstein appears, to the autistic reader, to invite a celebration of this supposed weakness as another kind of awareness. Wittgenstein's remarks, and Kerr's comments on them, are worth quoting at length: Kerr writes that

> The voice of common sense assures us that we describe things as well as we need to; but the idea of a description that is infinitely finer than our clumsy powers can ever achieve is not as easily expelled.
> According to students' lecture notes, Wittgenstein once made the following suggestion:

51. See Strochlic, "This Incredible British Artist."
52. Levinson, *Rain Man*.

> "One often has the experience of trying to give an account of what one actually sees in looking about one, say, the changing sky, and of feeling that there aren't enough words to describe it. One then tends to become fundamentally dissatisfied with language. We are comparing the case with something it cannot be compared with. It is like saying of falling raindrops, 'Our vision is so inadequate that we cannot say how many raindrops we saw, though surely we did see a specific number.'"[53]

Kerr further comments:

> The fact is that, since it makes no sense to talk of the number of drops we see during a shower of rain (people would smile patiently if we did), we need not reproach ourselves for being powerless to say precisely how many we saw . . . it startles us into realizing that we do have an ideal of exactitude or completeness at the back of our minds which very easily imposes itself inappropriately. (After all, I *must have* seen a specific number of raindrops).[54]

Kerr's language of "common-sense smiling patiently" at "inappropriateness" echoes the neurotypical difficulty in appreciating the value of Autistic Fascination's attention to fine detail. Again, the point here is not to digress into the temptation of the retrospective diagnosis genre, and to speculate on a notional Wittgenstein the autist, but to think about how Wittgenstein's remarks about faces and raindrops make sense if appropriated in a specifically literal autistic hermeneutic. In the "face" passage, the issue is that of the "meaning concealed behind the phenomena," which, in the last analysis, is unavailable. Again, this is bafflement, and *language seen as a collection of phenomena*

---

53. Wittgenstein, *Wittgenstein's Lectures*, 63.
54. Kerr, *Theology after Wittgenstein*, 165.

with unavailable resolution, for Incarnational metaphor, is the inscrutable face. Conversely, in the raindrops example, the issue for Incarnational metaphor is to see the "*ideal of exactness*" as a total seeing of phenomena as pure "things." The common-sense perception of a shower of rain is displaced by the absurd and impossible attention to each drop of rain, as a fascination of reverence and communion. It is, in reality, not impossible that an autistic savant could count the number of raindrops; savants defy our understanding.

Kerr expresses something similar when he writes that "Philosophy, traditionally, begins in wonder. There is a sense in which Wittgenstein's work puts an end to all our metaphysics by inviting us to renew and expand our sense of wonder."[55] Wittgenstein writes, in a letter to Paul Engelmann:

> The poem by Uhland is really magnificent. And this is how it is: if only you do not try to utter what is unutterable then *nothing* gets lost. But the unutterable will be—unutterably!—*contained* in what has been uttered.[56]

There are three points to make about this comment. Firstly, again it, of course, echoes those famous words from Wittgenstein: "Whereof one cannot speak, thereof one must be silent." Secondly, Wittgenstein is praising an economy of poetic style as exact, weighed, allusive and evocative.[57] Thirdly, and perhaps most usefully for how we will think through Incarnational metaphor, it describes an (un)saying within poetic discourse.

---

55. Kerr, *Theology After Wittgenstein*, 141.
56. Engelmann, *Letters*, 6–7, quoted in Kerr, *Theology after Wittgenstein*, 167.
57. Poetic style as a means to indicating the site of the holy will also be discussed further in chapter 5, with reference to Gerard Manley Hopkins' work.

> **This is not the common-sense perception of a shower of rain (dead, conventional metaphor) but the excess which counts the raindrops to observe and catch them poetically; paradoxically, this seems "prosaic," but the joy involved in this savant phenomenon is, we are arguing, akin to poetry.**

Kerr also discerns this "(un)saying" in one of Saint Augustine's sermons, where Augustine thinks of poetry as music:

> At the harvest, in the vineyard, wherever men labour hard, they begin with songs whose words express their joy. But when their joy brims over and words are not enough, they abandon even this coherence and give themselves up to the sheer sound of singing. What is this jubilation, this exultant song? It is the melody that means our hearts are bursting with feelings which words cannot express. And to whom does this jubilation belong? Surely to God, who is unutterable. And does not unutterable mean what cannot be uttered? If words will not come and you may not remain silent, what else can you do but let the melody soar?[58]

This overwhelming joy reflects, again, Ramsey's thinking of religious language as excess which attempts to say the unsayable. Crucially, it is excess as musical/poetic language, which will be explored as Incarnational literal metaphor as we progress. In what will really become (as we shall see) an apophatic, atheological thinking of this chapter's content, this is excess as an unsaying, beyond the logic of propositional language; by outwitting Descartes' pure logic and scientific method, in excess, it thereby escapes metaphysics. To make this deconstruction of metaphysics more explicit, we will now turn to an autistic reading of Postmodern deconstruction. This is a

---

58. On Ps 32, Sermon 1, 78, quoted in Kerr, *Theology after Wittgenstein*, 167.

demanding, but ultimately exhilarating, move toward a genuinely mythical autism.

INCARNATIONAL METAPHOR AS DECONSTRUCTIVE ATHEOLOGY

What Is Deconstruction?

When I was a much younger reader than I am now, a visiting professor came to give a seminar on Deconstruction. I will never forget his opening line: "You do realise this is all a joke, don't you?" That troubled me so much. Why would he say that, and then present a learned paper on the subject? It took me years to get the joke; because, in truth, Deconstruction is a game, a playful play on metaphor. It is also, and precisely by being so, utterly serious; do we need to, in some way, see even our most serious language as a game?

Deconstruction is an intellectual project which emerged in the later twentieth century, and seeks to highlight the inherent instability of language in a radical way, with radical consequences. Deconstructive thinkers, most famously Jacques Derrida, have argued that our post-Christian era has become uniquely aware and self-critical of what he terms "logocentrism." *Logos,* it will be remembered from the *theo-logy* introduction (Beginner's Guide), means "word," but also a deeply felt "meaning" or "structure" or "order." Readers of John's Gospel will remember the astonishing words spoken of Jesus in the famous prologue to the book: "In the beginning was the *Logos.* And the *Logos* was with God, and the *Logos* was God."[59] So throughout Western civilization's history, the source of Being and the object of worship is this *logos.*

59. John 1:1.

Derrida argues that we are tied to this intellectual model, and that, to escape it, we would have to escape language itself, because all our language emerges from this conceptual apparatus; from this *logocentrism*. The concept relevant to us from Derrida's work is the effacement of a metaphorical origin and the impossibility, for us, of regaining it. His translator Gayatri Chakravorty Spivak writes: "When Derrida claims for himself that he is within and yet without the *clôture*[60] of metaphysics, is the difference not precisely that he *knows* it at least?"[61]

Derrida focuses on the Enlightenment philosopher Jean-Jacques Rousseau in tracing an evolution of language from the spoken language of the emotions to the written language of ideas. Before conceptual language, Rousseau argues, comes poetic language; and before scientific literalness comes metaphor. Derrida explains: "In general, Rousseau gives a sacred and holy character only to the natural voice that speaks to the heart"[62]; quoting Rousseau that "(written language) substitutes ideas for feelings. It no longer speaks to the heart but to reason."[63] So Derrida argues that Rousseau (whose doctrine of the "noble savage" is relevant here) is right to distinguish an original "emotional" spoken language which is then, in anthropological terms, "corrupted" by a "rational" written language. We could say that writing changes everything; it is fixed on the page, it can be copied, circulated, replied to indefinitely, miscopied, forged . . . whereas, unless we repeat ourselves, and even if so, we are heard only once, in our immediacy.

60. Cloister.
61. Spivak, "Translator's Preface," in Derrida, *Of Grammatology*, xxxviii.
62. Derrida, *Of Grammatology*, 264.
63. Derrida, *Of Grammatology*, 271.

The atheologian Mark C Taylor has written about "an irreducible obscurity that both beckons and frustrates thought."[64] He is describing the phenomenon of language, which, in a deconstructive hermeneutic, is seen to yield no stable origin. This is all too familiar. Frustration in the face of the world's norms is a hallmark of living with autism, where an "irreducible obscurity" of the social world is baffling and overwhelming. The aim of bringing an autistic hermeneutic into literary-theological hermeneutics is not to sanitize or heal this bafflement and overwhelming. It is to live with it and, in Rowan Williams' powerful phrase, be "learning [its] difficulty." Williams writes:

> Our consideration of both the excesses and the gaps in language will underline the importance of acknowledging "learning difficulties" in our unfolding sense of what language is—and also the importance . . . of learning difficulty itself as a key to much of this.[65]

Here we will be working toward a kenotic atheology which embodies the wound that, to again use language from Mark C Taylor, both tears and involves tears.[66] This is similar to Ramsey's doxological language inasmuch as it escapes definition; but Taylor is more particularly writing about deconstructive theology, in its pain and loss, but also in its liberation and *jouissance* (play).

It is not difficult for us to see here a fundamental loss for autism, yet a paradoxical one. If we consider relative (actual, clinical) autism as lived by real-world autists, conceptual language is easier, more straightforward and more accessible; we know where we are, there are no metaphors to trip us up and lead us astray. Yet in our mythical

64. Taylor, *Tears*, 215.
65. Taylor, *Tears*, 125.
66. Taylor, *Tears*.

LITERAL METAPHOR AND INCARNATIONAL METAPHOR 131

autism, the poetic one, (impossible) "literal metaphor" is the realm of the sacred. The forgotten origin of language's metaphorical roots, in this case, is pure, affective empathy, which is effaced by Writing's[67] cognitive apparatus; and the loss happens when intentionality is complexified by a departure from that initial simplicity. In our myth, this cognitive loss is a Mindfulness of Separation. In pre-writing speech, we would have reveled in metaphor, taking it literally, immersed in the poem. Now, in dead metaphors such as "the branch of an organization," we are lost. For us, Derrida makes an interesting claim if both we and, in some sense, he, share a commitment to "literal metaphor":

> It is not, therefore, a matter of inverting the literal meaning and the figurative meaning but of determining the "literal" meaning of writing a metaphoricity itself.[68]

If we think of language as a pairing of signified (what is being described) and signifier (what describes it), Derrida writes about the evolution and increasing complexity of this written language:

> "Signifier of the signifier" describes . . . the movement of language: in its origin, to be sure, but one can already suspect that *an origin whose structure can be described as "signifier of the signifier" conceals and erases itself in its own production.*[69]

For Derrida, we are, culturally and linguistically, and always have been, situated within a Book which we call metaphysics. Metaphysics (see glossary), is the science of what can logically be said about the nature of Being, humanity, science, history and philosophical categories.

---

67. "Writing" as the concept of writing—how we tell the story of our logical world; metaphysics.
68. Derrida, *Of Grammatology*, 15.
69. Derrida, *Of Grammatology*, 7.

Western metaphysics has been founded on the *logos,* as if (to return to Heidegger) the event of a tree's existence could be reduced to its chemistry, its bi-ology, its physiology, its sum of -ologies. Metaphysics attempts to make being into a science; and to return to Wittgenstein, language is inadequate to the task. Derrida famously writes "At the end of the Book,"[70] playing games and taking liberties with the language of this logocentric book which we call metaphysics, to convey to us that, at base, we can at least imagine an (impossible) "destruction of the book" which liberates writing;[71] as Jesus says, "the truth shall set you free."[72] (And we can perhaps, here, stop to consider how much of the true speech of Jesus is metaphor, (humorous) hyperbole, and parable).

At this point, an autistic hermeneutic honors this joy, frustration, and obscurity with the insight of its presence. Autistic refusal to play the game outwits the willful ignoring of the instability of language, and for this reason, its "inability to make sense" will be its strength, as it is read into Derrida's words about an "undecidability." If we have the courage to live in this radical doubt and undecidability, Derrida writes, then:

> The very oscillation of undecidability goes back and forth and weaves a text; it makes, if this is possible, a path of writing through the aporia. This is impossible, but no-one has ever said that deconstruction, as a technique or method, was possible; it thinks only on the level of the impossible and of what is still evoked as unthinkable.[73]

70. Derrida, "End of the Book," in *Of Grammatology*, 24.
71. Derrida, "End of the Book," in *Of Grammatology*, 18.
72. John 8:32.
73. Derrida, *Memoires for Paul de Man*, 135, quoted in Taylor, *Tears*, 215; *Aporia* (Greek) literally means "opening," an existential chasm that cannot be crossed over.

To make the connection again, just as deconstruction thinks on the level of the impossible, so too does mythical, Absolute autism, and this will be even more evident in chapters 3 and 4. For now, we can suggest that Absolute autism recognizes itself here; Mindfulness of Separation finds a resonance in the aporia (chasm), and absolute Fascination inhabits it in weaving a beautiful, impossible text by means of Incarnational metaphor.

Derrida's words here are written as part of a memorial of the poet Paul de Man, and this connection is relevant in two ways. Firstly, this is a kenotic hermeneutic of sacrifice and loss; de Man's post-holocaust writing precludes any resolution, and this is why bafflement persists, in the absence of any adequate theodicy (justifying the existence of evil in the universe created by a good Gxd). Secondly, de Man is celebrated as a poet, and this autistic hermeneutic works, as we shall see, within the bafflement which inhabits poetry.

White Mythology

Derrida argues that metaphysics' certainty as propositional language works by forgetting its origin in metaphor, that originally language is not tied into certainty until a *logos* assumes control. This happens by our using linguistic constructions of the world and forgetting that they are subjectively thought models. The philosopher Paul Ricœur uses the term *métaphore vive* to indicate the (impossible) rescue of this awareness of the inescapable nature of metaphor. Reading this autistically, we could interpret Ricœur's words as a resonance with the metaphor we have rescued and resurrected, which we have called Incarnational metaphor.

Ricœur argues that onto-theology[74] as a master narrative exists only by betraying its origin in poetic language. He comments:

> (The Thomist doctrine of analogy's) express purpose is to establish theological discourse at the level of science and thereby to free it completely from the poetical forms of religious discourse, even at the price of severing the science of God from biblical hermeneutics.[75]

So, we have found ourselves thinking in terms of theology, forgetting the world as it was before we adopted *logos* and *-ology*. Derrida sees this complacency about language as a "White Mythology":

> What is white mythology? It is metaphysics which has effaced in itself that fabulous scene which brought it into being, and which yet remains, active and stirring, inscribed in white ink, an invisible drawing covered over.[76]

Western metaphysics as a master narrative is a forgetting of the fact that it is also a mythology. Derrida continues:

> What is metaphysics? A white mythology which assembles and reflects Western culture: the white man takes his own mythology (that is, Indo-European mythology), his logos—that is, the mythos of his idiom, for the universal form of that which it is still his inescapable desire to call Reason.[77]

---

74. The argument put forward by Thomas Aquinas and others that Being is secured by a theological underpinning
75. Ricœur, *Rule of Metaphor*, 322.
76. Derrida, "White Mythology," 11.
77. Derrida, "White Mythology," 11.

The key point here is the metaphor Derrida uses of white mythology, relevant to an autistic hermeneutic in both of its homonymic (punning) senses of *white*. White as race critiques imperialism and we will consider this in terms of capitalism in the next section. First, we must consider that Derrida's use of the color "white" also means invisible ink on the page. White ink on a white page is something invisibly there, which Derrida calls the trace; the ubiquitous White Mythology. Written on this page is the inescapable ubiquity of signs, with no black/white, subject/object dualistic referential stability. The trick of the white ink is that it leaves writing to lose itself in endless, circular, mutual referentiality. If we can escape the fiction of White Mythology, telling us that all is well on the page, we will see that there is no fixed place, because there is no anchor of the metaphysical God, as the transcendental signified. Is Derrida an atheist or a mystic? He plays games and asks questions. What he does make clear is that with no absolute referent, meaning (and the freedom to interrogate it), with an eye on the poetic and the playful, is kept open. This freedom and *jouissance* indicates the end of metaphysics because we have poetic freedom unbound from a rigid logic. We can, like the African myth-makers of the cooking of the sky, invent stories as houses where meaning lives. We can be poetic.

> **Of course, we have to operate within metaphysical "certainties" in order to function as human beings—but can we at the very least be aware of it? Can we consider moving from prose to poetry, from certainty to uncertainty, at least in principle; in some sacred corner of ourselves?**

Thinking of autism as the trace (Derrida's term for that absence we are aware of) means that the suppressed talk of it can be articulated, much as in the guilelessness of the boy in the folk tale *The Emperor's New Clothes*. As readers will doubtless know, in the folk tale of *The Emperor's New Clothes*, the little boy is the only person brave enough to say out loud that the Emperor is naked—his clothes are all imaginary.

Now this is exactly what the holy fool would do—and it is exactly what the autist "without guile"[78] would do. Autistic literal metaphor resurrects the dead metaphor indicated by white mythology, fittingly by its very quality of black and white thinking. A useful way to explain this is to refer back to the role of myth in another example, this time in Travis Knight's 2016 animated film *Kubo and the Two Strings*. The protagonist, Kubo, knows that the mythical power of ancestor worship is the magical force of the singing of memory, and he also knows that the magical force of the singing of memory is the mythical power of ancestor worship. White mythology needs to reduce this pairing of myth and song into a fixed system of causation and signification, which tries to fix meaning into stability; it looks for clarity (white light) to be the referee (adjudicator, and means of reference). Does singing *mean* myth, or does myth *mean* singing? White mythology, as Imperialism, is the myth of making a final, closed decision or a pronouncement; ironically having lost myth itself in its original quality of the spiritual discernment of the power of song as worship, and worship as song. Dead metaphor is the forgetting of metaphoricity, and autistic literal metaphor is the re-problematizing of it, in outwitting white myth, keeping writing open.

---

78. John 1:47.

Coinage

Derrida draws on a metaphor "coined" by Friedrich Nietzsche, of metaphysics as worn-out coinage. Nietzsche famously writes:

> What, then, is truth? A mobile army of metaphors, metonyms, and anthropomorphisms—in short, a sum of human relations which have been enhanced, transposed, and embellished poetically and rhetorically, and which after long use seem firm, canonical, and obligatory to a people: truths are illusions about which one has forgotten that this is what they are; metaphors which are worn out and without sensuous power; coins which have lost their pictures and now matter only as metal, no longer as coins.[79]

Derrida uses this metaphor to compare the use of coinage, in white mythology's Capitalist imperialism, with the use of the currency of words. He comments about this circulation or usage of Nietzsche's "coins":

> Moreover, to "usage" we may append the subtitle "wear and tear," and it is with this that we shall concern ourselves. And first of all we shall direct interest upon a certain wear and tear of metaphorical force in philosophical intercourse . . . it constitutes the very history and structure of philosophical metaphor. But how can we make it discernible, except by metaphor?[80]

The problem is that a "worn out" metaphor can only be replaced with another metaphor, itself subject to usage as wear and tear. In anti-Capitalist terms one might say, similarly, that in a Capitalist society, coins keep circulating, regardless of how defaced and defacing they are. The

---

79. Nietzsche, *On Truth and Lies*.
80. Derrida, "White Mythology," 6.

faceless consumer and the faceless producer lack value, because the only value is the worn-out face on the coin. True, the Royal Mint produces new coins, but by so doing will simply replicate the process by producing more faces to deface.

The Autistic Coin: Resisting Tokenism

In the Introduction, Mindfulness of Separation and Autistic Fascination were described as two faces of a coin. If we return to that metaphor, the autistic coin is aware that it lacks a face—there are no "Emperor's New Clothes." Recall autistic inability to "read" faces, and Wittgenstein's awareness of the inadequacy of taking people "at face value"; autistically approaching Derrida's thinking here, being face-blind is the asset of approaching the faceless coin as it really is. Incarnational metaphor already accepts and exposes them for what they are, these coins of dead metaphor, and brings the unseen *métaphore vive* back to life in the space of myth.

The phenomenon of the token minority representative in film and television indicates that the black, or gay, or trans, or disabled character has no value except as a token gesture to a politically shallow form of inclusivity which keeps the marginal other appeased and under control. Tokenistic autism now appears perhaps to be moving somewhat toward a genuinely neurotribal assertion of autism as valued in its own right, if Steve Silberman is right. Autistic traits seem to be asserting themselves in film and television in celebrations of the "unsociable but brilliant" geek (too many to mention). But still, they remain the odd one in a normal society.

However, in terms of white mythology, an autistic non-tokenism means that autistic metaphor has always absented itself from circulating defaced currency, and given that all currency defaces itself in its usage, this means that it has not used currency at all. Autistic people are drawn to shiny, spinning objects. When a coin ceases to be a coin, it becomes an object which can be polished to a (faceless) shine, and can be spun. A dead metaphor in endless circulation is "polished up" and "spun" by autistic value which sees the image of value only as itself. A £1 coin doesn't mean £1, but only a faceless coin, of value simply as a beautiful piece of metal. The autist is not in the business of reading faces. A transcendental signified (God as the *logos* of our the-*ology*), which is dis-credited has never been taken on credit; because the transcendent is transcendent, not amenable to circulation, and has always been, in Mindfulness of Separation.

The Emperor's New Coins

In the other sense of the homonymic "white," white mythology is an imperialist master narrative, and its use of coinage is capitalism.

In an anti-Capitalist reading, one might critique white mythology as follows. Capital-ism decap-it-ates itself by amassing capital without the value of the human face except as the face of a coin. The loss of the human face is the reduction of "thisness"[81], the sacred, intrinsic value of the individual person or thing, which we will discuss later, into a mere pragmatic sign; in Marxist terms, a unit of the means of production. Autistic metaphor resists Capitalist

---

81. Translating *haecceitas,* i.e., the existential/theological value of the individual, which will be discussed in chapter 5.

decapitation by having been *always already* penniless in terms of pragmatic purchasing power. Joel Bregman, describing what we term Autistic Fascination, writes

> [with] intense preoccupying interests . . . such individuals literally can become world experts on such topics, yet resist suggestions to transform this interest and knowledge into functional, meaningful or marketable skills.[82]

Fascination is cherishing "thisness" for its own sake, as chapter 5 will discuss; for now, "thisness" is the sacred individual nature of all beings. Incarnational metaphor as fascination inhabits the "thisness" of the metaphor (the poetic) without "cashing it out." Here, autistic love is revealed. A mythical autistic empathy can be found here, where fascination is the joy in the coin itself, defaced and valueless, meaningless; the holy fool is content to love the worthless piece of metal, absolutely free of avarice. She escapes Capitalist decapitation because she "has no capital" (as finance, as the capital letters in a name,[83] as a capital city, as the capital of a column, as *capus* (head)). In a sense, being "headless," it has always already been decapitated in terms of what Mark C Taylor calls art as the site of the Disaster, where "metaphysics trembles in the irreducible obscurity that both beckons and frustrates thought."[84]

Barthes and Iser: "Where Your Treasure Is"

Incarnational metaphor's abnormality contains the privilege of already, in its penniless freedom, understanding

---

82. Zager et al., *Autism Spectrum Disorders*, 14.
83. Autistic Fascination will be thought of as namelessness in chapter 6, in Pirandello's novel *Uno, Nessuno e Centomila (One, No-One and One Hundred Thousand)*.
84. Taylor, *Tears*, 215.

the glory of the clash of unresolved/decoded meanings described earlier as excess and bafflement. This is a privileged insight into what Postmodernism terms the "disaster" (the end of metaphysics), as prefigured in what the critic Roland Barthes terms "the death of the author." Anticipating Derrida, Barthes' phrase emanates from his thinking of the death of Gxd (which we will explore in chapter 4):

> We now know that a text is not a line of words releasing a single "theological" meaning (the "message" of the Author-God) but a multi-dimensional space in which a variety of writings, none of them original, blend and clash, and once the author is removed, the claim to decipher a text becomes quite futile. To give a text an Author is to impose a limit on that text, to furnish it with a final signified, to close the writing.[85]

Because our (mythical) autistic literal metaphor stays in the image, refusing to decode the branch of an organization into a bureaucratic structure, it similarly refuses the resolution of the "final signified" (God), and is living a resurrection which does not "close the writing." As we shall see more fully in chapter 4, the resurrection of metaphor is also the paradoxical trace of the death of the Author, Creator, Gxd.

Wolfgang Iser, writing even before Barthes' anticipation of Derrida's deconstruction, also foresees the anarchic power of the living text as the death of metaphoric stability. Iser's *Implied Reader* seems at first sight to exist in a neurotypical relationality, where the work of literature is realized in "an arena in which reader and author participate

---

85. Barthes, "Death of the Author," in *Image, Music, Text*, 146–47.

in a game of the imagination."[86] What kind of game is this, however? A *jouissance* weaving across the aporia?

As we read autistically, the work of literature, in fact, exists in autistic separation between reader and author;[87] where reading is the reader's utter separation from authorial intent; and Iser writes that reading is using "our own faculty for establishing connections—for filling in the gaps left by the text itself."[88] The reader is, then, ultimately a solitary figure, and reader and author are both separated by the implicit separation within the work itself, in its gaps. So Iser states that to perceive, "a beholder must *create* his [sic] own experience."[89] The writer becomes absent, leaving the reader to "engage his imagination in the task of working things out for himself [sic],"[90] and this is hospitable to conscious autism when read as Mindfulness of Separation. This autism in the text itself, seen as Mindfulness of Separation, is equally Autistic Fascination occurring precisely in the separation. In the supreme authority of the novel as a rich text which withholds the "prize" of configured meaning, Iser tells us, "awareness of this richness takes precedence over any configurative meaning."[91] So it is, when we read and reread a good novel, because we find ever deeper riches within—this is what makes a Classic.

This richness-in-absence works with a real power when it is read autistically as fascination, and in subsequent chapters it will be seen theologically as a fascination in/of the incarnate crucified Christ in the kenotic realization

---

86. Iser, *Implied Reader*, 257.

87. This separation will be examined further with regard to Maurice Blanchot's *Space of Literature* in chapter 3.

88. Iser, *Implied Reader*, 280.

89. Iser, *Implied Reader*, 288.

90. Iser, *Implied Reader*, 288.

91. Iser, *Implied Reader*, 285.

of the text. A fully Incarnational metaphor is a kenotic atheology—of a disaster where ultimate meaning (signification) is lost, and this Incarnational metaphor utterly embodied in the work of art. This is where the deconstruction conceived by Derrida is poetry, thought as, in his astonishing words, "trembling on the edge of prayer."[92] This is to be absent from the economy of the sign (that which functions to indicate meaning), laying up no treasure on earth.[93] On this basis, we can now move on to chapter 3, where Incarnational metaphor can be considered as an autistic discernment of apophatic fiction—which is contemplative prayer.

---

92. McDonagh, "Prayer, Poetry and Politics," 231.

93. "Do not store up for yourselves treasures on earth, where moth and rust destroy, and where thieves break in and steal. But store up for yourselves treasures in heaven, where moth and rust do not destroy, and where thieves do not break in and steal" (Matt 6:19–20).

Chapter Three

The Autism of Apophatic Fiction

It's the yellowness I'm in.
—Peter, a young autistic child

While with an eye made quiet by the power
Of harmony, and the deep power of joy,
We see into the life of things.[1]

What matters, most fundamentally, in this chapter, is to see apophatic theology, poetry, and the autistic hermeneutic in a perichoretic unity, that is to say, dancing together as one. Why, as we have pondered in early chapters, this strange, counter-intuitive choice of poetry? Here, we are at the heart of LTA (Literature, Theology and the Arts). The twentieth century contemplative Thomas Merton gives us a powerful entry into this thinking, reclaiming *logos* from the straitjacket of metaphysics which we saw in the

---

1. Wordsworth, "Lines Composed a Few Miles Above Tintern Abbey," in *Works of William Wordsworth*, 206.

previous chapter. Merton tells us that in our contemplation, Gxd acts by "awakening in us the awareness that we are words spoken in His One Word, and that Creating Spirit (*Creator Spiritus*" dwells in us, and we in Him."[2] These are words I will not attempt to analyse; I leave you, the reader, to contemplate them. Enough to say that *logos* and *our* indwelling creative spirit are brought together.

Autism, we have seen, can infuse itself mythically into this "space of literature," even if, in relative (real-life) autism, the autist would often turn away from it in bewilderment. But, as chapter 2 argued, it is precisely this bewilderment which matters. So now, we can enter the fullest bewilderment which is expressed in apophatic language.

In light of this, the next stage in the journey toward a full (mythically autistic) Incarnational metaphor is to step back for a moment from the postmodern and atheological writing of the twentieth and twenty-first centuries. We are going to explore some historical examples of apophatic theology, and then read them in the light of a postmodern hermeneutic.

As we saw in the theology introduction, kataphatic language shows that something between subject and object can simply be affirmed; for example, "God is good." It can be used to develop systematic theology which is a set of straightforward (if sometimes difficult!) statements.[3]

---

2. Merton, *Seeds of Contemplation*, 5

3. Much biblical commentary works by the reduction of the poetic power of metaphor to doctrinal formula. For example, referring to Isa 49:23, "And kings shall be thy nursing father, and their queens thy nursing mothers, in a letter to William Cecil (*Zurich Letters*, May 1559, 35). Calvin writes that "God promised by the mouth of Isaiah that queens should be the nursing mothers of the church." Calvin "does the job for the reader" by interpreting the narrative: the queens are nursing the church. Isaiah's prophetic genre as prophecy would require the reader (or hearer) to question what this narrative means *for her*, as a soul-searching response. Calvin as a theologian closes down the poetic space by appropriating the metaphor's ambiguity and reducing it to a dead metaphor, which propositional language; *the state* has a duty to safeguard *the church*. In this way an *apo-* opening is closed down into a *kata*-resolution. This is the

The reader relates directly and unproblematically to this statement.[4]

In contrast, apophatic theology works for thinking of the mystery and transcendence of Gxd. Apophatic discourse, as separation, is the breakdown of the relationship which kataphatic discourse employs. For this reason, apophatic theology is also called "negative theology" or "mystical theology." In fact, the apophatic and the kataphatic are inseparably related—systematic theology affirms through kataphatic language the site where apophatic language needs to disrupt it. This is in order to explore the paradoxes which are implicit within the kataphatic.

> **In fact, kataphatic theology without the complement of the apophatic would probably not truly be theology, in that it would fail to consider the issue of the transcendence of Gxd.**

Mutual Validation

As autistic hermeneuts, we are particularly interested in apophatic language. We are exploring, in this chapter, how there might be a mutual validation between apophatic and autistic theological thinking. This is firstly because this apophatic discourse can have an authenticity which receives new power, when we read it through the theological lens of an autistic hermeneutic. Both modes of thinking, the apophatic and the autistic, are marginal voices, deserving to be heard as theologically significant. As we

---

"task" of theology as theo-logy: to classify and organize *theos* into a (quasi-scientific) *-logy*. Here, we are establishing the distinction between the two different strategies of metaphor here to clarify how apophatic theology is distinctive. A useful remark on this is Teresa of Àvila's account of her divergent theological method, where she meditates on "the living poetry of this (Bible) verse," *Interior Castle*, 57.

4. Without the creative problematization of dead metaphor, which the autistic hermeneutic of literal metaphor involves [see chapter 2].

said earlier, margins can be fruitful places of exchange, able to see what the mainstream might miss. As we explore apophatic theology, we will see how this mutual validation unfolds. Secondly, apophatic theology is an important forebear of the atheological thinking which was read autistically in the previous chapter and which we will study more deeply in chapter 4. At this point, we will then see how atheological thinking offers us the richest place for the autism of Gxd; and this emerges through a series of connections which this chapter will now develop.

The apophatic discourses we will engage with are Pseudo Dionysius the Areopagite's *The Mystical Theology,* Saint Teresa of Àvila's *The Interior Castle,* and Saint John of the Cross' *Ascent of Mount Carmel.* These three writers of apophatic theology are chosen because they express a progression of narrative strategies which this chapter terms "apophatic fiction." I have coined the neologism "apophatic fiction" to explore how the genre of fiction might be a strategy for, as apophatic theology will explain, "expressing what cannot be expressed."

> **We will see how the three mystics considered are all using fiction as a narrative strategy to outwit the limits of kataphatic, propositional theology. They are writing apophatic theology as fiction, and fiction as apophatic theology—this is the confluence I am calling apophatic fiction.**

Developing the concept of apophatic fiction, we will now see how strategies of metaphor and imagery can, indeed, indicate what cannot be indicated. Working toward full Incarnational metaphor, apophatic fiction will offer us a hospitable place for the literal metaphor which can only be theological. This will be where the theological power of Incarnational metaphor truly emerges.

De Certeau's Mystic Fable

A good pathway in is the historian Michel de Certeau's thinking of mystical writing in the sixteenth century as "the mystic fable." De Certeau has written a multi-volume series under this title, but for our purposes, focusing on the sixteenth century, he is thinking of two different genres which co-exist in this period. The first is Courtly Love: extended pieces of poetic writing which recount the deeds of male heroes seeking to win their beloved female. These are poems which focus on the chivalry of the (high-standing) hero, and in reality, make the beloved into a god. The other genre de Certeau sees flourishing in the same time period is mystical writing; heresies and new sects abound.

De Certeau argues that *eros,* in both genres, has become "a 'nostalgia' connected with the progressive decline of Gxd as One, the object of love."[5]

(Why is there a "progressive decline" of Gxd as the source of love? There are a number of reasons which can only be mentioned here, as agents of social, intellectual and spiritual change—the Renaissance; the age of discovery beyond Eurocentrism; and Church schisms, not least in the Reformation and Counter-Reformation, are perhaps some of the main forces we could list here).

Bringing these two concerns together, it is fable, the fictional genre, which he uses to describe the outpouring of mystical writing. De Certeau describes "the fiction of the soul," which he argues is the "foundation of Teresa of Àvila's *The Interior Castle*."[6] We will see how this "fiction" categorization also works for John of the Cross. First, we

---

5. De Certeau, *Mystic Fable*, 4; one could also see the emergence of new religious movements as a response to this religious crisis, and as de Certeau points out, "heresy abounded" (*Mystic Fable*, 18).

6. De Certeau, *Mystic Fable*, 188.

will see how Dionysius the Areopagite sets in motion a kind of "prototype," centuries before Teresa and John.

PSEUDO-DIONYSIUS: THE RHETORIC OF NEGATION

> By a rejection of all knowledge,
> he possesses a knowledge that exceeds.[7]

How Dionysius Wrote, and Why

According to legend, *The Mystical Theology and Divine Names,* which we will now explore, was written by Dionysius the Areopagite, who is mentioned in the Acts of the Apostles as being converted by the Apostle Paul.[8] However, textual-historical research indicates that his work is more likely to have been written around the fifth or sixth century, by an anonymous author who fictionally adopts this persona. In his introduction to the English translation of Dionysius' *The Mystical Theology and The Divine Names,* C E Rolt discusses this and points out anachronisms where Dionysius draws heavily on Neo-Platonic sources, so that "The Dionysian writings may therefore be placed near the very end of the fifth century."[9] Rolt adds that "the pious fraud by which he fathered (his work) upon the Areopagite need not be branded with the harsh name of 'forgery,' for such a practice was in his day permitted and even considered laudable."[10]

---

7. Dionysius, *Mystical Theology*, 194.
8. Acts 17:34.
9. Rolt, "Introduction," in Dionysius, *Mystical Theology*, 1.
10. Rolt, "Introduction," in Dionysius, *Mystical Theology*, 1–2.

Dionysius' writing is an astonishing departure from kataphatic into apophatic theological thinking. As we saw in the Theology Introduction, apophatic discourse arises as "merely a bold way of stating the orthodox truism that the Ultimate Godhead is incomprehensible: a truism which Theology accepts as an axiom and then is prone to ignore."[11] This is so in Christian theology because "the various Names of God are . . . mere inadequate symbols of That Which transcends all thought and existence."[12] This means that, far from annulling or contradicting orthodox theology, apophatic theology expresses what is implicit in orthodox theology. Therefore, negative theology is best understood not as the negation of theology, but the theology of negation.[13]

In the face of the inadequacy of these "symbols," Dionysius relies on a narrative strategy of metaphor which deviates from the strategy of kataphatic theology—but is still a crafted discourse profoundly rooted in, and expressing, theological thinking. It is this strategy of abnormal metaphor which qualifies Dionysius as a creative writer of the apophatic.

Broadly speaking, Dionysius focuses on a Jewish source and a Greek one, fusing them in his work. Firstly, he draws on the biblical book of Exodus and the story of Moses' ascent of Mount Sinai,[14] where he is confronted by the darkness which hides the face of Gxd. He combines this Scriptural imagery with Plato's myth of the cave, where the prisoners in the cave mistakenly but inevitably "deem reality to be nothing else than the shadows of

---

11. Dionysius, *Mystical Theology*, 7.
12. Dionysius, *Mystical Theology*, 7.
13. See Turner, *Darkness of God*, 22.
14. Exod 24:16.

(unseen puppets)."[15] The theologian and historian Denys Turner argues that by fusing the imagery of the Exodus and Platonic narratives, Dionysius "made a theology out of these metaphors without which there could not have been the mystical tradition that there has been: 'light' and 'darkness,' 'ascent' and 'descent,' the love of God as *eros.*"[16] Dionysius is an original and creative thinker, with a profound legacy. Turner writes:

> "mystical theology" in the West is in itself unintelligible except against the background of (Dionysius') writings . . . if and insofar as "mystical theology" is the product of the convergence of sources in Plato and Exodus . . . then it is scarcely an exaggeration to say that Denys [*sic*] invented the genre for the Latin Church.[17]

However, Dionysius' apophatic theology is not simply "about" a hidden God—more than this, he is outworking what the "hiddenness of God" means for, and in, language; how we can articulate what cannot be articulated. Turner explains that apophasis means

> the breakdown of *speech,* which, in face of the unknowability of God, falls infinitely short of the mark . . . [if] theology means "discourse about God," or "divine discourse," so the expression "apophatic theology" ought to mean something like: "that speech about God which is the failure of speech."[18]

---

15. Plato, Republic 515C, quoted in Turner, *Darkness of God,* 14.
16. Turner, *Darkness of God*, 13.
17. Turner, *Darkness of God*, 13.
18. Turner, *Darkness of God*, 20.

Dionysius' linguistic strategy for apophasis is for metaphor itself to become a distancing from — or even within — itself. He does this by conjoining metaphors which consume each other, by negating themselves in their combination. This is why Dionysius employs light *as* darkness.

For example:

> where the mysteries of God's Word
> lie simple, absolute, unchangeable
> in the brilliant darkness of a hidden silence . . .
> [where thou] shalt be led upwards to the Ray
> of that divine Darkness which exceedeth all
> existence.[19]

Dionysius draws on the narrative of Moses on Mount Sinai as a way to express the apophatic opening, which is achieved not by rejecting intellectual (kataphatic) theology but by using the mind to advance to its limit, and then (and only then) going beyond it. In other words, as Turner explains, kataphatic theology ("knowledge") is the ladder and apophatic theology is the place where we step off the ladder ("unknowing"):

> His incomprehensible presence is shown walking on the heights of His holy places which are perceived by the mind; and then It breaks forth, even from the things that are beheld and from those who behold them, and plunges the true initiate unto the Darkness of Unknowing . . . united by his highest faculty to Him that is wholly Unknowable, of whom thus by a rejection of all knowledge he possesses a knowledge that exceeds his understanding.[20]

---

19. Dionysius, *Darkness of God*, 191–92.
20. Dionysius, *Darkness of God*, 194.

Expressing this paradox of "a knowledge that exceeds his understanding by a rejection of all knowledge" is attained by the linguistic strategy of the self-negation of language itself, as knowledge as the renunciation of knowledge. Denys Turner calls this a "self-subverting utterance" which "first says something and then, in the same image, unsays it."[21] Dionysius' theological thinking is that Gxd as absolute origin is beyond even any language of being; requires a strategy beyond affirmation or negation. He explains that this is because of the nature of Gxd as absolute origin:

> We do not say that the fire which warms or burns is itself warmed or burned. Even so if anyone says that Very Life lives, or that Very Light is enlightened, he will be wrong.[22]

(This is, at least in part, why Postmodern theologians such as Jean Luc Marion (drawing also on Tillich) can write of "God Without Being."[23] This is not a question of simple, positivistic atheism, but the very opposite; a profound expression of faith, as we shall see).

The need for this strategy is discussed at length in the discursive "learned" narrative of Dionysius' *Divine Names,* and it is a carefully reasoned work of 140 pages. In contrast, *The Mystical Theology,* in only 11 pages, puts this strategy to work as an experiment in the creative practice of metaphor with—and as—theological thinking. In other words, it is a theological poem, apophatic in its self-negating metaphors; for example

> unchangeable mysteries of heavenly Truth lie hidden

---

21. Turner, *Darkness of God*, 21.
22. Dionysius, *Mystical Theology*, 75.
23. Marion, *God Without Being*.

in the dazzling obscurity of the secret Silence, outshining all brilliance with the intensity of their darkness, and surcharging our intellects with the utterly impalpable and invisible fairness of glories which exceed all beauty![24]

While using this profusion of imagery, then, *The Mystical Theology* is also a theological treatise; but it can perfectly well be interpreted as fiction-within-theological-treatise similar, in a sense, to Michel de Certeau's idea of the "mystic fable." This holds good, so long as we read it in the light of all the weight and value of fiction, which we discussed when we considered myth in chapter 1. Of course, to use the cryptic words of Matt 24:15, "let the reader understand"—we are both invited and commanded to forge our own understanding of Dionysius' intention; literal, fable, apophatic? Let you, the reader, decide.

The Mystical Theology and Mythical Autism

This creative writing of theological thinking has potential to be thought of as hospitable to autistic literal metaphor, in its twin aspects of Mindfulness of Separation and Fascination, with Love at the center. Thinking autistically, when the story of Moses on Mount Sinai is thought through an autistic hermeneutic, the darkness hiding God's face is pure Mindfulness of Separation. Similarly, the Platonic myth of the cave is pure Mindblindness, because seeing "only shadows" is the inability to understand the face of the other. In *The Mystical Theology*, metaphor *as* separation is utterly radical; the self-subverting strategy of metaphor cuts off every connection except to its own paradox—Very Life "does not live," and Very Light "is not

---

24. Dionysius, *Mystical Theology*, 191.

enlightened." This takes us toward an important concept, namely the *coincidentia oppositorum* (identical/co-existing nature of opposites) where theological thinking might see literal metaphor as an "impossible possibility"; where Life and Light do not "refer" to living and enlightening. They are "shut up inside" the metaphor, and for us this is an autistic failure/refusal to decode them as an ostensive intent.

Light *is* darkness; and in the mythical autistic trinity, Mindfulness of Separation is where, and only where, Fascination can occur; and Incarnational metaphor requires both of these in order to exist. "Very Life" and "Very Light" which are closed off from Being (they do not live, they are not enlightened) are viewed mythic—autistically as absolute fascination, pure light-beyond-all-light and life-beyond-all-life. Absolute fascination is precisely that—an impossible Absolute, beyond the relativity of our normal living. It finds itself in the Absolute which is both nothing and everything. Very Light, which is Absolute darkness, is Absolute Mindfulness of Separation; yet as we are Absolutely fascinated, it shines as the Absolute of object of Fascination; pure Light. Recall the child Peter's words that "it's the yellowness I'm in." (Impossible) Absolute Fascination can be (impossibly) "in" that Very Light, in ecstasy. This is pure praise and worship ("worth-ship"): pure Love.

> **Very Light calls forth pure love, precisely, in our myth, in that cognitive empathy is negated (knowledge which exceeds all knowledge) while affective empathy, the pure love of God, is absolute. This is autistic love.**

> **Lastly, regarding the mythical autistic trinity, metaphor here is surely the Incarnation of mystery, emptying itself of common-sense signification. Self-subverting metaphors invite the myth of Incarnational metaphor by taking literally what cannot be taken literally; the paradox of Very Life which does not live.**

So literal metaphor becomes an apophatic theological reality as that which, mythically, inhabits mystical theology; Incarnational metaphor comes to life in the paradox of apophasis.

THE INTERIOR CASTLE: TERESA OF ÀVILA

> Today while I was beseeching the Beloved to speak through me . . . I had a vision that I will share with you now as a foundation we can build on.
>
> It came to me that the soul is like a vast castle made exclusively of diamond or some other very clear crystal. In this castle are a multitude of dwellings, just as in heaven there are many mansions.[25]

Saint Teresa of Àvila, born in 1515, was a Spanish nun and reformer, famous for her mystical writing. The most famous of her works, *The Interior Castle,* is an extended metaphor of the soul as an inner castle where Christ dwells. The soul's journey is to travel inwards in pursuit of that Christ at the deepest level within the self, through Christian practices of contemplation and action. Her translator Mirabai Starr describes her as a "wild child"[26] who was banished to a convent due to romantic indiscretions; however, at the age of forty, she underwent a kind of inner conversion (in contrast to the forced conversion of her

---

25. Teresa of Àvila, *Interior Castle,* 35.
26. "Introduction," in Teresa of Àvila, *Interior Castle,* 5.

Jewish grandparents, by the Spanish religious authorities). This conversion experience sent her on a genuine journey of theological and self-understanding, Christian practice, serving, teaching, and writing. *The Interior Castle* has become a spiritual classic, and we will explore it now, to see if it is a fruitful place for our autistic hermeneutic.

Teresa the Novelist?

Teresa calls her work "mystical theology," and yet, as we shall see, The Interior Castle is something very like a novel—or perhaps a piece of prose-poetry, with its extended poetic tone and imagery, its emotional charge, and its structured plot. What we will explore here is whether she is using fiction as a strategy for the apophatic (what she calls mystical); is *The Interior Castle* a work of apophatic fiction?[27]

Perhaps the most popular reading of *The Interior Castle* sees it as a spiritual autobiography, chronicling a series of inner events. Another reading, of course, sees it as the chronicle of a deluded woman's overactive imagination. Either way, it would be difficult to argue that the story is not on some level a narrative of some kind of inner events; in the preface to her 2003 translation of *The Interior Castle,* Mirabai Starr sees it as an account of "religious fireworks and divinely altered states of consciousness" in which, at the age of forty, "God-states started to descend like a monsoon on the parched landscape of Teresa's soul."[28] Teresa herself recounts this, and many other inner (and outer, worldly) events in her autobiography *The Life of Teresa of Àvila by Herself.*

---

27. See Teresa of Ávila, *Life of Teresa by Herself*, 85.
28. "Introduction," in Teresa of Àvila, *Interior Castle,* 9.

However, the crucial point we will consider here is the nature of "experience." The question Starr does not discuss is in what kind of discourse the text operates, and the *Castle* is a very different book than the *Life.* At times, in *The Interior Castle,* Teresa breaks into the narrative, moving from the nominative ("she") to the vocative ("try to understand"). On more than one occasion, she explicitly advises her reader in this way, for example, writing:

> Look. Try to understand what I'm saying. We don't actually feel heat or smell an aroma. . . . How, you may ask, could the soul see this truth and understand it if she is incapable of seeing anything? Well, it is not in the moment of union that the soul is cognizant of this truth, but she sees it clearly afterwards. It isn't some vision . . . it is an unshakeable certainty. . . . Don't be mistaken. This conviction is not built upon any physical forms. It is not like the invisible presence of our beloved Jesus Christ in the most holy sacrament. . . . It has nothing to do with manifestation; it's purely about divinity. . . . The soul didn't experience this with the ordinary senses that tell us there is someone next to us, but in a subtler, more delicate way that transcends explanation.[29]

Discussing the view of *The Interior Castle* as the autobiographical story of Teresa's mystical experiences, the theologian Denys Turner calls this reading "a common, informal view around that the 'mystical' [has] something to do with the having of very uncommon, privileged 'experiences.'"[30] However, he adds that "John of the Cross and Teresa of Àvila did make mention of 'experiences,' [but] attached little or no importance to them,[31] and cer-

---

29. Teresa of Àvila, *Interior Castle*, 99, 123–24, 225; see also Teresa of Àvila, *Life of Teresa by Herself*, 174, 187–88.
30. Turner, *Darkness of God*, 2.
31. Turner, *Darkness of God*, 2.

tainly did not think the having of them to be definitive of the 'mystical.'"[32] (In fact, the bodily effects of contemplation tend to be suffering, and "rapture" and "ecstasy," according to Teresa, "have little to do with" the body).[33] If Teresa does not think mysticism is defined by her experiences, then what form does her mysticism take?

Turner is rather harsh in his judgement; he uses the term "experientialism" to describe a form of mysticism which is "a rival practice which displaces that Christian ordinariness [of "worship, prayer and sacrament"]. . . . It abhors the experiential vacuum of the apophatic, rushing to fill it with the plenum of the psychologistic . . . [resulting in] deformations of the spirit."[34]

Basically, then, Turner is suggesting that chasing esoteric inner *experiences* is harmful because they are a distraction from the "ordinariness" of Christian practice; and they divert one from the awareness of the mystery of God by feeding into a subjective, ego-fueled state.

This is not to suggest that Teresa *the nun* (the writer) never experienced subjective experiences of divine presence; often she will say "a certain nun" when we are reasonably sure she is talking about she, herself, having mystical experiences; and her autobiographical *Life* makes this even clearer.

Be that as it may, however,

---

32. Turner, *Darkness of God*, 2.

33. Regarding rapture, "It is all about love melting into love. Pleasures of the body have little to do with this union; the spiritual delights the Beloved shares with the soul are a thousand times removed from the pleasures married people must experience" (Teresa of Àvila, *Interior Castle*, 145).

34. Turner, *Darkness of God*, 259.

our focus here is on *The Interior Castle* as a work of poetic-mystical theology—an apophatic fiction or, in de Certeau's words, a mystic fable. Whatever else it is, the *Castle* is certainly a beautifully poetic story of the soul's journey inwards.

This journey proceeds inwards, from the First Dwelling to the most interior, the Seventh Dwelling, where Christ, the Beloved, is most deeply found in mystical union. In this, it is strikingly similar to the male quest narratives of Courtly Love epic poetry, which influenced Teresa as a young woman; except that this time it is the female ("she," the soul) traversing inner, not outer, adventures in search of the (male, Christ) Beloved.

By reading the Castle as apophatic fiction (recalling that we are in the territory of truth-yielding story), it is here that we will be able to enshrine our myth and continue our approach to the autism of Gxd. So, to be clear, is the protagonist of the Castle an autobiographical self, or a fictional soul? To some extent, it is necessary to disregard the complex, and ultimately unverifiable, question of Teresa as an experiencing *person.* We, *for our purposes,* will treat the *Castle* as a story, from which we might learn. The crucial difference is to distinguish Teresa, the nun, the writer, from the (fictional character) soul she writes about in the book; not least because it would be naïvely and seriously underestimating her intellect to assume that the cornucopia of metaphors in *The Interior Castle* is not written by a skilled creative writer.

Teresa the Theologian

Similarly, for all that she ironically writes about being a "poor, unlearned woman,"[35] her work displays a theological understanding which she herself (in her autobiographical writing) says, and is clear in her work, she learned from reading Saint Augustine among other theologians. Teresa's first experience of monastic life was in an Augustinian convent,[36] and Rowan Williams writes about "her beloved Augustine."[37] Both Peter Tyler and Rowan Williams trace the influence of Augustine on her theological thinking. Tyler comments on insights from her autobiography, the *Life*:

> Throughout the *Life* Teresa tells us how important books had been . . . Augustine, Jerome and Bernardino de Laredo had initiated her into the spiritual language of the Catholic Church.[38]

Teresa's autobiographical *Life* records: "As I began to read [Augustine's] *Confessions*, it seemed to me that I saw myself in them."[39] This is also theological thinking in the context of the Spanish *alumbradismo*[40] movement as an influence on Teresa, where, with a "mind receptive to God," it builds on medieval Augustinian theology.

The Interior Castle is a work modelled on, yet different to, Saint Augustine's fifth century *Confessions*. The

---

35. For example, Teresa of Àvila, *Interior Castle*, 250, 67; also Teresa of Ávila, *Life of Teresa by Herself*, 75. Starr in her introduction to *The Interior Castle* states that she has edited the text to take away the extreme self-deprecating tone of many of Teresa's remarks (see Starr, "Introduction," in Teresa of Àvila, *Interior Castle*, 15–16).

36. See Starr, "Introduction," in Teresa of Àvila, *Interior Castle*, 6.

37. Williams, *Teresa of Àvila*, 140.

38. Williams, *Teresa of Àvila*, 102; see also 24–25.

39. Teresa of Ávila, *Life of Teresa by Herself*, 9.7–8, quoted in Williams, *Teresa of Àvila*, 53.

40. The Spanish *Alumbradismo* (Enlightenment) spiritual movement came perilously close to censure by the Inquisition, as a heretical sect; and Teresa had to skillfully write on the right side of a dangerous line.

Confessions is in the genre of autobiography, but it is written in terms of intellectual, theological, and moral exploration. It begins with accounts of Augustine's debauched life, his conversion and subsequent moral and spiritual change, but then moves much more into a kind of propositional theology which he discovers, or is revealed to him by God, stage by stage. So it could be said to be a theological statement written in the genre of an autobiography, of himself as a theological thinker and explorer. We could say that for the *Confessions*, his concept of self means that autobiography and theology are inseparable.[41]

Williams comments that Teresa's work "reproduces something of the technique of Augustine's *Confessions*,"[42] and *The Interior Castle* has similarities, in that it is an "inner quest" story. However, it differs from the *Confessions* in ways that are crucial for the concept of apophatic fiction. *The Interior Castle* is primarily, *as a text,* not a narrative of the self, but a poetic telling of the soul in a castle of metaphors. One, in this case, belongs in the non-fiction section, but the other, the *Castle,* belongs in the rich glory of the fiction section—or perhaps in a strange category in-between.

On top of this, it is worth noting that Augustine uses the first person for the narrative framework of his *Confessions* (but also using the third person to discuss the theology he discovers in his personal journey, and the second person in addressing Gxd); Teresa very sparingly uses the first person "I." Instead, the narrative perspective is of "she," the (third person) soul, in her riot of metaphors and similes. The point, then, is that, in terms of a *narrative of experience*, Christ ("He," "the Beloved") and "she," the

---

41. See Turner, *Darkness of God*, 50–73.
42. Williams, *Teresa of Àvila*, 45.

THE AUTISM OF APOPHATIC FICTION 163

metaphor-drenched soul, not Teresa the nun, are the protagonists. On rare occasions, as we have seen, Teresa, the writer, "breaks the fourth wall" to talk directly to the reader, to give advice.[43] However, in general, we are reading a poetic love story, not totally removed, as we have seen, from the love stories of Courtly Love which Teresa read, as a young woman—with the important proviso that the seeking soul here is not a gallant (male) knight, but a humble (female) nun; the story is of an inner, not outer, journey, and the beloved is in fact the ultimate Beloved, Christ. The narrative technique might be explained as follows.

Starr writes that Bernini's famous statue *Saint Teresa in Ecstasy* is "an unabashedly sensual image . . . the nun swooning blissfully backward while a clearly delighted androgynous angel plunges a flaming sword into her, leaving her on fire with love for God."[44] This is where the crucial point is. What Starr (and, of course, Bernini) do not explicitly point out (in fact, it is ultimately, possibly, unnecessary for either of them) is that, although Teresa the narrator, Teresa the actual nun, may be in an ecstasy of "musing on" this theological imagery and experiencing the text,[45] it is not "the nun" (Teresa, the narrator) who is "swooning in (literary, theological, and erotic) ecstasy," but the "soul," whom we are viewing as a fictional protagonist. As we

---

43. The effects of contemplation, which Teresa the narrator discusses, are not the same as the objects of contemplation. Teresa the narrator, in a didactic/pastoral role, alerts the reader to physical effects of intense contemplation (a "second order" consequence of the practice of cultivating awareness of the mystical), for example: "Pain . . . weak pulse, bones disjointed, hands rigid" (Teresa of Ávila, *Life of Teresa by Herself*, 140); "copious tears and splitting headaches" (Teresa of Ávila, *Interior Castle*, 90); "Sobbing . . . chest constriction . . . nosebleeds" (Teresa of Àvila, *Interior Castle*, 96–97).

44. Teresa of Àvila, *Interior Castle*, 10–11.

45. If contemplation often has physical effects such as nosebleeds, meditation on erotic imagery can have physical effects too; but this is not in itself the role of the erotic in the text.

will see even more when we read Saint John of the Cross, sexual imagery is not shied away from; Teresa's "soul" protagonist, as she approaches the innermost dwelling, describes raptures of delight (orgasmic experience is one interpretation) and the final prize—which is also death—is union with the Beloved.

For our hermeneutic, a non-experientialist *reading* can look for ways that the *text* works as a theological thinking and a narrative using the genre of fiction. Put simply, we are using a different pair of glasses; a different hermeneutic, to discern our own potential benefit from her writing. This outwits the experientialism debate if, for our purposes, the idea of "experience" in the text is rethought. This would be to see it as a poetic embodiment of apophatic theological thinking. A useful way to consider this could be to bring Teresa's work alongside the novelist Italo Calvino's thinking on *livelli di realtà* (levels of reality). Calvino writes:

> La letteratura non conosce la realtà ma solo livelli. Se esista la realtà di cui i vari livelli non sono che aspetti parziali, o se esistano solo i livelli, questo la letteratura non può deciderlo. La letteratura conosce la realtà dei livelli e questa è una realtà che conosce forse meglio di quanto non s'arrivi a conoscerla attraverso altri procedimenti conoscitivi. E' già molto.
>
> (Literature knows no reality, but only levels. If a reality exists of which the various levels are only partial aspects, literature cannot decide this. Literature knows the reality of levels, and this is a reality which perhaps recognizes this better than other ways of knowing do. And that, already in itself, is quite a lot.) [this author's translation].[46]

---

46. Italo Calvino, *I livelli della realtà*. See also Dunster, "Abyss of Calvino's Deconstructive Writing."

So how does the story of *The Interior Castle* work? Do Calvino's "levels of reality" work as a way to understand it? First and foremost, the level of reality is an *Interior* one—there is no physical castle but only one within the inner life, fictionalized. The next level of reality, in fact equally fundamentally, is that of the interior Christ—the startling proposition that Christ lives within the person, the self. We, ourselves, as mind and soul, can ponder on this theological assertion as we read the "soul" narrative. It is therefore not unreasonable that "musing deeply," she is thinking theologically of Augustine. We might say that in the inward journey to discover the Beloved within, she is following Augustine's theological reworking of Neoplatonic *anamnesis* (un-forgetting of the pre-existing soul).[47] In a Christian context, for Augustine and Teresa, this *is* the discovery of Christ within; as profound immanence.

Augustine writes:

> do not go outward; return within yourself. In the inward man dwells truth. . . .[48] You were within me, and I was in the world outside myself.[49]

and similarly, Teresa writes:

> I urge those of you who have not begun to go inside yourselves to enter now, and those of you who are already in: don't let warfare make you turn back.[50]

The trope of the interior castle reads as an outworking of Augustine's conviction that the person lacking spiritual consciousness is looking "outside," but Gxd is discovered

---

47. See Turner, *Darkness of God*, 58; and Augustine reworks *anamnesis* as Christian theology when he writes that unforgetting is a spiritual union with God: memory is the faculty of unforgetting where "our hearts are restless until they find rest in you" (Augustine, *Confessions* 1.1:1).

48. Turner, *Darkness of God*, 129.

49. Augustine, *Confessions*, 231.

50. Teresa of Àvila, *Interior Castle*, 62.

within. Augustine's thinking of a transcendent Gxd as being found most deeply and immanently in the self (also the self subject to original sin) is deeply paradoxical. Augustine stays within kataphatic language; but Teresa deepens this understanding for us. Just as with Dionysius' apophatic writing, the paradox of a transcendent Gxd, who is at the same time a deeply personal and immanent interiority, requires metaphorical language. We are reckoning with an apophatic thinking of Gxd within yet absolutely beyond.[51] Teresa's apophatic theological intent in negotiating this paradox in *The Interior Castle* is clear throughout. When she describes her visions as "mystical theology,"[52] as we have seen, she emphasizes that a grounding in theology is her foundation.[53] However, when Gxd suspends the understanding, as she tells us in her *Life,*[54] as well as at certain stages of *The Interior Castle*, this echoes Dionysius' surpassing of the intellect in apophatic theology. Teresa explains this to her reader, expressing her sense of inadequacy to the task, for example:

> In this moment of perfect clarity, the soul understands that God alone is truth. . . . I wish I could say more about this, but it's ineffable. . . . God has made the soul into an utter fool so that he can replace false intelligence with true wisdom. . . . In a state of union, the soul sees nothing and hears nothing and comprehends nothing. . . . Our intellects, no matter how sharp, can no more grasp (the concept of the soul and God dwelling in it) than they can comprehend God. . . . Yet when he unites himself with her at last, she understands nothing. She loses her senses and her reason.

---

51. See Turner, *Darkness of God,* 69.
52. Teresa of Ávila, *Life of Teresa by Herself,* 71.
53. Teresa of Ávila, *Life of Teresa by Herself,* 84.
54. Teresa of Ávila, *Life of Teresa by Herself,* 85.

> In the intensity (of) . . . such vivid knowledge, (the soul) feels estranged from God.[55]

(The theologically astute reader will immediately be drawn to her language of the soul which "feels estranged from God" precisely at the moment of union, because it echoes the mystic Meister Eckhart's famous words about "taking leave of God for God's sake."[56] This does indeed take us back to Dionysius' writing of Very Being which does not exist, and Jean Luc Marion's work on God without Being; and, of course, Jesus' utterly paradoxical cry on the Cross: "My God, my God, why have you forsaken me?").

Coming back to Calvino's levels of reality, the next trope in the story of the Castle is rooms; like the "house of many mansions" which Jesus promises in John's Gospel,[57] the interior castle is vast, and awaiting exploration. Each sequential chapter is another level of reality, which Teresa calls dwellings, and the journey inwards is a deeper knowledge of Christ in each successive, more advanced and more deeply inner room. If this seems too intellectual and lacking in *praxis* (practical outworking), this would be misleading. In fact, one of Teresa's maxims, frequently interjected in the text, is "practice, practice, practice!" Knowledge of Christ is of no value as purely intellectual theology alone; it is also a practical theology where knowledge is also union, achieved through very practical actions, particularly worship, prayer and service to others. Perhaps not unlike our own reading of the adventures in John Bunyan's Pilgrim in *Pilgrim's Progress*, the journeying nun, learning from the soul in the castle, has to *do* things.

---

55. Teresa of Àvila, *Interior Castle*, 246, 123, 36, 263.
56. Meister Eckhart, "Qui audit me non confundetur," in *Selected Writings*, 176–77.
57. John 14:2.

This is story; it is not literally an instruction manual; but by implication, as we learn from the story of the "soul" who journeys within the Castle, it certainly is. This is of great value to the practical Christian who reads the *Castle* as an exercise in worship and contemplation. There is certainly no conflict when we now need to focus on our approach here; which is to read Teresa's mysticism as a poetic work, written to express apophatic theological thinking.

Narrative Strategies

We have pointed out that, as apophatic fiction, Teresa's narrative departs from Augustine's *Confessions,* which are a spiritual/theological but kataphatic autobiography. In contrast, the *Castle* works almost entirely by relying on imagery. Its frequent, main tropes, beyond that of the Castle and its rooms include:

- the journey (inwards)
- the garden (God as gardener—provider, loving care, fruitfulness, beauty, nature, creation);
- the butterfly flitting from flower to flower, restlessly (recalling Augustine's famous words that "our hearts are restless till they find their rest in Thee"); also fragile, short lived and beautiful—glory and fragility/smallness of self);
- the silk worm, emerging from its cocoon as it awakens in its spiritual awareness;
- reptiles (the problem of sin and temptation—the snake in the garden of Eden)

These alone invite a reading which lingers in the richness of metaphoric potential, as polysemic (capable of different shades of meaning) but also organically "semic" (*seme* (Greek) = a seed to be planted). There is also the richness of a glorious excess of poetic crafted material, which amounts to a cascade of metaphors. This excess is entirely surplus to the skeleton which allegory would offer for pragmatically constructing a (kataphatic) theological system. To give a mere selection of the many examples used, she uses metaphors such as:

> "silent sandpaper" (50); "clash of arms and explosion of mortar" (57); "the desert of the soul" (74); "wounds, ointment" (78); "fledgling birds" (83); "storms" (83); "stars hurtling across the heavens" (92); "(the mind) wander(ing) from one extreme to another, like a fool who cannot find his assigned seat" (108); (mere humans as) "worms" (150); life as a "tempestuous sea" (150); spiritual strength as "streams of milk flowing from the divine breasts" (271); (inauthentic thinking as) "mud clinging to our boots" (80).

and there could be many other examples in this list. Unlike Dionysius, she does not "dive into" self-consuming metaphors, but works her way in toward them. Sometimes simple imagery, as listed above, can work in the way which, neurotypically, we use metaphor and simile to extract pragmatic meaning. So any one of these images is enough to carry a theological point which can be meditated on and imitated in "ordinary" Christian practice and prayer. For example, when we read about the worm in its cocoon, we might be reminded that we are not yet what we will be as we advance in Christian maturity. Or that the full emergence from the cocoon is only in the perfections of heaven. Or that as the humble silk worm spins its cocoon, it is already producing something as beautiful as silk, so we should be encouraged even if we feel ourselves as mere novices in spiritual development. Or we may feel a "wretched worm" (the narrative tells us we are "wretched worms," at more than one point and, in fact, when translating the *Castle,* Starr edits out many of these passages as too "self-loathing"). This is the polysemic[58] and open-ended nature of imagery; in Jesus' words in John's Gospel, "let the reader understand." No-one has the authority to lay down "what these images mean" for us (and therefore become our hermeneutical boss!). The above examples give my subjective thoughts at this time—you may be inspired to take other lessons from them, and both of us might evolve or deepen what we see in these images. (What we are practicing here is in fact, what is termed Reader Response theory; we have been doing it all along in developing our consciousness of different hermeneutics, and choosing one in particular; in the conscious knowledge that there are others).

However, her imagery, increasingly in the innermost rooms, follows Dionysius' literary technique of self-subverting metaphors. So her paradox, frequently, is of the sweetness of pain as part of the deepening journey; apparently an oxymoron but, within the fiction, and, by implication, in the reader's aims for spiritual growth and understanding, a simple fact; perhaps the extreme pain of repentance and humility within the extreme joy of a deeper knowledge of Christ, the soul's "Beloved." As in Dionysius' *Mystical Theology* (we cannot discount that the *Mystical Theology* was part of her studies), as the protagonist soul progresses into the deeper rooms, the narrative more and more uses the paradoxical imagery of darkness as light.[59]

58. Generating more than one possible meaning.

59. Often, at the beginning and end of sections, she begs for God's help because she finds writing so difficult, and her writing as inadequate. Is this surely (theologically) sincere? Or possibly an ironic proto-feminist comment, or even a way to protect

We may recoil at Teresa's humility when it casts us as mere worms, but she astutely points out that, for all of us, "Our intellects no matter how sharp, can no more grasp (the reality of the soul) than they can comprehend God."[60] It is clearly a theological statement, in the face of apophatic "expressing what cannot be expressed"; in the face of the greatness of God, therefore, she recognizes the vital need for humility.[61] It would be unthinkable to feel that her writing, or any writing, would be adequate. And yet, she writes!

True Erring: Monsignor Quixote, Teresa, and the Novel

Having rejected an autobiographical reading or an allegorical reading, we are now able to argue for *The Interior Castle* as a work of apophatic theological thinking. The argument here is crucial. It is that it is fiction itself which is an apophatic strategy, and therefore can be termed "apophatic fiction." This is crucial, as the point towards which the whole of this chapter has been working, and this is the concept of "apophatic fiction." I have created this term to indicate that Teresa and John are both apophatic theologians *and* creative writers.[62] More than this, their creative

---

herself from being seen by the Inquisition as too provocative a theologian? However, even if these are real strategies, the fact remains that humility can hardly be over-emphasized in Teresa's work, as a fundamental truth and an essential practice, e.g., Teresa of Ávila, *Life of Teresa by Herself*, 85, 88, 118; and Teresa of Àvila, *Interior Castle*, 80, 90, 141, 190, 226, 247, 289.

60. Teresa of Àvila, *Interior Castle*, 36; also, for example, 275: "These metaphors make me laugh at myself. I'm not satisfied with them, but I can't come up with any others." Often, at the beginning and end of sections, she begs for God's help because she finds writing so difficult, and sees her writing as inadequate; humility, but also apophatic theological awareness.

61. Humility can hardly be over-emphasized in Teresa's work, as a fundamental truth and an essential practice, e.g., Teresa of Ávila, *Life of Teresa by Herself*, 85, 88, 118, and Teresa of Àvila, *Interior Castle*, 80, 90, 141, 190, 226, 247, 289.

62. Dionysius, in a sense, is also a creative writer, creatively reworking metaphor into a new form.

work *is* the discourse of their apophatic theology. A remarkable part of the "story" is that, when Jesus appeared to Teresa, he asked who she was, and she replied "I am Teresa of Jesus. Who are you?" Jesus replied, "I am Jesus of Teresa." "Teresa's Jesus" can thus be a creation of Teresa the narrator, giving her power to create theological fiction.

A lateral way in to thinking of the idea of apophatic theological fiction will now demonstrate what apophatic fiction might look like, if Graham Greene, the "Catholic atheist,"[63] can similarly be considered as a novelist grappling with the unknowable God. This is particularly relevant in Green's novel *Monsignor Quixote*. Its similarities with *The Interior Castle* will become apparent.

In Greene's novel, Cervantes' Don Quixote and Sancho Panza are recast as a Catholic village priest and a communist atheist local politician. Cervantes' Quixote becomes the Don as he enters into the alternative reality of imagined participation in the grandiosity of the world of chivalric romance. Greene's Quixote becomes a Monsignor, mistakenly bestowed on him by the deluded bishop who promotes him on slender and improbable grounds.

However, there is a deeper and more fundamental play on delusion at work. When Monsignor Quixote and Sancho embark on a journey together, Sancho exchanges Father Quixote's book of moral theology for his copy of the works of Lenin. Sancho's Marxist ideals have been found wanting in Realpolitik at the level of mundane local politics, but it is Quixote who enacts that idealism in acts of resistance against capitalism.

Sancho in turn asks Quixote, "Do you really believe those stories?" of the faith. Quixote's answer is revealing:

---

63. Sweeney, *Almost Catholic*, 23.

"I want to believe, and I want others to believe."[64] Doubt is an inalienable part not only Quixote's faith but also, he implies, even the Pope's. If his faith is "only a fiction," does this render it "untrue?" His deluded quest "for the socks" to make him a "real" bishop is a comic reworking of the Don's equally comic quest for chivalric glory, and both fulfill that quest to its logical (apophatic) conclusion of madness. As a "knight errant," like the Don he is erring at every level—wandering in the "cock and bull story"[65] of shopping for the purple socks, wandering in the title of Monsignor given to him by the deluded, drunken Bishop of Motopo, and wandering in the space of fiction, as Greene's creative reworking of the original.

"Monsignor Quixote-enacts Don Quixote-enacts the knight errant" is a multiple play on levels of reality in the text, just as Calvino's *livelli di realtà* does, as was discussed earlier. In an autistic hermeneutic, levels of reality in the text collapse and coexist into one "literal" truth, just as they do in Greene's novel. In the space of the text (and only there, in the "literal" space) Monsignor-*is* the Don-*is* the knight errant. Autistic literal metaphor, by taking "the branch of the organization" as "the branch of a tree," is therefore the privileged entry into the text with its impossible reality.

Teresa's "Soul" as "Sister Quixote," the Knight Errant

The Interior Castle is also a narrative of the journey as quest. Speculating on authorial intention, it could seem

---

64. Teresa, like Don/Monsignor Quixote, wants "others to believe" too, and her rhetoric is both poetry and persuasion.

65. A "cock and bull story" is the title of Michael Winterbottom's 2005 comic metanarrative film about a film crew attempting to make a film of the novel *Tristram Shandy*, which is itself (as is the film) a purported autobiography that also errs absurdly.

reasonable to think that Teresa, like the Don, is modelling her work on the same genre of chivalric romance. This is borne out in the biographical account that she grew up reading chivalric novels,[66] and "believing in" the chivalric values of the quest for romantic conquest could be suggested in the reason for her being sent to the cloister, to protect a chastity under threat from amorous adventures.[67]

After her pivotal, transformative emotional reaction to the *Ecce Homo* (behold the *man* [my emphasis]) statue, Teresa's love is transferred to the quest for Christ. The question of "erotic experience" has been discussed above, but a reworked chivalric eros is now enacted in the story of *The Interior Castle*, which is also the enactment of the Scriptures as story. She is a "knight errant" as she errs in the space of fiction, "taking liberties" with theology. Teresa's "soul," like the Don[68] and the Monsignor, also, in her quest, becomes mad with love,[69] and her final destination and consummation can also only be death.[70]

Teresa's awareness of the apophatic theological dimension leads her to rework both the chivalric love quest of her youth and the sacred story of faith in a second-order story similar to both Cervantes' and Greene's. Teresa is Cervantes, not Quixote. She "spins a yarn," for example, in the trope of the silk worm spinning its own cocoon, to create an inner sanctum for the purposes of dying in Christ, in

---

66. Teresa of Àvila, *Interior Castle*, 5.

67. Teresa of Àvila, *Interior Castle*, 5–6, 8, describes Teresa as a "wild child" having "adventures," which include being in a teenage relationship that is "more intimate than was socially acceptable" and even as a nun becoming "an inveterate flirt" who becomes "perilously intimate with a man."

68. Dulcinea becoming for the Don the object of the chivalric love; living out the justice of Sancho's Marxism as Christian love for the Monsignor.

69. Teresa of Àvila, *Interior Castle*, 112, 113, 114, 115, 123, 210.

70. Teresa's seventh dwelling discusses death at length, as the consummation of the divine marriage; both Quixotes die, happy in their madness.

order to be resurrected in Christ as a butterfly.[71] The soul as a narrative character both casts itself poetically in the cascade of metaphors[72] and enacts itself in the narrative's plot of experiences of the quest, the dwelling, and their enabling encounters with God as sensory *gustoes*.[73]

Her fiction is apophatic in the sense that it is a rhetorical strategy to outwit kataphatic discourse, with the same theological intent of that used by Dionysius' strategy of self-subverting language.[74]

Crucial to this argument is that her rhetorical strategy is itself apophatic when the definition of apophasis is recalled. *Apo-* as a grammatical participle is the distancing of relationship where grammatical predication breaks down in discourse, in what Turner has called "that speech about God which is the failure of speech."[75]

The theology is expressed not as "hidden" in the plot, but as the hiddenness which the narrative form creates, existing by not existing anywhere, except *as* the plot. In this way, fiction is an apo-phasis, disrupting the kata-phatic relationship in which theological discourse would operate. Kataphasis would carry theological doctrine "straight to" the reader, but fiction instead creates an opening for the reader, and the theological is suspended in the text, "there for the taking," but not really "there" at all, in the sense of "telling the facts." Instead, it actually invites and questions the reader—"do you enter this world of the text, partaking of the story as a poetic sacrament of mystery?" In this sense, thinking theologically in the text is a wager

---

71. Teresa of Àvila, *Interior Castle*, 126ff.
72. See section 2.3.2.
73. The sensory metaphor is gusto (taste).
74. For example "Our intellects, no matter how sharp, can no more grasp (the reality of the soul) than they can comprehend God" (Teresa of Àvila, *Interior Castle*, 36).
75. Turner, *Darkness of God*, 20.

176   THE AUTISM OF GXD

of faith on the part of the reader. It depends on the reader to "let go" of (kataphatic) rhetorical security and enter a Coleridgean "willing suspension of disbelief."[76] The story isn't (necessarily) "real," but by faith it indicates a truth more real than "fact."

For fiction itself to be an apophasis speaks powerfully in the light of Incarnational metaphor. Literal metaphor is an apophasis where the reading of the metaphor, resisting decoding, exists in absence from kataphatic pragmatism, yet it is the full presence of the metaphor itself in the text. Yes, I am a mere worm! And simultaneously a butterfly! (Still not a rabbit though.)

The text within itself also offers a clear formula, to alert the reader to be anything but theologically naïve regarding the self-subverting utterance of *docta ignorantia*[77] in the comment that "as (the soul) cannot comprehend what it understands, it understands by not understanding."[78] When it also states that "knowing is not experiencing,"[79] a more meaningful reading of this than the experientialist understanding that "you will only know if you experience this" is the possibility of reading it instead as "(true) knowing is 'not-experiencing.'" This is utterly apophatic because, theologically thought, the nonexistent space of

---

76. Coleridge, *Biographia Literaria*, part 2.6, quoted in Jasper, *Sacred Community*, 106.

77. Referring to Nicholas of Cusa, *Of Learned Ignorance*: Nicholas argues from geometry that scientific reasoning, for example about tangents, will lead to the incalculable (an analogy which was discussed in chapter 1). Nicholas then goes on to apply the same reasoning to theology: "We, then, believers in Christ, are led in learned ignorance to the mountain that is Christ" (161); Nicholas also develops *docta ignorantia* into the term Negative Theology (59–64) and this is also an innate feature of knowledge itself: referring to Aristotle's analogy of owls trying to look at the sun, "since the natural desire in us is not without a purpose, its immediate object is our own ignorance. If we can fully realise this desire, we will acquire learned ignorance" (8).

78. Teresa of Àvila, *Life*, 127.

79. Teresa of Àvila, *Life*, 93.

apophatic fiction is superlatively existent, as what Dionysius describes as, in fact, "this hidden Super-Essential Godhead."[80]

In summary, the tropes of the soul's journey and her love affair form an apophatic strategy to carry the ineffable into the nonexistent space of literature. This is a progression toward her pupil John's development of her method. John's poem, "The Ascent of Mount Carmel," will be what the autistic hermeneutic views as a fuller poetic apophasis, where the ineffable as fiction carries great potential for literal metaphor to approach its fulfilment as Incarnation. But—what has this to do with autism? A great deal, if we ponder it in our autistic-LTA hermeneutic.

Teresa and Autism

Does Teresa's apophatic fiction prove a hospitable place for a mythic-autistic hermeneutic? For one thing, this is a solitary journey, hidden within an individual castle of the individual soul; this is a journey of the authentic *autos,* in pure separation. The inadequacy of any writing, which she has identified, would, furthermore, be for us pure, Absolute Mindfulness of Separation—we are forever cast out from the ideal of a perfect writing as a perfect approach to the divine. However, her strategy of apophatic fiction in the very building of the narrative Castle also embodies a Mindfulness of Separation, in that there is an existential gulf between author and protagonist; we might (and possibly, should) participate in the text as learners reading our own spiritual path within the metaphors, but to recall Calvino's levels of reality, the text itself is utterly divorced from both author and reader. This is another Mindfulness

80. Dionysius, *Divine Names*, 53.

of Separation; we might (or might not) learn profitably from this fiction (just as we used the example of a good novel in the Introduction); but Mindfulness of Separation finds itself in our ultimate distance from the text. We might sometimes say we are "immersed in a book"; but if we start, *psychologically*, to *become* part of the book, we are in the territory of psychosis.

Be that as it may, the myth of Absolute Autistic Fascination finds itself here too, perhaps in some ways possibly even more powerfully than in Dionysius. Here, the profusion of imagery gives delight to the mythical autism which inhabits this world of the text. As a mythical autistic hero/saint, I can revel in gardens, flowers, butterflies, a crystal castle, a Gardener who is my Beloved. So literal metaphor, too, can realize itself as Incarnational metaphor, where, *within the text,* there is only the non-sense of *becoming* a castle, a flower, a silkworm, a castle dweller, a lover. You may have noticed that we have just suggested that to inhabit the book, as opposed to "being immersed in it," would lead to psychosis. Am I not, now, suggesting the same thing? It depends how we view it. Recalling the boy Peter in the Introduction, who says "it's the yellowness I'm in," we could say that the boy is detached from reality; but in fact here, "autism speaks." Is it possible, even, to wonder if there is a Zero Positive of autistic empathy at work here, as we read as the mythical autistic hero/saint? Would this be the totally other mirror image of a psychotic Zero Negative, which succeeds all too well as a (perhaps rather too confident) cognitive reader, missing the apophatic secret, failing to inhabit the glorious impairment of cognitive empathy which is our (Zero Positive) autism, and the glorious joy of Peter's "yellowness"—the autism of the text, which inhabits the metaphor in rapt, literary, affective empathy? Our myth would be one of inhabiting the text not as "ourselves" (relatively autistic, or relatively not), but in the embodiment of our mythical autism. Why are we building this mythical autistic interior castle? Purely because an Absolute autism can give us a song which we, perhaps, in our relative autism, might catch in albeit faint but beautiful echoes; we are learning to be autistic literary-theological readers by reading our own, carefully-spun myth. If we were to take the view that the *Interior Castle* is an account of pathological delusions, which is sometimes done, we might be underestimating the power which Absolute Fascination discerns, and this is the power of this autistic myth. In other words, Autistic Fascination and Incarnational metaphor "take things literally," but we, as creators of this myth, know that, to paraphrase Rudolf Bultmann about the Bible, our myth *is not* truth, but *embodies* truth. Our autistic myth stands as myth, read-y to be read. We don't in truth know how to interpret Peter's statement of being "in" the yellowness, and perhaps we should not even try; but we have built a case in this chapter for *The Interior Castle* as apophatic fiction. So, within the fiction, myth can fix onto these images, and Autistic Fascination within its mythical space can delight in them. We can inhabit the silkworm, spinning silk and approaching emergence from the cocoon, knowing full well that this is not "reality," but we invest it with the reality of mythical significance, as a sacred story. And, of course, in this way, Fascination and Incarnational metaphor exist only within the isolated text with its Mindfulness of Separation. At the center of these inter-related qualities of the autistic sacred myth, we see the same love as we did with Dionysius; affective empathy grows ever deeper in the knowledge of the Beloved, precisely as, further and further into the mystery, cognitive empathy is disabled. Think of the young autistic man who gives a large sum of money to a beggar, from his own slender income; is he deluded, or a holy fool—and can we truly ever answer this question? This is a pure love which we will now see more deeply at work in John of the Cross' *The Ascent of Mount Carmel*.

THE ASCENT OF MOUNT CARMEL: JOHN OF THE CROSS AND MYTHICAL AUTISM

John's Theological Poem

On a dark night, Kindled in love with yearnings—oh, happy chance!
I went forth without being observed, My house being now at rest.
In darkness and secure, By the secret ladder, disguised—oh, happy chance!
In darkness and in concealment, My house being now at rest.
In the happy night,
In secret, when none saw me,
Nor I beheld aught,
Without light or guide, save that which burned in my heart.
This light guided me
More surely than the light of noonday,
To the place where he (well I knew who!) was awaiting me—
A place where none appeared.
Oh, night that guided me,
Oh, night more lovely than the dawn,
Oh, night that joined Beloved with lover,
Lover transformed in the Beloved!
Upon my flowery breast, kept wholly for himself alone,
There he stayed sleeping, and I caressed him, And the fanning of the cedars made a breeze.
The breeze blew from the turret As I parted his locks;
With his gentle hand he wounded my neck

> And caused all my senses to be suspended.
> I remained, lost in oblivion; My face I reclined on the Beloved.
> All ceased and I abandoned myself, Leaving my cares forgotten among the lilies.
>
> —John of the Cross[81]

As Teresa was writing, she regularly met with "learned men" to discuss theology. To one young man, she became a kind of mentor. This young man is the figure we now know as Saint John of the Cross. Like Teresa, he lived a monastic life, was a reformer, and wrote mystical theology; we will now, as with Teresa's Castle, approach John's poem as apophatic fiction with autistic potential.

John of the Cross is most famous for giving Christian spirituality the archetype of the "dark night of the soul," for two reasons. Firstly, he was kidnapped and imprisoned on charges of "disobedience" to his monastic order, so that he well knew darkness and suffering, and secondly, on the basis of the poem, which is commonly known as *The Dark Night of the Soul;* although actually, it is the Prologue to *The Ascent of Mount Carmel*, an extended theological treatise. Looking at the poem as it is written above, is this a homo-erotic fantasy, or is the dark night of the soul a deep depression[82]—or is John doing something different? *The Ascent of Mount Carmel*, in its entirety, goes on to explain how deeply, mystically theological the initial poem is. The extended commentary which follows the poem suggests that he is not writing about an erotic fantasy or encounter, and he is not talking about depression; rather, he is, like his mentor Teresa, writing apophatic fiction—or, more accurately, apophatic poetry.

---

81. John of the Cross, "Dark Night of the Soul," in *Ascent of Mount Carmel*, 65.

82. This archetype is well established in Christian mystical thinking; yet perhaps it overlooks somewhat the erotic element where John meets and melds with the Beloved.

There is an evolution from Teresa's (at first sight) rather homely extended story-telling to John's highly concentrated metaphors in this poem. It achieves something which is achieved only in fleeting images in Teresa's work. With *The Ascent to Mount Carmel* poem, John heaps metaphor upon metaphor in an intense concentration of the journey; it is breath-taking in how full and yet concise it is, and almost too rapid; every word counts—"blink and you miss it." Reading it aright requires that we linger in it, and inhabit every word. There is a real excess of imagery—why do we have "cedars," why do we have "breeze"? True, every image could be interpreted as a biblical trope; but why so many? It seems to me that John is adding in all these numerous images to create a poetic texture; as we have said earlier, to outwit kataphatic theology by turning to the apophatic, and doing so by "deviating" (these poetic writers were definitely suspect to the Inquisition)—deviating into poetic expression of truth which cannot be expressed by means of straightforward, propositional language. This is a poetry of apophatic fiction.

John's poem is, like Teresa's novel, both a journey and a love affair, with the journey toward the lover leading to the absolute union which can only be told as apophatic discourse; by resorting to metaphor. This is necessary as the poem reaches "oblivion" and "all ceasing," but not in a vacuum, as kataphatic language would tell it, but wrapped up, or rather, instantiated, in metaphors: "hand," "neck," "wounding," "face," "lilies." The fact that this is also orgasmic, abandoning oneself to the Beloved (as Teresa also describes), is akin to, and modelled on, the prototypical biblical book of the Song of Songs, where love for Gxd is cast as erotic longing. To return to Plato's myth of the cave, it is not difficult, in Platonic terms, to say that physical, human *eros* is merely a shadow of a spiritual eros. John is daring enough to express this.

The oblivion he experiences is in the context of darkness, which fills virtually all of the poem until the final union and consummation; but, as with Dionysius, it is a darkness as light, not a physical light but a light in his heart. This context of darkness being the journey to union follows the imagery Dionysius uses, of the paradox of seeing most brilliantly in utter darkness. This is ecstasy and, as absolute ecstasy, it takes place in the absolute *eros* of absolute unknowing [*ex-stasis*—displacement "out of the space" of normality]. This orgasmic "carnal knowledge" as complete unknowing takes on real power when it is read as apophatic fiction. Here, John is employing Teresa's strategy of using story as an apophasis of union. Like Teresa, John reworks the ineffable, but perhaps even more completely because he focuses so much on darkness; he is sexualizing Dionysius' self-subverting utterance of Light as Darkness into the place of absolute, erotic, union. Yet this is in a darkness full of negation; he can see no-one, and in the darkness (which figures in almost every line until the final lines of consummation) he has only the light of his heart to guide him. This self-subversion is, then, the total unknowing of the most intimate knowing, and in this sense, it can be read as a paradoxical re-expression of the pervasive imagery of darkness, night and concealment which, ultimately, is the place of true knowing and being. Remarkably, John tells us that

> All the doctrine whereof I intend to treat in this Ascent of Mount Carmel is included in the following stanzas, and in them is also described the manner of ascending to the summit of the Mount, which is the high state of

perfection which we here call union of the soul with God.[83]

If the poem "contains all the doctrine" of John's theological thinking, Denys Turner is right to interpret the "dark night" theologically. Turner comments that

> Faith, the darkness of unknowing, is the conviction—but also the practice of the Christian life as organized in terms of that conviction—that "our deepest center is in God." It is the conviction that our deepest center . . . is in us but not of us, is not "ours" to possess, but ours only to be possessed by. And so faith at once "decenters" us.[84]

Turner argues persuasively for the fundamental distinction between experiential depression and the dark night of the soul on which John dwells here. This is a fundamental safeguarding from experientialism. Turner explains the difference:

> In depression, it is the "self" which causes the distress of the sense of its loss, but "the dark nights" on the other hand are entered into as loss of that same self, for in that consists their pain, but the hope it acquires is of the non-recovery of that selfhood in any form, for what is lost in the passive nights was never the self at all, but only an illusion all along. But in saying that this conventional self is an "illusion" it is necessary to warn against an obvious, and tempting, misinterpretation. To say that the self is an illusion is not to say that it is not real, for, on the contrary, it is precisely in terms of such selfhoods that real people really live, most of the time . . . a live, dynamic falsehood.[85]

---

83. John of the Cross, *Ascent of Mount Carmel*, 63.
84. Turner, *Darkness of God*, 251.
85. Turner, *Darkness of God*, 244.

> **The theological conviction behind this, of faith as a decentering, turns the question of experientialism on its head. If the experience of the self is the real fiction, as Turner argues, then the "non-experience" which can only exist in its poetic telling is in fact the more theologically "true."**

This is why we will be able to read apophatic fiction as a mute language of being in the conclusion of this chapter; "mute language" as thought by the Postmodern thinker Maurice Blanchot, is a similar paradox in which we find the pure truth of Being. This is equally true in the sense with which Turner reads John's theological thinking; perhaps Turner's words, here, too, merit a contemplative reading:

> My true self consists in my transformation in God. I know myself in my not-knowing my difference from God. And "contemplation" is the power to rest in that not-knowing. There is no experience, then, of which that selfhood is the object. The experience of the loss of experience of the self . . . is what John calls "the passive night of the spirit."[86]

The reason that apophatic fiction offers a place to rest in that not-knowing is that it operates when theologically thought, but is embodied only as poetry—a text of what "is not," but "is only" the image.

An Autistic Reading of The Dark Night

We already have learned from Dionysius and Teresa how apophatic fiction offers a place for Mindfulness of Separation, Fascination, Incarnational metaphor, and at the heart, autistic love. However, an autistic reading will recognize a discourse here which speaks in its strongest form,

---

86. Turner, *Darkness of God*, 245.

particularly, to autistic love—that enhanced and deficient empathy. The impairment/refusal of cognitive empathy here would be a strategy to understand the darkness as a Mindfulness of Separation; without knowing or seeing, I love, and yet that "impaired" love is precisely where the perfect utter affective love is found. The poem's combination of *eros* and hiddenness/darkness is, in fact, a "loving without knowing." This is the risk of autistic faith which practices love with no guarantee, because there is no way to "assess" the object of love. It is simply trusting, unconditional love, receiving and giving.

This is also a discourse which the twenty-first-century theologian Jean Luc Marion develops, where the gift outwits ontological difference in the parable of the prodigal son.[87] *Eros* surpasses knowledge, because the father is supremely a Holy Fool, loving without knowing, or even asking, if the son deserves forgiveness. In autistic terms, the father practices total affective empathy precisely in this space of impaired cognitive empathy. This begins to show us something of the autism of Gxd, which will shine with its greatest intensity in chapter 4.

MAURICE BLANCHOT: THE MUTE LANGUAGE OF BEING

In (poetic) language the world recedes and goals cease; the world falls silent; beings . . . are no longer ultimately what speaks. Beings fall silent, but then it is being that tends to speak and speech that wants to be.[88]

—Maurice Blanchot, *The Space of Literature*

---

87. See Marion, *God Without Being*, 97–99.
88. Marion, *God Without Being*, 97–99.

We saw earlier that Denys Turner has suggested that we can take the mystical poetry we have studied "seriously," as apophatic theology. Recall that he also leads us in another, promising direction; to quote him again:

> Though I do believe we have been misreading (the Medieval mystics) . . . within the rather closed, anti-intellectual world of Christian "spiritualities," . . . [there is] the possibility that certain quite contemporary developments in Western thought, associated with "post-modernism," contain a revival of that awareness of the "deconstructive" potential of human thought and language which so characterized classical medieval apophaticism."[89]

Chapter 2 looked at readings of postmodern writers, particularly Derrida and Barthes, and the atheological thinking of Mark C Taylor. We saw how a deconstructive atheology was an important step toward Incarnational metaphor. Now we can go further, looking at apophatic fiction atheologically, as Turner has suggested. We will do this by exploring the thinking of Maurice Blanchot, the novelist/critic/philosopher, specifically, his poetic "theology"[90] of the work of art as he thinks of it in his 1955 study *L'espace littéraire (The Space of Literature)*.

Blanchot writes in *The Space of Literature* about a philosophy of art which is, we might strangely say, "beyond" the sacred. In his thinking, the deepest authenticity of a work of literature lies in a Heideggerian silence where Being speaks. Or rather, what Blanchot (and Heidegger, whom he is following) would term not Being but simply "being," which lies beyond the metaphysical construct of Being. We will now see how his work is not far from the

---

89. Turner, *Darkness of God*, 8.
90. This term is used advisedly, as will become clear.

hidden superabundance which apophatic discourse indicates and, in its paradoxical self-negation, embodies.

Blanchot and Heidegger: Mute Being and the Absence of God

To bring the conversation together between Blanchot and the mystical theologians' apophatic fiction, we need first to explain Blanchot's concept of mute being, in terms of the work's space and the absence of the gods. Chapter 2 followed Mark C Taylor into the atheological possibilities of Derrida's work, but in Blanchot we will see if an even more deeply authentic possibility begins to open up for an autistic hermeneutic. This is because Blanchot, following Heidegger, thinks in terms of the departure of the gods. This is a "clearing away" of our human representations of Gxd, to indicate the hyperessential.[91]

This, for us, is a move toward Incarnational metaphor as a theological understanding of the text itself as absolute kenosis; the emptying out of our representations as a sacrifice we make.

Just as, in chapter 2, Wittgenstein was shown to celebrate the ability of the Uhland poem to magnificently "utter the unutterable," Blanchot writes about a "pure" form of poetry which expresses what is evanescent, such as the work of Mallarmé where, for example, evanescence is conveyed in the image of cigar smoke. He writes about a place where language "expresses nothing"[92] because the pure work of art does not exist to represent but to be. The work of literature is, for Blanchot, something more and other than the mere fact of the existence of the book; it

---

91. "more real than reality."
92. Blanchot, *Space of Literature*, 22.

is the realm where being speaks. I came across perhaps a useful parallel this week, when a friend explained to me what his practice of yoga really meant. "It's not about how far I can stretch my leg compared to that person over there; it's about breathing in that moment, in that position, and being present in it."

To explain what this means for us, reading Blanchot, it is important to see how Blanchot is thinking in terms set out by Heidegger. Blanchot is writing within Heidegger's shadow, so it is important to discuss here, at least briefly, what this means for his thought. Ann Smock, Blanchot's translator, brings out the fundamental but implicit nature of Blanchot's Heideggerian thinking. Her words merit a careful reading, when she writes that:

> all of *l'espace littéraire* is imbued with [Heidegger's idea of] care [*Sorge*]: *le souci de l'origine, le souci de l'oevre,* anxious solicitude for a time before the time when beings supplant being and submit to the command of the objectifying, acquisitive subject; concern for a time other than the time measured by the gradual reduction of the irreconcilably alien to the homogeneity of all that is comprehensively mastered. To the extent that in the work of art the impossible is realized as such, art alone answers, with true fidelity, to the requirement of Heideggerian authenticity.[93]

Blanchot rarely uses Heidegger's name, but assumes that the reader will recognize what his use of the term implies in debt to Heidegger. However, he does, for example, occasionally explain that, for example, "When I am on *the worldly plane*, which I share with things and beings, being is profoundly hidden. (It is the thought of this concealment that Heidegger urges us to welcome)."[94]

---

93. Smock, "Introduction," in Blanchot, *Space of Literature*, 7.
94. Blanchot, *Space of Literature*, 251.

Heidegger's Turn to the Poetic

In the essay *What Is Called Thinking?*, Heidegger asks a fundamental question about thinking, suggesting that "normal" unreflective thinking does not question the representational assumptions it makes. If we could step back from these assumptions that representation "simply works," we would be aware of a withdrawal from the complacency of our logic:

> The real nature of thought might show itself . . . at that very point at which it once withdrew, if only we will pay heed to this withdrawal, if only we will not insist, confused by logic, that we already know perfectly well what thinking is.[95]

He illustrates this point by commenting very simply that "when we wait for the sun to rise, we never do it on the strength of scientific insight."[96] When we "step back from" metaphysical conceptualization (our unquestioning reliance on the scientific method[97] as a total explanation of being, for example), we step outside representational thinking. We might become aware of its inadequacy in the face of Being; in this sense, Heidegger can make the astonishing claim that "science does not think."[98]

Heidegger argues that the language which escapes the "trap" of scientific totality is poetry. His famous "turn to the poetic" indicates that poetry is akin to "thought" in its originary capacity preceding metaphysics. However, "thought and poesy, each in its own way, *are* the essential telling, [but not that] thought and poesy use

---

95. Heidegger, *What Is Called Thinking?*, 44–45.
96. Heidegger, *What Is Called Thinking?*, 36.
97. This is certainly not anti-science; it questions scient*ism*, not science's validity!
98. Heidegger, *What Is Called Thinking?*, 134.

language merely as their medium."[99] Words are "not merely terms [but] wellsprings that are found and dug up in the telling."[100]

> **Heidegger has suggested that being *is itself* the work; the poetic work is not the pragmatic representation of *text* or *writing*, when *used* for anything. Rather, being is disclosed, as the "unthought thought" itself.**

In this sense, Blanchot, following Heidegger, can speak about the work of art or literature as the non-representative space of pure being. (Recall that he suggests that our metaphysical concepts of "Being" would, in rethought thought, simply be "being"; this is what he terms ontological difference).

Heidegger's thinking of Being falling silent as a withdrawal of all representation reads powerfully in an autistic hermeneutic. In an (impossible) absolute autism, metaphor "represents" nothing, being only the pure being indicated by withdrawal. Theologically, this can be read as absolute Incarnational metaphor where the "Nothing" beyond representation is the (being of) the hyperessential All of God. If we think carefully here, this withdrawal of representation is told in the myth of Mindfulness of Separation, and the disclosure of being is told by Autistic Fascination, that total, rapt union with the object of obsessive love, pure being, as presence known only in the absence which is Mindfulness of Separation. We are able, in our mythology, to think of an Absolute autism of the "unthought" of a pure space of the work of art or literature.

---

99. Heidegger, *What Is Called Thinking?*, 128.
100. Heidegger, *What Is Called Thinking?*, 130.

The Space of Literature as Mute Being

Blanchot, then, draws on Heidegger's understanding of poetry as this originary "wellspring" of pre-reflective, pure thought. He considers the possibility of the work of art as "beyond thinking," as pure being representing nothing. He writes:

> The work brings neither certainty nor clarity. It assures us of nothing, nor does it shed any light upon itself. It is not solid, it does not furnish us with anything upon which to brace ourselves. These values belong to Descartes and to the world where we succeed in living.[101]

(Descartes, as we discussed earlier, advanced a metaphysics where logic and the scientific method were secure, knowing the certainty of *cogito, ergo sum* (I think, therefore I am)). Blanchot takes us into the world of a pure, authentic space of art as pure being. In that escape from rigid solidity, we will find silent speech:

> This is the Heideggerian withdrawal of being which speaks only by not speaking (not speaking as representation). In this sense, the work speaks by being-silent/silent-being.[102]

As we read at the opening of this chapter, Blanchot tells us that

> Beings fall silent, but then it is being that tends to speak and speech that wants to be.[103]

We have used the metaphor of speech, too, in our mythical autism. Recall that at the outset of this book we reclaimed the slogan "Autism Speaks" from a

---

101. Blanchot, *Space of Literature*, 223.
102. Blanchot, *Space of Literature*, 223.
103. Blanchot, *Space of Literature*, 223.

THE AUTISM OF APOPHATIC FICTION 193

quasi-eugenical "cure" agenda to a place where autism, pure and unashamed, "speaks," and this speech forms the basis of our myth. How perfect, then, that Blanchot can tell us that in the place of our poetic metaphor, "beings fall silent" and "being tends to speak." In our mythical autism, all the beings of this world have fallen silent in our ears and we exist in the place where Leneh Buckle tells us that she is blissfully "in a world of her own," in perfect Mindfulness of Separation. There, and precisely there, "being tends to speak," pure being itself, because we are the ideal listener; our absolute autism presents itself as a total Fascination which, in love and joy, obsessively "hangs onto every word"; it is, impossibly and utterly, the glorious mythical geek who can tell the story of the Space of Literature.

There is an essentially apophatic nature of the work when it is thought of in this way. Blanchot writes:

> Why is art so intimately allied with the sacred? It is because in the relation between art and the sacred, between that which shows itself and that which does not . . . [where they are] realized only as the approach of the unreachable—the work finds the profound reserve which it needs.[104]

This is because

> when art is the language of the gods, when the temple is the house where the god dwells, the work is reduced to the vehicle of representation, and the work invisible and art unknown. The poem names the sacred, and men hear the sacred, not the poem.[105]

It is the absence which is the sacred—of the gods, of man-made religion—which gives the work "the profound

---

104. Blanchot, *Space of Literature*, 233.
105. Blanchot, *Space of Literature*, 230.

reserve which it needs,"[106] and this must be the sacred of the divine as absence. We are not far, as Turner has realized, from the absent presence of hyperessentiality. This is the authenticity of the "wellspring" Heidegger has described.[107]

Thinking through the apophatic works this chapter has considered, apophatic fiction is similarly the removed sacred of the absent Gxd who speaks by being silent and is seen by being invisible. This means that apophatic fiction can be understood as the language of mute being, "where beings fall silent and being speaks," but only in the space of the work itself, which regarding all representation is silent, beyond all thinking. From here, we can see how Blanchot's thinking has, *in terms of mythical autism, for yielding an Incarnational metaphor,* now even surpassed Derrida's postmodern thought for us. We can see this by a careful reading of Derrida's approach to negative theology.

DIONYSIUS AND DERRIDA

In *Denials: How to Avoid Speaking,* Jacques Derrida writes an extended commentary on Dionysius' *Mystical Theology* but insists "what I write is not negative theology."[108] In Derrida's work, jokes and games are never far away—so how are we to understand his relationship to Dionysius, the negative theologian supreme? Derrida seems at first glance to be doing something similar—but the clue is in the word *Denials*. We could say that Derrida is denying denial. The difference is in how absence is thought,

---

106. Blanchot, *Space of Literature*, 223.

107. Recall that earlier we read Heidegger's words that, poetically thought, words are wellsprings: "Words are not merely terms [but] wellsprings that are found and dug up in the telling" (Heidegger, *What Is Called Thinking?*, 130).

108. Derrida, "How to Avoid Speaking," 8.

within or without the wager of faith. The wager of faith is, famously, Blaise Pascal's phrase for faith which knows that it operates without proof but, totally within this awareness, makes the decision, we could say, to "bet on it."

> **This is a "wager" not in terms of the assent which Bonhoeffer, we recall, terms "cheap grace," but a radical commitment and deeply considered way of life. Derrida sees in Dionysius' thinking something which also distinguishes John's dark night of the soul as the "ontological wager of hyperessentiality."[109]**

An ontological wager is a step of faith regarding Being (ontological), which stakes everything on "hyperessentiality," the "total being beyond being" that is at the heart of negative theology. This, however, Derrida writes, is "not the deconstruction" that he writes.[110] Quite the opposite; Derrida is writing an absence which "blocks every possible relationship to theology"[111] and is simply meaningless absence. Yet it is not valueless. Derrida writes:

> Only pure absence—not the absence of this or that, but the absence of everything in which all presence is announced—can inspire, in other words, can work, and then make one work.[112]

This is an absolute emptiness, and when he writes about it working and making one work, we could perhaps think of (the terror of) the blank page or the empty vessel;

---

109. We could, in fact, think of this wager of faith as having some similarity to John Henry Newman's nineteenth century "grammar of assent." Newman is an enthusiastic believer in science, but realizes that he can (and, at a personal level, must) give his assent to a Christian faith, which operates at a level totally to that subject to, or supported by, scientific evidence; simply in a realm other than that which "proof" guarantees.

110. Derrida, "How to Avoid Speaking," 8.

111. Derrida, *Positions,* 40, quoted in Taylor, *Erring,* 6.

112. Derrida, *Positions*, 40.

both must constantly stay empty if filling them is to continue; perhaps, even, a broken vessel through which the work flows. But this absence is not a mystical presence.

Derrida, is, in fact, using a very deconstructive irony *to subvert Dionysius' subversion* and demolish its theological power. This does indicate a potential for atheological thinking, but Derrida is not equating this with his deconstructive narrative project.[113]

In *The Mystical Theology* Dionysius writes of an absent trace:

> the understanding and contemplation of [this hidden Super-Essential Godhead]'s nature is not accessible to any being; for such knowledge is super-essentially exalted above all [names] unsearchable and past finding out, since *there is no trace* of any that have penetrated the hidden depths of Its infinitude.[114]

Dionysius writes of a trace which is not; but Derrida's trace is the ubiquitous lack of identity in a labyrinth of "everything always already inhabited *by the trace of something that is not itself*."[115] It is the denial of Dionysius' denial. We saw in chapter 2 that, for Mark C Taylor, the trace is an emptiness atheology can articulate, perhaps even denying Derrida's denial. Derrida's language of absence is tempting for an atheologian in its apparent echo of hyperessentiality.

Blanchot instead, as we have seen, is following Dionysius's (not Derrida's) trace as absence itself, the Heideggerian space where being speaks. At this point, we see laid bare the radical difference between atheism and atheology, at the deepest level.

113. Derrida, "How to Avoid Speaking," 77.
114. Dionysius, *Mystical Theology*, 53.
115. Spivak, "Introduction," in Derrida, *Of Grammatology*, lxix, quoted in Taylor, *Erring*, 138.

APOPHATIC "USELESSNESS" IN THE SPACE OF LITERATURE

We can also consider a certain "uselessness" as a mark of authenticity in Blanchot's terms; and this holds good, equally, when we read John's and Teresa's apophatic fiction as authentically useless. This is an inversion of worldly values enacting the Kingdom of Gxd in the Beatitudes;[116] yet this inversion will reveal this authenticity of uselessness to be the only thing of any use that there is. Teresa's text is written to be of "use," but of "dubious use," only as inspiration, suggesting images which are, using the term advisedly, erotic fantasies. The book is "useful," but she explains this "use" as nothing more consequential than "consolation" and "delight."[117] However, what use is the story (the pure work) as within itself? Teresa interjects again and again about "good works,"[118] and there is a mutual interplay, in the holism of the charism, where contemplative prayer, sisterly love and loving service are "useful," each supporting the other. Teresa's stance toward praxis (and she was a very efficient and practical Abbess), is simply for the furthering of goodness, not "civilization," empire or any achievement at all.[119] What use is love? And is the book a manual or an inspirational work? Surely the latter. At another level, one could outwork love without contemplation, instead solely by means of loving service; and Teresa the narrator makes it clear that this is equally

---

116. Matt 5:3 expresses perhaps the deepest reversal of the eight "blessed are they" statements that comprise the Beatitudes: "blessed are the poor in spirit, for theirs is the kingdom of heaven."

117. Teresa of Ávila, *Interior Castle*, 297.

118. For example, Teresa of Ávila, *Interior Castle*, 293, 294, 288; Teresa of Ávila, *Life of Teresa by Herself*, 19.

119. Teresa of Ávila, *Life of Teresa by Herself*, 76, 147, 150–51; also Teresa of Ávila, *Interior Castle*, 47, 294.

valid, for some, as a means to achieving authentic Love.[120] So this begs the question again of what "use" the Castle is. Its "use" is to indicate a journey which has no use at all, because it doesn't exist at all. The contemplative orders "do" plenty,[121] but in contemplation—what do they "do?" Teresa the woman, and John the man, do plenty,[122] but Teresa's "soul" and John's "lover" as narrative protagonists, can only wait, in Taylor's terms, "After God." What "use" is the dark night where John's lover "abandons himself" (abandons his self)? Both journeys lead nowhere—by definition, to an ineffable no-where.

Blanchot honors this quality of "uselessness" as the authentic nature of the work. When the work speaks, it speaks not as, or in the service of, anyone; it simply speaks:

> The writer belongs to a language which no-one speaks, which is addressed to no one, which has no center, and which reveals nothing. He may believe that he affirms himself in this language, but what he affirms is altogether deprived of self.[123]

---

120. For example, Teresa of Ávila, *Interior Castle*, 113.

121. "Carmelites speak of contemplation as a gift of God that can be nurtured by a life of prayer, community, and service. These three elements are at the heart of our charism. In prayer (or worship) we build up a friendship with "the God whom we know loves us," as St. Teresa of Ávila described it. In community building (or fraternity) we encounter God in our brothers and sisters, who comfort and challenge us. In service (also known as mission, apostolate, or ministry) we open ourselves to be God's hands in the world, responding to the needs of others, especially the poor and marginalized" (The British Province of Carmelite Friars).

122. See Teresa of Ávila, *Life of Teresa by Herself*, 18, 74, 79; Teresa of Ávila, *Interior Castle*, 12; *The Life of Saint Teresa by Herself* not only prefigures the metaphoric structure of *The Interior Castle*, but also recounts a life story of tremendous activity. However, the goal of the activity is to further the Kingdom of God, which is "useless" in earthly terms, as the "foolishness of God."

123. Blanchot, *Space of Literature*, 26.

THE AUTISM OF APOPHATIC FICTION   199

This nothing place "reveals nothing" in a "pure passivity of being."[124] This "pure passivity of being" is the place where the work of art—the pure poem—does not act, but is. Action would be a mimetic function which the pure poem resists. So we might say that the authenticity of the "useless" apophatic discourse is not far removed from the authenticity of Blanchot's "useless" art work. Similarly, Incarnational metaphor is "useless"; it does not respond to pragmatic demands for what ostensive intent requires (the branch of the tree needs to be the branch of an organization for business to function). The Holy Fool is a useless lay-about and an embarrassment to all decent people who collude in the fiction of the Emperor's new clothes. "Not for nothing," (or perhaps precisely "for nothing") does David Jasper write in *The Sacred Desert* that doing nothing might be the most important thing we can do.

NEGATION, ERROR, AND BETRAYAL AS AUTHENTICITY IN THE SPACE OF LITERATURE

Teresa and John are both rebels, running the gauntlet of heresy,[125] and audaciously going beyond merely reforming their own orders but establishing new ones, and these new orders are unconventional enough to suggest walking barefoot in the park.[126] John is actually denounced, incarcerated and tortured as a traitor to his order. At the level of the text, they are also traitors by deviating from

124. Blanchot, *Space of Literature*, 27.
125. See Tyler, *Teresa of Àvila*, and Starr, "Introduction," in Teresa of Àvila, *Interior Castle*.
126. The Discalced order (founded by Teresa) literally means those who have renounced footwear. Gene Sax's 1967 film *Barefoot in the Park* is described in this way: "Paul, a conservative young lawyer, marries the vivacious Corie. Their highly passionate relationship descends into comical discord in a five-flight New York City walk-up apartment" (https://www.imdb.com/title/tt0061385/). It hinges on whether Paul will dare to walk barefoot in Central Park.

propositional common-sense theological narratives. Negation itself is a betrayal of affirmation. Erring (as used by Mark C Taylor)[127] is also a betrayal. Erring is risky, and there is no ironic tone when Teresa the narrator inserts comments on the dangers of "grave error."[128]

Teresa is sometimes censured, even ridiculed, by some, as a hysterical or deluded person. ("Hysterical" — the instability of the womb-an). Is taking her "literally" and emulating the book a recipe for facilitating the distress of psychosis?

An interesting consideration on delusion/psychosis is the contemporary movement in the mental health world which listens to delusional voices for their message, befriending rather than attacking the enemy.[129] Similarly, Ron Hansen's novel *Marietta in Ecstasy* "leaves us hanging" as we wonder if a contemporary nun has visions and mystical experiences — is she mentally ill or genuinely experiencing Gxd? We are back at the experientialism argument.

If "experience" is read as other than a metaphoric, poetic space, fanatical devotion is the danger. Denys Turner, as we have seen, has argued that this is a seriously dangerous misreading, which deviates entirely, as we saw earlier, from Teresa's interjections into the poem of warnings about precisely this.[130] She "grounds" us by insisting time and again, that humble service, in the spirit of love as a spiritual discipline, creates the only conditions for the poem's outworking.[131] However, by writing as they have

---

127. Taylor's 1984 book *Erring* explores how one might think of a deconstructive atheology of the arts.

128. Teresa of Ávila, *Interior Castle*, 41–42.

129. Hearing Voices Network.

130. Teresa of Ávila, *Interior Castle*, 99, 123–34, 225; see also Teresa of Ávila, *Life of Teresa by Herself*, 174, 187–88.

131. The "ordinariness" of Christian practice discussed earlier.

done, in such a deeply poetic way, John and Teresa are both erring, perhaps not on the side of caution. They might seem traitors to kataphatic stability, politically as well as theologically.

Blanchot's thinking of the work itself as betrayal adds a deeper substratum to this idea. A reading which brings in the respect accorded by Blanchot to figurative language does not rescue Teresa or John from "error," but validates their error as authenticity. Blanchot recounts that the poet Hölderlin ("already veiled by madness") describes the necessary betrayal which enacts the "infidelity" of the gods who depart. Hölderlin writes that, in an act "less facile than humanism," "man forgets himself and forgets God: he turns back like a traitor, although in a holy manner . . . in the form of infidelity where there is a forgetting of everything."[132]

This language, which reads as an echo of Meister Eckhart's "taking leave of God for God's sake,"[133] is describing a "holy treachery." It is holy in its authenticity which reckons with how "facile" humanism is, precisely in the terms Heidegger has used about science, which "does not think." Apophatic fiction then becomes an act of authenticity which enacts the infidelity of the gods.

In other words, to have faith at all, it is necessary to be both betrayer and betrayed (in a strangely Tillichian betrayal). In the end, in this ultimate faith, it becomes possible, and necessary, to follow Meister Eckhart, as Gxd takes leave of us, to find ourselves also, in absolute faith,

---

132. Hölderlin, *Poet's Vocation*, quoted in Blanchot, *Space of Literature*, 272.
133. Eckhart, "Qui audit me non confundetur," in *Selected Writings*, 176–77.

"taking leave of God for God's sake."[134] "We walk by faith, and not by sight," the Apostle Paul tells us.[135]

What deeper Mindfulness of Separation could there be?

Similarly, Incarnational metaphor, indifferent to the world's pragmatic demands, betrays the common-sense business contracts of the world. Neither can it conform to the expectations of community, with its autism "cured" (the shadow of evil lurks also in the eugenic "cure" narrative of *I am Autism,* with which we began). It is literally "other-worldly," with the autist irremediably (yet also, as Eckhart understands, salvifically) "in a world of her own," as we have come to find autism.

Distress: Ridiculous Amounts of Suffering and Authenticity

Betrayal is distressing, and this distress is another sense in which Blanchot's thinking of the artwork sheds light on apophatic fiction.

Teresa might be a hypochondriac, manufacturing the symptoms of the Passion (the famous image of her heart's (phallic) piercing by God mimicking the spear in Christ's side). Equally, Teresa might be genuinely chronically ill,[136] so possibly therefore the venerated saint who endures

---

134. "Therefore Paul says: 'I would be willing to be eternally separated from God for the sake of my friend and for God's sake' (Rom 9:3). . . . Taking leave of God for the sake of God is the greatest act of renunciation that someone can make. Now St. Paul renounced God for the sake of God: he left all that he could get from God . . . he never gave anything to God, nor did he ever receive anything from God" (Eckhart, "Qui audit me non confundetur," in *Selected Writings*, 176–77).

135. 2 Cor 5:7.

136. She discusses (bodily, physical) illness in both the *Interior Castle*'s didactic narrator voice and in her *Life of Teresa by Herself*, most often using the anonymity trope "a certain woman" (see e.g., Teresa of Àvila, *Interior Castle*, 89, 159-60; and Teresa of Ávila, *Life of Teresa by Herself*, 140). Due to her reports of frequent, severe headaches, she is commonly known as the patron saint of migraines!

suffering with courage and longsuffering. Who can say. At the level of the text, however, suffering is a huge element of the soul's necessary experience.

Suffering in the struggle for/of authenticity would read the suffering in Teresa's text in terms of enduring in the absence which John poeticizes as the "dark night of the soul." This would read the narrator character's suffering as the embodiment of atheological faith. Negative theology is a theology of "not"; it is the privation which Hölderlin describes as the "lack" which "helps" poetry.[137] Hölderlin (as Blanchot points out, approaching madness) "calls the empty, distressful present 'bountiful suffering.'"[138] Teresa also, numerous times, describes her suffering as a blessing and even a delight.[139] Like Hölderlin, she writes that "the joy she felt in that pain (in the context of 'becoming a poet') . . . [was] agony."[140]

Being welcoming of suffering echoes Paul's entering the suffering of Christ (Col 1:24, in Young's Literal Translation, "I now rejoice in my sufferings for you, and do fill up the things lacking of the tribulations of the Christ in my flesh for his body, which is the assembly"). In fact, reading Teresa as an apophatic theologian, it is tempting to read "the things lacking of the tribulations of the Christ" not as the (rather awkward) notion that Christ's sufferings are somehow "not enough." An intriguing possibility might be to read Christ's suffering *as* the things lacking, in the cry of desolation.[141] So "filling up" this "lack" would be, in

---

137. Blanchot, *Space of Literature*, 246–47.

138. Blanchot, *Space of Literature*, 246.

139. Suffering as bliss is the pervasive concept throughout the dwellings, which become increasingly inner in union with Christ.

140. Teresa of Ávila, *Life of Teresa by Herself*, 113.

141. Which Teresa echoes in the soul's experience; see Teresa of Ávila, *Life of Teresa by Herself*, 140, 157.

apophatic terms, entering into the nothingness (the lack of Gxd) of the Crucifixion. Indeed, Teresa's abandonment by Gxd, the closer she gets to Gxd, is what she describes as "being suspended between heaven and earth (like Christ on the Cross)."[142]

Exactly the same point applies to John's "dark night," which could even be construed as indistinguishable, Turner argues, from "clinical depression" except in how it is conceived theologically and expressed poetically. In other words, do I see my darkness as a place where Gxd's absence is also Gxd's presence? It is clear that John suffers not only in the "literal" sense of the incarceration and torture recorded in his biography, but also with a "dark night" which is not merely, even if also manifested in, clinical depression. Both Teresa and John write a lot about suffering. Even in the erotic bliss of the nighttime tryst, the lover in John's narrative is (phallically? Or a bite?) "wounded" by the caress of the beloved. This makes sense in terms of the work of art, in Blanchot's terms. It might mean the following.

Blanchot, discussing Hölderlin's words "what use are poets in the time of distress," writes

> Forgetting, error, the unhappiness of erring can be linked to an historical period: to the time of distress when the gods are absent twice over, because they are no longer there, because they are not there yet. This vacant time is that of error . . . and nevertheless error helps us . . . the force, the risk proper to the poet is to dwell in God's default, the region where truth lacks. The time of distress designates the time which in all times is proper to art.[143]

---

142. Teresa of Ávila, *Life of Teresa by Herself*, 138–40; Teresa of Ávila, *Interior Castle*, 249–58.

143. Blanchot, *Space of Literature*, 246.

THE AUTISM OF APOPHATIC FICTION

This is, however, what Hölderlin calls a "bountiful suffering, bountiful happiness."[144] This is a self-subverting strategy as has been seen in Dionysius, and John in *The Dark Night of the Soul* describes this dark night as "O happy night!" Teresa too employs self-subverting language of exquisite pain.[145] At the level of the work, is there an authenticity which conflates suffering with happiness? Blanchot argues that

> when Hölderlin speaks of poets who, like the priests of Bacchus, go wandering from country to country in the sacred night, is this perpetual departure, the *sorrow of straying* which has no place to arrive, to rest, also the *fecund migration,* the movement which mediates, that which makes of rivers a language and of language the dwelling, the power by which day abides and is our abode?[146]

This is certainly how Mark C Taylor views Derrida's dissemination,[147] as fecund migration, invoking the parable of the Sower and the Seed,[148] so that a new atheological thinking can be "assured." Blanchot rests his case in his identity as a poet: "To this question there can be no response. The poem is the answer's absence."[149]

There can similarly be no answer, ultimately, to the question of "experience"/experientialism in the apophatic fictions of Teresa and John. She might be hysterical and deluded,[150] and he might be chronically depressed; or

---

144. Hölderlin, "Dichterberuf," quoted in Blanchot, *Space of Literature*, 246.
145. Teresa of Àvila, *Interior Castle*, 140, 167–68.
146. Blanchot, *Space of Literature*, 246–47.
147. Derrida's term for the way in which metaphors are scattered as seed in order for new metaphors to sprout, in an endless process.
148. Taylor, *Erring*, 118–20.
149. Blanchot, *Space of Literature*, 247.
150. This is the dubiety at the heart of Ron Hansen's novel *Mariette in Ecstasy*; is the novice Mariette a true stigmatic (someone whose body develops wounds in the

both might be superlative apophatic theologians, writing knowingly in a crafted poetic register. The poem, solely and entirely as the poem, is the answer's absence.

Fundamentally, the point here is to think of autism as Mindblindness/zero degree of cognitive empathy/Mindfulness of Separation, and precisely at the same time fascination/affective empathy/presence. This is to be in that decentered place of faith which Turner describes, and to be "suspended between earth and heaven" with Teresa (and with Christ). It is true of autistic metaphor, suspended in the space of fiction, as chapter 2 argued. This deeply theological space of apophatic fiction can be embodied in autistic metaphor because autistic poet-faith understands the impossibility of "cure," and finds great joy in its being. In an act of autistic authenticity, the betrayal of Gxd and by Gxd is the inhabitation of absolute Mindfulness of Separation. In this space, it is necessary to read on, and see where Meister Eckhart's words lead:

> When (St Paul) took leave of these things, he renounced God for the sake of God, and yet God remained with him, as God exists in himself, not according to the manner in which he is gained or received but according to the being which he himself is.[151]

This is, again, fascination/Mindfulness of Separation in the forgiveness of betrayal, and the acceptance of its necessity. Autism has a privileged insight of this, as we can now most fully see.

---

places where Christ was wounded on the Cross) and does that mean bearing the wounds of Christ inflicted by the society [and the reader] judging her also? Or is she "simply another neurotic emo kid" who would listen to heavy metal music and self-harm? Would Pilate find her "innocent?"

151. Eckhart, "Qui audit me non confundetur," Iin *Selected Writings*, 177.

AUTHENTIC APOPHATIC DISCOURSE: TOWARD INCARNATIONAL METAPHOR

Each section of this chapter has indicated how it is a progression toward Absolute Incarnational metaphor. In a sense, there is little more to say, but in a deeper sense, there is Nothing to say. Autistic metaphor can be thought of as Incarnation, when the mystery of the Incarnation is the absolute apophasis of Mindfulness of Separation; Gxd, as a human being, is "the child who was born to die."[152] In the paradox which apophatic discourse expresses in self-subverting utterance, it is also the union of total absence in, and as, total presence. This total presence is indicated in discourse as the expression of Autistic Fascination. Autistic Fascination, in saintly terms, is absolute autistic affective empathy as *eros*. That *eros* is also, in saintly terms, the absolute unknowing of faith, in the face of the Mindfulness of Separation in the darkness of God. This is the Absolute "zero positive," in Baron-Cohen's terms. The literal metaphor discussed in chapter 2 becomes a theology of the Incarnation as hyperessential Presence in apophatic language, thought also as the authenticity of mute being. Self-subverting apophatic fiction is a metaphor which is, for us, in our mythical autism, literally (within our story, for us) "real," and actually, theologically, more "real" than anything else. In true Platonic fashion, following Dionysius, Teresa indicates this inversion of "reality": "there is nothing in the world but the soul" and the world is, in the end, illusion.[153]

When an autistic hermeneutic takes apophatic discourse "literally," as we have argued, the distance between

---

152. 1 Tim 1:15 tells us that "Christ was born to die."

153. Teresa of Ávila, *Life of Teresa by Herself*, 91; Teresa of Ávila, *Interior Castle*, 246–47.

figuration and theological thinking collapses. In this sense, the saints are absolutely autistic when they "literally" (unseeingly) see God *in the discourse* of mystic beatific vision. Apophatic discourse embodies this vision, but the vision itself is "dazzling darkness" and the words are silent. Pure autistic apophasis, as the Incarnation itself, is silent, and ultimately, in absolute purity, "cannot be spoken of." This would be an absolute and total autism; the autism of Gxd, which we will now explore in chapter 4.

Chapter Four

The Autism of Gxd

Reborn, he cried in exaltation and surrender,
"The Godhead is broken like bread. We are the pieces."
And sat down at his desk and wrote a story.[1]

A woman burdened by the legacy of a judgmental, rigid Christianity in her upbringing, told me that her earliest memory was of being read to by her great-grandfather from the Bible, about judgement and punishment of sin (what does a guileless, small child understand of sin?). Fear of the Lord was not the beginning of wisdom but the beginning of a crippling, lifelong anxiety. How did you even begin to recover? I asked her. Her answer shocked and fascinated me. A wise nun, she said, told me to write God's name on a piece of paper, and burn it. You mean you burned God? I asked her. Yes, she said—it was utterly terrifying and utterly liberating.

---

1. Auden, "Herman Melville," in *Collected Shorter Poems,* 146.

THE DEATH OF GOD MOVEMENT

We are entering territory, in this chapter, where there is material which is demanding and possibly shocking, unless you are familiar with the strange and remarkable work of Thomas J. J. Altizer—but his "death of God" theology is essential for our theology of the Autism of Gxd. Personally, my journey with Altizer has been a series of glimpses gained over a period of time, rewarding and exciting. I hope this chapter will make at least the basics of his thought clear.

In this chapter, we will see how the autism of Gxd flows, for us, from the death of Gxd. In order to get there, first I want to argue that the much maligned "death of Gxd movement" of the mid-to-late twentieth century has been greatly misunderstood and undervalued. This is, I feel, because its nature as poetic, existential statement has perhaps been mistaken for systematic theology. If we can take this approach of reading the death of Gxd as a kind of parable, we can then, specifically, read Thomas J. J. Altizer's "death of God" thinking in the light of autistic myth. This is a neurotribal reading, so that we can, for us, rethink the death of Gxd as the autism of Gxd, if it is read aright—namely, mythologically.

The April 8, 1966 cover of TIME magazine was the first ever, in the magazine's history, to feature only type, and no photo.[2] The cover—with the traditional, red border—was all black, with the words "IS GOD DEAD?" in large, red text. This brought the "death of God movement" into the view of the American public, creating very visible controversy, most famously played out a year later in the debate between Thomas J. J. Altizer and John W. Montgomery

---

2. *TIME* magazine, 8th April 1966.

at the Rockefeller Chapel, University of Chicago.[3] Looking back, Altizer writes of the period:

> I think that I became one of the most hated men in America, murder threats were almost a commonplace, savage assaults upon me were widely published, and the churches seemed possessed by a fury against me.[4]

In the UK, also in the early 1960s, Bishop John Robinson had done something similar in achieving public prominence through his SCM paperback *Honest to God,* arguing for a similar Christian atheism based on his reading of Paul Tillich.[5] Atheologians including Harvey Cox, William Hamilton, Gabriel Vahanian, Paul van Buren and Altizer came to be known as proponents of the "death of God movement" generating the article in TIME magazine and *Honest to God.* In 1968, for example, William Hamilton draws on Dietrich Bonhoeffer's "religionless Christianity" as a forebear of the death of Gxd, quoting Bonhoeffer's letters from prison, when Bonhoeffer writes:

> So our coming of age forces us to a true recognition of our situation vis-à-vis God. God is teaching us that we must live as men who can get along very well without him. The God who is with us is the God who forsakes us (Mark 15:34 ["My God, my God, why hast thou forsaken me?"]). The God who makes us live in his world without using him as a working hypothesis is the God before whom we are ever standing. Before God and with him we live without God. God allows himself to be edged out of the world and onto the cross. God is weak and powerless in the world, and that is exactly the way, the only way, in which he can be with us and

---

3. Altizer and Montgomery, *Altizer-Montgomery Dialogue*.
4. Altizer, *Living the Death of God*.
5. Robinson, *Honest to God*.

> help us. (Letter of 16th July 1944).[6] . . . Man is challenged to participate in the sufferings of God at the hands of a Godless world.[7]

However, as early as 1961, Altizer is moving toward a non-theistic Christianity in his *Oriental Mysticism and Biblical Eschatology*.[8]

> **Death of Gxd theology is certainly not simply atheism, but on the contrary, a deeply theologically thought response to secularism.**

In *The Secular City,* Harvey Cox envisions a harmony between the secular and the religious, which celebrates both: "God can be just as present in the secular as in the religious realms of life, and we unduly cramp the divine presence by confining it to some specially delineated spiritual or ecclesial sector."[9]

Altizer is profoundly Christian, and when he writes *The Gospel of Christian Atheism* in 1963, he is articulating a vision of a new form of faith, which attempts to rescue an authentic Christianity, paradoxically, by subverting Christianity. His thinking is in fact not "secular" but "profane,"[10] and this important distinction comes from his reading of Tillich and Eliade. His Christian atheism offers a mythological thinking which ironically re-mythologizes what Bultmann has de-mythologized. This makes his work a hospitable discourse for a myth of the autistic hermeneut.

---

6. "Dietrich Bonhoeffer," in Altizer and Hamilton, *Radical Theology*, 120.

7. "Dietrich Bonhoeffer," in Altizer and Hamilton, *Radical Theology*, 123, quoting Bonhoeffer, letter July 18, 1944.

8. Altizer, *Oriental Mysticism*.

9. Cox, "Secular City 25 Years Later," in *The Secular City*, 1025–29.

10. "Secular" meaning within the confines of a worldly vision; "profane" etymologically as pro-fanus, outwith (not within) the temple (the temple still in sight) but also with overtones of profanity as blasphemy/obscenity/offense—in other words, as heresy.

ALTIZER, TILLICH, AND ELIADE

Altizer is building upon the theological foundations of Paul Tillich and Mircea Eliade. First, then, we turn to Tillich. Tillich writes from the existential threat of the First World War, so much so that the title of his collected sermons is *The Shaking of the Foundations*.[11] He is also writing within a theological and cultural context where early twentieth-century Existentialism has raised questions of what he calls "threatenedness"; a sense of chronic anxiety and emptiness. Tillich's theology of culture is a response to this threatenedness, which listens to Existentialist thought and argues that

> the human condition always raises fundamental questions which human cultures express in various ways in the dominant styles of their works of art, and to which religious traditions offer answers expressed in religious symbols.[12]

Tillich has been called an atheist, but his "atheism" is not the rejection of Gxd, in fact the very opposite. When he writes that "The modern way to flee God is to rush ahead and ahead. . . . But God's Hand falls upon us,"[13] this is an existential statement, because "The God whom he cannot flee is the Ground of his being."[14]

---

11. Tillich, *Shaking of the Foundations*.
12. Kelsey, *Fabric of Paul Tillich's Theology*, 64.
13. Tillich, *Shaking of the Foundations*, 48.
14. Tillich, *Shaking of the Foundations*, 54.

> As we saw in the theology Introduction, Tillich's atheism is the expression of the majesty of Gxd conceived beyond theism. David Kelsey comments on Tillich that Gxd cannot "be a supreme being" for, by definition, *any* entity is finite. Hence, Tillich refuses to speak of the "existence" of Gxd.[15] His famous term, *The Ground of our Being* is some-"thing" which is not a thing, but underlies all things. Even the word "God" is an object.

Whatever concerns us ultimately, says Tillich, is our "God."[16] Religion can easily displace a thinking of this God (which Tillich calls "the unconditioned"), so that

> . . . religious ritual, myth or institutions are ambiguous, "functioning religiously" to express the unconditioned . . . [but] they invite for themselves the ultimate concern appropriate only to the unconditioned. Thereby they become "demonic," powerfully destructive of the life trying to "transcend" itself.[17]

False gods, when we form religion careless of the Unknowableness of Gxd, can mean that religion can be demonic, and this is something to which Altizer will return. Tillich, in the 1940s and 50s, then, provides a thinking almost of theology as "a-theist" existentialist authenticity, in the light of Existentialism; and the 1960s death of Gxd movement can be seen very much to extrapolate from this. I believe it is time, long overdue, to revisit it, when much religion has become all too crude and lacking in existential depth. And it is through the power of autism, the marginal voice, that we can validate it and offer it new power *from our own strength and integrity*; if only, when autism speaks, the Church will listen.

---

15. Kelsey, *Fabric of Paul Tillich's Theology*, 66.
16. Kelsey, *Fabric of Paul Tillich's Theology*, 65.
17. Kelsey, *Fabric of Paul Tillich's Theology*, 70–71.

Tillich has already sown the seeds of an "existential faith" which listens outwith (i.e., not within) the temple. In George Pattison's words, an existential faith requires "as a prerequisite, the "shaking of the foundations" of being, by the shock of non-being."[18] Pattison is describing an Existentialist theology which is an expression of Modernism but at the same time, anchored in a Christian humanism of Tillich's "theonomy" (rule of God; more akin to a natural law than a judicial one) where "the 'Will of God' . . . is not a strange voice that demands our obedience, but the 'silent voice' of our own nature as man [sic], and as man with an individual character."[19] The collection of meditative essays *Radical Theology and the Death of God*,[20] co-written by Altizer and William Hamilton in 1966, is dedicated to the memory of Tillich, and his influence is central to the emergence of the radical atheological current. Graham Ward has remarked that Altizer "reverses Tillich's priorities—judging God in the darkness of modern culture rather than culture by the ultimate revelation of God."[21] This perhaps could tend to imply that Altizer is not fundamentally grounded in Christian theology, but this is far from the case. His subversion of theology is itself deeply theological, engaging as first principle with Protestant and Catholic theologies along with Buddhist thought. We could perhaps say that what is distinctive is the way in which Altizer writes, and what he is writing.

Where Tillich thinks of authentic being so that art and culture ask questions which theology answers, Altizer thinks of this authenticity differently.

18. Pattison, "Fear and Trembling," 227.
19. Tillich, *Morality and Beyond*, 24, quoted in Pattison, "Fear and Trembling," 228.
20. Altizer and Hamilton, *Radical Theology*.
21. Ward, "Postmodern Theology," in Ford and Muers, *Modern Theologians*, 136.

> **In Altizer's (poetic, rhetorical) work, art is not the question to which theology can respond, but *art itself (in this particular enactment) is the mode in which theological thinking operates.***
>
> In other words, we are called upon to be poets and artists—able, at least, to adopt an art-lover's appreciation in our hermeneutic—if we are to grasp what Altizer, the poet of atheology, is saying to us. His atheology is not written in the genre of systematic or dogmatic theology, but is more truly read as a poetic form which has similarities to what chapter 3 called apophatic fiction.

Altizer's theological thinking is an evolution of the "non-existence" of Gxd, in the existential sense meant by Tillich. For Altizer, Gxd and culture articulate each other existentially, in an inseparable identification which could be called a theological poetics or equally a poetic theology.

Another key to this synthesis might equally lie in Altizer's reading of Mircea Eliade. As we saw in chapter 1, Eliade views religion within an anthropological, Religious Studies viewpoint when he discusses the sacred and the profane (non-sacred). Recall how he writes that

> In imitating the exemplary acts of a god or of a mythic hero, or simply by recounting their adventures, the man [sic] of an archaic society detaches himself from profane time and magically re-enters the Great Time, the sacred time.[22]

Altizer, however, employs a more radical mythologizing strategy. Here, the secularized narrative in Western Modern art, and particularly literature, *is* the expression of the mythologized biblical narrative; it is the sacred profane. So Altizer reads James Joyce's irreverent textual games with

22. Eliade, *Myths, Dreams and Mysteries*, 23.

the language of Catholicism in *Finnegan's Wake*, in terms of a mythic retelling of the sacred profane.

Where Eliade has designated separate realities for sacred time and profane time, *Altizer's idea of the sacred profane thinks of all as sacred, and all as profane*. The narrative of authenticity in secular art and literature is as sacred as biblical narrative, and in fact *is*, in his chosen hermeneutic, an enactment of core biblical narrative.

ALTIZER'S SACRED PROFANE AND INCARNATIONAL METAPHOR

This offers possibilities straight away for Incarnational metaphor. In Altizer's work, *the poetic and the theological are not available for pragmatic "appropriation"* (as Tillich would envisage) by each other. Instead, if anything, (and here we can heartily agree with Graham Ward), it is a confluence where theological thinking (silently) "listens to" the poetic as the discourse of its own being. If it is true that the Christ event is incarnate *in* the poetic, this means that the poetic is not a metaphor *for* the theological. Instead, the poetic-theological simply "is," and there is no theistic referent for metaphor to "carry between" the two. For us, this is Incarnational metaphor. As Tillich has suggested, the function of theistic referent disappears,[23] and this, we could say, is what Altizer calls this living within metaphor—the "sacred profane." For example, an allegorical hermeneutic might say that the biblical story of Exodus *is a symbol of* our own sense of exile from God, or from past idyllic days of Christian culture; but in Altizer's poetic hermeneutic of Scripture, the Exodus and consequent wandering in the

---

23. This follows on, in our thinking, from chapter 3's concept of apophatic fiction, and Altizer's work also refers to the connection between Christian atheism and apophatic theology.

desert *is* our own sense of exile, in whatever form. He is not an allegorist but a poet; the difference may be subtle, but allegory does not enter into this poetic universe where metaphor supplants simile. Just as we saw with the Rabbits and Ruth, we are taking our poetry with the utmost seriousness; "we are not pretending."

Literal metaphor, as our thinking of apophatic fiction argued, does not allegorize metaphor into a "useful" theological schema, referring *to* that which theology formulates.[24] Instead, literal metaphor was read there as being *in* the space of apophatic discourse, so it does not formulate, but inhabits, that "object" which is the text. Altizer himself makes this connection explicit; for example, on the anonymity of Gxd, he writes: "the naming (of the anonymity of God) echoes the highest expressions of our mysticism in its call for a total transfiguration, and possible only by way of a full union with the depths of anonymity itself."[25] The "echo" is made possible only through a poetic-mystical "full union."

Looking at the sacred profane as the sacred outwith the temple offers another way to think of the marginal space of apophatic theology, which operates outwith the temple of (propositional, kataphatic) theology. This way is to read the sacred profane autistically, as fascination. Art (including literature) does not *lead to* a theological outcome but *is* the theological object, and this is in fact

---

24. Chapter 5 will develop this idea further, by reading a fully Incarnational literal metaphor in Manley Hopkin's *ecceitas* (poetic Scotist *haecceitas* or "thisness"). In chapter 5, at that point, this will be a fuller space of Autistic Fascination. Here, though, regarding Altizer, this reading prepares the way for chapter 5's reading fascination as an *ecceitas* of the sacred profane. The reason for this is that the possibility of reading back into Hopkins's *ecceitas* autistically is made possible in the light of Altizer's sacred profane death of Gxd.

25. Altizer, *Godhead and the Nothing*, 2.

a non-theological object without meaning.[26] It takes us close to Blanchot's thinking of the work of art (including literature) as *lacking ostensive meaning.* Is this even possible? Can we be cast out even from our very name, in anonymity, at an existential level? The paradoxical naming of anonymity is, for us, literal metaphor which, as we have seen, works only, ultimately, as a theologically thought Incarnational metaphor. It exists without meaning—"outwith meaning"—because it simply *is* itself, as we consciously enter into it, simply *are* it, in spiritual terms. This hinges on our adopting an autistic (or atheological, ultimate) hermeneutic.

To approach this connection, it is useful to go back to how fascination was introduced in the Beginner's Guide. Fascination was described as joyful immersion, being overwhelmed in the object of fascination. This is the phenomenon of RRBIs[27]—it could be as an Asperger's obsession or a "severely impaired" autistic behavior of repetitive, restrictive behaviors of touch, smell, hearing, tasting. For example, what could be more "profane" (in Eliade's sense of non-religious) than certain objects of autistic sensory fixations or special interests—deep fat fryers, shiny spinning objects, twinkling lights, electric pylons, a running tap, a piece of velvet cloth? (All of which are either sensory or intellectual, but recall, in Bregman's terms, (of monetarily) valueless delight to some autists). Yet this is

---

26. This is the opposite of Rudolf Otto's thinking of the numinous as *"Mysterium tremendum et fascinans"* (Otto, *Idea of the Holy*). This is not a sacred that overwhelms in an eerie unknown, causing trembling terror and mesmerization. It is instead joyful being in the sacred mystery, which remains mystery precisely because it does not need meaning. Autistic Fascination as sacred profane is not a fascination of encountering the other, but a fascination of being in what representation would convert into the other. This seems the opposite of Mindfulness of Separation at first glance, but it is the mystical union of separation that was indicated by chapter 3's autistic hermeneutic of apophatic discourse. The next section will explore this paradox.

27. Introduction, see "RRBIs" and "Sensory Connoisseur."

the sacred autistic space of "meaningless meaning." It is the place most fully to *be*. In Heidegger's terms, it outwits ontological difference,[28] if we are considering a mythical absolute autism.

A sacred profane of meaningless communion does not theologize this into symbolic appropriation: water could be thought in biblical tropes, but electric pylons? (stretching metaphors to think of electric pylons as carriers of the power of the Spirit, for example, would be absurd). Fascination simply *is*, full of spiritual power in sensory delight.[29] For the autist, it is sacred in the sheer delight it brings. The clear distinction here is that in the autistic sacred profane, the biblical archetypes of the sacred (ultimately, the absolute kenosis of Gxd into the world, as what we will see as a universal sacrament) do not *represent*, but *are,* the sacred profane [my delight in seeing the wonder of deep fat fryer design]. This might seem all too ridiculous, but in the following incident I was all too humbled and forced to reconsider my assumptions about fascination and meaning/fulfillment. I was invited to attend a school assembly at a school for children with intellectual disabilities, most of whom were non-verbal and some of whom had profound autism. I wondered how the school chaplain, Sandy Finlay, would approach the assembly. It was Mother's Day, and Sandy spoke very briefly about how wonderful our mothers are. He then brought out some cleaning cloths and a feather duster, saying that mothers do a lot of cleaning (I wish this were true of myself!). He passed them around for children to smell the perfumes and feel the textures of these dusters and cloths. The children loved this. Sandy

---

28. In the sense that we see past our metaphysics of "Being" to stand in the presence of Heideggerian simple, pure being.

29. Or horror, in the distress of being overwhelmed in a too stimulating, crowded, noisy, too bright environment.

closed the assembly with a simple Christian song—and to the staff's (and our) delight, a number of children, in one way or another, sang along.

What was happening there? Sandy's words held a simple meaning, which the staff and we enacted, perhaps on behalf of the children, but where the assembly came alive for the children was in their delight, sniffing and touching the household objects they might associate with their mothers, but presumably at a non-verbal level. Now here is where we transmute that non-verbal response into our mythical thinking of absolute autism. In absolute fascination, we approach the poetic text (thinking of apophatic fiction, our recent, hospitable home); and we find that we can be absolutely immersed in that text ("feeling" it, "sniffing" it, and tasting the words); our response is beyond the function of words as ostensive intentionality. In the same way, fascination as Incarnational metaphor approaches the atheological thinking of Altizer's sacred profane. How so? To explain, we could turn first to non-verbal art as a living text. For example, Altizer writes that the sacred profane is embodied in

> the greatest landscape paintings of Monet and Cezanne, and even in the late landscapes of Van Gogh, wherein the very incarnation of chaos in the dazzling space before us poses an inescapable call for union with that chaos.[30]

Similarly, many of William Turner's watercolors "enter into chaos," as being, not representation. The Victoria and Albert museum guide discusses this:

> William Hazlitt commented that Turner's "pictures are . . . too much abstractions of aerial perspective, and representations not properly of the objects of

30. Altizer, *Gospel of Christian Atheism*, 2.

nature as of the medium through which they are seen . . . they are pictures of the elements of air, earth and water." . . . Turner was less concerned with painting specific places than with the dramatic possibilities of sea and air, and with the motion of the elements. Light was his theme. . . . Joseph Farington noted that "Turner has no settled process but drives the colours about."[31]

When Altizer describes this as an "incarnation of chaos," this indicates something which the phenomenon which Modernism presents, and the role of art is to invite an apocalyptic (revelation/revealing) chaos, to dazzle, not to signpost. For this reason, the landscapes are manipulated into form and texture which *catches, rather than represents,* the landscape. The distortions which prevent a simple image emerging, in fact, capture more of the landscape, but as what, in chapter 5, we will call an *ecceitas,—*a poetic "thisness," a sense of pure being, not a representation ("re-presentation").

To see the "dazzling space" of the artwork as Autistic Fascination would mean that a theologically thought fascination within metaphor honors a similarly, mythically thought atheological narrative. This would be because literal metaphor, not "signposting anywhere," might find itself in the space where, increasingly in Impressionist, Expressionist and abstract/non-representational art, representation is eclipsed by the pure power of the work which "dazzles." In this way, through the lens of our autistic hermeneutic, these landscapes function as literal metaphor because they do not "fold back to" pragmatic interpretation, staying instead in the mute power which was indicated by Blanchot, as discussed in chapter 3.

31. Victoria and Albert Museum, "British Watercolours."

Its relevance to literal (and therefore Incarnational) metaphor is firstly, that being *in* the profane as a sacred space is to be *literally* there (impossibly), within the art work; this, we recall, existentially, (as Tillich would understand) in the sense we considered in Ian Ramsey's thinking of doxological language—more literal than the material world, in fact. This is the fascination which autistically inhabits an art breaking free of representation. Secondly, this sense of profanity's relevance to Incarnational metaphor is also a Mindfulness of Separation, where Autistic Fascination as the profane is marginalized from religious discourse (as was Altizer), cast out from the temple of theology by the blasphemy which speaks the Incarnation in a deep fat fryer. Perhaps at a deeper level, too, this glorious fascination can only take place within the space of autistic separation from the neurotypical world by its very nature. So the mythical being of the sacred profane is approached by the mythical being of Mindfulness of Separation, as well as fascination; so Mindfulness of Separation is, again, active as the third element of this trinity. Also, fascination is pure love, even if cognitively blind or divorced from social (or representational) norms; its affective power is very real, and autistic love (in its cognitive darkness and affective light) lies at the heart of how Incarnational metaphor, Fascination, and Mindfulness of Separation co-inhere.

THREE PROPHETS OF BLASPHEMY AND THE END OF CHRISTENDOM

This sacred profane, we have seen, is irreligious, but Altizer's argument is that, precisely by being so, it is paradoxically, and profoundly, Christian. When Christian atheism is read as the blasphemy of the death of Gxd, this blasphemy is articulated as, and because of, the end of Christendom. So the sacred profane in both senses, as "outwith the temple" and as holy blasphemy, can be envisioned in a Western culture which is living the (holiness of the) end of Christendom. Modernism both articulates and makes possible its end; Altizer argues that "it cannot be denied that there is an epiphany of nothingness in full modernity which is unique in history."[32] Altizer writes about "seers" who bring this end into view and into being: it is "deeply and comprehensively envisioned by Blake, Goethe, Dostoyevsky and Mallarmé . . . called forth by Joyce, Kafka, Stevens and Beckett."[33]

Being outwith the temple entails living the death of Christendom, and Altizer reads this death in terms of Modernism, but also in his nineteenth-century "three prophets"—the philosopher G. W. F. Hegel, the Existentialist Friedrich Nietzsche and the poet William Blake. It is worth looking at them briefly now, in order more fully to understand Altizer's thinking of the death of Gxd.

Blake's "Honest Indignation"

A starting point is Blake's words in *The Marriage of Heaven and Hell:* "The voice of honest indignation is the voice of God."[34] (We might also think of Tillich's "honest atheist," beloved of Gxd).

> **Altizer, like Blake, sees Jesus as the heretic who overturns the structures of religion, and both see their task as a recovering of that heretical Jesus.**

---

32. Altizer, *Gospel of Christian Atheism*, 51.
33. Altizer, *Godhead and the Nothing*, 13.
34. Blake, "Memorable Fancy."

Blake's indignation is against Christendom as a loveless, oppressive structure. In *The Garden of Love,* Blake writes:

> the gates of this Chapel were shut
> And "Thou shalt not," writ over the door . . .
> And I saw it was filled with graves,
> And tombstones where flowers should be;
> And priests in black gowns were walking their rounds,
> And binding with briars my joys and desires.[35]

An autistic hermeneutic reads Blake's "honest indignation" and the poem's defense of Christ as pure Love in terms of autistic integrity. Pure autistic affective empathy boldly steps past the priests, disregarding the neurotypical cognitive structures of the "chapel"; and the autistic truth telling of a "garden of fascination" does not recognize any compromise in its indignation. This is also a dangerous, anarchic thinking of Jesus[36] because it also emancipates the artist; Blake writes: "I know of no other Christianity and of no other Gospel than the liberty of both body and mind to exercise the Divine Art of Imagination."[37] This is dangerous, because the artist, as we saw in chapter 3, errs. Who knows where the "Divine Art of Imagination" might lead? It might lead to deep fat fryers, or Tracy Emin's unmade bed. Autistic faith might be dangerously unconventional, and the autist might be a disturbing, alien presence in the community of faith. We might think back to Brother Juniper and the Holy Fools we considered. Another example from George Eliot's work would be an intriguing parallel. Reading Eliot's *Felix Holt the Radical,* the story of a radical political campaigner, in an autistic hermeneutic, we rejoice in Felix Holt's uncompromising stand for justice, which

---

35. Blake, "Garden of Love."

36. Altizer writes about the Incarnation of Jesus, rejecting the Messianic or triumphalist theologies of the names "Christ" or "Lord."

37. Blake, "Jerusalem," in *Complete Poetry and Prose*, 77.

marks him out as odd and inconvenient. Similarly, autistic faith asks the awkward questions of "elephants in the room," disregarding tactful or pragmatic conventions. Holt is an interesting parallel, in the context of Eliot's theological and political radicalism, where he is critical equally of both ecclesial power and (a)moral pragmatism.[38] George Eliot and William Blake might well be kindred spirits! In any case, it is easy to see that Altizer finds inspiration in Blake's impatience with Christendom, as we shall see.

Profanity as Blasphemy: Friedrich Nietzsche

Friedrich Nietzsche is most often represented as a savage critic of Christianity, and his *Antichrist,* among other works, certainly seems to be, although he is not an enemy of Jesus, perhaps, but of what religion has become. However, most gravely, most of all, his concept of the *Übermensch* (Super-humans) has been thought to have inspired Hitler's concept of the Master Race, in Nazism. In spite of this, we can be fairly sure, reading Nietzsche more fully, that Nazism is a demonic distortion of Nietzsche's intent. It is worth remembering that Nietzsche wrote in aphorisms; if we read them as poetry, rather than as dogma, perhaps we will be less scandalized when we see a poetic dynamic in action. (The Psalms are best read as poetry, in a similar way; what is an adequate hermeneutic when the Psalmist writes that "happy is the one who seizes your infants and dashes them against the rocks"?)[39] Nietzsche expresses rage against a Christianity which has exalted weakness at the expense of courage, and this is a "No" which Altizer sees as hugely significant, as we shall see.

38. Eliot, *Felix Holt the Radical*.
39. Ps 137:9.

Here, we can see how Barth, Nietzsche and Blake have all influenced him. Recall Barth's *Krisis* where a divine No-saying (to sin) becomes a divine Yes-saying (in forgiveness and grace). Altizer subverts this *Krisis* of the divine "No" to make it a Nietzschean No-Saying. Where Barth argues that theology is "a service serving the Church—an "ecclesiastical science,"[40] Altizer follows Blake in assaulting Christendom as the place where "The footsteps of the Lamb of God were there; but now no more."[41] Altizer argues that, in Blake's symbolic universe, "Luvah's sepulcher, most simply interpreted, is the repressive body of the Christian Church—and, as Nietzsche remarks, Christianity is "the stone upon the grave of Jesus."[42] This, however subversive, is not alien to even an apparently more unorthodox Tillichian thought: we need only recall Tillich's words that

> . . . religious ritual, myth or institutions are ambiguous, "functioning religiously" to express the unconditioned . . . [but] they invite for themselves the ultimate concern appropriate only to the unconditioned. Thereby they become "demonic," powerfully destructive of the life trying to "transcend" itself.[43]

Altizer writes:

> Karl Barth was the first theologian to maintain that the "secret" of the creation can only truly be known by faith in Christ . . . it beautifully illustrates the quandary of the modern theologian who is forced to speak about God in a world in which God is dead.[44]

---

40. Hardy, "Karl Barth," in Ford and Muers, *Modern Theologians*, 24.
41. Blake, "Jerusalem" 24:23, in Altizer, *Gospel of Christian Atheism*, 42.
42. Blake, "Jerusalem" 24:23, in Altizer, *Gospel of Christian Atheism*, 43.
43. Kelsey, *Fabric of Paul Tillich's Theology*, 70–71.
44. Altizer, *Gospel of Christian Atheism*, 99.

Barth expresses Gxd as known through Christ, but Altizer shifts the emphasis so that "what is known" is, in Jesus, the crucified Gxd. This is actually (for the autistic hermeneutic, *literally*) a profoundly Trinitarian thought of *homoousios:* Jesus fully human *and fully divine* as the death of Gxd.

In Altizer's thought, Nietzsche, like Blake, is a "modern Christian seer"[45] of this death. God, for Nietzsche, is "the deification of nothingness, the will to nothingness pronounced holy!"[46] A classic Existentialist statement, the parable of Nietzsche's Madman, reads:

> Whither is it moving now? Whither are we moving? Away from all suns? Are we not plunging continually? Backward, sideward, forward, in all directions? Is there still any up or down? Are we not straying, as through an infinite nothing? Do we not feel the breath of empty space? Has it not become colder? Is not night continually closing in on us? Do we not need to light lanterns in the morning? Do we hear nothing as yet of the noise of the gravediggers who are burying God? Do we smell nothing as yet of the divine decomposition? Gods, too, decompose. God is dead. God remains dead. And we have killed him.[47]

The death of the metaphysical God is both chaos and gospel, as emancipation. Altizer writes: "only by means of a realization of the death of God in human experience can faith be liberated from the authority and the power of the primordial God."[48] This means that the demonic nature of Luvah is taken absolutely seriously by the autistic reader who is able to follow Blake's honest indignation

---

45. Altizer, *Gospel of Christian Atheism*, 95.

46. Nietzsche, *Twilight of the Idols*, section 18, in Altizer, *Gospel of Christian Atheism*, 93.

47. Nietzsche, *Joyful Wisdom*, in Altizer, *Gospel of Christian Atheism*, 95–96.

48. Nietzsche, *Joyful Wisdom*, in Altizer, *Gospel of Christian Atheism*, 112.

into Altizer's theological thinking. The autistic literal hermeneutic reads this literally ("idiotically," we might say; at face value, seriously, with integrity) as an absolute No. An autistic serious following through of the critique of Christendom as Blake's "sepulchre" sees Gxd dead, here, in the midst of our religion. The metaphor is "real," here, as the embodiment of Gxd's absence.[49] The autistic hermeneutic "takes Altizer seriously" when subversively, he also deviates from the norms of theology, as we autists do in society.

A Short "Deviation": Chop Suey!'s Betrayal

A twenty-first-century deviation from the narrative here perhaps helps to work into thinking of the fully radical nature of this thinking of Christendom as the demonic. This deviation is the deconstruction of any possible theodicy (justification of the problem of evil in the world of a loving Gxd), in the music of System of a Down's "Chop Suey!"[50] System of a Down (SoaD), an American heavy metal band of Armenian ethnic origin, express "honest indignation" as raw rage, where reflecting on Armenian genocide[51] leaves religion as a shallow formula which mocks the actual carnage by seeming to offer sanitizing power: in the middle of

---

49. Altizer's memoir is entitled *Living the Death of God*, and that impossible, intolerable paradox, read autistically, will become the narrative of intolerable, impossible absolute autism.

50. "Chop Suey!"'s original title was "Suicide" and was changed for legal reasons; this new title fits well with their surrealism.

51. SoaD's lead singer, Serj Tankian, has campaigned long and hard for international recognition of the events of 1914–15 as an Armenian genocide by the Ottoman Empire. At the time of writing this (April 2021) Tankian raised this issue during a BBC interview (Victims of a Down, "Serj Tankian Talks"); within a fortnight, President Joe Biden made a statement officially recognizing the genocide (see Kreps, "Serg Tankian").

an angry, surrealist heavy metal rant comes a gentle, plaintive, lyrical refrain, and they sing:

> I don't think you trust
> In my self-righteous suicide
> I cry when angels deserve to die
> In my self-righteous suicide
> I cry when angels deserve to die / Father, father, father, father
> Father, into your hands I commend my spirit
> Father, into your hands
> Why have you forsaken me?
> In your eyes forsaken me
> In your thoughts forsaken me
> In your heart forsaken me, oh
> Trust in my self-righteous suicide[52]

Yet, in our hermeneutic, its "self-righteous suicide" formula is also a poetic enactment of the insane choice of the "suicidal self" of the "righteous" Christ at Calvary. In this lyrical refrain, again comes the voice of rage, echoing Jesus' cry of abandonment, "Father! Why have you forsaken me?" How are we to interpret this conjunction of the Crucifixion and a "self-righteous suicide?" Isn't "self-righteous" a little too righteous for its own good? Autistic integrity, with its black and white thinking, will grapple with this dubiety/duplicity, and refuse to ignore the betrayal upon betrayal inherent in it, grappling with what, for us, is an absurdity. Betrayal upon betrayal, as Jesus' death is founded on Judas' betraying him with a kiss; and at another level, we ourselves, in our actual lives, betray this reality. David Jasper explains this in his theologically ironic essay, *Evil and Betrayal at the Heart of the Sacred Community*:

---

52. System of a Down, "Chop Suey!"

> we prettily talk of paronomasia[53] while this poor guy is dying on the cross, for Christ's sake; We have to step outside this fictive nonsense, this mythical realm, confronting two worlds whereby the banality of evil ("Jesus, be sensible [we would say] and grow up, we do love you, you don't need to do this . . .") is exposed in its truly mythic dimensions[54]

So, do we trust in a "self-righteous suicide"—what do we even make of these words? Is it possible, in pure affective empathy bereft of cognitive empathy, to be utterly beyond making sense of atrocity, and sing by howling in the death of Gxd, at the existence of a culture's felt need for "self-righteous suicide" as escape or atonement?

Jasper points out that the apostle Peter is also both betrayer and betrayed: "his hopes dashed—for which he had given up everything? To hell with everything, we understand very well how one can prefer the banality of everyday evil . . . to this awful, overturning, unbearable, unnecessary violence."[55] He links this back to the idea of the reader "confronting two worlds whereby the banality of evil ('Jesus, be sensible [we would say] and grow up, we do love you, you don't need to do this . . .') is exposed in its truly mythic dimensions," and these "two worlds" are where the reader chooses which betrayal to make:

> Through the looking glass of fiction, the question is how we tell the difference between real and unreal. Or perhaps the real question is, in a world where finally only truth really matters, should we even try to do so, and simply remain content to be mad out of duty?[56]

---

53. Paronomasia: word-play.
54. Jasper, *Sacred Community*, 37, 39.
55. Jasper, *Sacred Community,* 35, 37.
56. Jasper, *Sacred Community*, 38.

This is surely a place where the Holy Fool can find echoes of herself; so, too, in autistic "foolishness" and innocence, she will be mad out of duty, and duty, as Jasper suggests, to the truth. For an autistic hermeneutic, we see here a discourse which can be read as the autistic integrity of "black and white thinking" which resists compromise. Tactless, totally committed to love and truth, the little autist who speaks up about the Emperor's new clothes; who exposes the Emperor's nakedness. One might even think of Nick Cave's lyrics in the song "Today's Lesson": "Underneath all of her clothes she was completely naked,"[57] the integrity of a love for truth, however absurd and tactless. A fusion of Mindblindness and autistic affective empathy, loving truth.

Chop Suey!'s Betrayal: Our Holy Blasphemy

"Chop Suey!" is also singing a double betrayal, blaspheming the Christ who fails (betrays) the Armenians, abstaining from salvation by remaining "self-righteous" in indifferent absence. In an Altizerian reading, we would say that for us to remain indifferent, is to collude with another betrayal; denying the Crucifixion as the death of a Primordial Gxd, who kills and betrays Love, thereby requiring the suicide of the righteous self, and this, on one level (among others) is a cosmic enactment of the Armenians' horrific suffering.

If this is dismissed as "mere emo music" (as which it certainly also is perceived, for a certain audience), this dismissal is perhaps because the authentic (and even, in a sense, autistically sensitive) "emo" teenage questions are unheeded,[58] and teenage rebellion is honest indignation.

57. Nick Cave and the Bad Seeds, "Today's Lesson."
58. Doesn't Heidegger remark that children are the true philosophers, when he writes of "the *Geschick* (art) of being: a child that plays" in *The Principle of Reason*?

SoaD's discography also critiques Western indifference to the Tiananmen square massacre, for example, in *Hypnotise* (2005), or the Iraq war in *Boom* (2005). Their concern for social justice is expressed as the music of rage, and its scrutiny is relentless.[59] "Chop Suey!" questions Christendom's claim to goodness, exposing its demonic nature and simultaneously suggesting the possibility of trusting the demonic "self-righteous suicide" as a necessary betrayal.

The reason for digressing into this strange reading of heavy metal music (and I strongly recommend you watch the official video on YouTube),[60] is to approach the moral power of a shocking holy blasphemy, as a "mythical dimension" of truth telling where autistic integrity can be "mad out of duty" in facing layers of betrayal. What option do we have but to be mad for the truth? We autists are guileless; we do not lie or betray, and how can we comprehend betrayal?

It articulates the consequences of Altizer's radical deconstruction of the "salve" of Christendom, which is also a shocking holy blasphemy. The Nietzschean No-Saying for Altizer issues from a reading of Blake's "Jerusalem" where "the Great Selfhood, Satan . . . [is] the Devouring Power."[61] In Altizer's words, Nietzsche's Gxd of Christendom is the Christian Gxd as "the embodiment of an absolute No-saying, because it is the only epiphany of the sacred which is a total reversal of a forward-moving divine process."[62]

In this sense, the ultimate paradox of Barth's *Krisis* is, radically and heretically, inverted by taking the theological

---

59. Like Blake, SoaD also have a liberated view of sexuality, which they see as oppressed by Christian morality.

60. System of a Down, "Chop Suey!" official video, YouTube.

61. Blake, "Jerusalem" 33:17–24, in Altizer, *Gospel of Christian Atheism*, 100.

62. Altizer, *Gospel of Christian Atheism*, 101.

position that Christ, becoming sin for us, does so to the point of being an embodiment of sin, and Gxd is Satan, as the negation which is itself (as SoaD have expressed, in sacred, profane rage) negated in the Crucifixion as the death of Gxd. Altizer writes:

> [T]he Christian God can be manifest and real only by means of a faith engaging in an absolute world and life-negation, a negation that must occur wherever there is energy and life. When the radical Christian confronts us with the liberating message that God is Satan, he is stilling the power of that negation, breaking all those webs of religion with which a regressive Christianity has ensnared the Christian, and unveiling the God who had died in Christ.[63]

SoaD's Gxd is the "self-righteous" Satan in whom "I don't think you trust," and yet, for Altizer thinking atheologically, and SoaD thinking equally authentically, there is a strange meeting of this evil and death with the suffering of John of the Cross in the apophatic discourse of *The Dark Night of the Soul*. Altizer writes:

> All our deeper Christian vision has known the presence of God as the presence of an absolute abyss, as here total presence can only be the total presence of an absolute abyss.[64]

Inverting the model of clinical depression (as we did with John of the Cross' Dark Night), this is not an abyss of suffering but a suffering of abyss. Both Altizer and SoaD's lyrics invite a reading of Gxd *as* abyss. Altizer writes:

> Is an absolute abyss possible apart from a realization of God . . . a voice that is a pure and absolute abyss,

---

63. Altizer, *Gospel of Christian Atheism*, 101.
64. Altizer, *Godhead and the Nothing*, 129.

one whose realization silences every other voice, or silences every voice that is not the voice of abyss?[65]

The abyss is the place of the gospel. When it is possible glibly to assent that Christ is "made sin for us,"[66] what is harder to consider is the utter self-righteous suicide where Gxd is in Hiroshima, Auschwitz, Armenia, as Satan. Altizer's mythology is outrageous, but it is outrage at Christendom, whose Gxd is perhaps indeed a little too self-righteous. Justly, His angels as agents (Lucifer, the angel of light) "deserve to die," and so, in holy blasphemy, does "He." (But, then, did the innocent civilian "angels" deserve also to die, we also wonder).Theodicy is obscene; a Primordial Gxd must die.

Altizer knows full well that he is mounting an assault on the religious establishment, and frequently says so. So how can he be, as William Hamilton writes, both "evangelical" and "pastoral?"[67] Strange as it may seem, his concern is to be faithful to the truths of twentieth (and now twenty-first)-century Christianity. He argues that nineteenth-century textual criticism has effectively destroyed the credibility of a unified and literally inspired biblical voice, undermining the Church's authority:

> A century and a half of historical scholarship has demonstrated that the Bible contains a diverse body or series of traditions and imagery that resists all attempts at harmonization or reconciliation. No longer is it possible to speak of a biblical faith or a biblical religion or even of a distinct and singular biblical God; nor is there any possibility of rationally or logically uniting the self-contradictory biblical images of God.

---

65. Altizer, *Godhead and the Nothing*, 131.

66. 2 Cor 5:21.

67. "A lucid, joyous, wise, evangelical—even pastoral—piece of theological work" (Hamilton, cover matter, *Gospel of Christian Atheism*).

> Nevertheless, a radical and dialectical theology can lead us to grasp the necessity of the contradictory language of the Bible.[68]

The end of a (straightforwardly) "biblical faith" opens an abyss which is the death of Gxd, and yet as such is the epiphany of the cosmic Jesus; the total "righteous suicide."

This, as Jesus' disciples would say, is a hard saying.[69] Are we really so bereft as to be at the point of Christian atheism? As far as our dominant worldview is concerned that may, in some places, be true (missionaries from the Global South now come to evangelize the godless developed world, after all) but we cannot say that Christianity as a worldview is dead. Altizer, instead, is describing something which has always been true, not merely in terms of our cultural "emancipation" from the evils of a Western (Colonialist/Capitalist/Imperialist/Judgmental/Opiate of the People etc.) Christendom. Instead, he is taking that moment of emancipation, as we might grasp it, and making of it an opportunity to say something profoundly spiritual. If we recall the performance of "Chop Suey!" by System of a Down, we might tap into that rage at a God who is not Gxd.

Recall the woman who burned God (would she have been a witch in another lifetime?) Perhaps we can discern in Altizer a similar crucial (and cruciform) thinking. Do we dare to say that the Primordial God is Satan? As System of a Down so cryptically sing, "I cry when angels deserve to die." Can we liberate an anonymous Jesus resurrected amongst us where we exchange those longstanding judgements between sinner and saint, saved and unsaved,

---

68. Altizer, *Gospel of Christian Atheism*, 89.
69. John 6:60.

with what Altizer calls the Universal Jesus? This is a radical Incarnation, one which follows Blake.

Now, can we see a way for autistic authenticity to validate and be validated by this thinking of Christian atheism? For an autistic hermeneutic, a "sacred profane" of metaphor-as-atheism-as-the-Incarnation offers a way to validate its way of seeing. Sacred profane can be thought of in two senses. Firstly, the sacred profane is honoring a sacrality of the space of the secular, divorced from religion [archaic *pro* (outside)-*fanus* (temple)]. Secondly, it is the profanity (blasphemy) of taking God's name in vain by speaking the death of Gxd. First, then, we can consider a sense of (sacred) profanity, as outside the temple and irreligious. This *pro-fanus* reads autistically as Autistic Fascination in the space of Mindfulness of Separation. We are, eternally, but gloriously, forever "cast out."

Secondly, our mythical autistic integrity is exposing the Ultimate and Absolute Emperor's fictional clothing to be nakedness. After all, Jesus himself was stripped naked as they gambled for his clothes at Golgotha.[70] Our particular mythical autism is, in the more common sense of the word, profane—taking God's name in vain, blaspheming. It is for this reason (although probably all the other uses of "x" are true—not least, the chasmic)[71] that I can write of Gxd. Furthermore, can I dare to say that Gxd also writes this of Gxdself? Altizer explores this possibility at the deepest possible level, and our Absolute Incarnational metaphor will dare to go there with him. We will now see how Altizer mythically approaches and appropriates

---

70. Matt 27:35.

71. Referring to x as the Greek letter *chi* (pronounced "kai"—the symbol of inversion, here in ways of Christian atheism, of the Beatitudes, of the paradoxes we have encountered and will do).

Hegel's more discreet blasphemy; and how this takes us closer to our own mythical possibility, the autism of Gxd.

HEGEL AND THE SELF-EMBODIMENT OF GOD

Hegel and Geist

In 1977, Altizer wrote *The Self-embodiment of God*, and it seems to me the most complete statement of his view of Bible as myth.

> **In *The Self-embodiment of God*, Gxd's self-embodiment is a universal sacrament where Creation, Fall, Incarnation, Crucifixion and Resurrection are all one cosmic event, which is Gxd's exile from Gxdself—the self-embodiment of Gxd is the self-exile of Gxd.**

It is here at the self-exile of Gxd where we can most clearly see Altizer's deep commitment both to Bible and to his "third prophet," the philosopher Hegel.

Perhaps Hegel's most famous contribution to philosophy is the dialectical process (which informed Karl Marx's atheist socio-economic concept of dialectical materialism). The dialectical process is a vision of history and philosophy where one reality or idea will meet another opposing one and, from their meeting, there is a mutual negation, creating a synthesis, which generates a new reality or idea in turn to meet its opposite, and so on; the process evolving, for Hegel, from primordial emptiness toward a completion. Shockingly, for the pietism of his (and our) generation, Hegel sees the dialectic fundamentally as *Geist* (Spirit); a Gxd who evolves in human consciousness and history, from Nothing, through the meeting and evolving overcoming of contradictions, as Becoming, toward ever greater Completion. Hegel presents the dialectical unfolding of Being as the Becoming of Mind or Spirit (*Geist*). Altizer quotes Hegel:

> This incarnation of the Divine Being, its having essentially and directly the shape of self-consciousness, is the simple content of Absolute Religion. Here the Divine Being is known as Spirit; this religion is the Divine Being's consciousness concerning itself that it is Spirit. . . .[72]

> Spirit alone is reality. It is in the inner being of the world, that which essentially is, and is per se; it assumes objective, determinate form.[73]

In this, the dialectical process has a definite teleology (end, purpose), where history is the increasing self-realization of Spirit in its own (and our) consciousness. As Ernst Cassirer remarks,

> In Hegel's philosophy, the formula of Spinoza, *Deus sive Natura*, [God as nature] is transformed into *Deus sive Historia* [God as History]. Yet the apotheosis[74] is not concerned with particular historical events, but rather with the historical process as a whole.[75]

So the unfolding of Being in Becoming is *Geist* in the form of "God as History." There is here, however, an interesting reversal in Altizer's use of Hegel. Hegel writes:

> In the Christian religion God has been revealed as truth and as spirit. As spirit, humans can receive this revelation. In religion the truth is veiled in imagery; but in philosophy the veil is torn aside, so that humans can know the infinite and see all things in God.[76]

---

72. Altizer, *Gospel of Christian Atheism*, 66 (citation not given).
73. Altizer, *Gospel of Christian Atheism*, 64 (citation not given).
74. Revelation or appearance of Gxd.
75. Cassirer, *Werke*, 368, in Lucas and Lucas, "Spinoza, Hegel, Whitehead," 40.
76. Knox, "Hegel."

In Altizer's reading of this, truth is indeed "veiled in (an) imagery" of religion, but history becomes a cosmic *biblical* story; a story where the Christian narrative is not a "veil" but a mythical enactment of Hegel's Being and Becoming. This is not merely as a historical process; it is a Cosmic (mythical) story, although history and culture enact and embody the cosmic Story. In Altizer's narrative, as we have seen, religion is a bankrupt entity. *What remains is the Story* in religion not as Hegel's "veil" but as the embodiment of Spirit in (crucially, *in*, not *by*) the metaphors of biblical narrative. "Living the death of Gxd"[77] is an exercise in Existentialist Scriptural poetics, not theological doctrine.

Altizer's Universal Sacrament

In Altizer's reading of Hegel, the "inner being" of *Geist* is known in, and as, the sacred profane. In his atheological reading of him, he carries the dialectic of *Geist* into a poetic/existential reading of biblical narrative events.

The primordial emptiness (and, in a *coincidentia oppositorum,* fullness) is the silence of a primordial Gxd before the Creation, which is then broken, as spoken as *logos (Logos*: the metaphysical logocentric construct of chapter 2, rethought here also as the Genesis myth's Creative words *"let there be light").* This spoken Creation as a departure from primordial silence brings the primordial Gxd into the dialectical process—a history, cosmically thought—*and this is the Fall, not of humanity, but of Gxd.* Gxd is no longer pure and undifferentiated, but entering into the "messiness" and Becoming of a historical process. This primordial Fall into the dialectical process is embodiment;

---

77. Altizer, *Living the Death of God*; his theological memoir.

at once Creation, Incarnation, Crucifixion and Resurrection. So Altizer envisions a Hegelian reading of biblical myth, where the utter *kenosis*[78] of salvation history, as the death of Gxd, is told as the dialectical outpouring of *Geist.* In the Resurrection, there is no Ascension back to a primordial heaven; rather, Jesus is resurrected in humanity. For this, Altizer draws on Blake's idea of the anonymous Jesus, present in all of us (recall the story of the monks who bickered until they were told that one of them was actually the disguised Christ; seeing the possibility of Christ, each monk saw and recognized the Christ in all of the others; perhaps even in himself).

The Self-Embodiment of Gxd

So, when he draws on Hegel, the third of his "prophets" of the death of Gxd, Altizer (radically, mythically, deconstructively) re-enters the "religion" that Hegel has described as the "veil," and he thinks through Hegel's dialectical philosophy of Spirit in terms of biblical narrative. Effectively, biblical narrative becomes Hegelian dialectic, and Hegelian dialectic becomes biblical narrative.

Spirit descending and entering into dialectical process is what Altizer casts as the Fall. A cosmic Fall from the silence of pure Being into dialectical Becoming is not only Fall, but also Creation, by the production of determinate being from that Fall.[79] This is a move from silence to speech (we think again of *logos* and the initial cosmic

---

78. *Kenosis*, as the Guide to Theology told us, is the sacrificial outpouring of self, attributed to Jesus in the New Testament.

79. Altizer would have been more than aware of Hindu Creation myths where the cosmos is the sacrificed body of the god; we will see that his thinking draws also on Buddhist philosophy.

words of the divine fiat ["let there be] . . .) He expresses it in this way:

> Mythically envisioned, the advent of speech is both creation and fall. For speech is simultaneously both the origin of all meaning and identity and a fall from the quiescence and peace of silence.[80]

We might recall Tillich's thought of the Divine as the Ground of Being which is known authentically here as the inner speech of a theonomy [theonomy, we recall, being the rule of Gxd—perhaps thought more as a natural law than a judicial one]. This speech is Hegelian Spirit, and at the same time, mythically, Gxd's acts in Scripture.

Speech as the Voice of Gxd

The Fall of Gxd in the biblical narrative, for Altizer, then, is the dialectical synthesis of pure Being and pure Nonbeing into determinate Becoming; and this dialectical history of Becoming is the myth which is spoken by Gxd in sacred history. A "silent voice" of "our own nature" (if we can hear it), is also thought by Altizer as atheological and mythical, expressed in Hegelian terms. This is where the "silent voice" becomes the voice of Gxd in Scripture, which is also the silent voice of Hegelian Being or *Geist*. Thinking mythically of our own deepest selves, *we truly do own that power of subjective realization. It is our Interior Castle.* However, Altizer observes that in the times of the Hebrew Bible prophets, and of the New Testament, there are obstacles to authentic speech,[81] out of which prophecy emerges as a new authentic speech. The fullest speech,

---

80. Altizer, *Self-Embodiment of God*, 5.
81. The Hebrew Bible prophets repeatedly preach to Israel (and to us) of our falling away from Gxd; the Gxd, particularly, of social justice and compassion.

in authentic response to the Divine, arises from the deepest silence, as Altizer knows well from the mystics. The language of faith needs to be not "merely repeating the words of faith"[82] but something alive, and dialectically new. True speech (our creative and revelatory *logos,* at an existential level) is the way in which faith emerges; faith is the fullness of speech and not just any speech (which Altizer calls "chatter") but, in language echoing Tillich's Gxd as "the Ground of our Being," "speech embodying its own ground."[83] Speech as authentic *logos* is fundamental, and not a mere vehicle[84] but something more profound, which actually creates faith; "faith responds to the mystery of speech."[85]

So we can see that Altizer is really doing something unique; as a poet, he is drawing on the mystic language of apophatic theology, and doing so in a deeply Hegelian way. Silence is "both our origin and our end," and it is actually present in speech and is "speakable in speech."[86] Silence passes into speech when speech emerges out of silence. It is a presence in speech. He writes:

> Silence can dwell in speech, but its emptiness is negated by the presence of speech. When silence is present in speech it is not a mere emptiness, just as it is not a simple absence, it is far rather a presence.[87]

Just as we understood earlier that apophatic theology is not the negation of theology but the theology of negation—now, similarly, we can say that this silence is not an

---

82. Altizer, *Self-Embodiment of God,* 2.
83. Altizer, *Self-Embodiment of God,* 3.
84. Recall how Heidegger writes of the poetic word as not a vehicle but a wellspring of being.
85. Altizer, *Self-Embodiment of God,* 3.
86. Altizer, *Self-Embodiment of God,* 5.
87. Altizer, *Self-Embodiment of God,* 9.

empty silence but a silence of emptiness (pregnant with the depths of silent fullness).

Autism's Silent Speech

At this point, can we see an autistic hermeneutic—a legitimate theological listening of absolute autism—as a possible way to validate Altizer's Hegelian reading of the narrative of Gxd's acts? The wording here is deliberate; *validating,* not *validated*. With a reading of this radical atheology which is powered by a mythical autistic hermeneutic, can we dare to perform this neurotribal reading? Can we offer our autistic friendliness (yes, we are faithful when we can be friends) to a hospitable atheological silent speech? We can. Here, however, we need to recall all that the mythical autistic trinity has been for us: Mindfulness of Separation, Fascination, Incarnational metaphor, in perichoretic unity dancing in autistic Love at the center. But there is more. This following paragraph is one which needs to be pondered. It is at the heart of our autistic Gxd.

Firstly, autistic integrity and black and white thinking has no place for what Altizer calls "chatter." Its absolute Mindfulness of Separation, which is also absolute fascination, recognizes a fundamental authenticity of the silence of pure being as the voice of Gxd, Absolute Spirit, as silence within speech. Mindfulness of Separation, which nurtures Fascination, understands the silence within authentic consciousness (thought of as *Geist* and therefore, also, of ourselves). This impossible territory is expressed only through paradox, as we saw in apophatic fiction; the moment of absolute union (speech) is the moment of absolute absence (silence). Furthermore, that moment of absolute union is absolute, rapt, fascination immersed in the love at the heart of the autistic trinity. Need it be said that Incarnational metaphor is working powerfully here? Indeed it is, in the sense that Altizer's Scriptural-Hegelian *poiesis*[88] takes Scriptural metaphor all too poetically and real-ly; this is not an exercise in frivolous game-playing but one where the stakes are high; this is a wager of faith.

Now, in the light of the myth of the death of Gxd, it can be thought of as pure autistic affective empathy in absolute *kenosis*.

To do this, we need to step back and see what Altizer's Hegelian reading of Scripture means by *kenosis*. We will then also see the absolute, autistic, affective empathy of sainthood atheologically, as the absolute *kenosis* which is the autism of Gxd. Our autistic myth will honor Altizer's Salvation History. Autism speaks, proclaiming this myth of the death of Gxd as something which can be intuited autistically and spoken to the Church, if the Church will honor its insight.

Incarnation and Exile as Kenosis

We are now in a position to see how the mythically told salvation history of biblical narrative can be recast as an epic telling of the outpouring (*kenosis*) of pure Being and Nonbeing into Becoming or determinate being. To reiterate, this Hegelian descent of the absence which is pure quiescent Being, into presence which is determinate Becoming, is the universal dialectical Fall. This Fall is enacted in the total salvation history as embodied in the mythology of Creation, Exodus, Incarnation, Crucifixion,

---

88. Type and method of poetic writing.

and Resurrection. Not for nothing did Altizer write of *The Gospel of Christian Atheism*[89] in perhaps his most accessible work.

> This is an apocalyptic *kerygma*[90] of the death of Gxd. This is in the sense of Gxd revealed as emptying Gxdself totally and lovingly into the world, so that Jesus is known in the Incarnation which is also Fall and Crucifixion. Resurrection is the kenotic emptying of the crucified Jesus, anonymously poured out into the world in the death of the transcendent Gxd.

Christ's Ascension to heaven is viewed by Altizer as a Hellenistic accretion,[91] and instead, ascension is subverted into the utter, absolute descent of Jesus into Hell. If this shocks us (and it should), we can call to mind Dietrich Bonhoeffer, the Christian theologian of the Confessing Church which spoke out against Nazism, and his radical thinking of Gxd's suffering in the Camps, telling us that only a suffering God can help us;[92] we can think also of System of a Down's paradoxical word-games with the "self-righteous suicide" which is also, musically, a lament in the midst of their rage. This self-embodiment of Gxd as exile is an absolute kenotic choice, and in all its moments is enacting the apocalyptic gospel of Gxd with us *in* death. This is both terrible and wonderful; as Nietzsche writes, "Even God hath his hell: it is his love for man."[93] The death of Gxd which liberates the world is Gxd's self-emptying, so that also in Nietzsche's words, for the atheist Christian,

---

89. Altizer, *Gospel of Christian Atheism*.
90. The message of the gospel as preached in an authentic Christianity.
91. A later theological appendage to the original gospel, which emerges from Greek philosophical thought.
92. Bonhoeffer, *Cost of Discipleship*, 479.
93. Nietzsche, *Thus Spake Zarathustra*.

"I tell you: one must still have chaos in one, to give birth to a dancing star. I tell you: ye have still chaos in you."[94] The gospel of Christian atheism is "a hard saying,"[95] but it is ultimate hope, of Gxd with us, even in our hell, and this is the faith of John of the Cross' dark night of the soul.

This, in Altizer's view, is a return to a primitive gospel without Messianic[96] or Hellenistic[97] elements. It is the embodiment of the Christian myth in faith, and *The Self-embodiment of God* traces Christian myth as these biblical archetypes:

> . . . to embody the fullness of the biblical moment of faith . . . it evolves by way of an evolutionary yet interior movement of the biblical moments and movements of Genesis, Exodus, Judgement, Incarnation and Apocalypse. *The sacred history of the Bible here becomes interiorized and universalized.*[98]

The universal cosmic Fall is the fall of Gxd, and the myth of Exodus is not only the Exodus of the people of Gxd. When Gxd enacts their redemption, revealing Gxdself in the burning bush, this is, in mythical terms, Gxd's choice at a far deeper level, to exile Gxd as determinate being from Gxd as pure Being. This is therefore Gxd's exile:

> God is the name of exile . . . the name of God makes exile manifest in its source, and thereby in its finality, a once and for all finality eradicating every possibility of the Nonbeing of actuality. And to speak the name of God is not simply to speak the name of the ground

---

94. Nietzsche, *Thus Spake Zarathustra*.
95. "Many therefore of his disciples, when they had heard this, said, This is a hard saying; who can hear it?" (John 6:60).
96. From the thinking of sects awaiting the coming of a Messiah.
97. From the Greek philosophical thinking, which influenced early Christianity.
98. Altizer, *Self-Embodiment of God*, 6.

of actuality, it is to sanction actuality, it is to speak that name whose utterance seals the finality of the actual.[99]

Actuality: the real presence of Jesus in us, and in the *actual world.* Here, using language of "actuality,"[100] is this not, in a sense, "dangerously" close to pantheism? Altizer, we recall, wrote *Oriental Mysticism and Apocalypse* in the early stages of his career; and here, in *The Self-embodiment of God*, he is not slow, particularly as the book approaches its end, to see parallels with Buddhist thought. Gxd, as the writer of John's Epistles tell us, is love; and compassion is central to Buddhist understanding and practice. It would almost be possible to discern a slight element of syncretism, as Altizer increasingly invokes parallels with Buddhist thought as *The Self-embodiment of God* approaches its climactic end.

Autistic Kenosis

This *kenosis* is absolute love poured out absolutely, even entering into our world's hells; shockingly, the Ascension is not an upward movement into Heaven but a downward movement of Love present, as Bonhoeffer well knew, into Auschwitz; into Hiroshima; into Armenia, Tiananmen Square, Iraq; into our hells. Just as Bonhoeffer has said, decades before Altizer's radical theology, "only a suffering God can help us."[101] What use is a Friend who pontificates from on high? This is shocking—and we should be shocked, unless we are numb to the sufferings of the world.

---

99. Altizer, *Self-Embodiment of God*, 29–30.
100. What is, in the material world.
101. Bonhoeffer, *Cost of Discipleship*, 479.

Can we now see how *kenosis* might be read in an autistic hermeneutic? Truly readily. To put it very succinctly, working toward Absolute Incarnational metaphor, we could discern *kenosis* in all the facets of our mythical autism. Firstly, as kenotic fascination, it is Jesus utterly present, all in all, in the world as full Incarnation, known as the liberation of the dancing star, the glittering object which fascinates the autist in joy. Secondly, as pure affective empathy, utter autistic *kenosis* gives unconditionally; even in the unknowing of the lack of cognitive empathy which is the death of the omniscient Gxd. Thirdly, Mindfulness of Separation is the kenotic self-exile of Gxd, and the faith which chooses to affirm itself as faith in Gxd, (even as we affirm the loss of the absent, dead Gxd), in the chaos where, as Nietzsche writes, we are "straying, as through an infinite nothing . . . [with] night continually closing in on us . . . [because] God is dead."[102] Faith for the autist is difficult. Black and white, literal thinking does not find a resolution to the question of faith when it applies positivist logic. Pure affective empathy in the face of the bewilderment of impaired cognitive empathy is painful and costly (as I well know). Mindfulness of Separation is inescapable. The supreme validation for autistic faith would be faith in an autistic Gxd, which we can now suggest as a profound way to think the embodiment of Gxd's self-exile.[103]

---

102. Nietzsche, *Joyful Wisdom*, in Altizer, *Gospel of Christian Atheism*, 95–96.

103. This autistic Gxd is underpinned by the assumption that it is possible to conceive of a Disabled Gxd (see Eiesland, *Disabled Gxd*, 100).

THE AUTISM OF GXD

Universal Autism as Hegelian Nonbeing

We are now ready to consider a total, cosmic self-exile as the autism of Gxd. The myth of autistic integrity can now find a way to read itself into this self-exile as total, Absolute Mindfulness of Separation and total, Absolute Fascination; and this exile's embodiment will, at last, enable total Incarnational metaphor to come into being.

As a myth which recognizes itself here, absolute autism as Mindfulness of Separation actually becomes creative, dialectical Hegelian Nonbeing. It is the Nonexistence which is the necessary opposite of Being in Becoming. Recall that for Altizer's mythical Hegelianism, ultimately, there is a return to the Pure Nothing of Pure Being, in apocalyptic consummation of the Divine. Altizer understands from the mystics that the moment of total union is the moment of total abandonment; the meeting of lovers in John's Dark Night of the Soul. So, implicitly within the embodiment of Becoming is total absence, which is total presence in this apocalyptic consummation. For the trinity of mythic autism, we will see this consummation of synthesis[104] itself as an absolute, apocalyptic revelation of pure, Absolute autism. We can see Absolute autism in its trinity of absence (separation), presence (fascination), and, as we will see, the paradoxical absent presence which is Incarnational metaphor. Autistic affective empathy, as we have consistently seen, will be at the heart. As we have also seen, each one of these is the necessary complement of the others.

---

104. Synthesis is the process of being and nonbeing meeting and cancelling each other out to form a new being.

THE AUTISM OF GXD   251

We can continue to bring our autistic myth alongside Altizer's Hegelian biblical myth. Altizer extends Hegel's argument that Absolute Spirit is determinate being. In this myth, if Gxd is determinate, speaking in the acts of salvation history, the transcendent primordial Gxdhead is dead, and apocalyptic consummation is thought of as the final *telos* of that death. Being Nonbeing as Absolute Spirit is the kenotic totality of Gxd's acts, as Love poured out even unto death. Mythical absolute autism is then this creative absolute separation in determinate being itself. In the play of Being and Nonbeing in determinate being, autism as the dialectical other is the perpetual existence of their separateness and negation, which continually plays in the shimmering of Becoming. The Becoming of determinate being cannot exist without the continual separation which creates the dialectical tension of Nonbeing and Being. Autism, as the phenomenon of separation itself, is this perpetual moment of separation. Autism is the moment of Nonbeing which itself encounters Being, thus generating the separation of Being-Nonbeing and it is also, as a consequence, the distress of determinate being's separation from the transcendent primordial Plenum of pure Being.[105] Autism is the embodiment of the primordial Fall which is the fall of Gxd.

We can also think of this Hegelian *telos* (purpose, end, consummation) theologically, in Altizer's language, as a new Plenum (Absolute Fullness).[106] This mirrors the Primordial Plenum which was the silence before the creation and the fall of Gxd. The final and complete resolution of Being and Nonbeing which is the silent speech of a new Plenum,

---

105. Pure being, thought theologically, as what was earlier considered as Tillich's atheism of the inescapable Ground of Being which Is Not, because it is beyond all being.

106. Absolute fullness of all.

is achieved only by the absolute absence (death) of Gxd, which actually *is* Gxd. Living in kenotic death, death is life (are we to take the Apostle Paul at his word when he writes that "we die daily?")[107] and the presence of Gxd is the absence of Gxd. This death, for us in our mythical autism, is Absolute autistic Love, which shines in the sparkling beauty of Fascination precisely as it abandons itself in the darkness of Absolute Mindfulness of Separation. This is unconditional love, which gives without knowing. This is, in fact, an autistic Jesus, dying in Absolute Love for humanity, entering into the suffering of the world; "My God, my God, why hast Thou forsaken me?"

In the trinity of mythical autism, presence (absolute fascination) and absence (absolute Mindfulness of Separation) coincide as a *coincidentia oppositorum*, finally and apocalyptically (in total revelation), as the consummation of Incarnational metaphor. *In its consummation, Incarnational metaphor is the final, absolute kenosis where silent speech is total metaphor, beyond being*. It is the fullness of joyful poetic being which has no referent, becoming nothing. This is the total presence of metaphor, as the total absence of its decoding into pragmatism. It is totally literal metaphor made holy by its Incarnation of Nothing (which is, equally, Everything); a metaphor which goes nowhere and is nowhere, because language has broken down in the impossible paradox of this *coincidentia oppositorum.*

---

107. 1 Cor 15:31; also, we could consider the radical inversions we call the Beatitudes (Matt 5), as the "upside-down" Kingdom of Gxd.

> **In this way, mythical absolute autism can be expressed as the Hegelian negation which is total absence as total presence—which Altizer expresses as the death of Gxd. With autism as the negation which is simultaneously total affirmation, as manifestation of the kenotic fullness of the death of Gxd, it is possible to arrive at an Autistic Gxd. The autism of Gxd is the mythical Absolute of Mindfulness of Separation, Fascination, Incarnational metaphor and autistic Love.**

Altizer sees the mythical narrative of Creation, Exodus, Incarnation, Crucifixion, Resurrection and Apocalypse as the speech of Gxd, and it is also possible to think of universal, absolute autism as a mythology of this Gxd whom we have killed. If absolute autism is the embodiment of an utter separation which is kenotic fullness, the death of Gxd is the embodiment of a now universal autism. This is an autism which has "come of age" by finding its autonomy as Mindfulness of Separation of the death of Gxd. This "coming of age" of a conscious autism was thought of earlier in terms of Modernism, and it is equally a *felix culpa*[108] of emancipation in terms of the heretical vision of Nietzsche and Blake.

In relative, person-specific autism, as we saw in the Introduction, the fundamental separation is between (human) being + (human) being; there is a finite degree of communication breakdown and the lack of meeting. The fusion of horizons envisioned by Gadamer is impaired.[109] However, in Absolute terms, this is a fundamental and irreparable tear in the fabric of the universe, where horizons cannot and will never meet.[110] By the act of speaking

---

108. Fortunate Fall.
109. See fig. iii, 105.
110. See fig. iv, 106.

(relationality), as we have seen, Gxd falls from a primordial Plenum into separation from that Plenum, so that Gxdself is exiled from Gxdself. Therefore, paradoxically, relationality carries within it its own exile; and so even relationality carries within itself its other as autistic separation. The Introduction explained that, in terms of the human autistic spectrum, this is a universal phenomenon in which we all, to some degree, partake. Recall Batalvi's love poem, *Separation is King.* Even without this participatory spectrum, however, autism's very existence as a phenomenon would speak as a way in which the human universe contains something which embodies disunity and separation, with its strange presence and communion implicitly within it. This is not the Barthian separation of the "sin" of fallen humanity; this is independent of any flawed moral apparatus of dysfunctional relationships, or the disharmony of competing egos, which might be the cause of the separations of sin. Rather, this is a structural feature which cannot (and should not) be "fixed." It asks, instead, to be understood and accepted, and, much more than this, validated and cherished. It is, in fact, vitally important. When autism speaks in this way, it brings these mystical and atheological ways of thinking into alignment with itself so that they are celebrated as a glorious and mystical, mythical autism of Gxd. This is an autistic Gxd who validates these places on the margins, where mysticism and paradox are reached. Absolute autism speaks the pure speech of Gxd for us.

Gxd as Isolation

Altizer describes a cosmic separation and isolation in Gxd and, consequently, in all reality. An autistic hermeneutic would read the following almost as a textbook definition of universal autism:

> Now the Fall can be envisioned as a fall of an original Totality or All; it is the center or primordial ground of reality which becomes darkened and broken by the Fall. As a consequence of the movement and actuality of the Fall, alienation and estrangement penetrate the center of reality, as the primordial Totality becomes divided and alienated from itself. Nothing whatsoever stands apart from the "descending" and chaotic movement of the Fall, as every individual entity now stands out in a new solitude and isolation. For with the loss of an original unity, harmony or coherence, distance arises and creates every new experience, thus bringing about *a new and solitary selfhood which is its own individual center or ground. From a radical Christian perspective, we could say that God Himself is the primary embodiment of a solitary and isolated selfhood*. (my italics)[111]

Where this chapter has earlier discussed Gxd as carrying an internal autism of inner exile, Altizer's work here now discusses Gxd as isolated. This cosmic and divine isolation emanating from the Fall is an utter separation; in the language which I am using here, it is Absolute autism. The isolated Gxd is pure *autos:* Absolutely autistic, and the autistic Gxd is isolated. The isolation of Gxd is the autism of Gxd.

"It Is Finished"

As he dies, Jesus cries *telesthai!* (it is finished!) Can this be read within an autistic, Hegelian myth? Altizer writes:

---

111. Altizer, *Descent into Hell*, 183.

> A fully self-actualized presence can only be total presence, and a presence in which speech and silence are one. A total speech must also and necessarily be a total silence . . . such silence speaks . . . insofar as presence is actually absent, or inasmuch as absence is actually present.[112]

This is an apocalyptic speech which is, to say, a revealed (paradoxical) divine speech; where the All is realized in the total presence of total absence. The All is real presence—it is total presence—and yet what is the "where?" There is no heaven which would be separate from the All—what could be separate from the All? Total presence is everywhere and nowhere, and yet it is "here"—it is an actual presence and *the* actual Presence. Yet, we cannot "grasp hold of" totality or total presence. So total presence is also total absence.

This language employed by Altizer is, indeed, utter paradox, echoing the apophatic fiction discussed in chapter 3, and it is the paradox of the *coincidentia oppositorum* (the meeting of opposites in unity) of presence and absence, silence and speech, which is the apocalyptic fulfilment of the death of Gxd in the Incarnation of Christ Crucified. It is profoundly Christological; an utter immanence of the Incarnation really does mean that Christ is "all in all."[113] Jesus is Savior in the sense of being thus the total presence which not only dies but in so doing, in this absence which is self-silencing, completes the self-realization of All: "*It is finished*" truly means "it is completed."[114] Now, we can see the cosmic dimension of salvation. Where there has been the Fall from a

---

112. Altizer, *Self-Embodiment of God*, 91, 89.

113. Col 3:11.

114. The Greek word in the New Testament is *telesthai!* (it is finished/complete!) with the sense of an ending as a completion (we could think of Hegel's *telos*).

primordial Plenum (which we cannot have known) into the particularity of the transcendent Gxd as actor in salvation history, the cosmic reversal of this Fall is the death of the dualism of the transcendent Gxd and humanity, and the gathering of all in fullness. As the All, it is silence which speaks in its being. It is the completion of Christ's total Incarnation. Rather than the book of Revelation's mythical "four horsemen of the apocalypse" vision (although a gxdless world is, perhaps, a world of the darkness which these mythical horsemen bring[115]), this apocalyptic[116] consummation is a poetic enactment of the fullness and completion ("*It is finished*") of Christ as something we can enter existentially in faith: Altizer concludes that "as we hear and enact that impossibility, then even we can say 'it is finished.'"[117]

Faith enables us to speak by enacting this fullness, in living the sacrament of the death of Gxd in faith. The gospel saying "*I am the door*," can be seen differently as "*The door is I*" where Christ is pure subject—a universal "I." This completes the impossible possibility of the All and the Nothing as a *coincidentia oppositorum* in apocalyptic fulfilment:

> All self-identity is realized in this act: "The door is I."
> "The door is I" when "I am the door." Yet this is a door leading to nowhere . . . presence loses itself as presence . . . "I am the door" only when "The door is I."[118]

This is the total immanence of Jesus, *Geist,* in us— *we really do have that authenticity of subjectivity* if we can take hold of it. Why is this important for an autistic

---

115. See Rev 6.
116. *Apokalypsis* (Greek) means revelation.
117. Altizer, *Self-Embodiment of God*, 96.
118. Altizer, *Self-Embodiment of God*, 88.

reading? Simply because when "the door is I," this is the total *autos* (auto-nomy, authenticity) of our self as pure subject, in kenotic Christianity as a wager of faith. The door is I when I, present only to myself, in my own authentic (and autistic) choice, independent of you, realize presence as the absolute subject's act of faith.

> **This is why faith as conscious autism is the ultimately impossible demand as our Mindfulness of Separation; our absolute unknowing. The call to autistic discipleship means forsaking all and following Christ, where the all we let go of is all we know. It is, of course, impossible — again, we must remind ourselves of the pitfall of experientialism. We are not angels, and we need to keep our feet on the ground. Yet, as the saints and mystics devote themselves to this faith, is there not a certain autism of sainthood?**

In terms of an apocalyptic gospel, which is completed in Jesus,[119] what is the consummation which would be a fullness of autism come of age? What is the Autistic Gxd? The autistic Gxd is silence. The autistic Gxd is silent speech. This is beyond the "garrulousness"[120] of religion. In degrees of fascination almost exceeding speech, the garrulous autist speaks obsessively about her special interest, but no-one listens, because no-one can tolerate it by entering that obsessive world. She can only, finally, retreat into that world of solitary fascination — and yet, as we have abundantly seen, this is a joy and fulfilment few others can comprehend. In more "impaired," non-verbal, profound (or, in mythic terms, more profoundly self-validating) autism, "chatter" is forsaken because deeper fascination in deeper isolation is the deeper silence.

---

119. The title "Christ" holding messianic overtones is rejected by Altizer.
120. Altizer, *Self-Embodiment of God*, 3.

The Autistic Gxd is the fulfilment of absence (I have accepted my fundamental separation from you, become absent from you, and passed into a silence of pure presence). The Autistic Gxd has ceased to speak, because by being all in all (total presence) the Autistic Gxd is beyond all words and images. The Autistic Gxd, ultimately, communicates so fully, paradoxically, that Gxd does not communicate beyond silent speech. Furthermore, Gxd is not simply autistic but is actually autism itself. Gxd is that silence which is beyond words (not less than, but more than). If the Gxd of Totality is absolute Mindfulness of Separation—pure autism—then pure autism—its silence—is Gxd. Here, again, it is vital to recall that we are not discussing autistic people with a (relative) autism but the myth of an absolute quality of pure autism. Pure or absolute autism, as the introduction made clear, does not exist. But neither does Totality—as total Being, how can it have being?[121] How can we, as fish, find that object which is the ocean? Heidegger would understand this as ontological difference, and Tillich would understand it as the Unconditioned.

Yet, the Autistic Gxd is also speech, but a silent speech. This moves us into the presence which is Autistic Fascination. The Autistic Gxd is that pure, wordless presence which holds the autist in the unity of Absolute fascination; the union of seer and seen holds the autist within the world of the sensory, or obsessive, object of love. This is the sensory connoisseur's incomprehensible joy, where Gunilla Gerland takes refuge in the texture of the brown armchair,[122] and the way in which Katie Bridges

---

121. Recalling Tillich.

122. Gunilla "found the place to be left in peace—behind the armchair, where she was able to shut out everything and simply be—absorbed in the material of the brown armchair" (Bogdashina, *Autism and Spirituality*, 191).

can "stare at a drawing of a futuristic city all day long"[123] in rapt fascination. This is the solitary genius who, in Autistic Fascination, immerses herself in mathematical formulae in sheer delight, revealing answers to the world. As the autist Christopher, in Mark Haddon's *The Curious Incident of the Dog in the Night-Time* aces his math exams, he asks us "Now I can do anything, can't I?" And the answer is, absolutely yes—and absolutely no.

Is this union an ecstasy? People frequently say that the sensory or the obsessive are the autist's "escape from the world," (ex-stasis = away from the equilibrium of being) but fascination is more than this, it is excessive joy (ex-stasis = ecstasy). Autistic Fascination is a separation from the world which leads into the ecstasy of joy. The outpouring of the garrulous autist is the attempted return into language, from the pure joy of the communion within the sensory and the obsessive which are Autistic Fascination. This is akin to doxological language's attempted return into language from that which cannot be spoken. Yet the object of fascination speaks to the autist in silence,[124] more powerfully than anything the words of the neurotypical world can offer. This is a kind of presence unlike anything in the neurotypical world.

The Autistic Gxd, then, is the object of fascination, and the Autistic Gxd also embodies fascination. In this very particular sense, chapter 3 demonstrated Teresa of Àvila to be fascinated by Gxd. Her fascination, beyond words, requires the non-language of the non-being of apophatic fiction, which is Incarnational metaphor. So, is the Autistic Gxd also fascination itself? Is Gxd fascinated?

---

123. Bridges, "Special Interests."

124. Recalling the autist Leneh K. Buckle's words that she was happier before she could speak ("Is Increasing Functionality Always Good?" in *Autism, Ethics and the Good Life*).

Fascination is not only aesthetics, but also passion and love. The language of the moment of Absolute, Autistic Fascination is a mythic language of the holy. So Gxd might not merely be *in* that moment, but actually *be* it.

In Altizer's thought, the Incarnation as the utter *kenosis* of Gxd is love, and not merely the love *of* or *from* a transcendent Gxdhead but the pure embodiment of love itself. So Jesus is ubiquitously and anonymously present,[125] and ultimately, it is Blake's poetic vision, not theology, which can be an articulation of it.[126] This embodiment is profane—utterly immanent and therefore secular—and yet, as Blake would argue, also holy. It is the embodiment of the sacred profane. The Autistic Gxd's love is the expression of love which is realized in death. This is the acceptance of the death of all the "normal" (neurotypical) comforts of interaction, and yet remains love as fascination.

> **Gxd's love is fascination, in the sense of being completely immanent, just as Autistic Fascination is an inner and immanent experience, "in a world of her own." The Autistic Gxd of Love is fascinated by the All in which Gxdself is embodied, and this All is Gxd. Gxd is fascinated by Gxd's own self and in love with All, as that Self.**

Gxd, the embodied presence which is the active, present *Geist*, is the fascination inherent in the dialectical development of both creativity and the history of ideas, so that the process of pure idea is the immanence of Gxd as Idea in history. In our mythology of autism, the creative thinking generating this process of idea happens in a

---

125. Drawing on Blake's idea of Jesus as Universal Humanity; see Altizer, *Gospel of Christian Atheism*, 69.

126. See Altizer, *New Apocalypse* (his study of William Blake); also reading Nietzsche's aphorisms as poetry, so that the "three prophets," Blake, Nietzsche, and Hegel, are read poetically with Scripture to form a mythic, existential telling of the gospel.

space of autistic separation. Thinking of universal autism as Baron-Cohen's all-pervading autistic spectrum, might we even dare to say (following the psychiatrist Michael Fitzgerald's concept of autistic "genius genes" by implication) that there is a speck of autism gleaming through all humanity and history? Paradoxically, the separation of the thinker creates the immanence of the independent thought. This is an autistic archetype, of the "odd but brilliant" autist, in Baron-Cohen's work, and Fitzgerald's *The Genesis of Artistic Creativity*.[127]

The Silence of Jahweh

What is at stake here is an apocalyptic silence. The autistic Gxd is absolute autism and hence absolute silence. As the absolute isolation of the dead transcendent God, the Autistic Gxd is absent. Furthermore, the inner exile of Gxdself means that Gxd is isolated even from Gxdself. This isolation is so utter that there can be no speech, other than authentic silent speech. Yet, thinking of the Gxd we have killed, do we not also have a silenced Gxd, struck dumb in order to become what Eiesland calls the Disabled God? True, the Gxd of exile speaks in revelation, but this is, in the critic Eric Auerbach's terms, the alien speech of Yahweh.[128] Briefly put, Auerbach argues that there is a contrast between the style and registers of Greek and Hebrew canonical story. With the Greek story of Odysseus, *the Odyssey*, the story is full of foregrounding details which give a sense of place and context. By contrast, Auerbach looks at the biblical narrative in a way which is obvious

---

127. See Baron-Cohen and Craig, "Creativity and Imagination"; and Fitzgerald, *Genesis of Artistic Creativity*.

128. See Auerbach, *Mimesis*, in particular his chapter "Odysseus' Scar" on the Hebraic versus Homeric literary world views.

to us as soon as we consider it as story—there is almost no context, no small, everyday details, to set the scene. Auerbach sees this as a Yahweh who speaks, starkly, from a void, and it is this which he calls the alien voice of Yahweh. There is still more alienation as the biblical prophets speak, repeatedly; and almost without exception, nobody listens. Jesus himself tells us that "a prophet is never heeded in his own land."[129] In terms of Yahweh's inner exile as alienation, it is as if this fissure widens and widens—Israel itself is cast out into captivity and a new exile.[130] The fissure widens still more, until Christ bursts it open in His death which is the consummation of Gxd's absence, and yet, simultaneously, it releases a new presence which is, as we have seen, present in, and as, absence. The Gxd in exile cannot even "talk to Gxdself." The Autistic Gxd is silence, a silence which grows with an increasing degree of autism manifesting until, in the Crucifixion, there is the Autistic Gxd's total silence; Jesus cries *"My God, my God, why have you forsaken me?"* and there is no answer. This is, as Blanchot expresses it, the place where "There can be no answer to that question. The poem is the answer's absence."[131]

"I am the door" when "the door is I." This is a door leading to nowhere; an entry into silence but yet speaking in the apocalyptic *coincidentia oppositorum* of silence and speech, absence and presence. Christ's ministry in the gospels is speech, but it is a silence where he speaks in parables so that no-one can understand him.[132]

---

129. In all four canonical Gospels: Matt 13:57; Mark 6:4; Luke 4:24; and John 4:44; see also Jer 26:5, which he is echoing.

130. In the Babylonian and Assyrian empires (as recounted in the books of I Chronicles, II Kings, and Ezra).

131. Blanchot, *Space of Literature*, 248.

132. "Many therefore of his disciples, when they had heard this, said, This is a hard saying; *who can hear it?*" (John 6:60).

Understanding is only possible in devotion to the enactment of the Beatitudes—as a friend told me, "don't understand it in order to do it—do it in order to understand it." (In the Last Supper, after all, we hear Jesus' words, "*Do this in memory of me.*") The ministry of Christ now is silent and anonymous, where faith becomes the acts of Jesus absolutely "in His absence." Yet the silent speech and total presence of Christ can be figured in the holy space of the Autistic Fascination of Gxd, and it is a space of love and joy. Joy, even in our hells, which is a mystery of faith. Fascination in Mindfulness of Separation—that strange joy "in a world of our own"; pure subjective, existential faith, precisely as the auto-nomous subjectivity of *autos*.

Full Incarnational Metaphor

Our goal all along has been the Autism of Gxd as an atheological love story; and this is realized inseparably in the facets of the autistic mythical trinity. As myth, it works by means of a fully realized Incarnational metaphor. We can now express Incarnational metaphor in the light of the autism of Gxd, as the total love we enact in the Eucharist. The speech of the self-embodiment of Gxd becomes the embodiment of Gxd, thought at the deepest level, the level where Altizer, also, has been aiming all along—the self-embodiment of Gxd in Eucharist. There is, in the sacred profane, a poetic Eucharist of the epic. In Altizer's tapestry of myth, he sees this Eucharist enacted in epics such as Melville's *Moby Dick*, where Gxd escapes us and ultimately overwhelms us, as the great white whale; or in James Joyce's irreverent Catholic word-games in *Finnegan's Wake*.[133] However, the epic poem itself of *The*

---

133. Biblical narrative as epic, but also the sacred profane of Joyce, for example, in *Finnegan's Wake*, or in Melville's *Moby Dick*, as Modernism is the enactment of the death of Gxd (see Altizer, *Gospel of Christian Atheism*, chapter 1).

Self-Embodiment of Gxd culminates in the most sacred moment, the consummation of the death of Christ. Here, at its deepest level, it is sacred speech which embodies that consummation, and so it is the voice of Christ who pronounces "It is finished*.*" Altizer writes of this as "the impossible possibility" which is the actual death of Gxd and the moment of Christ's total entry into world, death and hell. This is the realization of total absence *(*"My God, my God, why hast Thou forsaken me?"*)* and total presence (it is the fullness of the transcendent Gxd who dies in the Crucifixion). As such it is a totality, and ultimately the pure speech of Gxd. Altizer conveys the utter holiness of this moment as divine consummation, and that consummation as the sacrificial emptying which is divine love. It is divine perfection and the mystical paradox of the self-emptying and self-embodiment of Gxd; it is both the death of Gxd and the life of Jesus, a Jesus who is the embodiment of the death of Gxd. Therefore Jesus can truly say, "It is finished," in New Testament Greek the cry *telesthai!* which is a cry of victory that "it is completed." Does it end there? Of course, the answer is yes, but it is also no. Altizer asks whether we can enact this moment by hearing this silence. The answer is the hearing which is the embodiment of grace:

> The otherness of silence disappears and is reversed when silence is fully actual and immediate in its presence. Such silence is grace, the one grace that is possible in actual presence, and it is a grace that is everywhere in the actuality of total presence; indeed, only when voice passes into silence.[134]

This is what language can approach, but ultimately only express in a non-language in mysticism. It is only at

---

134. Altizer, *Self-Embodiment of God*, 95.

the finishing of language, and it is enacted again and again in the testimony of the mystics who articulate it as a finality of language which, being beyond language, is beyond time and participates in the "once for all" event of silence:

> Even if it happened fully and finally only once, it occurs again and again, and once again occurs even now because of the finality of that once and for all event. And it does occur even now, and even occurs to us, and occurs when we say "It is finished."[135]

It is also the enactment of the Eucharist of "Living the Death of Gxd," in faith, as Altizer has expressed in his memoir of that title. The enactment of the death of Gxd happens in the outpouring of the Spirit of Jesus. For us, also, there can be an enactment in our lives through mindfulness of the mystery implicit in the "impossible possibility" which is embodied in the Eucharist's deepest meaning.

In the end, Incarnational metaphor embodies, and is the essential means, for us, for all this myth to manifest itself. Incarnational metaphor is a Eucharistic language where literal-mindedness speaks as silence, because in "it is finished," language is finished. Chapter 2 indicated the possibility of Incarnational metaphor as the doxological religious language of excess which Ramsey describes. It also demonstrated the post-Cartesian language of deconstructive theology which discerns the gaps inherent in language, so that metaphor does not "do," but "is." Chapter 3 suggested that Incarnational metaphor could be thought of in terms of apophatic fiction which can indicate, but not touch, its object. Now, an atheological thinking of metaphor as the autistic death of Gxd means that to say "It is finished" in Eucharistic enactment is language where metaphor is incarnate by meaning "nothing."

---

135. Altizer, *Self-Embodiment of God*, 95.

> **This is a nothing which is everything. An absolute Incarnational metaphor of absolute autism is silence, the silence of *kenosis*, the absolute absence and absolute presence of Gxd when "It is finished."**

As holy autists, we mythically enact the deeds of the Great Hero as we come to the poetic Eucharist, an autistic Eucharist in which we partake through faith in the Autism of Gxd.

Chapter Five

The Autism of Poetry

This particular tree will give glory to God by spreading out its roots in the earth and raising its branches into the air and the light, in a way that no other tree before or after ever did or will do.

—Thomas Merton, *New Seeds of Contemplation*[1]

SOMETHING FAR MORE DEEPLY INTERFUSED

> And I have felt
> A presence that disturbs me with the joy
> Of elevated thoughts; a sense sublime
> Of something far more deeply interfused,
> Whose dwelling is the light of setting suns,
> And the round ocean and the living air,
> And the blue sky, and in the mind of man[2]

Why write this chapter if chapter 4 has already brought us to the completion of the Autism of Gxd? Wordsworth, in

---

1. Merton, *New Seeds of Contemplation*, 29.
2. Wordsworth, "Lines Composed a Few Miles Above Tintern Abbey," in *Works of William Wordsworth*, 207.

the above lines, tells us why. In strictly positivist research-language terms, we could refer to this chapter as a test case; but, thinking theologically and poetically, we could better call it an enactment. We think of Jesus telling us of the sacrament, "*Do this* in memory of me," and we recall how, in the previous chapter, we noted Altizer saying that Jesus' words, "It is finished" (completed) are completed in us *when we can enact* those words in a poetic Eucharist. Thus, we are going to enact a theo-poetic fascination of poetry in this chapter.

The twentieth-century monk and mystic, Thomas Merton writes:

> A tree gives glory to God by being a tree. For in being what God means it to be it is obeying Him. It "consents," so to speak, to His creative love. It is expressing an idea which is in God and which is not distinct from the essence of God, and therefore a tree imitates God by being a tree.
>
> The more a tree is like itself, the more it is like Him. If it tried to be like something else which it was never intended to be, it would be less like God and therefore give Him less glory.
>
> No two created beings are exactly alike. And their individuality is no imperfection. On the contrary, the perfection of each created thing is not merely its conformity to an abstract type but in its own individual identity with itself. This particular tree will give glory to God by spreading out its roots in the earth and raising its branches into the air and the light in a way that no other tree before or after ever did or will do.[3]

Before we even begin, we can surely discern here something of glory for the autistic reader (and many others); I am created to be myself, *exactly as I am*, and this

---

3. Merton, *New Seeds of Contemplation*, 29.

is not only acceptable but perfect, and beautiful in its uniqueness. My unique autistic self is perfect and glorious, created to be like Gxd by being my deepest and truest self.

However, we can go deeper still, for a mythical autism, by looking for a *theological* telling of this glory. We could say that Merton is giving a poetic expression of a Medieval concept which the theologian-philosopher John Duns Scotus termed *haecceitas*. In this chapter, we will explore why this is a hospitable place for mythical autism. Simply put, *haecceitas* means "thisness"—the sacred identity of one leaf on one tree, even if there are umpteen millions which are, to all intents and purposes, identical—each is imbued with its own *haecceitas*. We will be looking for *haecceitas* in poetry, and exploring whether poetry seen this way might contain an inner autism. This chapter will delve into poetry and discuss the surprising thought that autism could be seen in its essence. We are not speaking about the autism of poets, but of something inner, the autism of Gxd as the autism of poetry.

REPRISE

> It wasn't so much a garden as a corner of wilderness on the hillside and, each inch of it, the beech, the sycamore, the brambles, wild raspberries, gorse. . . all had a sense of sanctity or, in her childish mind, magic. One spot was particularly imbued with strong magic, and for sure the fairies lived there. Under a silver birch tree there was a shady hollow of moss, and this little dimple in the hillside held a strong magic. From the kitchen she stole a piece of bread, broke it into crumbs, and left it there. Had she known more, she might also have stolen a thimbleful of wine too. In

the morning, no doubt the foxes had eaten it, but for her there was no doubt. The fairies had accepted her offering.

For her eighth birthday, she was surprised with an exquisite cake in the shape of a house—perhaps her mother ordered it from a baker's shop but equally possibly, she could have constructed and decorated the little house herself. It was delicious, but far too big for the small gathering around her as she blew out the candles, and the remainder of it went into a large cake tin. In the days after the little birthday party, it seemed too special—sacred—just to eat casually, and perhaps her busy mother forgot about it. The girl finally, one day, decided to sneak a slice for herself as a post-birthday treat. The opened the tin, and the cake was decorated with tufts of spotty black mold and fernlike blue mold. She shut the tin quickly. It was her first real sense of the demonic.

My sacred places—what the Celts call thin places, where the dividing line between heaven and earth is narrowed—they are unmistakable. Clava Cairns, Machrie Moor, the little lochan on Dava Moor, the ruined motte above Holm Burn. There must be so many more out there, which I'll discover when heaven reveals all splendor.

GARDEN SWING
for Alice Walker

Swing swing swing swing
Creak creak swing swing
Language of a little girl
In her secluded little garden
On her swing swing swing

A thrush begins to sing, swing swing
A fragile dusk
As lucid as green glass, swing swing
A silent bubble in confusion

> Then cathedral bells
> Ring out for miles
> Until the dark
> And cold begin
> Swing swing
>
> One day I will look back
> And tell her she was right
> Crying for beauty and failing light[4]

I couldn't resist putting in these examples of my own (unique) autistic self here, to illustrate my relation to *haecceitas*. No doubt many readers will relate to the belief of the child in magic, or even an invisible friend or two—childhood, as Wordsworth knows well, is a time of awe; perhaps even where humans are closest to the simplicity of the divine. Certain readers, perhaps not so few, will relate to the sense of the thin places where heaven and earth seem somehow to converge, almost. Not for nothing are many, otherwise "rational," people, content when pressed to confess that they experience a sense of the divine in the hills or in the woods, regardless of whether they consider themselves religious.

We have earlier quoted Wordsworth's "Lines Written a Few Miles above Tintern Abbey," and the key phrase for us is "something far more deeply interfused," what Wordsworth, as a thinker of the divine, glimpses in nature.

---

4. Dunster, *Garden Swing*, Nomad 9, p.10

> What I want to explore in this chapter is the possibility that the overwhelming sense of awe and communion which, as adults, we may have lost, or sidelined, can be conceptualized as an enduring reality in autism. One might even argue that these moments of grace might be the streak of autism, tiny or considerable, which lies in all of us, on the universal autistic spectrum. We might also, even, say in this sense, that poetry can perfectly well be understood as autistic fascination.

Firstly, we will stay within theological thinking, and then, secondly, see how a sacred quality might be discerned in poetry. Turning, thirdly, to autism, we will construct an autistically thought conceptual framework for this phenomenon. We will see how it hinges on Alistair Clarkson's narrative of the Sensory Connoisseur, which was discussed in the Introduction. From there, we will explore how this might manifest itself in myth as a pure essence of autism, an absolute connoisseurship, which is seen to relate in resonance and companionship, communion, even, as it comes to the work of art and rejoices. Lastly, we will then be in a position to test this theory of an autism of poetry as we read the work of the poet-priest Gerard Manley Hopkins.

WHAT IS HAECCEITAS?

Thomas Aquinas and John Duns Scotus

To begin our theological thinking, we will first explore the word introduced earlier in this chapter, *haecceitas.* In order to discern the autism of poetry as the autism of Gxd, we will do well to unpick this word *haecceitas* and explore its theological meaning. Before we look at its origins, we must acknowledge that Scotus was not the sole creator of this way of thinking; the Buddhist word, *tathātā*, translates best as "thisness," and soon after Scotus, the Dutch mystic Meister Eckhart also appropriated "thisness" as part of his, almost atheological, mystical theology. For more on Meister Eckhart and his similarity to Scotus, the theologian Bernard McGinn has given an excellent lecture, which may be of interest.[5] Our focus, however, is the Scottish theologian Duns Scotus, who laid the groundwork for "thisness" in a philosophical-theological sense (the two were, in Christendom, at that time, in many ways simply one discipline).

To put this in context, in the early thirteenth century a pivotal discovery was made, which will help us understand that the Middle Ages were not perhaps such benighted and pre-rational times as people sometimes assume. The Greek works of Aristotle and Plato had been lost to the Western world. However, unknown to Christendom, some important texts of their work had survived in the Islamic world and had been translated into Arabic. It was not until these works were translated from Arabic into Latin by Islamic scholars that they were suddenly made available to scholars in the West. They were seen ambivalently as an exciting source of insight but also a potentially dangerous threat to Christian beliefs, and Christian scholars studied and responded, particularly, to Aristotle. Most influentially, the Dominican theologian-philosopher Thomas Aquinas took Aristotle's philosophical understanding of the divine and translated it into Christian terms. This, as we shall see, contrasted with the thinking of the Franciscan theologian philosopher John Duns Scotus, who responded differently to Aristotle and developed the term *haecceitas*.

The pagan Aristotle's approach to what we would call theology is to consider in what ways human language can

---

5. McGinn, "Mystical Language."

talk about the Absolute Other. He concludes that this Being must be so utterly different to human understanding that our feeble words must in that context carry a meaning utterly different to their normal meaning. Aristotle calls this the analogical method. No matter which words we use to describe Gxd, they can only be an analogy of what we are seeking to describe. Thomas Aquinas follows Aristotle's reasoning and brings analogical thinking into Christian philosophy-theology.

In contrast to this, Duns Scotus argues that language, in some terms at least, can be used for the divine and the human in exactly the same way, so that language is one, and so human and divine being can both, to some extent, partake in one linguistic world. The term for this is univocity (one voice). In his dense, highly analytical style, Scotus writes:

> Univocity: Notwithstanding the irreducible ontological diversity between God and creatures, there are concepts under whose extension both God and creatures fall, so that the corresponding predicate expressions are used with exactly the same sense in predications about God as in predications about creatures.[6]

At first sight, reading it closely, this seems to negate all that we have until now said about the inadequacy of human language to describe Gxd; and yet, we have seen in apophatic fiction and the myth of the death of Gxd that there *are* certain ways in which we can speak of Gxd. For Scotus, one way is for language to be sacramental. Scotus follows the earlier scholar Hugh de Victor in developing a concept of sacramental participation. So, Denys Turner writes that "truly, for Hugh, the sacramentality of things

---

6. Scotus, *Ordinatio*, 1, d. 3, pars 1, q. 3, n. 163, quoted in Williams, *Cambridge Companion to Duns Scotus*, 578.

is universal."[7] The difference between sacrament and symbol is conflated into one, however, so that Turner can write that, for de Victor, "all nature, all history and all Scripture are, within the dispensation of grace, a complex of symbolic representations of the divine, a universe whose reality is sacramental."[8]

That being said, we must be careful to observe that, for Scotus, univocity is a union in predicative terms, not ontological terms. That is, we have union and identity with Gxd in our language and concepts, not in our being/Being. Sacrament and symbol operate in such a way that, at least in some senses, human language is not separated from divine language, but language is one. This union at the level of language opens up the possibility of what the theologian Mary Beth Ingham calls a "Franciscan optimism" of language (this takes us back to the *naïf optimism* of Francis of Assisi, the founder of Scotus' Franciscan monastic order; perhaps even of the (far from *naïf*) reforms of Pope Francis in the twenty-first century, although he is not himself a Franciscan). We have the hope that our language really "works" when we describe Gxd. Again, this might seem the very opposite of our discussion of the autism of Gxd as silence and utterly other and isolated. However, the crucial point here is that, for our approach, univocity taps into what we have called the presence-in-absence of Gxd; in other words, fascination. More than this, we can recall our concept of apophatic fiction as a strategy where language can indeed describe the indescribable. This is poetry.

---

7. Turner, *Darkness of God*, 106.
8. Turner, *Darkness of God*, 107.

Quidditas and Haecceitas

In this context of univocity, we can now see what *haecceitas* truly means in its full context. Aquinas followed Aristotle in a concept still used in Western philosophy; in Latin, it was *quidditas,* which we translate as quiddity or "thatness." This is a philosophical mode of describing individual objects in order to define them.

Aquinas stays within the Aristotelian predication (linguistic attribution) of individuation in the use of analogy in his philosophy. In his metaphysics, the individuation of an object is *quid-itas* (that-ness), amenable to classification and definition in the hierarchy of being. In other words, we look at objects in the natural world and we can capture them, so to speak, with a description of their physical properties. This is the work that language does to describe the individual object; this is an adequate and logical individuation. We can classify objects through their properties.

We can now see why, in radical opposition, Scotus coined the term *haecceitas.* Where Thomist (i.e., of Thomas Aquinas) individuation, *quid-ditas* is "that-ness," Scotist individuation is *"haecc-eitas"* (this-ness). This, like univocity, is utter theological optimism. This is the *thisness* of a particular and unrepeatable individual, captured not as *that* but as *this*. It is unrepeatable because it does not depend upon a quiddity which could be replicated. *"This"* is the valued creature of the individual sparrow, when Jesus tells us that "not one of which falls without your Father knowing."[9] *Quidditas* belongs to being and matter according to material properties. *Haecceitas* hangs freely in what Scotus daringly calls less than numerical unity. *Haecceitas*

---

9. Matt 10:19.

is the non-quantitative nature of the individual. Scotus writes:

> Anything with a real, proper, and sufficient unity less than numerical is not of itself one by numerical unity — that is, it is not of itself a *this*. But the proper, real or sufficient unity of the nature existing in this stone is less than numerical unity. Therefore the nature existing in this stone is not of itself one by numerical unity.[10]

We could interpret this, perhaps, by saying that the *haecceitas* of the sparrow is a non-material quality. We could think of quantum particles which lack the property of physical mass; we could think of the theology of angels as beings of pure energy without physical reality so that the question of how many angels can sit on a pinhead yields the incredible answer that both an infinity of angels can, or, thought differently, none can; we could think of the wave/particle enigma of quantum physics.

For Aristotle, and, following him, Thomas Aquinas, Gxd is the ultimate cause behind the entire chain of cause and effect — of all causality. This Gxd is the force which causes all movement, the Cause beyond all causality, infinitely removed; the Prime Mover. In contrast, Mary Beth Ingham's incisive reading of Scotus gives us a creation celebrated in Franciscan love, which is Gxd's handiwork. Gxd is artist, and creation is the artwork.[11] Where Aquinas' Dominican metaphysics of analogy could be read as the pessimism of alienation from the Prime Mover as distant Creator, Scotus' Franciscan optimism sees the world as a creative poetry written by Gxd, and able to be

---

10. Scotus, *Ordinatio* II, d. 2, p. 1, q. 1, n. 8 7: reproduced in Williams 395.

11. Scotus is writing as a Franciscan, not long after the order's inception. "God as artist" can be seen in terms of Francis' love of animals as part of the created order (also preaching to the fishes) and in his famous canticle to brother sun and sister moon, where Francis himself is also the artist, as the poem's author.

read directly as such in sacramental poetic participation. Univocity is the metaphysics of this audacious theological claim. If Scotus' *haecceitas* appears perhaps to slide from linguistics to ontology, we must remember that

> **in our thinking of Gxd as the Poet who creates the spiritual poem of the world, this is really all about language. Language, poetically thought, could indeed be more than ontological Being.**

We have considered earlier how, for Heidegger, poetry might outwit ontological difference. This inverts the hierarchy of language and material reality—coming back to the very beginning, this is the deep truth-telling of myth, although Scotus would not have seen it that way.

Now, can we mythically equate Autistic Fascination with *haecceitas*? Recall that we are dealing with language. Could a *haecceitas* of poetic language be, in the light of our mythical autistic hermeneutic, Autistic Fascination? The way we will test out this hypothesis is to have a test case, of a poet who would be utterly in sympathy with Thomas Merton's description of the sacred individual tree where we began this chapter. This is the poet-priest Gerard Manley Hopkins. First, however, it will be helpful to think through the poetic potential of the autistic Sensory Connoisseur concept.

THE AUTISTIC SENSORY CONNOISSEUR IN POETRY

In the "Our Approach to Autism: A Beginner's Guide" section in the Introduction, we encountered the Sensory Connoisseur model of autism put forward by Alastair Clarkson. To recap, the Sensory Connoisseur is the autistic person whose attention to detail and responsiveness to the sensory means she has extraordinary powers of appreciation. As Francesca Happé puts it, and she is worth quoting again,

> Repetition is not repetition, for example, if you have expert levels of discrimination. Listening to different recordings of the same symphony might strike some as repetitive, but these sound entirely different to an expert. The child with autism who would happily spend hours spinning coins, or watching drops of water falling from his fingers, might be considered a connoisseur, seeing minute differences between events that others regard as pure repetition.[12]

Clarkson takes this understanding even further, in a radical way:

> Within discussion of an alternative view of "pure repetition" in ASD, let us try to think more expansively regarding what is "repetitive," by considering behaviour within the neurotypical world. Can we form an alternative behavioural view of the neurotypical person who typically watches television for many hours a day—a person who may sit every day staring at a flickering screen, displaying limited communication with others as a result? Or can we consider the over-anxious and neurotic house-cleaner, repeatedly cleaning away invisible dirt? A key question remains: "how far is our notion of 'repetitive' actually influenced by sociological value systems?"[13]

Can we see RRBIs[14] as an instantiation of *haecceitas*? This is not to suggest, of course, that autists are all Medieval theologian philosophers unawares. Rather, it is

---

12. Happé and Frith, *Autism and Talent*, xvi.
13. Clarkson, "Sensory Connoisseur," 11.
14. Restricted and Repetitive Behaviors and Interests (see "Our Approach to Autism" A Beginner's Guide").

to wonder whether, if Scotus had looked aright, today, he might not have seen something of sensory connoisseurship in his predicative theology of *haecceitas*.

> **Perhaps we can see the link to Autistic Fascination as Gxd's loving delight in the artwork of creation, which sidesteps pragmatic, ostensive language in a poetry of free flowing, unconditional love. This is a language of poetic being, which we will come to see as a kind of *haecceitas*.**

This is where a mythical Autistic Fascination of poetic faith can *be*, inhabiting metaphor only as the truly real, beyond quiddative being. By being excluded from quiddative being it more truly inhabits Being, and this, when it is read autistically, is the paradox of absolute autism existing as absence and presence. It hangs by a thread, impossibly.

GERARD MANLEY HOPKINS: ECCEITAS

In light of this possible poetic *haecceitas*, we might even dare to assert that it is the destination where autism already, intuitively is. The Sensory Connoisseur, in that case, possesses the "second naïveté" which we saw in Paul Ricœur's thought, so that, as we also suggested earlier, autism is privileged with an insight only hard-won by the neurotypical world, if at all. This, for our purposes, might apply powerfully when our mythical autism's fascination meets the poetic fascination of the English Victorian poet, Gerard Manley Hopkins. Hopkins was both a priest who was a poet, and a poet who was a priest—an uneasy tension in his life. However, his poetry is therefore informed by both poetic and theological sensibilities. For example, his epic poem *The Wreck of the Deutschland*, based on the true story of a group of nuns who die in a shipwreck, is a profound meditation on the nature of prayer and abandonment. We will largely be focusing on a sense of presence as Autistic Fascination, but it would be a mistake to think that Hopkins' work is an eternal sunshine of divine Presence in poetic form. Hopkins, the poet/priest, also knew despair and the darkness of Gxd in what are known as his "terrible sonnets," for example in "Carrion Comfort," where he describes "that night, that year / Of now done darkness I wretch lay wrestling with (my God!) my God."[15] He also, in "No worst, there is none," writes:

O the mind, mind has mountains; cliffs of fall / Frightful, sheer, not man-fathomed. Hold them cheap / May who ne'er hung there.[16]

This is truly a dark night of the soul; yet, just as we have seen with Teresa, there is much poetry of Presence, and this is where we will discern a theological thinking which reads in a strong sympathy with Autistic Fascination. What we want to do in this chapter, then, is to look for particular examples from his lyric poetry where we might discern a poetic *haecceitas;* which we could read, in our mythical autistic hermeneutic, as the autism of the poem. In this way, we can read through eyes which see, and celebrate, the glory of autism within the poem.

Hopkins and Scotus

The critic Carol T Christ comments on Hopkins' poet-priest identity, and argues that Hopkins' work flows from a theological source in his own quest for holistic integrity as poet-priest. She captures this poet-priest sensibility by describing how, in Hopkins' conception of Gxd, there is

---

15. Hopkins, "Carrion Comfort," in *Works of Gerard Manley Hopkins*, 62.
16. Hopkins, "No Worst, There Is None," In *Works of Gerard Manley Hopkins*, 62.

a divinely ordained poetics inherent in creation. She describes his view in this way:

> In the creation of the universe, God charges it with a rhyming capacity which enables man's imagination, his capacity of instress, to realize the divinely ordained instress of the world.[17]

The word "instress," meaning the poetic potential or essence of an object, is one of Hopkins' neologisms, and it is frequently used by him because it is crucial to his poetic vision. (His other neologism, "inscape," is very similar). Here we can note how theologically thought this poetics is: instress is a "rhyming capacity" not only as realized in "man's [sic] imagination," but also as something with which creation is "charged" by divine creation and ordination. Instress is thought of simultaneously as theological and poetic. The critic F R Leavis writes that Hopkins has a "habit of seeing things as charged with significance," so that this significance is "not a romantic vagueness, but a matter of explicit and ordered conceptions regarding the relations between God, man and nature."[18]

However, instress as both theological and poetic might also, perhaps, mean that poetic vocation might be what leads him into danger of straying from doctrinal orthodoxy. Martin Dubois speculates on Hopkins' attraction toward Scotus as "(an) opposition to the dominant mode of Catholic theology at the time, a rigidified Thomism which ran contrary to Hopkins' instinct for discerning God's animating touch in nature's diversity as in human uniqueness . . . the world is charged with the grandeur of God."[19] This argument for an attraction for Scotism might

---

17. Christ, *Victorian and Modern Poetics*, 70.
18. Leavis, *Common Pursuit*, 512, quoted in Dubois, "Hopkins' Beauty," 549.
19. Dubois, "Hopkins' Beauty," 552.

be seen in a reading of Hopkins' *Duns Scotus' Oxford,* and how it expresses a deep appreciation of Scotus, even approaching veneration:

> Towery city and branchy between towers:
> Cuckoo-echoing, bell-swarmèd, lark-charmèd, rook-
>   racked, river-rounded;
> The Dapple-eared lily below there; that country and town did
> Once encounter in, here coped and poised powers;
>
> The hast a base and brackish skirt there, sours
> That neighbour-nature thy grey beauty is grounded
> Best in; graceless growth, thou hast confounded
> Rural keeping-folk, flocks, and flowers.
> Yet ah! This air I gather and I release
> He lived on; these weeds and waters, these walls are what
> He haunted who of all men most sways my spirits to peace;
>
> Of realty the rarest-veinèd traveller; a not
> Rivalled insight, be rival Italy or Greece;
> Who fired France for Mary without spot.[20]

This is a richly crafted sonnet, using the rhetorical devices which characterize much of Hopkins' work when he is most lyrical; alliteration, enjambement, sprung rhythm, inversion, the crafted sonnet rhyme scheme, and densely packed imagery. This is a powerful admiration of Scotus. One could suspect that by being in sympathy with Scotism over against Thomism, Hopkins, a Jesuit not a Franciscan, is courting theological "eccentricity."[21] There is also a very

---

20. Hopkins, *Poems of Gerard Manley Hopkins,* 40.

21. On the contemporary Catholic theological context: "Decisive support for (the revival of Thomist thought) came with Pope Leo XIII's encyclical *Aeterni Patris* (1879; "Eternal Father"). . . . Leo asked especially for a recovery of the wisdom of Aquinas, whom he hailed as 'the special bulwark and glory of the Catholic Faith.' . . . In 1880 Leo made Aquinas patron of all Roman Catholic schools. The code of canon law of 1917, the official compilation of church law, required that Catholic teachers of philosophy

real sense of wonder in the journal entry where he names Scotus as the source of a possible "mercy from God":

> After the examinations we went for our holiday out to Douglas in the Isle of Man . . . At this time I had first begun to get hold of the copy of Scotus on the Sentences in the Baddely library and was flush with a new stroke of enthusiasm. It may come to nothing or it may be a mercy from God. But just then when I took in any inscape of the sky or sea I thought of Scotus.[22]

If inscape is here thought of as somehow linked to Scotus as a "mercy from God," could it be considered as a theological-poetic possibility which might, even, lead to a concept of poetic *haecceitas*?

Hopkins Poetic Technique: An Embodiment

We could consider whether instress and inscape have a flavor of *haecceitas*. In his notebooks, examples of the term inscape are prolific. Two examples suffice:

> May 11, 1871—It was a lovely sight—The bluebells in your hand baffle you with their inscape, made to every sense: if you draw your fingers through them they are lodged and struggle with a shock of wet heads . . . then there is the faint honey smell[23]

> April 8, 1873—The ashtree growing in the corner of the garden was felled . . . looking out and seeing it maimed there came at that moment a great pang and I wished to die and not to see the inscapes of the world destroyed any more.[24]

---

and religion follow the method and principles of Aquinas. This established Thomism as the official philosophy of the Roman Catholic Church" (O'Meara, "Thomism").

22. "Journal, June 29–August 3, 1872," in Hopkins, *Journals and Papers*, 162.
23. "Journal, May 11, 1871," in Hopkins, *Journals and Papers*, 145.
24. "Journal, April 8, 1873," in Hopkins, *Journals and Papers*, 174.

Instress is hard to pin down as something separate to inscape except for perhaps having a different emphasis, for example:

> Sept. 1, 1868 — The all-powerfulness of instress in mode and the immediateness of its effect (in the architecture of a chapel) are very remarkable[25]

> July 13, 1874 — The comet — I have seen it at bedtime in the west, with head to the ground, white, a soft well-shaped tail, not big: I felt a certain awe and instress, a feeling of strangeness, flight (it hangs like a shuttlecock at the height, before it falls) and of threatening.[26]

Both words, as these passages suggest, have a strange fusion of the objective physical object and the subjective emotional response. However, they do not stop there for the poet, Hopkins. He seeks to bring inscape and instress into being in his poetry. The critic Charles Williams explores how Hopkins achieves this, not merely by emotional inspiration but also by the hard work of poetic craft. The craft of poetic creation is rightly seen by Williams as resulting in the poem as a level of being into which the reader is drawn. Williams expresses this graphically:

> Alliteration, repetition, interior rhyme, all do the same work: first, they persuade us of the existence of a vital and surprising poetic energy; second, they suspend our attention from any rest until the whole thing, whatever it may be, is said . . . (phrases) proceed, they ascend, they lift us (breathlessly and dazedly clinging) with them, and when at last they rest and we loose [sic] hold and totter away we are sometimes too concerned with our own bruises to understand exactly what the experience has been . . . (his) experience

---

25. "Journal, Sept. 1, 1868," in Hopkins, *Journals and Papers*, 119.
26. "Journal, July 13, 1874," in Hopkins, *Journals and Papers*, 198.

(of "inner wrestling") is expressed largely in continual shocks of strength and beauty.[27]

Williams sees Hopkins' work as approaching, but not actually being, mysticism.[28] He sees a fusion, in Hopkins' poetry, of two elements. Poetic response (i.e., the poet's sensibility to the world which generates his poetry) co-exists with the (hard) intellectual work of processing that response—he refers to "a passionate emotion" and "a passionate intellect."[29] If Hopkins "approaches" the territory of mysticism, this might be seen in theological thinking related to chapter 3's apophatic fiction. However, instead of absence being the main focus, presence is more apt. This is because his "passionate intellect" and "passionate emotion" work in his poetry to be an (apparently spontaneous) outpouring of the Latin term *ecce!*: "behold!"

Pitch and Ecceitas

Another term Hopkins uses is pitch, and he uses it to encompass several different meanings, more than our general consideration of pitch as how high or low a musical note is. He extends this concept in three ways. Firstly, he uses it to mean the singsong nature of tonal language, where a change of pitch, indeed in the conventional sense, denotes a change of meaning; in Mandarin Chinese, for example.

However, secondly, pitch means individuation; it is contrasted with quiddity:

> Two eggs precisely like, two birds precisely alike: if they had been exchanged no difference would have

---

27. Williams, "Introduction," in Hopkins, *Journals and Papers*, xxii–xxiii, xiv.
28. Williams, "Introduction," in Hopkins, *Journals and Papers*, xiv.
29. Williams, "Introduction," in Hopkins, *Journals and Papers*, xv.

been made. It is the self then that supplies the determination, the difference, but the nature that supplies the exercise, and in these two things freedom consists. This is what I have before somewhere worked out in a paper on freedom and personality and I think I used the terms freedom of pitch and freedom of play: they are good at all events and the two together express moral freedom.[30]

Thirdly, pitch is, it seems, following on from this, equivalent to both a poetic and a moral/spiritual instress:

> It is to be remarked that choice in the sense of the taking of one and leaving of another real alternative is not what freedom of pitch really and strictly lies in. It is choice as when in English we say "because I choose," which means no more than (and with precision does mean) / I instress my will to so-and-so. And this freedom and no other, no freedom of field, the divine will has toward its own necessary acts. And no freedom is more perfect; for freedom of field is only in accident. . . . So that this pitch might be expressed, if it were good English, the doing be, the doing choose, the doing so-and-so in that sense.[31]

In fact, Hopkins will use exactly this formula when he writes that "the just man justices,"[32] creating another neologism by unilaterally deciding to use justice as a verb, not a noun. From here, crucially, Hopkins is now in a position to conclude, "Is not this pitch or whatever we call it then the same as Scotus' *ecceitas*?"[33]

Seeing pitch, both moral-existential and poetic, as *ecceitas* (when he "really meant to say *haecceitas*"), could then be a real and powerful fusion and inner reconciliation

---

30. Hopkins, *Journals and Papers*, 323.
31. Hopkins, *Journals and Papers*, 328.
32. Hopkins, "As Kingfishers Catch Fire," in *Works of Gerard Manley Hopkins*, 53.
33. Hopkins, *Journals and Papers*, 328.

THE AUTISM OF POETRY

for Hopkins as poet/priest. The critic John Llewellyn speculates that *"ecceitas"* was not a slip of the pen by Hopkins, but another of his neologisms, and one which is crucial for us, if so.

Llewellyn's argument is convincing. He argues for Hopkins' neologistic strategy as an "unorthodox orthography" (spelling).

Hopkins' unorthodox orthography gains some legitimacy from the fact that an earlier form of haec is haece, where ec is the root of the Latin word oculus, eye. . . . "Is not this pitch . . . eicceitas?"[34]

Hopkins was also an excellent classical scholar, and therefore aware of the nuances of the Latin word *ecce,* which can be translated as "here is," or "look at this!" (with your eye=*ec)* which is more archaically expressed as "Behold!" In fact, a genre of Christian sculpture and painting is the *"ecce homo"*—"behold the man" (Christ). This is associated with the Crucifixion because it is at Christ's trial that Pilate says "behold the man."[35] Llewellyn argues that *ecceitas*—whether it is an unconscious slip of the pen or not—is a profound understanding of Hopkins' poetry. He explains that this is not least because *ecce* is grammatically not nominative but vocative, (not stating a fact, but appealing to the hearer, as an address to the person). He comments:

> Address is the appeal that the sheer existence of something or someone makes in which the goodness for that entity of its existence attracts our attention. The appeal is the call (*Geheiss,* vocation) "Listen!" or "Look!" It is the ecce that can be heard or seen in the haecceity of the individual singularity that according to

---

34. Llewellyn, *Gerard Manley Hopkins,* 94

35. John 19:5; in the Latin translation, Pilate says *ecce homo*—"behold the man"—just as Teresa saw in the statue with that title.

Scotus, followed by Hopkins, is in a relation of formal distinction with a thing's common nature.[36]

Llewellyn concludes that "No less than Hopkins, Scotus is concerned to provoke in his reader a sense of 'as if for the first and last time.' That is one way of spelling out what they both mean by haecceity."[37] "Behold the sacred individualization!"—"*ecce haecceitas!*" could be read as a manifesto for writing which is a theo-poetic celebration of the sacred individual thing. It is as if Hopkins' writing blesses the object to realize its sacred potential—he is performing as poet-priest.

ECCEITAS AND AUTISM

The Windhover: An Autistic Reading

Now, can we discern an autism of the *ecceitas* of Hopkins' poetry?

First, we will aim for pure fascination, of words beyond words; here is a poem which is best read "in a single breath," and then reread to catch the words—as opposed to an initial reading's catching of the rhythm and sound of the words purely. Read it first just for the sound, as if you were listening to music. . . it is a poem to read, and read, and savor.

> The Windhover
> *To Christ our Lord*
>
> I caught this morning morning's minion, king-
>   dom of daylight's dauphin, dapple-dawn-drawn Falcon, in his riding
> Of the rolling level underneath him steady air, and striding

---

36. Llewellyn, *Gerard Manley Hopkins*, 94.
37. Llewellyn, *Gerard Manley Hopkins*, 7.

> High there, how he rung upon the rein of a wimpling wing
> In his ecstasy! then off, off forth on swing,
>> As a skate's heel sweeps smooth on a bow-bend: the hurl and gliding
>> Rebuffed the big wind. My heart in hiding
> Stirred for a bird, –the achieve of, the mastery of the thing!
>
> Brute beauty and valor and act, oh, air, pride, plume, here
>> Buckle! AND the fire that breaks from thee then, a billion
> Times told lovelier, more dangerous, O my chevalier!
>
>> No wonder of it: shéer plód makes plough down sillion
> Shine, and blue-bleak embers, ah my dear,
>> Fall, gall themselves, and gash gold-vermilion.[38]

As we let the poem hang in the air, we could usefully revisit all the aspects of fascination we have explored up to now, and see if they resonate with an *ecceitas* of the poem. Like Hopkins' poem, we will allow the connections between poem and autism to tumble out in a medley, because, in truth, they can't ultimately be separated. The only way to approach this fascination of *ecceitas* within the territory of myth is to *experience* the poem, whether it takes one or several readings. What then do we find? Undoubtedly you will see things which I don't, and vice versa. *Ecceitas* is experienced as reveling in the poem. Fascination clings hold of it; if you also cling hold, perhaps you are entering the myth of the autism of the poem. Is this a legitimate claim? Recall what we have considered earlier, that poetry can be read, for us, as an escape from ostensive language into excess and the place of the Holy Fool; the glory of a magnificent poem like this is its density not of meaning (which we can also extrapolate if we wish), but its density of evocation, where, as we saw in chapter 2, metaphor becomes *more than just* its (decoded) meaning.

---

38. Hopkins, "Windhover," in *Works of Gerard Manley Hopkins*, 29.

We could say that the relationship of poetic texture and the words which create it, and our receiving of them, is a poetic universal sacrament, in Franciscan optimism. Margaret Ellsberg comments:

> The particularity of what Hopkins said in his poems revealed more about his theology than most of his carefully groomed arguments: the poems stressed out his faith. Each poem became a credo, with words as sacramental elements, his experience as the transcendent force, and Hopkins himself as the celebrant.[39]

I am reluctant to intrude into your reception of the poem, but if this is new territory, I will give one or two examples of my own (subjective) response.

- *morning morning's minion*: the repetition, alliteration and para-rhyme seem to enclose me in a world other than my own; I feel transported. The rhythm feels like wing strokes.
- *minion, kingdom . . . Falcon*: the internal rhythm and pararhyme hook me into feeling captured and captivated by a textured, poetic universe; again, its rhythm-rhyme is not "symbolizing" but something more akin to poetically "being" the wing beats.

The whole poem, read as a rush of sounds and half-glimpsed concepts, invites us in the way that Charles Williams described earlier when we looked at Hopkins' poetic technique. After that initial shock of sound, these sorts of details which create the sound can be savored. It is subtle and difficult to describe; these are words beyond the telling of words, we might say, or, as Bob Dylan tells us, definition kills.

---

39. Ellsberg, *Created to Praise*, 96.

> **Being (being) *as* words; here we have all of our mythical autism—absence (from propositional language); poetic sacramental presence and the surpassing of ostensive language in Incarnational metaphor; the poetic texture and presence yielding both Autistic Fascination and complete autistic love. This is all Incarnational, not least, because, if we are lucky, we have been caught up in the poem *as an incarnation,* and we are participating in the love of creation in which it is written.**

Not for nothing does Hopkins preface the poem with the words *To Christ our Lord.* We could perfectly well parse the poem for Christological meaning (and find it, in excess), but love—love for the bird, the windhover (more commonly known as kestrel)—is what binds this bird in Hopkins' poem to his universal sacrament where Christ can be a bird (again, we think of St Francis of Assisi preaching to the birds). This, for us, is total autistic empathy at the stage where we are immersed in the sound-world, glimpsing meaning along the way, yes, but too busy being fascinated and in love to want to stop right now. We could take a sound-bite—*a skate's heel sweeps smooth on a bow-bend*, for example, and cherish it, even glimpsing half or less of the meaning, but playing with the sound of it and its texture.

Can we enact this a little further, to cement the mythical relationship between autism and the theo-poetic? Here are some thoughts, drawn from a little more interaction with Hopkins' poems. As we have repeatedly seen in previous chapters, insistence on "taking things literally" does not mean that metaphor dies. On the contrary, it lives more fully by our autistically inhabiting the metaphor in a creative relationship. For example, in Hopkins' *The May Magnificat,* an autistic reading of metaphor would ask "*why, how* is the bloom on the apple a 'drop-of-blood-and-foam-dapple?'" and "*why, how* is the earth 'mothering?'"[40] Blood and foam apple blooms—what a color and texture!—and the earth mother can, at the very least, exist in the space of the poem. Coleridge's willing suspension of disbelief[41] is thought autistically as taking things literally, and reveling in that autistic privilege. Hopkins' metaphoricity dwells in the poetic intensity which is driven by a theological conviction rooted in sacrament. This offers us a deeper suspension of belief, perhaps; it is sacrament, not symbol. This *is* (mystically) a blood and foam apple blossom; and the Earth *is* mothering me.

Attention to Detail: The Geek

We have begun to see that an autistic hermeneutic can recognize its own mythical autism in terms of fascination in Hopkins' writing. If we recall the traits of fascination, we might see how they might play out in a reading of his work.

Firstly, absolute fascination is present in "geeky" extreme attention to detail. The "geek" archetype of autism[42] draws on the first aspect of Autistic Fascination, which is an immersion in phenomena through extreme attention to fine detail, often to the point of obsession. Hopkins' notebooks are full of his detailed observation of what he sees—art, language, architecture, music, science, (his paper *Statistics and Free Will* is sadly lost) and most of all

---

40. "When drop-of-blood-and-foam-dapple / Bloom lights the orchard apple," Hopkins, "May Magnificat," in *Works of Gerard Manley Hopkins*, 37.

41. Recall how, in the Introduction, we looked at the poet Coleridge's concept of "willing suspension of disbelief" when we read a poem or story.

42. A reference to Luke Jackson's influential autistic teen autobiography (Jackson, *Geeks, Freaks and Asperger Syndrome)* and Silberman's *Neurotribes:* "geeks" are inverted from figures of ridicule, pejoratively labelled "odd," to figures of creative, lateral thinking and of great value.

the natural world. His sketches complement his writing and are a fusion of scientific curiosity and aesthetic appreciation.[43] Attentiveness is key to this. We see the same deep commitment to the object in his poetry. For example, a stream merits a detail-rich stanza in *Inversnaid:*

> Degged with dew, dappled with dew
> Are the groins of the braes that the brook treads through,
> Wiry heathpacks, flitches of fern,
> And the beadbonny ash that sits over the burn.[44]

Clearly, Hopkins has observed this brook with attentiveness, and has made, as we will see, a commitment to bringing this locus of attention to life through poetic texture.

(The geek in me recognizes this poetic texture observed in nature! A family story worth recounting: as a young man, Ernie was hill-walking with a friend, who suddenly realized Ernie was not by his side as he walked. Looking back, he saw Ernie lying flat on his stomach in the midst of the bracken and heather. His friend rushed back to see if Ernie was hurt. "No," he replied—"but just look at the petals of that tiny white flower!")

Sensory Sensitivity

Inversnaid also offers a hospitable discourse for the second facet of Autistic Fascination, sensory sensitivity. It is, for our theologically thought fascination, inseparable from attentiveness to detail because both are extreme sensitivities to the environment. Sensory sensitivity means

---

43. There is a wonderfully diverse and eclectic proliferation of line drawings and maps in his notebooks, e.g., Hopkins, *Journals & Papers*, 144–47, 448.

44. Hopkins, "Inversnaid," in *Works of Gerard Manley Hopkins*, 52.

that what is perceived through the senses is so intense as to be a source sometimes of torment, and sometimes of delight. Immersion operates in the poem as not merely observation but union with the nature of the poetic inscape. So, what is also evident in this example is the immersion in sound through alliteration. It seems to me that his alliteration has an onomatopoeic character, creating sound-texture. So in this case, for example, the parallelism and clustering of D sounds could be the tricking of the stream, and in line three the F sounds could be the rustling of the fern. This is an immersion in the sounds, as well as the visuals, of the minute observation which is recognized, and honored, by Autistic Fascination.

Alliteration, rhythm, rhyme and conjoining poetic neologism ("beadbonny") create a texture of attentiveness to sound-image which is a meticulous seeing of nature, a meticulous evoking of image, and a meticulous listening to language. The metaphors of groin and tread, and the neologistic joining of bead and bonny are also the fruits of attentiveness to groins, treads and beads so that the metaphoric relationship of groin and the cutting of a stream path into the brae, of treading and the descent of a stream, and beads and dew, work by an attentive seeing of phenomena. These relationships are strange and atypical in their depth of crafted and intuitive response, even up to the commitment which needs to invent neologisms, because existing language is not enough; and, as such, in their very oddness, also in deep sympathy with Autistic Fascination.

"THIS IS ALL NONSENSE"

> Of course, this is all nonsense. I could send this poem to half a dozen autistic friends and guarantee their response; "I can't make head nor tail of poetry." We are in the realm of absolute autism, where no human eye can behold the glory of Gxd. I am recording the imaginary thoughts of it, and I inhabit perhaps some of it, but to inhabit all of it would be impossible or, at the very least, producing insanity, sainthood, death, or all three.

But we can persist with the myth. Why? The object is not to make autistic people theologians and poets. The converse; the object is to approach theology and poetry and tug at their sleeve, and ask "can you hear a beautiful autism in your work?" At the start, we stated that not all places are equally hospitable; in my own case, Fundamentalism was (finally, for me) a desert without potential or fulfilment. Whereas, in Altizer's work and, increasingly, in lyrical poetry, my own, personal degree of autism has been drawn there because, as a poet and a theologian, I have discerned there the autism which is uniquely part of me to be absently present, literal, fascinated and deeply in love against all odds. Thus, I can imagine and extrapolate to a mythical Absolute Autism where these hospitable places would listen, purely on a speculative/mythical level, and recognize something of the beauty of autism which empathizes with their discourses. Recalling the neurotribal nature of autism, the atheologian or the poet might respond to this autism of Gxd and say yes, I am in good company! because, to come back to the glory of individual trees where we began this chapter, it is possible to be a sole beech tree in a forest of birch trees and feel a little alone.

In an era where "queer" meant simply "odd" and not part of the LGBTQI community, Hopkins himself wrote that

> It is the virtue of design, pattern or inscape to be distinctive and it is the vice of distinctiveness to become queer. This vice I cannot have escaped.[45]

Being a queer tree, one looks out for a fellow, similarly queer tree, to validate it by one's friendship, and by which to be validated oneself.

---

45. Hopkins, *Gerard Manley Hopkins: Poems and Prose*, vol. 1, 66, quoted in Ellsberg, *Created to Praise*, 90.

Chapter Six

The Autism of Nothing

Suddenly in this doorway where I stand
in this house I see this place again,
this time the night as quiet, the house
as well secured, all breath but mine borne
gently on the air—

And where I stand, no one.[1]

WHO IS LUIGI PIRANDELLO?

There could be an almost limitless number of poems, novels, plays, symphonies, songs, statues, paintings, films, video games, art installations, where our mythical autistic hermeneutic could search for hospitable environments. We have danced with some of them, and now, lastly, we will dialogue with one more discourse, where we can find a home for a mythical Autism of Nothing. This will bring the death of Gxd, *haecceitas,* and Incarnational metaphor all toward an autistic consummation in that Nothing.

So, in what will emerge as a fitting choice, this last chapter brings an autistic hermeneutic to two novels by the nineteenth/twentieth-century Italian playwright and

---

1. Stafford, "At Our House," in *Darkness Around Us,* 5.

novelist Luigi Pirandello. We will see that the novels can be read, for the privileged reader (armed with a conscious autistic hermeneutic), as an object lesson in the gift of being autistic. This is a comparative study between a lesser and a greater autistic potential for Incarnational metaphor. The comparison, for discerning "levels of autistic potential," is between an earlier and a later Pirandello novel. The first, earlier novel is *The Late Mattia Pascal*, (*Il Fu Mattia Pascal*), from here on abbreviated as *Mattia Pascal*. The second novel, Pirandello's last, is *One, No-one and One Hundred Thousand*, (*Uno, Nessuno e Centomila*) from here on abbreviated as *Uno, Nessuno*.

We will see that that *Uno, Nessuno* is a narrative offering the poetential (another slip of the pen, like Hopkins'?)—offering the poet-ential, as poetic potential of the full gift of autism, as Incarnational metaphor. In comparison, *Mattia Pascal* journeys toward this gift but turns back (like Lot's wife, who looked back, in Genesis, and was turned into a pillar of salt[2]) into neurotypicality, missing the theological power of conscious autism. Crucially, this absolute, fully conscious autism is an autism of the Nothing.

> **You will have noticed that we are now using the term "conscious autism" as a mythical absolute autism which the protagonists do, or do not, achieve. In other words, are they autism-conscious, as some people would talk of being Gxd-conscious?**

I have been struck by how apt they seemed, as I read these novels; there are good reasons for selecting them for this "case study" or enactment. Firstly, Pirandello is foundational to the Theatre of the Absurd. We will see how the Absurd's emergence from Modernist writing is

---

2. Gen 19:26.

an arena where Mindfulness of Separation can be seen as increasingly conscious. This is similar to the way in which we saw in Altizer's work, influences such as Joyce and Hermann Melville. In fact, as we will see, Pirandello's radical, innovative, experimental technique could even be read as proto-postmodernist. So, another aim of this chapter is, in a small way, to use our autistic hermeneutic to bring his generally overlooked significance to light, and validate it with the voice of autism. In fact, this is not least because, in 1934, Pirandello was awarded the Nobel Prize for Literature, but his contribution to European literature has perhaps been overlooked or forgotten by the English-speaking world, although his dramas are still fairly popular as stage productions. James McFarlane explains how Pirandello is foundational to the Theatre of the Absurd as it develops in the twentieth century:

> By his insight into the disintegration of personality, Beckett; by his assault on received ideas, Ionesco; by his exploration of the conflicts of reality and appearance, O'Neill; and by his probing of the relationship between self and persona, actor and character, face and mask, the work of Anouilh, Giradoux and Genet.[3]

McFarlane sees in Pirandello's work:

> a deeply and destructively ironic attitude to naturalistic reality, a determination to replace the illusionistic counterfeiting of reality by the recognition of the profounder reality of illusion.[4]

With this "profounder reality of illusion" we could at once say that Pirandello's thought is akin to our understanding of truth-telling myth. However, Pirandello goes further. His "illusion" does not seek mythically, merely to

---

3. "Neo-Modernist Drama," in Bradbury and McFarlane, *Modernism*, 569.
4. "Neo-Modernist Drama," in Bradbury and McFarlane, *Modernism*, 651.

embody our truth; it aims to subvert it in order to wake us up, and shake us out of our complacency. He certainly achieved this. There were riots at the première of one of his first plays.[5]

Secondly, the presence of "madness" or "schizophrenia" in Pirandello's own family life hugely influenced his work. At one point, actually after, not before, Pirandello was writing, autism was wrongly labelled as a form of schizophrenia;[6] who can say what the reality of his wife's "madness" was? What is certain is that he kept her locked away—who knows but whether she might have been a holy fool, teaching Pirandello. He repeatedly referred to her as his muse.[7] There might be, as we shall see, areas where a perceived "pathology" of autism will recognize some traits.[8]

Thirdly, and most importantly,

> **the central concern of Pirandello's work, to question and even uproot our comfortable assumptions, is redolent with potential hospitality for the death of Gxd, and, for us, the autism of Gxd as we understand it.**

The novels are selected here in contrast to Pirandello's more widely known plays, for two reasons. Firstly, it is little known that Pirandello spent many more years as a novelist than a playwright, and his novels are worthy of attention in their own right. However, secondly, and more

---

5. See Bassnett-McGuire, *Luigi Pirandello*, 7.

6. See Bassnett-McGuire, *Luigi Pirandello*, 18–19; Büdel, *Pirandello*, 24, states that "it is ironical that Pirandello the misogynist should have found in woman his most fruitful source of inspiration."

7. See Büdel, *Pirandello*, 22–23.

8. We are (very) far from equating schizophrenia with autism, even though early diagnostic thinking in the first half of the twentieth century at times did so. Rather, the ironic "madness" of the holy fool in Pirandello's work comes into dialogue with the gift of autistic seeing.

fundamentally, a novel offers something different to a play. In contemporary Western culture, ultimately, I read alone and you read alone. We may discuss our appreciation of Middlemarch, but my Middlemarch is my Middlemarch and yours is yours. This is another aspect of innerness and solitude which predisposes the novel for giving a hospitable welcome to an autistic hermeneutic. These novels' first-person narrative offers an inner psychological space. Pirandello's drama is much more celebrated, but it is the inner voice of the first-person narrator's psychological space in these novels, rather than the acted words and actions in the social arena of drama, which lends itself to the success of an autistic hermeneutic. Autistic Mindblindness makes the "reading" of a live performance enactment difficult, with the difficulty of grasping ostensive action and the Mindreading needed to decode the actors' expressions and gestures. In the novel, I am alone and undisturbed in my fascination of the novel; I am "in a world of my own." We will look briefly at the plays, to outline the context in a general discussion of Pirandellian thought and its possibilities for an autistic hermeneutic. For a close reading, however, it will be his novels which offer possibilities for a deeper response to the call of a mythical autism.

PIRANDELLIAN DRAMA

Pirandello is best known for his many plays, perhaps most famously *Enrico IV (Henry the Fourth)*, *Sei Caratteri in Cerca d'autore (Six Characters in Search of an Author)*, and *Il Gioco delle Parti (The Rules of the Game)*. What makes Pirandellian drama innovative and challenging is that he distorts form, and (at that time) innovatively breaks the fourth wall. He creates a metanarrative which makes the work subvert itself. It has a strong sense of anticipating Barthes' Death of the Author, which we discussed in chapter 2.

In his drama, a common technical device is the play-within-the-play. However, this is more than its previous usage in the pre-Modern period. Where the Shakespearean play-within-a-play is a set piece, clearly bounded within the primacy of the play itself, Pirandello's plays-within-plays "take over" the setting of the purported play to subvert it from within. The critic James McFarlane describes the play-within-the-play as "the spectacle of a spectacle which is . . . not so much a play *within* a play as a play *beyond* a play."[9] McFarlane is right, but the even more subversive nature of this *beyond* is the inversion where *beyond* itself takes primacy over the foreground, becoming more real.

In *Sei Caratteri,* for example, a play is about to begin, but six protagonists emerge out of the audience and onto the empty stage. They announce that they are six fictional characters in search of an author. They have a desperate need to make their story real, in order to resolve its problems by a literal en-act-ment. They proceed to replace an "original" play planned by the "director" with their own play, which they then act out. This play completely displaces any trace of the purported original play. It ends in violence and death, not resolving the problems the characters bring to the plot but enacting their tragedy. This device, briefly stated, is really an existential challenge to the audience, to enact a similar questioning of their own constructed realities.

Something not dissimilar happens in *Enrico IV.* The central protagonist is a grandfather who is cared for by his

---

9. Bradbury and McFarlane, *Neo-Modernist Drama,* 567.

family. He becomes delusional and believes that he is King Henry the Fourth. The family decide to play along with his delusion, and treat him as this eleventh century Holy Roman Emperor. When the farce becomes unbearable and the family cannot keep it up any longer, the grandfather reveals that he has long since ceased to believe in the delusion; but he has decided to "play along with their playing along."

What is happening in these plays? The forces at work are vital for us to understand Pirandello. He was born in the hamlet of Cavasù, in the district of Caos in Sicily. *Cavasù* in Sicilian dialect means literally digging things up and turning them upside down, while Caos in Italian (although not Sicilian dialect) means Chaos. Whereas contemporary Sicilian culture was oppressively conformist, Pirandello struggles with and challenges norms, enacting this chaos. He writes:

> So I am the son of Chaos.
> Nietzsche said that the Greeks raised white statues against the black abyss, to hide it. Those times are gone. Instead, I shake them to reveal it.[10]

There is an aloneness in this iconoclastic approach to art, where one must forge one's own path by choosing what she assents to, and how. The critic Carlo Salinari writes that:

> At the base [of Pirandello's work] . . . one can find . . . a feeling of the anarchic condition in which modern man finds himself, of the lack of an organic social fabric which sustains him and binds him to others, of the mastery of man by things which are external to his will,

---

10. Autobiographical fragment, 1923, quoted in Büdel, *Pirandello*, 7.

of the inevitable defeat to which man is condemned in the society in which he finds himself living.[11]

Straight away Salinari's vocabulary of the individual who is unable to be "bound" (connected) to others speaks to the condition of autism and is a condition to which autism speaks. Profoundly living Mindfulness of Separation, we know what it is not to be bound to others. This lack of "being bound" emerges in Salinari's sense, as the unfavorable lack of social cohesion experienced both in Pirandello's technique and in his protagonists. However, there is an ambivalence here. We lack the cohesion of being "bound" together, and this is a crisis. However, more importantly, being bound is also in itself oppressive; the nineteenth-century Sicily of Pirandello's early life was a closed and conformist place where it was easy to feel stifled by these bonds. He complained of its "boredom and tedium,"[12] seeing a wider sense of what Jean Paul Sartre would name *ennui.* We, in our mythology, can read this conformity ultimately, as we will see, as neurotypicality, in what Pirandello will call "the web of life." Freedom from "the web" reads for us as a figuration of the gift of autism. In his non-conformity, Pirandello's passionate rhetoric already starts to make him seem like a good autist, choosing "difference over indifference"[13] in glorious ex-centricity and its authenticity and integrity.

---

11. Salinari, *Miti e Coscienza del decadentismo italiano*, quoted in Pirandello, *Uno, Nessuno e Centomila*, ix. (Translations by the author of this book unless otherwise indicated.)

12. Pirandello, "Arte e Coscienza," in Giudice, *Pirandello*, 56.

13. A reference to the Scottish National Autistic Society's 2015 campaign slogan, "Difference, not Indifference."

RELATIVISM AND IRONY

Oscar Büdel entitles a chapter of his study of Pirandello *The Relativist*. He recounts the following story:

> When Pirandello toured Germany with his Teatro d'arte, Albert Einstein reportedly approached him after one of the performances and said: "We are kindred souls."[14]

This is anecdotal, but the critic Martin Esslin also describes Pirandello as "the 'Einstein of the drama.'"[15] In her essay, *Pirandello's Philosophy and Philosophers,* the critic Daniela Bini writes:

> With his violent polemic, Pirandello was giving the final blow to an idea of philosophy on which Western thought had rested for two thousand years: philosophy as order, as systematic thought.[16]

Bini also quotes Pirandello's 1893 essay *Arte e Coscienza d'oggi (Today's Art and Consciousness):*

> The old laws having collapsed, the new ones not yet established, it is natural that the concept of the relativity of everything has widened so that . . . nobody is any longer able to establish a fixed, unshakable point.[17]

This philosophical relativity is certainly important, and he puts it to work through his use of subversive, deconstructive irony, which he is able to employ *in* and *as* his writing. In his essay *L'idea Nazionale* (The National Idea),

---

14. Büdel, *Pirandello*, 35.
15. Esslin, *Reflections*, 47.
16. Bini, "Pirandello's Philosophy and Philosophers," in DiGaetani, *Companion to Pirandello Studies*, 17.
17. Pirandello, *Saggi e Interventi*, in Bini, *Pirandello's Philosophy*, 18.

he refers to three of the great nineteenth-century German philosophers:

> Hegel explained that *the subject, the only true reality, can smile at the vain appearance of the world. It stipulates it, but it can also destroy it*; it does not have to take its own creations seriously. Hence we have irony, that force which, according to Tieck, allows the poet to dominate his subject-matter. And, according to Friedrich Schlegel, it is through irony that the same subject-matter is reduced to a perpetual parody, a transcendental farce.[18]

Perhaps it is in looking at this idea of irony that it becomes possible to cut through the numerous crosscurrents of critics who repeatedly affirm and deny Pirandello as a philosopher.

> **If his philosophy *is not merely ironic but actually irony itself*, then this philosophy-as-irony cancels itself out, leaving *Maschere Nude* (*Nude Masks*);[19] "nude masks" are not masks at all, except as a paradox, and ironic (non)philosophy underpins and imbues his work.**

Pirandello remarks "I have never taken upon myself any philosophical responsibility. I have always intended to make art, not philosophy,"[20] stating in another interview that "In Italy there is a trend started by some critics to see in my work a philosophical content that is not there, I assure you."[21] Yet it is hard to deny that his work is brimming over with philosophical ideas. How can we square this circle? When we read the earlier words he writes about

---

18. "L'Idea Nazionale," 27 February 1920, quoted in Giudice, *Pirandello*, 113–14.
19. The title of the collection of dramas published in 1919.
20. Interview in DiGaetani, *Companion to Pirandello Studies*, 17.
21. Bini, "Pirandello's Philosophy and Philosophers," in DiGaetani, *Companion to Pirandello Studies*, 17.

Hegel, Tieck, and Schlegel, all European philosophers, how can we reconcile this with his denial? Perhaps we can, if we return to the Postmodernist thinking of chapter 2. Could it be that the dead metaphors of metaphysical narrative are being deconstructed, so that Pirandello is, indeed, even making fun of them? These remarks of Pirandello's, in fact, sound similar to Derrida's ironic denials of Dionysius, where Derrida's point is to interrogate narrative; like Pirandello, he seems to flirt with it.[22]

Daniela Bini then performs a fruitful retrospective reading of Pirandello through the twenty-first-century philosopher Gianni Vattimo. If this holds good, it can be argued that Pirandello's work as *farceur* (mocker) of philosophy in a sense has helped, historically, alongside the philosophers she cites, to prepare the ground for Vattimo's "non-foundationalist" thought. Bini writes:

> The Weak Thought of Gianni Vattimo's school . . . has suggested the theory[23] that the only possible philosophy left to man is that which constantly questions itself, totally aware of the precariousness of each statement as of the weakness and limitations of his tool: thought.[24]

Is this, as some critics have said, the evil of Postmodernism paving the way for a culture where we see our own thought—our own truth—as "precarious, limited and weak?" After all, this is a language of there being only relativism, rather than fixed truth/Truth. Is it for this reason that the culture employing ideas of Fake News is possible, or even inevitable? Perhaps Postmodern irony can be twisted

---

22. See Derrida, "How to Avoid Speaking," discussed in chapter 3.

23. Bini's choice of the word "theory" betrays a reluctance to break with rationalism, whereas Vattimo's work is perhaps more fruitfully read as an existential choice, taking cognizance of the subjectivity of the living and thinking subject.

24. Bini, "Pirandello's Philosophy," 18–19.

into cynicism and manipulation, or a confused openness to misinformation. One might see a parallel to Hitler's appropriation of Nietzsche. In fact, however, it seems to me that the duty Vattimo (and Pirandello) is presenting to us is the very opposite; we must relentlessly question ourselves, our sources, and our assumptions, but in the end make a decision based on the thin air of our own personal responsibility to the best truth we can find; in fact, it is a concept which invites us to a deep humility. This is what Postmodernist thought would describe as a non-foundational "place"; and it is also anti-metaphysical in the sense that, as Derrida did in chapter 3, it refuses to take our metaphysical assumptions for granted. It is Pirandello's shaking of the Greek white statues, and we need courage to walk the tightrope over the abyss which is revealed to us.

Setting the undeniable presence of philosophy in his work alongside his disavowal of being a philosopher raises interesting possibilities for autistic Incarnational metaphor. In Incarnational metaphor, we hover between absence and presence, paradoxically being both; we have Mindfulness of Separation precisely enabling fascination; isn't this what Pirandello's games do? We could see a mythical identity of these two, because Pirandello is operating within metaphysics (because we must, if we are to preserve any rational ability) and yet simultaneously and ironically deconstructing it; absence and presence; Fascination clinging to the artistic and intellectual beauty of the act of deconstruction instantiated in his fictions, while Mindfulness of Separation deconstructs metaphysics (even as it relentlessly still endures), as absence. This is why Pirandello's work is a place where an autistic hermeneutic can recognize and read itself. The non-foundational anti-metaphysics of Pirandello's work offers the possibility of giving Mindfulness of Separation an existential home, just as earlier chapters have identified in Teresa, Altizer and Blanchot. Critically, this happens because Pirandello writes art, and short-circuits the labyrinth of metaphysics where we yearn for stability from the author. Drama and fiction bear this heavy responsibility of rhetoric, but can deny philosophical accountability by offering the text as a living enactment rather than a formula subject to logical rules.[25] This is the cryptic method of the Holy Fool, speaking truth through what seems foolishness. This is precisely the point Paul Ricœur will make in 1975:

> Philosophical discourse sets itself up as the vigilant watchman overseeing the ordered extensions of meaning; against this background, the unfettered extensions of meaning in poetic discourse spring free.[26]

Pirandello's art deconstructs metaphysics by subjecting it to scrutiny in the form of art, which is able to stand outside it by "springing free." The existential backdrop of Pirandello's Absurd is that, if philosophy is unmasked as rhetoric, then only rhetoric remains.

Pirandello is not "ir-rational," lacking philosophical ballast, but actually "anti-rational," knowingly deconstructing philosophy by means of the rhetorical strategies of drama and fiction.

Daniela Bini makes this point, drawing again on Vattimo's "Weak Thought":

> As Vattimo says, the borderline between philosophy and art has disappeared. Philosophical statements can often be made through art much more forcefully,

---

25. Pirandello, ironically referring to the ideological construct or "form" of Fascism, states publicly that he aims for "life, not form" in his work and thinking (interview in *L'Impero*, September 23, 1924, quoted in Büdel, *Pirandello*, 12).

26. Ricœur, *Rule of Metaphor*, 308.

since it uses as a vehicle the synthetic power of imagination . . . having learned Heidegger's lesson, (quoting Vattimo[27]) "the work of art can be an actual realization (*messa in opera*) of the truth, because truth is no longer a metaphorically stable structure, but an event."[28]

To return to our mythology, autistic archetypes would be able to read Pirandello's "anti-philosophy" as Incarnational metaphor in the following terms. If Pirandello's work is read as an embodiment of Vattimo's assertion here that "truth is no longer a metaphorically stable structure," Mindfulness of Separation will see this undermining of a stable relationship between "reader" and "truth." This is realized in the text when literal metaphor has the guileless inability/refusal to "decode" into a "stable truth";

> **Pirandellian "anti-rationalism" is the problematizing of metaphor, to enter into the space of fiction, atheologically, exactly as previous chapters have discussed. Here, then, is our direction of travel; Incarnational metaphor might "work" as an expression of Pirandello's anti-philosophy and, equally, be an anti-theology.**

How very ironic, that we autists, so frequently unable to engage with (or even identify) irony, find ourselves so uniquely, mythically inhabiting irony! Perhaps we are all Chauncey (chancy) Gardeners, talking about sick trees while others hear us talking about the White House.

"Pantheism?"

Büdel sees the short story *Quand'ero Matto (When I was Mad)* and the play *Lazzaro* (Lazarus) as "permeated with

---

27. Vattimo, *La Fine della Modernità*, 84.
28. Bini, "Pirandello's Philosophy," 19.

pantheistic ideas," so that "death is neither a limit nor an end of life."[29] The danger here is to confuse pantheism with mysticism.[30] Not all forms of mysticism are pantheistic—perhaps they might, in some cases, approach panentheism,[31] but even so, we must beware with how we use language. Pirandello calls himself a mystic[32] (although it is always important to bear in mind his ironic attitude) but if he uses mysticism, it is more in the sense which views it as a form of unknowing; an immersion in how his work was famously described "Life, not Form."[33] Büdel returns to the essential point of Pirandello's work as a subversive meta-narrative:

> When we look for the origin of Pirandello's relativism, we find, not surprisingly, that it comes to him from his anti-rationalist convictions and beliefs, consonant with contemporary philosophical insights. Pirandello sees the basic evil in *ratio*, in human reason, which creates, indeed fabricates all the fictions with which man (sic) lives.[34]

A *ratio,* even of pantheist theology, would miss the point of Pirandello's doubling of "fiction" as the narrative of his writing and the "fictions we live by." This sets the stage for an ironic conscious autism, which consciously refuses to "play the game" (*Il Gioco delle Parti*).[35]

---

29. Büdel, *Pirandello*, 42.
30. Pantheism is the belief system where the physical cosmos *is* the divine.
31. Panentheism is the belief that the cosmos is *part of* the divine.
32. Büdel, *Pirandello*, 42.
33. Interview in *L'Impero,* September 23, 1924, quoted in Büdel, *Pirandello*, 12.
34. Büdel, *Pirandello*, 36.
35. Pirandello's play of that name.

The Loss of Faith

Pirandello's essay *Arte e Coscienza d'oggi* (Today's Art and Consciousness) articulates a profound sense of the loss of faith, and he writes here with a rhetorical style not unlike Nietzsche's:

> I am amazed that something which is in fact pitch dark should be called God . . . science has assigned man a pitiful place in nature compared to the place he once thought he occupied. . . . What has become of man? What has this microcosm, this king of the universe become? Alas poor king! Can you not see King Lear hopping before you, armed with a broom, in all his tragic comicality? What is he raving about?[36]

> As for the old . . . they return to God. . . . The young present a still sadder spectacle. Born in a feverish moment, when their fathers thought less of love than of war to reconstruct the country; born in the din of debates . . . amid the swirl of opposed political and philosophical currents . . . we feel dazed, lost in a huge, blind labyrinth, surrounded by an impenetrable mystery. . . . The old norms have vanished and new ones have not yet been established: so it is not surprising that the concept of the relativity of everything should have succeeded in making us lose our sense of judgement almost completely. . . . Nobody manages to have a firm and unshakeable viewpoint . . . never before has our life been more disjointed ethically and aesthetically. Disconnected, with no principle of doctrine or faith.[37]

This is Modernist loss of faith, closely approaching Matthew Arnold's sentiments in *Dover Beach,* where the sea of faith has retreated:

---

36. "Arte e Coscienza d'oggi," in *La Nazione Letteraria*, Florence 1893, quoted in Giudice, *Pirandello*, 55.
37. "Arte e Coscienza d'oggi,' in Giudice, *Pirandello*, 55–56.

> And we are here as on a darkling plain
> Swept with confused alarms of struggle and flight,
> Where ignorant armies clash by night.

or W B Yeats' *The Second Coming* where "the centre cannot hold; things fall apart."

Now we are able to see how high the stakes are; and in light of this, we can approach Pirandello's novels in search of hospitality for our mythical autism.

ONE, NO-ONE, AND A GENUINE AUTISTIC INTEGRITY

Constructions, Mindreading, and Their Deconstruction

Uno, Nessuno is a novel about the erosion of epistemological assumptions (what we assume we know), leading to a descent into madness, and this is an expression of the kind of anti-metaphysical games we have already discussed.

The plot is tragi-comic and absurd. Following his wife's comment that his nose is crooked in a way which he has not himself been aware of, the first-person protagonist, Vitangelo Moscarda, looks at his nose in the mirror[38] and from there, he descends into obsessive doubt, of himself, of all identity, and ultimately of epistemology itself. He sees "the outsider, opposite me, in the mirror,"[39] arriving at

---

38. The chronology of Moscarda's nose yields a quirky speculation: Pirandello is working, intermittently, on *Uno, Nessuno* between 1909 and 1926. Before this, in 1836, thirty years before Pirandello's birth, Gogol's satirical short story "The Nose" has its main character Kovalyov becoming co-protagonist with his own nose, and immediately after Pirandello published about Moscarda's nose in *Uno, Nessuno* in 1927, Shostakovich wrote his opera *The Nose*, based on Gogol's "The Nose." This writer has so far found no references to this in the secondary literature, but wonders if there could have been something in the air.

39. Pirandello, *Uno, Nessuno*, 17.

"the awareness of madness, fresh and clear . . . precise as a mirror."[40]

The descent into radical doubt is expressed repeatedly as a negotiation of constructions which Moscarda demolishes, one by one. Pirandello uses the trope of construction several times in the plot,[41] until Moscarda states that everything "for (humankind) is building material,"[42] and history is merely a construction.[43] Identity, too, is a construction:

> Man takes as material even himself, and he constructs himself, yes, sir, like a house [and] . . . I accept the fact that for you inside yourself, you are not as I see you from outside.[44]

Moscarda journeys from the role of a "toothless conformist"[45] to the madness which is truly wise, by means of radical doubt leading to madness, and the madness is the cure for itself in his final identity as a holy fool. Pirandello's comic irony operates at full stretch in the novel, but its final supreme irony of the holy fool can equally and thereby be read as the irony of ironies, where the biggest irony of all is the final ability to transcend irony, but only by way of the biggest irony of all, the wisdom of the holy fool.

---

40. Pirandello, *Uno, Nessuno*, 75.
41. Pirandello, *Uno, Nessuno*, e.g., 25, 33, 34, 37.
42. Pirandello, *Uno, Nessuno*, 41.
43. Pirandello, *Uno, Nessuno*, 79.
44. Pirandello, *Uno, Nessuno*, 31.
45. His wife's pet name for him is "Gengè" (Gummy).

THE NEUROTYPICALITY OF THE ONE AND THE ONE HUNDRED THOUSAND

For us, the narrative's critique of the construction of identity makes sense, in an autistic hermeneutic, as a critique of neurotypicality and the complacency of its assumptions of Mindreading: "No one doubts what he sees, and every man walks among things, convinced they appear to others the same way they are for him."[46] For an autistic reading, Moscarda's critique resonates with neurotypical resistance of the challenge of a universal autism: "Solitude frightens you. And then what do you do? You imagine many heads. All like your own . . . the presumption that reality, as it is for you, must be and is the same for everybody else."[47]

> **These "presumptions" read as a refuge from a fear of autistic insight. The people Moscarda sees around him can be read as suffering from unconscious autism, since they too, equally are victims of the gaps between differing views, but remain unaware of these differences. Autism is all around them and within them, yet they remain unconscious of it.**

Moscarda's awareness that epistemological certainty (as absolute, or complacent, neurotypicality—for us) is a sham, brings him to the moment of his own fear of this insight, where he realizes that there is a fundamental separation even in the intimacy of his marriage. He becomes painfully aware that "her" (nicknamed) Gengè (gummy—toothless)[48] is not Moscarda himself, but only her image of him. So, he comes to view himself as an enigma, simply because his wife's trivial remark about his nose has led

---

46. Pirandello, *Uno, Nessuno*, 102.
47. Pirandello, *Uno, Nessuno*, 25.
48. Pirandello, *Uno, Nessuno*, 42.

him to question the reality of his own perception when measured against the perceptions which others have. A moment of horror holds him, because at this stage he is still "hostage" to the need for a construction which is denied to him: "I was unable . . . to see myself as others saw me."[49] "An outsider whom only the others can see and know, but not I."[50] The "One, No-one and One Hundred Thousand" of (neurotypical) constructions is being "deconstructed," in his scrutiny of it:

> I still believed this outsider [himself as he sees himself in the mirror] was only one person: only one for everybody. But soon my horrible drama became more complicated: with the discovery of the hundred thousand Moscardas that I was, not only for the others but also for myself.[51]

Communicating adequately with others or even with himself has become an insoluble problem. William Weaver's translation of this book in the 1992 Marsilio edition has the following cover matter:

> It is Pirandello's genius that a discussion of the fundamental human inability to communicate, of our essential solitariness . . . elicits such thoroughly sustained and earthy laughter.[52]

Pirandello's novel is certainly humorous but he himself makes it plain that the novel's aim is not only or merely to entertain, as there is a deeper agenda: the same cover matter, quoting Pirandello himself, says that

---

49. Pirandello, *Uno, Nessuno*, 12.
50. Pirandello, *Uno, Nessuno*, 13.
51. Pirandello, *Uno, Nessuno*, 13–14.
52. Pirandello, cover matter, *Uno, Nessuno*.

> One, No-One and One Hundred Thousand arrives at the most extreme conclusions, the farthest consequences.[53]

The ultimate consequence is to expose the One and the One Hundred Thousand as constructions, to recognize the No-One in an act of ironic affirmation. In an autistic hermeneutic, Moscarda is breaking free of the complacency of neurotypical Mindreading. His consciousness of imperfect Mindreading fails to be able to construct even the self in the mirror, of the one hundred others' view of him in the social world: "I could see [my eyes] in me, but not see them in themselves. . . . He [Moscarda's reflection] knew nothing, nor did he know himself."[54]

The autistic nature of language as holding an inherent hermeneutical gap finds a further resonance in the novel when Moscarda says "the trouble is that you, my dear friend, will never know, nor will I ever be able to tell you how what you say is translated inside me."[55] This "loss in translation" is the hermeneutical gap where our horizons do not meet, and Moscarda is becoming so mindblind that he cannot even read himself. His journey is to travel from experiencing this as horror, to the recognition of conscious autism as an emancipation. His journey is, ultimately, toward being liberated from his names—the impotent, toothless Gengè, the religiously constructed Vitangelo (living angel), and the irritating Moscarda (*mosca* is an irritating, buzzing fly) all need to be left behind as he travels toward the *Nessuno* ("No-one").

---

53. Pirandello, cover matter, *Uno, Nessuno*.
54. Pirandello, *Uno, Nessuno*, 18.
55. Pirandello, *Uno, Nessuno*, 31.

APPROACHING CONSCIOUS AUTISM

As Moscarda becomes "The outsider inseparable from [him]self,"[56] increasingly he now exists "[w]ithout . . . giving any thought to the others."[57] When he looks at people who have been coming into his garden for years, suddenly he sees their presence not as normal features of his everyday life but as an "[i]nvasion by others."[58] Under the mosquito nets, he feels happy, with "the bed isolated; the sense of being wrapped in a white cloud."[59] He becomes unconventional, an outsider to society's norms. Where others go ahead "pulling the cart" of their daily lives, Moscarda tells the reader "I wasn't pulling a cart, no, not I; and so I had neither reins nor blinders."[60]

In an autistic hermeneutic, Moscarda can be seen in his journey to be travelling into the solitude of Mindblindness, excluding him, as autist, from the social world. So this begins, now, to seem a liberation, where he has neither reins nor blinders, and in autistic terms, he is approaching autistic non-conformity and autistic integrity. The exclusion from the social world leads Moscarda into the gift of being "in a world of his own." Moscarda exhibits the characteristics of this as the gift of Autistic Fascination. This is manifest in another autistic feature, namely his close attention to detail. This is reminiscent of St Francis who "was too busy looking at the beauty of individual trees to care about seeing the forest; he didn't want to see the wood for the trees."[61] Fascination gleams

---

56. Pirandello, *Uno, Nessuno*, 12.
57. Pirandello, *Uno, Nessuno*, 15.
58. Pirandello, *Uno, Nessuno*, 26.
59. Pirandello, *Uno, Nessuno*, 29.
60. Pirandello, *Uno, Nessuno*, 5.
61. Chesterton, *Saint Francis of Assisi*, 89, 178. This also echoes Hopkins' *ecceitas,* with the intense mindfulness to what is seen; equally, to Chauncey Gardener's

through the novel from the very start, as early as page 3, although Moscarda has to undergo the distressing aspect of it before he is able, finally, to see beauty in it. He has become obsessed with detail, staring at his nose in the mirror. This quickly becomes a narrative of intense obsessive rumination:

> I . . . was made to plunge, at every word addressed to me, at every gnat I saw flying, into abysses of reflection and consideration that burrowed deep inside me and hollowed my spirit up, down and across, like the lair of a mole, with nothing evident on the surface.[62]
>
> I would pause at every step; I took care to circle every pebble I encountered, first distantly, then more closely; and I was amazed that others could pass ahead of me paying no heed to that pebble . . . a world where I could easily have settled . . . my spirit filled with worlds—or rather pebbles; it's the same thing.[63]

THE (DE)CONSTRUCTION OF GOD: MARCO DI DIO

Stepping back from the protagonist's point of view, the plot's narrative again plays games with names, this time for an allusion to the post-Christian ideas we saw in Pirandello's essays and letters. Moscarda's experiments in shattering others' expectations of him include his odd speech and primarily his experiment in being an active decision-maker at the bank where he has previously been only the passive, titular head. One example of how he does this is by evicting his tenant Marco di Dio from his

---

ability to see the tree instead of the White House.

62. Pirandello, *Uno, Nessuno*, 4.

63. Pirandello, *Uno, Nessuno*, 5; echoing William Blake's words about seeing eternity in a grain of sand.

rent-free house and then giving the property back to him as a gift. It might be possible to see Marco di Dio as a figure for Gxd—his name, "Mark of Gxd" could suggest that Moscarda's experiment is also an eviction of Gxd, then to invert Gxd as humanity's gift, not its giver. Pirandello suggests elsewhere that God has been "living rent-free" for too long in Catholic Italy.[64]

In fact, it is the novel which enacts the eviction of God; a precursor of the death of God, half a century later.[65] The *Marco* in the original Italian has the name not only of the Gospel evangelist and author of the second Gospel book—Mark, but also the meaning of "marco" as the note (mark) in the margin of a financial ledger—he is erasing the trace of Gxd from the ledger. A nameless Gxd, free of the "ledger mark," is evicted and welcomed simultaneously, and this will be the madness ultimately of Moscarda as the holy fool.

This will become significant when viewed alongside the spiritual material which emerges later in his madness. In the distress of madness, he finds salvation in absolute renunciation, divesting himself of this ownership of the same bank's capital. The case becomes even stronger when Moscarda finds his ultimate spiritual rebirth in the novel's conclusion, with its overtones of Christian death and resurrection, and the text's close echoes of Paul's remark that as a Christian he "dies daily"—precisely what Moscarda does, minute by minute, in order to escape the tyranny of images and names.

---

64. See e.g., the burlesque/blasphemous "holy stoup" scene in *Mattia Pascal*, where he uses a bedside holy water stoup as an ashtray.

65. Anticipating (for our purposes) Altizer and the Death of God movement.

"GXD WITHIN"

A Gxd who has been evicted and erased becomes significant when Moscarda "finds Gxd" by the discovery that this evicted, erased Gxd is within him, but "hostile to all constructions."[66] Religion, which he sees as the church building which people have built for Gxd,[67] is as much a neurotypical "construction" as any other; he has, instead, "the sense of God inside, in [his] own way."[68]

This interior God is reminiscent of the inner fictions we saw in the writing of the mystics. It is "madness" because it has absented itself, removed itself from the social fabric of material gains and losses. Moscarda tell us: "That *quick* wounded in me when my wife had laughed . . . was God, without any doubt: God who had felt wounded in me"[69]. This "quick" of Gxd within him comes into view precisely as Moscarda is losing his own identity. This Gxd appears within the "no one" which escapes definition and construction. The "God within," "hostile to all constructions," can be read in sympathy with the mystical theology of Gxd which exists by not existing in any construction, beyond being, in the terms used by Dionysius and Meister Eckhart, as we have previously discussed.

Moscarda gives away all he owns. His act of surrendering all his assets to convert them to pure gift, is resonant of the twenty-first-century theologian Jean Luc Marion's thinking of Jesus' parable of the Prodigal Son.[70] The father's (true) prodigal generosity to the (falsely) prodigal (profligate) son is, for Marion, the gift which outwits

---

66. Pirandello, *Uno, Nessuno*, 144.
67. Pirandello, *Uno, Nessuno*, 139.
68. Pirandello, *Uno, Nessuno*, 139.
69. Pirandello, *Uno, Nessuno*, 139–40.
70. Luke 15:11–32.

ontological difference.[71] We will see, in our (non)conclusion, that this pure gift is an embodiment of absolute autism in its total affective empathy. It looks like madness.

TOWARD INCARNATIONAL METAPHOR: THE GREEN WOOL BLANKET

In his journey of discovery, Moscarda sets out to "undo" the images others have of him, and people react by seeing him as insane: "Have you heard? The usurer Moscarda has gone crazy!"[72] The play between sanity and insanity reaches a climax when the crowd denounce him as a madman, but he gives his own very sane reasoning: "All because I had wanted to prove . . . that I could be someone different from the man I was believed to be."[73] In fact, it is Moscarda, penetrating the falsity of constructions, who is sane, and this irony persists, at the next level, when being is possible only as Nonbeing. This is where we will see that Incarnational metaphor can be seen in a theological thinking of fascination.

The climax of Moscarda's movement away from the human world to a mystical union with the non-human happens in chapter 8.II, in his description of his experience with a green wool blanket. Whereas Moscarda's self has been a "hundred thousand" in his journey through self-doubt, at this point he says, "I found myself truly there."[74] This is authentic self-knowledge, but in Pirandello's supreme irony, it takes the guise of apparently puerile fascination. In Moscarda's contemplation, as he convalesces

---

71. See Marion, *God Without Being*, 97–99.
72. Pirandello, *Uno, Nessuno*, 75.
73. Pirandello, *Uno, Nessuno*, 95.
74. Pirandello, *Uno, Nessuno*, 155.

THE AUTISM OF NOTHING   325

after being shot, a green blanket becomes a microcosm of an idyllic natural world in his imagination:

> I stroked the green down of that blanket. I saw the countryside in it: as if it were all an endless expanse of wheat; and, as I stroked it, I took delight in it.[75]

> Ah, to be lost there, to stretch out, abandon myself on the grass to the silence of the heavens; to fill my soul with all that empty blueness, letting every thought be shipwrecked there, every memory![76]

From there on, there is only one place where he can continue to live, and that place is detachment and asceticism; because a life enmeshed in social conventions and material possessions would simply keep Moscarda prey to the workings of the One Hundred Thousand from which he needs to escape. Therefore, he gives away everything he owns and becomes a beggar and an ascetic.[77] His experience with the green blanket has figured a kind of salvation, and all his language is of delight—he is consoled and contented. By stroking and touching the green blanket, Moscarda finds a pathway out of obsession and into serenity—just as the autistic subject finds solace in an extraordinary relationship to the sensory world. In fact, there is a strikingly similar image from the autist Gunilla Gerland:

> Gunilla found the place to be left in peace—behind the armchair, where she was able to shut out everything and simply be—absorbed in the material of the brown armchair.[78]

Can literary green blankets be compared to autistic brown armchairs? If so, when we autistically mythologize

75. Pirandello, *Uno, Nessuno*, 155.
76. Pirandello, *Uno, Nessuno*, 155.
77. Pirandello, *Uno, Nessuno*, 158.
78. Gerland, *Real Person*, quoted in Bogdashina, *Autism and Spirituality*, 191.

them, Moscarda's similar "green blanket" experience is fascination; lost "in a world of his own," he perceives the "expanses" of it in fascination. This is prefigured in his attention to detail as he contemplates the natural world as an escape from "constructions,"[79] and fascination happens precisely in the place of the end of religious or metaphysical concepts which the narrative calls "no conclusion."

Büdel sees a dichotomy between tragedy and "mysticism," where Pirandello apparently gives up his lifelong ironic stance and "plays it straight":

> A further way out for Pirandellian characters is to die the death of the unio mystica. Of the two modes of experience which . . . lead to a complete loss of the Self, the tragic and the mystic, Pirandello has chosen the latter . . . in the tragic experience the Self is destroyed at the very moment of its truest, highest, and most complete realization and assertion; whereas the mystic in fusing—as it were—with the All and One, gives up, renounces his individual essence.[80]

It is perhaps unwise to lose alertness to ironic strategies at work in the text. Religion is anathema to Pirandello, as we have seen, and a conversion to "mysticism" seems improbable, as he is writing this, his last and greatest novel, immediately prior to his greatest output as an extremely ironic, tragicomic playwright. Perhaps Moscarda is simply a fool, addled and insane, and a figure of fun, stroking his green blanket and giving away his fortune.[81] Yet, in the end, after all his absurd, neurotic introspection, he

---

79. Pirandello, *Uno, Nessuno*, 36–39.
80. Büdel, *Pirandello* 52
81. Pirandello's output has to increase to salvage the family fortune after bankruptcy. He is unlikely to subscribe to idealism about poverty. (See Büdel, *Pirandello*, and Giudice, *Pirandello*.)

becomes a sympathetic character in the unusually lyrical language of the final chapter.[82] Moscarda states in his final, most "mystical" state, that the church bells, ringing for prayer, are irrelevant for him. He has killed God by evicting Marco di Dio, and Pirandello has not suddenly become a Christian. We can perhaps glimpse, in fact, that the novel is playing yet another Pirandellian language game, where the "mystic fusing" which "renounces individual essence" is in fact closer to what we would recognize as an atheology of the text.

NO CONCLUSION

The wording of Pirandello's last chapter, 8.IV, "No conclusion," is a paradox. "No conclusion" is the paradoxical dilemma of the author who must bring the book to a close while leaving its characters still alive beyond the book; since the imaginary construction of fiction leaves any arbitrary conclusion detached from the imaginary space where the characters might continue to live in the mind of the reader. So, in this sense, the conclusion is "no conclusion."

However, there is another possible reading of this title. "No conclusion" might mean a conclusion where "no" is itself the book's conclusion. If this is the case, it is a profound conclusion because the "no" is the "no" of the "no one" of the book's title. In the experience of the green wool blanket, Moscarda has arrived at a place where he wants to be no one. The one and the one hundred thousand appear to have been left behind; he tells the reader "I no longer look at myself in the mirror, and it never even

---

82. Pirandello's earliest writing was poetry, and he is, perhaps, "allowing" poetic diction to enter the text here.

occurs to me to want to know what has happened to my face and to my whole appearance."[83] He discusses his old self which bears his name, in the third person. So he says, "No name . . . leave it in peace, and let there be no more talk about it. It is fitting for the dead . . . life knows nothing of names."[84] Moscarda's name is dead—and this is the only way he can be alive. This life is a kind of death. In the loss of all names and constructions, he is free from "conclusions." His freedom from the selfhood of his name means he can experience life in any form: "I am this tree. Tree, cloud; tomorrow book or wind; the book I read, the wind I drink."[85] It is easy to see here why Büdel would read this as pantheism; but pantheism is a "theism" and an "ism," and Moscarda is free from all "isms."

It is also important to remember that Pirandello's ironic subversion is always playing games with the reader. While the whole novel has worked to construct a character as the first-person subject, it has been easy to overlook that the character Moscarda, who works so hard to rid himself of constructions, is himself only a fictional construction. "No conclusion" pulls the rug out from under the reader's feet. Moscarda/non-Moscarda is not, at the end of the day, a pantheist, or anything else, but a fiction. He "gives the game away," finally, when he tells the reader that "I am. . . . this book."[86] The whole narrative construction of the self-less self collapses into a mere playing with words, bringing the first person to re-attach itself to "tree, cloud . . . book or wind," so that the "I am" exists purely rhetorically as

---

83. Pirandello, *Uno, Nessuno*, 159.

84. Pirandello, *Uno, Nessuno*, 159; earlier, he has alluded to his name as an irritant, because *Moscarda* is so close to *mosca*, the irritating fly that buzzes around (49).

85. Pirandello, *Uno, Nessuno*, 159–60; nb. It would be easy to read "the wind I drink" as a mis-spelling of "the wine I drink" but "the wind I drink" is a translation of "il vento che bevo" (Pirandello, *Uno, Nessuno*, 224).

86. Pirandello, *Uno, Nessuno*, 160.

part of "the book." In a sense, this is nothing new. In Pirandello's drama, the action tends to hinge on the disruption of the willing suspension of disbelief. (As atheologians, we cannot but be struck by a parallel where the nameless (non)Moscarda utters "I am" statements: the Great I AM of Jahweh, the "I am" statements of Jesus in John's Gospel; are we *sure* that Moscarda hasn't got religion? Or does he think he is God?)

What is at stake here, however, is Pirandello's own statement that *Uno, Nessuno* "arrives at the most extreme conclusions, the farthest consequences."[87] "The most extreme conclusions" are, in fact, "no conclusion," because as universal subject, I/We/One/No-one/One Hundred Thousand draws "one's own conclusions." Moscarda is "no longer inside (him)self, but in every thing outside,"[88] and this is, decades before Barthes or Derrida, the Death of the Author as the death of the Transcendental Signified, the Creator who takes responsibility for "who" or "what" their protagonist "is."[89] Decades after Pirandello, Barthes writes:

> . . . today the subject apprehends himself elsewhere, and subjectivity can return at another place on the spiral: deconstructed, taken apart, shifted, without anchorage: why should I not speak of "myself," since this "my" is no longer "the self?"[90]

and Derrida writes:

---

87. Pirandello, cover matter, *Uno, Nessuno*.
88. Pirandello, *Uno, Nessuno*, 160.
89. The death of the author: "We know now that a text is not a line of words releasing a single 'theological' meaning (the 'message' of the Author-God) but a multidimensional space in which a variety of writings, none of them original, blend and clash" (Barthes, "Death of the Author," in *Image, Music, Text*, 146).
90. Barthes, *Roland Barthes*, 168.

> One must be separated from oneself in order to be reunited with the blind origin of the work in its darkness.[91]

This act is anticipated by Moscarda, who confronts the reader with what it is to be separated from oneself, in order that the pure work, the living of constant death and rebirth, can be experienced. Derrida adds that

> Only pure absence—not the absence of this or that, but the absence of everything in which all presence is announced—can inspire, in other words, can work, and then make one work.[92]

Pirandello's novel "works" by exploring the absence of Moscarda's self—finally Moscarda is able to function (or "work") with some sense of authenticity by embracing pure absence, even from his own name.

Derrida describes this "non-place":

> This universe articulates only that which is in excess of everything, the essential nothing on whose basis everything can appear and be produced within language.[93]

In this way, Pirandello's most supreme irony is realized, that when the subject dies ("No Names"), the universal subject can speak in fullness ("I am"—"I am this tree. Tree, cloud; tomorrow book or wind; the book I read, the wind I drink.").[94] Derrida's anti-theology or Dionysius' apophatic theology? So, close, it seems, to both! Yet with Pirandello's proto-Postmodernism and resolute atheism in

---

91. Derrida, "Writing and Difference," in *Of Grammatology*, 8.
92. Derrida, "Writing and Difference," in *Of Grammatology*, 8.
93. Derrida, "Writing and Difference," in *Of Grammatology*, 8.
94. Pirandello, *Uno, Nessuno*, 159–60; atheologically, we read Jahweh's "I am that I am"—is this a mockery or a genuine feeling of supplanting Catholic spirituality with a pure Nothing?

mind, perhaps we can place him as an antecedent in Derrida's camp.

THE GREEN BLANKET AS (AUTISTIC) UNIVERSAL SUBJECT

To return to the aim of seeing *Uno, Nessuno* in an autistic light, the green blanket offers a theological thinking which might bring an absolute autism of Incarnational metaphor into view. Moscarda's fullest life is as fullest death:

> I die at every instant, and I am reborn, new and without memories: live and whole, no longer inside myself, but in every thing outside.[95]

This is the death of Gxd and the death of the subject, and the resurrection and complete Incarnation of both. It might be remembered, here, that the site of this death-unto-resurrection is the green blanket.[96] It is as Moscarda strokes the green blanket that he becomes able to perceive "eternity in a grain of sand," and be liberated into "this wind I drink."

Thinking of (non)Moscarda in terms of Incarnational metaphor, he is the subject who is "mad"—he is the holy fool who "makes no sense." As autistic metaphor, in terms of the pragmatism of language, by "making no sense" and having no constructions, he is dead, having no name. Equally, as autistic literal metaphor, in terms of the resurrection of dead metaphors, he is alive to the image, in a state of *ecceitas*:

---

95. Pirandello, *Uno, Nessuno*, 160.

96. Moscarda is wrapped in the green blanket as he convalesces after being shot by the family friend Anna Rosa—or is this in fact (or fiction), life after death?

> I go out every morning, at dawn, because now I want to keep my spirit like this, fresh with dawn, with all things as they are first discovered.[97]

This is, autistico-atheologically, the incarnation of the kenotic Christ in the text, embodying nothing which is everything, poured out utterly in total autistic affective empathy which delights in the fascination of the text. Fresh with dawn, we see everything new (as our already present second naïveté).

> **In our autistic hermeneutic, the myth of absolute autism is read most fully at this "most extreme conclusion," where the green blanket offers the sensory connoisseur the absolute death and absolute life of Incarnational metaphor which is nothing and everything.**

THE LATE MATTIA PASCAL: THE UNSUCCESSFUL AUTIST

In light of (non)Moscarda's final, insanely saintly autism, we can move to a comparable novel. We will be able to compare *Il Fu Mattia Pascal*, in its autistic potential, to the autistic possibilities we have seen in *Uno, Nessuno*. We will see that in *Mattia Pascal,* the narrative stops short of a space where the absolute autism of Gxd can recognize itself. This comparison will highlight the autistic "badge of honor" which belongs to *Uno, Nessuno*, in order to show that as Incarnational metaphor, it has achieved what neurotypicality in this novel fails to do. *Uno, Nessuno's* Moscarda achieves what an autistic hermeneutic recognizes as autistic integrity, in a way that *Mattia Pascal's* eponymous protagonist does not. However, Pascal's failure reads,

---

97. Pirandello, *Uno, Nessuno,* 160.

equally incisively for an autistic hermeneutic, as a critique of neurotypicality. Here, a retreat from autism to neurotypicality is read as the failure to attain the spiritual insight which chapter 4 described as the autism of Gxd. So, where Moscarda has been shown to attain a full autism of Incarnational metaphor, we will now see how Mattia Pascal travels toward it, but stops short and turns back to neurotypicality.

Il Fu Mattia Pascal narrates the story of how the narrator-protagonist Mattia Pascal bizarrely fakes his own suicide in order to escape family and financial problems. The novel turns on Pascal's difficulty in constructing a new identity for himself, involves him in some rather bizarre tragi-comic episodes, and ends with his return to his home and family, to resume his old identity. This is, as we have seen, a key Pirandellian theme, where the idea of identity is challenged in comic enactments of its difficult nature. Pascal re-invents himself with the name Adriano Meis, only to return ultimately to the name Mattia Pascal, styling himself *Il Fu Mattia Pascal (*The Late Mattia Pascal*)*. This means that the protagonist will appear under either or both names at different points.

Mattia Pascal: The Character

The narrative chooses the protagonist's first name to be Mattia (Matthias), not the more common Matteo (Matthew). Matthias is one of Christ's lesser disciples, easily confused with Matthew, the Gospel writer. In contrast with Matthew, all that is known about Matthias is that he replaced the dead Judas.[98] Playing with the name, the narrative casts

---

98. Acts 1:12; and even Matthias' status as a (lucky or unlucky?) thirteenth apostle rests on mere chance, because he is chosen by casting lots. In the same way, Mattia Pascal, both character and plot, relies on the narrative device of chance throughout the novel.

Mattia Pascal as an obscure figure, aimless and marginalized, and as a "replacement Judas" he also betrays Christ, commits suicide, and becomes, in the end, a replacement disciple, if an obscure one without identity, who is "dead," in the sense that he exists only to replace Judas, the suicidal apostle who dies after betraying Christ.

His second name, Pascal, suggests the philosopher Blaise Pascal as an archetype, firstly for Pascal's famous wager of faith (Mattia Pascal's wagers, instead, are both at the casino and in his choices to bet on the opportunities offered by outrageous coincidences); and secondly, for that wager's significance in deconstructing philosophy. Both of these symbolic references to religion and philosophy will be fundamental for us, but at this point it is also important that Pirandello's narratives always use comic irony, so that the disciple Matthias and the philosopher Pascal are also being used as figures of fun.

Metaphysics and Religion

As we discussed earlier, Pirandello can be seen as a proto-postmodernist, challenging the conventions of fiction. In his drama, we saw his plays as the enactment of an anti-metaphysical project. This is also evident in *Mattia Pascal,* as the "fiction of the fiction" (the reader is reading the fictional identity of a protagonist who creates a fictional identity). *Uno, Nessuno* contrasts Moscarda's Gxd as the "quick" of his wounded soul with the "constructions" of religion and philosophy. However, religion and philosophy are approached differently and more bitingly satirically in *Mattia Pascal.*[99]

---

99. Names invite allusive possibilities: as already noted, Mattia is the lesser-known disciple of Christ, and Pascal the philosopher of the leap of faith. Pascal is unable to think of a new name for himself, so he appropriates names from an overheard farcical

Stepping back from the protagonist's point of view to look at the games the narrative plays with him, satire of religion is most obvious when the narrative plays with echoes of the resurrection. For example, Mattia mockingly refers to himself as having "come back from the dead" in chapter 17, and the narrative echoes the resurrected Christ's words in John 20, when Mattia says "It's me, Mattia! Don't be afraid, I'm not dead . . . can't you see me? . . . Touch me! It's me, Roberto! I've never been more alive than I am now!"[100] At the most basic level, his (hardly self-righteous) suicide hinges on a case of mistaken identity; after Moscarda has fled his village and family, a mysterious stranger's corpse is pulled from the water and mistaken for him—in other words, he didn't really die at all; the Resurrection of the ultimately returning Mattia Pascal/risen Christ is just a confidence trick.

Catholicism is lampooned most explicitly of all in the irreverent image of Meis using a holy water stoup as an ashtray, just as he has irreverently disposed of the sacrament of marriage by flushing his wedding ring down the toilet. Before he leaves his family, the narrative has him working in a library housed in a deconsecrated church, where the books have "the smell of mold and old age."[101] Pascal immediately adds that "this fate befell me too," with the joke turning on whether he means the fate of the previous inept librarian or the fate of the books. People don't use the library, because they believe the books are

---

conversation between theologians, and facetiously comments that "they've baptized me!" When a genuine suicide is mistaken for him, enabling his escape, he makes an allusive joke of Christ's substitutionary death: "Fortune had strangely smiled on me . . . another man had died in my place" (72). Is his home village of Miragno something to admire, or a mirage?

100. Pirandello, *Mattia Pascal*, 222.
101. Pirandello, *Mattia Pascal*, xiv.

about "religious matters,"[102] and when he returns to the library at the end to write his story, it is preserved by the curator there "as within a confessional."[103] "Books" and "papers" both suggest living within the law, whether civic or religious, but in leaving the church/library and his name behind, he is outside the law, and cannot even buy a puppy for company, let alone remarry, because he doesn't have identity papers to buy a dog license or get a marriage license.[104]

If Meis manages to discard Catholicism, or at least thinks he does, the next set of "books" to deal with is that of his landlord, Paleari, who sets out to convert Meis to theosophy. As a synthesis of theology and philosophy, theosophy was in vogue when Pirandello was writing in the early twentieth century, basing many of its claims on the paranormal as demonstrated in séances and developing a quasi-religious Gnosticism of "enlightenment." The narrative plays with its claims, as follows. After undergoing corrective eye surgery, Meis has a forty-day recuperation[105] in the dark where he becomes the captive audience for Paleari's extended rhetoric on enlightenment and "the lamp of faith."[106] Meis undercuts Paleari's arguments, exposing them to ridicule—but the narrative plays with the reader as the narrator himself is literally "becoming enlightened" through the healing process in the dark. It also teases the reader by drawing her into the narrator's suspense and doubt, and waiting for a verdict on whether the séance is bogus or proof of theosophical claims. The reader, waiting for Meis' vindication as the rationalist sceptic, is

102. Pirandello, *Mattia Pascal*, 1.
103. Pirandello, *Mattia Pascal*, 243.
104. Pirandello, *Mattia Pascal*, 93, 226.
105. Another satirical biblical echo of Jesus' forty days in the wilderness.
106. Pirandello, *Mattia Pascal*, 116, 154.

confounded by the inconclusive end of the evidence. The narrative, and Meis, both hang in an emptiness where truth as a construction is always an empty concept, implicitly offering the kind of detachment from metaphysics which *Uno, Nessuno* achieves. So, it would, initially, seem that *Mattia Pascal* can be read, in the terms discussed regarding *Uno, Nessuno*, as a journey into the freedom of death from the world, through Mindfulness of Separation.

However, the difference is whether this is an authentic understanding, because the protagonist and the narrator are both unreliable, and, more than this, liars. In this sense, the novel functions as the failure to attain the truth-telling of autistic integrity. The question is whether to read him as a "true" liar or not.[107] Meis tries to break free of the book (religion and civic law) but we will see that ultimately, he fails to do so. Where Moscarda in *Uno, Nessuno* has broken free of "constructions," it will be seen that Meis/Pascal fails to do so, not least because he constructs fictions which are not "true lies," but morally inauthentic lies. It might be good to examine his credentials as an autistic truth-teller, or otherwise.

Mattia Pascal: The Liar

For Mattia Pascal, a lie is just a lie, part of the kind of construction Moscarda has truly renounced. Pascal has no awareness of the possibility of true fiction such as the kind discussed as apophatic fiction in this thesis. In no sense do his elaborate lies realize themselves as creative acts; Adriano Meis is "an absurd fiction" to be destroyed

---

107. His view of the job of librarian as merely a "rat catcher," conserving the book but oblivious to the text (*Mattia Pascal*, xiv); "Novels, what do I care about any of that? Copernicus, my dear Don Eligio, Copernicus has ruined humanity for ever" (*Mattia Pascal*, 3). Ironically, as a liar, (and a fictional creation—of the author, Pirandello's) he has no insight into the truth of fiction.

when he becomes inconvenient.[108] Pascal is a liar who works by cognitive rather than affective empathy. In terms of Baron-Cohen's theory of impairments of cognitive and affective empathy, Pascal (and the text) operates more as psychopath than autist.[109] The psychopath is an expert at reading people, with excellent Mindreading skills, but with cruel and manipulative intent. He lacks affective empathy. At the very outset, before his suicide, Pascal has excellent "people skills" which he uses to exploit his friend Pomino's gullibility, stealing Pomino's girlfriend from him. Next, his entire reason for faking his own death is to escape his family responsibilities, filled with hate for them all.[110] When he returns, at the end, back into the truth of his real identity, it is not out of remorse or a sense of responsibility but for his own comfort, to be able to live a normal life again. His attitude to his family is still unloving: "I'll come alive again! I'll revenge myself!";[111] "Go to hell, you old shrew! I'm alive!";[112] "I want to have my papers in order. I want to feel alive, even if it means having to take back my wife."[113] Earlier, when Meis' lies to the Paleari family unravel, he is faced with a possible moment of truth, to redeem himself morally. He has the chance to be honest with himself about his elaborate fiction: "to avoid lying to her now, must I admit that I had told her nothing but lies till now?"[114] Instead of facing this potential moment of truth, he re-enacts the entire lie of his existence by faking a second suicide.

    108. Pirandello, *Mattia Pascal*, 213.
    109. A "zero-negative" empathy profile.
    110. When his wife is in labor, he hurries home not to be with her but to run away from himself (*Mattia Pascal*, 45); when his brother sends money for their mother's funeral, he spends the money on himself (*Mattia Pascal*, 47).
    111. Pirandello, *Mattia Pascal*, 212.
    112. Pirandello, *Mattia Pascal*, 231.
    113. Pirandello, *Mattia Pascal*, 226.
    114. Pirandello, *Mattia Pascal*, 198.

He also shows himself a psychopath as he doesn't take responsibility for his situation, but blames others: "they [his family] had got me into this situation."[115] This lack of self-accountability extends into lying not only to others but also to himself, where he defends the morality of his seduction of his friend Pomino's girlfriend, and when he has abandoned his family, states that he was "forced to seem fickle and cruel."[116] An alert as to the unreliability of the narrator is the aside to the reader, only a single line, in the narrative: "But out of pique now, I won't describe what happened."[117]

Of course, the deeper possibility is always that it is the narrative, not the protagonist, which is lying; is Pascal lying to others, to himself, or to the reader? An ironic reading of his self-justification would lift the narrative into using an unreliable narrator as a way of becoming a lying narrative, inviting the reader to examine its fictive status by casting doubt into the narrative itself. (And indeed, we should be wary of the tall tales wherein we willingly suspend our disbelief). This is not unlikely, given Pirandello's tendency to play games with the reader; does this make *the text itself* into a psychopathic narrative? After all, are we really to believe the phenomenal coincidences which enable this story to work? In an autistic hermeneutic, the question lies precisely here. The issue is how much the portrayal of impaired empathy in Pirandello's narrative invites a psychopathic interpretation, and how much it would, in contrast, be autistic.

The narrative itself invites the reader to view not only Pascal's actions but also the narrative itself as a tissue of

---

115. Pirandello, *Mattia Pascal*, 212.
116. Pirandello, *Mattia Pascal*, 190.
117. Pirandello, *Mattia Pascal*, 242.

lies. The plot rests on outrageously improbable *deus ex machina* devices. The success of his initial alibi of suicide depends on the highly improbable co-incidence of a mysterious stranger committing suicide on the very same day of his departure. The success of his new identity depends on the hugely improbable luck of winning a fortune at the casino. This raises the question of Aristotle's theory of dramatic plot which argues that a plausible impossibility is better than an implausible possibility, and by this logic the novel would be a failure; the outrageous coincidences are certainly possible, but implausible. However, Pirandello writes in an ironic way about this in his epilogue, justifying himself (like Pascal) about his "lies" of fiction.[118] Given the anti-Catholic subtext, it is reasonable in fact to read the entire story of a man who dies and comes back to life as a satire of the gospel narrative, and the fiction of Meis as a "lie" which Pirandello wants to equate with the "mere story" of Christ in the gospels; most pointedly, the Risen Christ.

To see how this relates to an autistic hermeneutic, *Mattia Pascal* as a "tissue of lies" does play the kind of textual games which invited a resonance with Mindfulness of Separation in *Uno, Nessuno*. However, the narrator is not embodying a philosophically necessary retreat from the known world (where Moscarda's doubt about his nose leads him away from any epistemological security). Instead,

---

118. See Pirandello, "Epilogue," in *Mattia Pascal*.

> Pascal the unreliable narrator/protagonist is choosing to deceive, tricking the others in his life into an illusory Mindfulness of Separation. The reader knows throughout that Pascal is not really dead, so any genuine Mindfulness of Separation is replaced by the portrayal of someone who is only *pretending* to enter the gift of autism.

More fundamentally, *Mattia Pascal* would be read in an autistic hermeneutic as an unsuccessful approach to the apophatic fiction of Incarnational metaphor. Pascal may be an elaborate liar, but as a poet and a contemplative he has no ability. Initially, in the rather sinecure and vague post he occupies in the library, he lazes around with no interest in books, and he has no appreciation for story as a source of truth. His capacity for fascination is absent, because his entry into the story of Adriano Meis soon changes from bliss to lonely torture where, in his lack of real agency, he cannot get close to people and is romantically frustrated. Whereas Moscarda observes his environment and muses on it, and comes to cherish a *haecceitas* of the green blanket, Pascal/Meis refers the world always to himself.[119] If Moscarda offers a narrative in sympathy with apophatic fiction's fascination, Pascal/Meis has no sense of celebration. He "tries the water" of separation, but because it is an inauthentic act, his separation does not lead to any kind of union of fascination. In fact, "trying the water" is an apt comparison: if the fake drownings of Pascal and Meis are spoof baptisms, the resurrection of Pascal as Meis is as a "corpse,"[120] like the "putrefied corpse"[121] of the real

---

119. E.g., The closed windows representing the world closed to him (*Mattia Pascal*, 211); the suicide of the gambler at the casino prefigures (perhaps inspires) his own fake suicide (*Mattia Pascal*, 64).

120. Pirandello, *Mattia Pascal*, 181.

121. Pirandello, *Mattia Pascal*, 69.

suicide who is pulled from the water "in [his] place."[122] The fascination of the glory of the resurrected body, for him, is simply putrefaction, and Pascal is no poet, least of all an apophatic or atheological one.

Failing to Be Autistic

So, the most important way in which he fails to attain the gift of autism is in his retreat from Mindfulness of Separation. We can see a contrast between *Mattia Pascal* and *Uno, Nessuno*, such that together, read autistically, they can demonstrate the difference between autism and neurotypicality, where to be neurotypical is (within our myth) to fail to experience the gift of autism.

We have seen how *Mattia Pascal* can be read as a narrative of resisting the book, in terms of religion and of the law. Initially, both suicides are blissful escapes, but separation soon becomes torture. Freedom is "a tyrant";[123] he must "kill that fiction,"[124] and his dilemma becomes clear:

> I saw myself excluded from life forever . . . the fear of falling again into life's trap would make me stay farther than ever from mankind; alone, utterly alone, distrustful, gloomy; and Tantalus' torment would be renewed for me.[125]

Inevitably, here, we find ourselves straying back into comparisons with Dionysius, or perhaps more pointedly, John's Dark Night of the Soul, and Teresa's agonies suspended between heaven and earth. An autistic reading of Pascal/Meis which examines him as a candidate for

---

122. Pirandello, *Mattia Pascal*, 72.
123. Pirandello, *Mattia Pascal*, 93.
124. Pirandello, *Mattia Pascal*, 212.
125. Pirandello, *Mattia Pascal*, 191.

apophatic fiction finds him wanting. Tempted by separation, he is then unable to bear it, not least because it is morally inauthentic but also in its lack of fascination for him. A comparison with *The Interior Castle*'s soul makes this clear. Separation for the *Interior Castle* soul character is in order to withdraw and enter into an authentic castle; it is morally grounded (the whole point of the exercise is to be rooted more deeply in love which enables genuinely good works), whereas Pascal's entry into separation is selfish and irresponsible. Separation for him is only, in the end, intolerable loneliness: "sentenced to lie, I could never have another friend . . . friendship means confiding"[126] [confiding: con(with)-fides(faith); his loneliness is intolerable because he is without faith]. In contrast, *The Interior Castle*'s soul character suffers anguishes of loneliness, but it is also a blissful loneliness because it happens within the fascination of the presence of Christ. In contrast, in *Uno, Nessuno,* Moscarda has, in fact, become closer to *The Interior Castle*'s soul, living a saintly life of renunciation and charity empowered by the mystical experience of fascination in the green blanket. Where the *Interior Castle*'s soul enjoys holy madness as bliss and Moscarda is similarly blissfully and holily mad, the joy of madness terrifies Pascal/Meis. Even at the very start, he says "I felt so drunk with freedom I was almost afraid I'd go mad, that I couldn't bear it very long,"[127] and eventually, facing "Tantalus' torment, I left the house, like a madman,"[128] and at that point he cannot endure madness, so decides to return from the fiction of Meis to the reality of Pascal. Pascal, in the end, only "played dead and ran off,"[129] but *The Interior*

126. Pirandello, *Mattia Pascal*, 101.
127. Pirandello, *Mattia Pascal*, 88.
128. Pirandello, *Mattia Pascal*, 191.
129. Pirandello, *Mattia Pascal*, 233.

Castle's soul knows death as the consummation of the spiritual marriage, and Moscarda, too, lives only by dying, and thereby lives completely.

Pascal's retreat from the anti-metaphysical freedom from the book is indicated when with the Palearis, he realizes that he is once again "caught in life's net."[130] Seeking a second freedom through a second suicide, however, he can only return to the "slavery" of the original identity he sought to escape, because freedom is "a tyrant."[131] Here, we could read a suggestion of Dostoyevsky's parable of The Grand Inquisitor.[132] The freedom of living in Christ is, for the Grand Inquisitor, a torment too great for humanity. It is also beyond Mattia Pascal's capacity. So Pascal returns to the deconsecrated church which is the site of lifeless religion, and his story is held in safekeeping by the "rat catcher" custodian as if "in a confessional."[133] With a deft double meaning, the narrative at the outset prefigures this. When Pascal describes his job at the library, he writes that the previous incumbent "didn't even have to look at [the books]; all he had to do was bear for a few hours a day the smell of mold and old age. This fate befell me too."[134] Is this the fate of the custodian, or the fate of the moldy old books? It is certainly the fate of the retreat back from freedom into the metaphysical Book which kills the freedom of the true book, and back into the letter of the law. This is most evident in the final persistence of the lie, which ends the book:

130. Pirandello, *Mattia Pascal*, 160.
131. Pirandello, *Mattia Pascal*, 93.
132. Dostoevsky's parable in *The Brothers Karamazov*; the Grand Inquisitor is confronted by Christ, who has returned to Earth, and complains to Him that free will is too great a burden for human hearts to bear. Christ is burned at the stake as he is an obstacle to the Church.
133. Pirandello, *Mattia Pascal*, 243.
134. Pirandello, *Mattia Pascal*, xiv.

> Every now and then I go out there [to the cemetery]
> to see myself dead and buried. . . . Who are you, after
> all? I shrug, shut my eyes for a moment, and answer:
> "Ah, my dear friend . . . I am the late Mattia Pascal.[135]

This is a false death, but also a false name: the person in the grave is not Mattia Pascal, but the real unknown, who is nameless. Pascal has moved from false name to false name, unable to be nameless. This previsages Samuel Beckett's novel *The Unnameable,*[136] and it apparently echoes Moscarda's triumphant death-into-life where "I am alive and I do not conclude. Life does not conclude. And life knows nothing of names."[137] Mattia Pascal, however, may affect to be "dead," but his "death" is diametrically opposed to (non)Moscarda's constant death and rebirth. Moscarda renounces names, but Pascal goes back to his dead, old name as the late Mattia Pascal, having learnt nothing of conscious autism.

At the start of this chapter, Pirandello was quoted saying that *Uno, Nessuno* "reached the most extreme conclusions,"[138] and as his last novel it might be seen as the goal toward which his oeuvre has been working. Thinking of it as a triumph of autism over psychopathy would make sense because (non)Moscarda has found humility, reverence and charity. In comparison, *Mattia Pascal* is the portrayal of the non-autistic, manipulative cognitive empathy which fails to attain the costly, selfless Incarnational metaphor of apophatic fiction. This makes *Mattia Pascal* a salutary tale for the neurotypical reader. Recalling the earlier autistic reading of Karl Barth, the gift of an autistic

---

135. Pirandello, *Mattia Pascal*, 244.

136. In Beckett's *The Unnameable,* the nameless protagonist muses continuously; there is only existential reflection as monologue and no action.

137. Pirandello, *Uno, Nessuno*, 159.

138. Pirandello, cover matter, *Uno, Nessuno (*Mondadori edition).

Krisis is offered to the neurotypical reader, as the gift of failure; a failure which Mattia Pascal fails to attain.

THE "ARTIST OF FAILURE"

In an interview late in life, Pirandello reflects:

> When I was a child I had difficulties even with my mother, and as for my father, it appeared to be quite impossible to communicate with him, not just when I was preparing myself to do so but when I had actually tried and had failed abysmally. As an artist I owe a great deal to him for the agony of those moments.[139]

A good example of Pirandello's art as the failure of communication is in the father's words ("F/father," for us, as the Autistic Gxd), in *Sei Caratteri*:

> But if it is all here, the evil! In the words! . . . And how can we understand each other, dear Sir, if I put into the words I say the value of things as they are in me; whereas whoever listens to them inevitably understands them in the sense and with the value they have for him, of a world as he has it inside himself? We think we understand each other; we never do![140]

Pirandello (the man) is not being read as autistic here—but he is articulating a "failure" which autism might inhabit in a theologically creative way. To be an artist of failure is to return to the starting point of our journey, and to think through Rowan Williams' words that we must endeavor to be "learning 'difficulty' itself."[141] To be an artist of failure could be seen as a supreme ability for the articulation of what a universal autism can recognize as

---

139. "L'Illustrazione Italiana," June 23, 1935, quoted in Giudice, *Pirandello*, 6.
140. Büdel, *Pirandello*, 57.
141. Williams, *Edge of Words*, 116.

the authentic understanding of a tear in the (metaphysical) fabric. This is an endless "Chinese box" of enactment without the possibility of final answer.[142] Susan Bassnett McGuire writes that

> [In Sei Caratteri] Pirandello has created a play about the processes of artistic creation, a study of the relativity of form enclosed within a formal framework. It is therefore not only a play that contains within it another play, it is a play about the nature of the play constructed on a Chinese box principle, where the answering of one question merely opens the lid to another.[143]

The "Chinese box" is the play-within-the-play:

> Like Shakespeare, Pirandello is concerned with using the stage as a metaphor for life, but unlike Shakespeare there is the added ironical dimension arising from Pirandello's particular vision of the dichotomy between art and life, between the fixed and the movable.[144]

Bassnet-McGuire is right to see irony as the contrast between Shakespearean and Pirandellian absurd tragedy, but the issue is not of a dichotomy between art and life, but their confluence in the gestalt psychology of "construction" used by Pirandello, as we have seen in the construction trope in *Uno, Nessuno.*

To think of this enactment of the tragi-comic, a surprisingly apt image takes us back, in conclusion, to the metaphor of Gxd's universal autism as a tear in the metaphysical fabric. In *Mattia Pascal,* the narrative relentlessly lampoons the theosophist landlord Paleari's imagery

---

142. Which can be seen as an influence in Samuel Beckett's work, for example, *Waiting for Godot* or *Happy Days,* in the hoping for a definitive message that never arrives.

143. Bassnet-McGuire, *Luigi Pirandello,* 47.

144. Bassnet-McGuire, *Luigi Pirandello,* 69.

348 THE AUTISM OF GXD

of enlightenment,[145] but the narrator Pascal/Meis remarks "Who could contradict him, after all?"[146] Paleari comes up with a strangely comic image—"the tragedy of Orestes[147] in a marionette theatre!"[148]

Paleari speculates on this event, telling Meis that if a hole were torn in the paper sky, "(Oreste's) eyes . . . would go straight to that hole, from which every kind of evil influence would crowd the stage, and Orestes would suddenly feel helpless. In other words, Orestes would become Hamlet. There's the difference between ancient tragedy and modern, Signor Meis—believe me—a hole torn in a paper sky."[149]

It seems that Paleari, despite his quasi-Platonist metaphysics, has expressed something essential both to Pirandello's thought and to the autistic hermeneutic. A "hole torn in a paper sky" works to "pierce" the illusion of the play—Orestes becomes Hamlet, tortured and rendered paralyzed by doubt. This hole in the sky is for Pirandello the fundamental interrogation prompted by his disruption of the willing suspension of disbelief; it "tears open" the conventions by which we live. The hole in the sky, for a universal autism, is the tear in the fabric which challenges all neurotypical mindreading complacency. Neither Pirandello nor the autistic myth-maker will let the reader off the hook, and as marionettes, we readers are left hanging irrevocably in this "suspension of suspension." The absolute autism which Pirandello's last novel achieves is its "no

---

145. Particularly in chapter 13, "The Little Lantern," 154ff; Meis comments that Paleari's eccentric fascination with the metaphor of enlightenment could be called *lanternosophy* (155).

146. Pirandello, *Mattia Pascal*, 160.

147. Orestes, the subject of Greek tragedy and myth, endured madness as a purification of guilt.

148. Pirandello, *Mattia Pascal*, 139.

149. Pirandello, *Mattia Pascal*, 139.

conclusion." After that, Pirandello turns to play-writing, because only play-acting is now possible. Absolute autism well understands Teresa's matter-of-fact humility when she tells us that writing the mystical is impossible—we know Mindfulness of Separation all too well. And yet she has blazed a trail for us, and we have followed her.

The paper sky has been torn, meaning that we now know it to be only paper, yet it remains our sky. Our paper sky is where we draw our paper fairies, and write our autistic, apophatic, absurd, and haecceic stories.

By One-Self
In the End, One Is by One's Self

In the end, also, we have seen, there is no conclusion. Here, as (non)Moscarda has taught us, there is no need for names. So, like him, I can be this book—or this book can be me. I will consider this—but first, to attempt a "proper" conclusion. For this book-self, which has travelled toward Tillich's, Altizer's and Pirandello's "honest atheism," the task of this conclusion is to articulate what this non-conclusion means for our deepest faith within this void. It needs to come to a conclusion about (or in) a non-conclusion.

In the Introduction, the initial premise was that "deep called to deep," in a meeting of LTA[1] and autism. We found ourselves standing in a paradoxically dazzling darkness; finding identity at the margins, which might, we speculated, in fact be a truer center. Love became a disability, and thus became the most sacred, divine, kenotic Love as a result. Within all this, we wove a myth of autistic love in all its apophatic literary facets; fascination, Mindfulness of Separation, and Incarnational metaphor. It called out from deep to deep: to mystical theology; to atheology; to poetry; and finally, to a novel of Nothing.

---

1. Literature, Theology and the Arts.

Perhaps our most (politically?) significant achievement will be to bring the divergent, creative modes of autistic being into view of theology, to hope that the theological reader will hear autism speak not as the monster of the "I am Autism" scaremongering narrative, but as a spiritual gift, in the terms suggested by John Swinton of autistic love. Could this, perhaps, offer a deeper understanding of the kenotic Jesus?—and of the Beatitudes which invert ability and disability, as we stand in the grace of God who stands with us?

This is, as Carl Raschke reminds us,[2] forever a Barthian[3] *theologia viatorum*,[4] where autism is not "cured" or "resolved," and we can never really draw conclusions anyway. The poor (whose spirits are blessed in the Beatitudes) are, in Jesus' words, "always with us,"[5] and the gift is, to return to Rowan Williams' phrase, "learning difficulty itself."[6] There will always be the glorious, subversive power of autism's (dis)ability, in the universal autism of Blake's and Altizer's universal humanity of the anonymous Jesus. There will always be the spiritual insight of a second naïveté where we inhabit T S Eliot's Little Gidding and "know the place for the first time" precisely by not knowing. Like (non)Moscarda we are free by having no name and no conclusion. We will keep coming back to our uncured selves in all our glory.

---

2. Raschke, *Theological Thinking*, 2.
3. Of Karl Barth.
4. A theology of journeyings.
5. Mark 4:17.
6. Williams, *Edge of Words*, 125.

AN ANONYMOUS, ANECDOTAL (NON) CONCLUSION

Now, to answer to the non-conclusion to which, finally, Pirandello's *Nessuno* led, an inconclusive conclusion might be possible, by returning to the beginning. We can "begin again" (the non-ending to Joyce's *Finnegan's Wake*) with Heather Walton's thinking about the poetic as answering to that to which theology cannot answer. This might outwit the illusory compromise of a conclusion, and yet conclude. It is an answer, thereby, which, in Blanchot's terms, is a non-answer; in other words, the answer's absence is in this poem which I am now writing to you. Moscarda relinquished his name, but in so doing he became the pure "I" of the text ("when the door is I"). Now, "I" will follow Moscarda, as the I of the text, and I am now speaking to you, in the first person. I will count the ways of the improbable journey to the nexus of autism, literature and theology. I am an autistic voice. I am, in Aristotle's terms, an implausible possibility.[7] I am improbable, on multiple levels, or rather, as an autistic person, I have ended up in improbable places. Or perhaps not.

Aristotle also writes:

> as Agathon says,
> One might perchance say that was probable—
> That things improbable oft will hap to men.
> For what is improbable does happen, and therefore it
> is probable that improbable things will happen.[8]

Things improbable also happen to women, and the confluence of improbable probability is a marginal place. It is perhaps also the place where moments of unexpected

---

7. Aristotle, "Rhetoric," in *Complete Works*, II.24:9.
8. Aristotle, "Rhetoric," in *Complete Works*, II.24:9.

interdisciplinarity can come to be. Margin of margins, not without intersectionality, that the "I" of this book would be a woman, a literary reader, a theological thinker, and an autist.

The stereotypes of autism:

1. Autism is a male condition
2. Autism occurs in children
3. Autistic people only read non-fiction[9]
4. Autistic people don't believe in religion[10]

And yet, here we are. Is this an outrageous improbability? Perhaps not:

1. Catriona Stewart's work with SWAN (Scottish Women's Autism Network)[11] has pioneered deeper understanding of autism and gender, and argues persuasively that autism is under-diagnosed in women—we are socially conditioned to learn to adopt roles—we mask our autism, learning to mimic, at the cost of expressing our real selves. Also—"New research suggests the disorder often looks different in females, many of whom are being misdiagnosed and missing out on the support they need."[12]

2. UK NICE (National Institute for Clinical Excellence) guidelines for assessing adults for an autism diagnosis: "core autism signs and symptoms (difficulties in social interaction and communication and the

---

9. But special interests often include the imaginary worlds of TV dramas—texts that are read obsessively, avidly, and perhaps more deeply than by neurotypicals.

10. The large number of people with autism who attended the ASPARRG (Autistic Spectrum People and Religion Research Group)/Glasgow University one-day seminar on autism and religion in September 2013 suggested that this might be an over-generalization.

11. http://www.swanscotland.com/.

12. Szalavitz, "Autism—It's Different in Girls."

presence of stereotypic behaviour, resistance to change or restricted interests) that have been present in childhood and continuing into adulthood."[13] Autistic children grow up into autistic adults—diagnostic structures only came into general use around the 1970s, and only in the framework of looking for developmental delays in children. So, untold generations born before the 1970s have been creatively peppered with undiagnosed autists, and some of us twigged that we might belong to that branch of the family tree.

3. And oh, of course, Autistic people don't do metaphor. But, oops, I just did—with the branches of the tree where I "twig," and relentlessly as the rhetorical base of this whole myth. Which is

4. in the end, really all about Gxd.

Gxd as known in autism? Was that even possible? How improbable is it that somebody mindblind and woefully lacking (asked at one point in life, how "someone so clever can be so stupid"), can be so clearly autistic and yet still—somehow—feel the irresistible need for poetry and for Gxd? I didn't come to poetry, or the novel, or film, or drama easily. They baffled me. Watching an episode of the police drama *Z Cars* as a child, I saw a scene where the police discovered a dead body in a boat. I was baffled by how the producers managed to find a dead body to use. And yet. Words, music, art, held something, just as behind all the incomprehensible nonsense of religion, something was also there. Words described, and the world cried out to be described. The branch of an organization was the branch of a tree, and somehow trees, and organizations, and genealogies, and things to hang shoes on, all cried

---

13. "Autism Spectrum Disorder in Adults."

out to be described. To de-scribe is not to de-cipher. Ciphers are the conventions of the Neurotypical world, too easy for autistic creative perplexity.[14]

Dante's pregnant words as he begins the journey through Inferno, Purgatorio, and Paradiso:

> nel mezzo del cammin di nostra vita,
> mi ritrovai per una selva oscura,
> ché la diritta via era smarrita.
>
> [Midway in the path of our life
> I found [rediscovered] myself in [by means of] a dark wood
> Whose right path was lost][15]

Deep calls to deep in the overwhelming of the waters, and in overwhelming darkness we feel the urgency of Bishop David Jenkins' words, which permeate LTA as witnessed by both Walton and Jasper, that theology is inadequate to the task, and we are "in the dark."

I had a strange experience of understanding darkness as personal reality—as autism *in mezzo del cammin,* with an autism diagnosis, not in childhood but "midway in the path of our life," and I began to wonder whether autism might also be a way to approach the darkness of LTA's abyss.[16] This felt anything but negative (since, as the whole of this book, really, has argued, negativity/disability is the paradoxical key), as it assumed a profoundly positive

---

14. An echo of Italo Calvino's phrase "systematic perplexity." Calvino's work, in its poetic taxonomies of the visible world, has also been a hospitable environment. See also Dunster, "Abyss of Calvino's Deconstructive Writing."

15. Dante Alighieri, *La Divina Commedia—Inferno* 1.1 [this writer's own translation]; *mi ritrovai* suggests, perhaps (another direction to be reserved for future research) re-finding the self is *as per* the wood, not as an unfortunate error.

16. This "I" was midway through writing on a literary-theological abyss in Italo Calvino's work when the "thunderbolt" of the autism diagnosis arrived (recalling Mark C Taylor's use, in the Introduction to *Tears,* of the *paysage foudroyé* (thunderstruck landscape) image, could this be both a shock and an illumination—a "light bulb moment?").

negativity. The hell of Milton's darkness visible is to languish in the diminishing returns of the de-cipherment project. So, the decision to look unflinchingly at the dark wood, and the path in it. The decision to look at autism, and to look at the un-de-cipherment of theology. Instead, permission to "not understand" liberated something. I think it was the Emperor's New Clothes of "what the text means."

I'm not convinced that honest autistic atheists are spiritually "thin" people (to return to John Swinton's considerations about autism). Listening to some young, bright autists, I sense that they have wonderful creative potential and need only to be given permission (which also means support). Like them, I "need my own space." I'll always be mindblind, I'll always need to escape from noisy, overstimulating environments. Am I sad to miss the party? To be honest, it's kind of boring to be at a party, when I could be reading a poem instead.

Another level of autistic understanding emerged as my research progressed. The oft-sung lines from my childhood, of the Glasgow Victorian hymnist George Matheson came back again and again, from childhood: "Oh Love that wilt not let me go/I rest my weary soul in Thee."[17] Matheson's lines can seem sentimental, with their images of oceans, rainbows and blossoms, but Matheson was no happy-go-lucky penner of cheap lines but a blind poet of theological thinking.[18] When Matheson writes: "O light that followest all my way, I yield my flickering torch to thee," he too is invoking a dazzling light in darkness;

---

17. Matheson, "O Love that wilt not let me go," in Church of Scotland et al., *The Church Hymnary* no. 424.

18. Where another blind poet, John Milton, writes "they also serve who only stand and wait," Matheson is, with great difficulty, getting a Divinity degree from the University of Glasgow, and then, as an ordained minister, engaging in parish work.

the light is behind him, not before him, and he has only a flickering torch. Too easy, perhaps, to conclude with the happy ending of "seeing" God in the darkness. Matheson "trace(s) the rainbow through the rain" (tracing it with his blind eyes), holding on only to the conviction that "Thy promise is not vain." He does not sing in triumph that "mine eyes have seen the glory of the coming of the Lord."

It did, however, come to me that just as God "would not let me know" (my slip of the pen at the keyboard, like Hopkins'—I meant to say "let me go"), it was just as true that, despite every darkness, I would not let God go. Perhaps this was another aspect of autism, where we "simply won't let go," following things relentlessly to their conclusion (even the autistic bafflement of the non-conclusion). So I have written my way into this search for the painful autistic integrity of self-knowledge and acceptance. Finding Gxd within?

When I see Jesus in a fallen sycamore leaf, I am incomparably blessed. Like Matheson, I stay (mind)blind, but the promise can exist, perhaps more profoundly, in the space of the lack of ciphers. Is this lonely, without belonging to the ciphering community of religion? Not really, when I have the un-deciphering Osip Mandelstam as my friend.[19] Mandelstam sees only the swallows in his poem of exile, symbolizing nothing. And when, as Hopkins would, I trace Jesus in the veins of a fallen sycamore leaf, the promise is not vain but vein. This vein is also not only a seam in the rock, yielding precious stone. It also became the vein of the kenotic Christ, blood poured out in communion with the suffering discerned by intolerable affective

19. Mandelstam's poetry of exile: Jacques Rancière examines the way in which Mandelstam's poetry is a reaction against a symbolist poetry co-opted to Soviet propaganda. In contrast, the swallows of Mandelstam's poem fly free of constraint, exiled from referentiality, see Rancière, *Flesh of Words*.

empathy. Nevertheless, this is all emphatically word games, not "serious," kataphatic, systematic theology. The promise "not vain" is only a promise held in poetry, and Jesus does not "appear before me" in an allegorical conclusion. So my truest autistic self, with the support of all that my patient teachers have taught me, resists the symbolic temptation and traces simply the fragility of the autism (another slip—the autumn) leaf with its color, texture, shape; and, as irreligious as an Altizer or a Pirandello, I am incomparably blessed.

I learned it all back-to-front. For a start, I was making heavy weather, not least of writing a literature and theology thesis, when I learned I had autism, or, rather, received the name for it, so literature and theology was already the site of the disaster where autism, right at the end, entered the field.[20] Looking at my theological searching, I had the shock of surveying it and exclaiming, "But this is all autism!" In the light of conscious autism seeking coping strategies, my teachers helped me learn to read texts, and read people. "Reading" people can be learned when it is not intuitive.[21] Learning *that* I didn't know, and then, slowly, *what* I didn't know, made it possible to adapt.

In terms of reading, permission not to know meant that the reading journey was a back-to-front, archaeological historical project. Starting (as instinctively I did) with postmodern fiction, I found a hospitable space where the emperor's new clothes were already out the window, and the game was to not know. This was a text I could enter. Moving backwards from there, Modernist fiction's unreliable narrator also gave me permission to not know, and to validate my Mindblindness. Armed with this permission, I

20. Dunster, "Abyss of Calvino's Deconstructive Writing."
21. Samuel Baum's 2009 Fox TV series *Lie to Me* and Alex Gardiner's 2015 UPI film *Ex Machina* are two imagined examples of learned Mindreading.

could now travel back, forwards, and in any direction with permission to enter the text and wonder, and work at empathy with an act of conscious imagination. So, I allowed myself to picture the read room (another slip—red room) where the child Jane Eyre is locked up by her cruel aunt, and to linger on the description of her distress, and imagine it happening. What was happening was the nuts and bolts of the learned pleasure of reading. My instinctive, fascinated awareness of *ecceitas* finally could be coherent because it had been liberated with room to breathe. My honest atheism with its longing for Gxd finally validated that *ecceitas*. Truly, it has been a love story. Gxd—"x"—multiplication, marked incorrect, place x in the box, x marks the spot, gender-non-specific, kiss, chiasmus, unknown quantity? All of these. Gxd is Gxd, and I . . .

I feel like a child whose stabilizers have been removed from my bicycle, Gxd. I wobble, I veer around, I am afraid of falling. This book's not finished—can it really be complete?

You are alone.
You are not alone.
You are alone.

Let it be.

Didn't someone once say it is no sin to limp?

Piety and Divinity ©Paul Douglas Dunster

A Last Word from Paul

This book is dedicated in part to my son Paul, who has faithfully stayed with me on the journey of its writing. It is fitting that Paul should have the last word.

> Without generalising too heavily, I think it's fair to say that one of the core, universal experiences shared across all walks of Autistic life must be that of frustration in communication; in a literal sense, as well as in a myriad of metaphorical ones. Why is it difficult to communicate what we care about, and what about it is special? Why is there such a gap between what we think and feel, and our methods of showing it to others? Perhaps that is why art and creative pursuits appeal so much to people on the spectrum - where one language fails to convey, another may be substituted. Where explanations of the beauty of an ordered system may sound like anal retentive and accusatory nit-picking, a beautifully cultivated garden may

communicate that love just by being witnessed. Where words might not occur at all to convey fondness, a masterfully-baked custom birthday cake may appear from out the blue to get the message across. And for those more inclined to colours and shapes, a picture may paint a thousand words (more than just a thousand, in my experience, but so goes the classic idiom.) In my experience, that lifelong pursuit, of the means to discover the language by which I can help people understand what I feel, has defined my adult life, and like many others, I've spent so long learning new mannerisms and etiquettes in order to socially pass as neurotypical, that that inner feeling of what's special, important and beautiful sometimes feels like the core foundation of my identity, such as it is.

I know for sure that the author of *The Autism of Gxd: An Atheological Love Story* has experienced some of what I've detailed here, but what surprises me most about her book in reading it, has been the robust harmony between two subjects which I—alongside several people I know who've proofread for Ruth at varying stages in the book's creation—skeptically pondered the tenuous relation between Spirituality and The Spectrum. The reading was hard, initially: I'm not well-accustomed to academic language at the best of times, and at several points I chuckled to myself at the irony that I, a person with Asperger's Syndrome, should struggle with a text that is, at least in some minor sense, about me.

But I think it's a testament to the skill of writing and the extensive thinking and debate that have gone into the book's creation, that I did begin to see myself in it, and to understand that there is a connection between the subjects, an important message about the sense of wonder and of sensuality, of indescribable beauty which is greater than the sum of its definable parts, and what scholars and spiritually-minded philosophers in the past described as a blessed sense of divinity, before anyone had a name for Autism, or a spectrum for the experiences of those who live with it.

That is what I take away from *The Autism of Gxd*, as a person who does have an Autism Spectrum Disorder, and does not remotely believe in God, or in the concept of faith. In that vein, the art I made for the book portrays what I understand the book to be about, in my modest way: "Piety and Divinity," one figure with his focus narrowly and surely on scripture, and another figure looking broadly toward the sun.

Well done, mum—you finally finished it. If there is a heaven, Altizer and Gran are hopefully in each other's company there, resting easy and proud to know that you completed your opus, and found your love language.

Paul Douglas Dunster

Glossary

absolute autism	see autism, absolute
Absurd, Theatre of the	early twentieth century drama genre which embodies a sense of futility and absurdity, to make an existential claim about life as such
accretion	something added on to the original, in the sense of being picked up unintentionally, e.g., a build-up of dust
actuality	actual fact; a reality
aesthetic	regarding the appreciation of art
affective	relating to the emotions
affective empathy	empathy at a felt level
alliteration	poetic technique which repeats letters or sounds
anachronism	piece of information which betrays that the writer has inserted something from the wrong time period

Analogical language	language which compares things by analogy, eg, "my love is like a red, red rose"
anamnesis	literally "unforgetting" (Greek); the Platonic concept of coming to an awareness of a great truth, or deeper, eternal self, which we had forgotten
anthropology	academic study of human societies and cultures
anthropomorphism	seeing things from a human point of view; ascribing human nature to non-human objects
Antichrist	i, Satan in the form of an enemy who wreaks havoc on earth before the return of Christ; ii, The, a collection of writings by Friedrich Nietzsche
apocalyptic	revealing a sacred truth or object
apophatic	regarding language which speaks about what exceeds speech, by using paradox
apophatic fiction	(neologism in this book) poetry or fiction which is used as a strategy to express apophatic theology
aporetic	in the way of an aporia
aporia	opening or chasm which cannot be crossed

GLOSSARY

apotheosis	the appearance or revelation of a god
archetype	symbol, person or object, usually imaginary, invested with (often sacred) meaning in which other people or objects partake, based on it as the original source
AS	Asperger's Syndrome
Ascension, the	Christ's rising up to heaven after his resurrection
ASD	Autistic Spectrum Disorder
Asperger (also Asperger's) Syndrome	high-functioning form of autism first conceptualised by Hans Asperger in the 1940s
atheology	way of thought which affirms belief in Jesus, in the light of God having died in the cosmic event of Jesus' Crucifixion; a paradoxical faith where propositional theology is subverted
Augustinian	i, relating to the thinking of Saint Augustine; ii, belonging to the Augustinian monastic order founded by him
authorial intention	what the author intended her work to mean
autism, absolute	the imaginary, mythical state of total Mindblindness (qv) and autistic isolation

autism, conscious	a consciously chosen entry into a mythical autistic hermeneutic
autism, mythical	this book's imaginary construction of a cosmic, absolute autism based on the features of everyday, lived autism, as an archetype
autism, relative	the varied degrees of real, lived autism which can be observed clinically
autism, universal	the imaginary, mythical, all-pervading autism of the texts we read, seen when we read them autistically
autist	person with autism
autistic hermeneutic	(in this book) strategy for reading texts as if through the eyes of a mythical autism
autistic spectrum	continuum in the human species from being less autistic to more autistic
autos	self (Greek)
Beatitudes	Jesus' sayings, which begin with "blessed are"; they invert normal expectations of what blessedness is (see Matthew Ch. 5)

Becoming	(Hegelian) ever-evolving emergence of changing Being into new forms which in their turn will evolve into another new form of Being
borderline personality disorder	psychological condition involving emotional instability
causality	mechanism where cause produces effect
CE	Christian Era; the calendar based on time elapsed since the time of Christ's birth; an interfaith/non-Christian alternative to using "AD" *Anno Domini* (Latin) "year of the Lord"
charism	spiritual gift to be used in service to Gxd, humanity and nature
Charismatic	movement, church, or person who practices a belief of being filled with the Spirit of Gxd, often resulting in exuberant and informal worship and the use of spiritual gifts
Chi [X]	(pronounced "kai") a character of the Greek alphabet similar in shape to the English letter X

Chiasmic	inverted in a way which reminds the reader of the X-shape of the letter Chi, for example when Jesus inverts norms and expectations by saying that the last shall be first
Christendom	Christian civilisation; particularly Western culture as shaped by the dominance of the Church
Christology	study of the nature of Christ
chronos	scientific, chronological time
clôture	literally "cloister" (French); a set-apart place
cognitive	regarding intellectual function
cognitive empathy	intuitive ability to understand another person's feelings and intentions at an intellectual level
coincidentia oppositorum	(Latin) identical nature of opposites which paradoxically meet as one
co-inherence	condition of existing together as one
configurative	describing and giving meaning to
conscious autism	see autism, conscious
Conservative theology	theology which tends to stress traditional values and theologies; in some cases, though not necessarily, associated with Right-wing politics

GLOSSARY

contemplative	Person or mode of practicing contemplation, particularly by meditating on sacred subjects
Courtly Love	Medieval poetry genre in which the hero accomplishes feats of bravery in order to win the woman he loves
credo	literally "I believe" (Latin); a statement of faith
Dasein	literally "the one" (German); as used by Heidegger, it means a sense of authentically being fully present; "being there"
Deconstruction	As first discussed by Derrida in the 1960s, that which within language which tends to question its complacency about simple acts of predication; a challenge to the Western tradition of metaphysics
Deism	nineteenth century concept of a philosophical God, rather than the God revealed through Scripture
demythologizing	process of stripping away a literal understanding of the miraculous in order to see a spiritual, rather than literal, meaning in Scripture
determinate	conditioned by other causes; part of a chain of causality

dialectic	meeting of opposites which resolves into a synthesis, which then meets another opposing idea or entity, thereby evolving
differentiation	scattering of different elements into the formation of diverse and composite objects
doctrine	teaching sanctioned by the Church to be acceptable and true
doxology	language of praise and worship
DSM-5	American Psychiatric Association's Diagnostic and Statistical Manual (Edition 5)
ecce homo	"behold the man!" (Latin); the words spoken by Pilate at Christ's trial prior to the Crucifixion; a genre of Christian art which focuses on Christ as he was at that moment
ecceitas	neologism by Hopkins meaning a poetic version of *haecceitas* (Latin; literally *ecce* (behold) plus *haecceitas* (thisness))
embodiment	the state of being made real in an object
"emo"	youth subculture which focuses on emotion and angst; emo young people often wear black clothes, make up or hair dye

GLOSSARY

empirical	which can be tested by scientific methods
enjambement	poetic device using a line of poetry whose sense runs into the next line
ennui	literally "boredom" (French); in Existentialism, a sense of world-weariness which borders on despair
epic	poetry genre where a story is told in the form of a long poem
epistemology	science of how things are known; a person or intellectual framework's own mode of knowing
eros	sexual love
eschatology	study of the end times before the coming of the Messiah (in Christian terms, the return of Christ)
esoteric	accessible only to initiates or those with specialised knowledge
etiology	clinical cause which produces the symptoms of a medical condition

Eucharist	the "Lord's Supper"; a ritual re-enactment of Christ's last meal with the disciples where he says "do this in remembrance of me; this bread is my body, this wine is my blood," and believers consume bread and wine which mystically are, or symbolise, the body and blood of Christ
Evangelicalism	literally, focusing on evangel, ie, salvation as "good news"; a religious movement which emphasises personal salvation through faith; also personal commitment to the (often fairly literal) teachings of Scripture, and evangelism (winning others to the movement)
Existentialism	early/mid twentieth century philosophical/literary trend which emphasises Being as an act of personal autonomy and responsibility with a certain sense of aloneness; often with a sense of futility or despair
Expressionist	early Twentieth century art genre using bold colours and stark lines to express, rather than meticulously represent, a person or object
farce	humour which is absurd or ridiculous

farceur	comedian performing farcical humour
fiat	(Latin) "let there be"; the words spoken by God in creating the world
figurative	not literal; eg, "you are my sunshine"
Fool, Holy	archetypal religious figure whose behaviour seems (or is) foolish
Franciscan	relating to the monastic order founded by St Francis of Assisi; a member of that order
fundamentalism	religious movement which focuses on a literal interpretation of Scripture; often connected with strict evangelical doctrines based on the Protestant Reformation
garrulousness	tendency to speak at great length or excessively
geek	person who may be ridiculed for their obsessive intellectual interests
Geheiss	literally "behest" (German); a sense of calling out for how things should truly be
Geist	immanent World Spirit (German); God-in-and-as the world; particularly as developed by G. W. F. Hegel

haecceitas	literally "thisness" (Latin); a quality of uniqueness of an individual object
haecceity	the concept of *haecceitas* as it is used in modern philosophy
Hegelian	Related to the philosophy of G. W. F. Hegel
heresy	belief which runs counter to the orthodox teaching of the Church
hermeneut	person using a hermeneutic
hermeneutic	strategy for reading, and more broadly, for understanding the world
hermeneutics	academic study of how different hermeneutics operate
historical-critical	see textual-historical
Holy Fool	see fool, holy
homoousios	literally *homo* (same) plus *ousios* (being) (Greek); used of the doctrine of Christ as having the being of God and the being of a human, simultaneously and eternally in one person
hyperessential	of a higher kind of reality
hyperlexia	excessive skill in reading and writing
illusionistic	describing art which creates a strong sense of reality, as if the object were actually there

immanence	dwelling within, especially as the indwelling of God in a person or world
Impressionist	early Modern art genre where a deliberate vagueness of style does not represent an object literally line for line, and yet captures its essence
incarnation	becoming flesh
Incarnation, the	God becoming flesh in human form
Incarnational metaphor	neologism used in this book, meaning an autistic "literal metaphor" which becomes a poetic form, where Christ is also embodied in a theologically powerful form, as atheology
individuation	philosophical concept of what makes an object individual
ineffable	incapable of being expressed in words
inscape	(in the thinking of Gerard Manley Hopkins) inner, spiritual/poetic quality of an object
instress	similar to inscape
Intense World Syndrome	theory that autistic people experience the world in a very intense way, with heightened sensitivity

internal rhyme	rhyme which happens within a line of poetry, rather than being repeated at the end of different lines
irreligious	lacking in religion; or, often, lacking in religious morality
islet of ability	exceptional talent in a person who seems otherwise cognitively impaired
Jesuit	of the monastic order of St Ignatius of Loyola
jongleur	(French) an early Renaissance travelling performer of songs and humor
jouissance	"play" (French); in Deconstruction, the play of linguistic signs treated as a game
kairos	(Greek) special, heightened, significant and sacred time
kataphatic	concerning language which is straightforward in theological terms
Kenosis	(Greek) self-emptying; total self-sacrifice (of Jesus)
kerygma	(Greek) the message of the gospel as it is preached in the early Church

GLOSSARY

Krisis	(German) in Barth's theology, the cosmic, existential crisis in which humanity's sinfulness and damnation is met with God's grace and forgiveness
Liberal Theology	theological movement which emerged in the nineteenth century; seeing the Bible as a collection of human documents which nevertheless contain divine truths about God
literal metaphor	(neologism in this book) autistic processing of metaphor which takes it literally
Literal-mindedness	the autistic trait of interpreting figurative language literally
logos	(Greek) spoken or written word in the sense of meaning; Word as cosmic event in the person of Jesus
LTA	Literature, Theology and the Arts
lyrical	poetic style which usually describes nature in loving appreciation
metanoia	(Greek; literally "turning around"); repentance
metaphor	poetic language where one thing is said actually to be another, because some attribute is shared by both

metaphore vive	(French) term used by Paul Ricœur to mean literally "metaphor which lives"; the way in which poetic language can break free of an oppressive metaphysics
metaphysics	literally *meta* (above) plus *physios* (the physical) (Greek); the study of reality understood in non-material terms
metonym	word which can be used as a shorthand of another expression because it forms part of what that expression involves; eg,"Westminster" as a word to describe "the parliament which meets in the Palace of Westminster"
mimetic	representative; for example, a portrait is mimetic of the person whose likeness it is
mindblindness	difficulty understanding the meanings and intentions of other people's speech
Mindfulness of Separation	(In this book) A hermeneutic and a way of being which inhabits a radical autistic hermeneutic. Here, the absence of Gxd is, paradoxically, the only way to inhabit the presence of Gxd.

Modernism	late nineteenth/early twentieth century artistic and intellectual movement where what is made is radically new, but so also is the method by which it is made
mystical theology	theological language which is concerned with the ineffable nature of God, and attempts to "say the unsayable"
myth	truth-telling story, with a sacred dimension
mythical autism	(in this book) the imaginary hermeneutic and voice of what autistic traits would be like if they were made into a sacred story of spiritual meaning
naïveté, second	deliberate return to simplicity, which values it as if for the first time
narcissistic personality disorder	psychological condition involving intense self-preoccupation
natural philosophy	pre-modern scientific reasoning about the natural world
Natural Theology	nineteenth century belief that God can be discerned through logic extrapolated from the created order

naturalistic	adhering to a strict faithfulness to the material facts without interpretation which could be imaginary or non-material in any way; in art, of a close and detailed representation
neologism	new word invented by a writer or speaker
Neo-Platonism	second to sixth century CE revival and further development of Plato's teaching
neurotribe	class of people who are cognitively different to the world around them, for example, autists
neurotypical	of people or brain functions which do not diverge from the normal
Nicene Council	fourth century CE Church Council which adopted the doctrine of Christ's oneness of being with Gxd the Father
nominative	form of grammar written in the third person (eg, it is, she knows, he feels)
Nonbeing	negating force; the necessary opposite of Being in Hegel's dialectical process
non-foundationalist	not acknowledging any stable foundation, e.g., metaphysics or Gxd

onomatopeia	in language, an effect where the word sounds like what it is describing, eg, thud, splash, miaow
ontological difference	the way in which philosophy can assert that beyond our doctrine of Being we could imagine a simpler being without our cognitive "baggage" (particularly in Heidegger's thought)
ontology	philosophical discipline which concerns what the nature of being is
onto-theology	belief that Being is anchored in Gxd
Orestes	mythical Greek character also in Greek tragedies; a murderer with madness and the desire for revenge
ostensive	expressing a message or meaning
paradox	proposition where two mutually exclusive propositions are both true
paranomasia	word-play, e.g., puns
para-rhyme	two sounds which do not exactly rhyme but almost do, e.g., storm/torn
parse	to analyse a sentence in terms of its grammar and syntax; to dissect it

pathology	diseased condition; study of disease
perichoresis	literally *peri* (around) plus *chore* (dance) (Greek); the doctrine of the Trinity, where Father, Son and Holy Spirit are one Gxd in three Persons, dancing together
perichoretic	operating as, or similar to, perichoresis
play-within-a-play	dramatic device where characters in a play are scripted to stage their "own play" within it
plenum	literally fullness (Latin); in philosophy, a totality
poetics	strategy or strategies used to write poetry
polysemic	capable of more than one meaning
Postmodernism	artistic/philosophical movement from mid/late twentieth century which challenges metaphysical certainties and conventions
pragmatic	intended for a particular use, to be used practically
praxis	(Greek) practical outworking of a theory or belief
predication	in grammar, the act of relating an attribute to an object, e.g., this apple is for you
predicative	relating to predication

GLOSSARY

Presence	In philosophy or theology, a presence of ultimate and total significance—see also Real Presence
primal	before written civilisation and history
Prime Mover	in Aristotle and Aquinas, the ultimate Cause of all there is; Gxd
primitive Christianity	an ideal of what Christianity might have been in its very beginnings, before being shaped by the institutions of the Church and New Testament
primordial	see primal
propositional	expressing a point of view or argument in a straightforward way
prosaic	not poetic
psychopathy	clinical diagnosis involving lack of empathy and often cruelty
quidditas	literally "thatness" (Latin); the nature of an object defined by describing its physical properties
quiddity	*quidditas* as used in modern philosophical reasoning
quiescence	quietness or peacefulness
Rationalism	philosophy which bases knowledge on the power of reason

Reader Response Theory	the idea that the meaning of literature exists within the relationship between the reader and what is being read
Real Presence	The actual, mystical presence of the body and blood of Christ in the Eucharistic bread and wine
redaction	recording and interpreting, as undertaken by scribes
Redaction history	the way in which different writers in history have used different content and style, and the study of how to interpret these differences in a historical context
relationality	the state of being or expressing a relationship
relative autism	see autism, relative
relativism	the belief that all truths are relative, and there is no absolute truth
relevance theory	theory that in the normal brain, we are guided in how we interpret speech, in a way that seems relevant because of the context
Religious Studies	academic study of different religions in a way which does not assign value judgements but merely observes and explores them

remythologizing	(in this book) taking scientific or theological content and building a myth to express it
Renaissance	historical period in the West of extraordinary flourishing in intellectual advancement and artistic expression, circa. sixteenth to seventeenth centuries
RRBIs	(In autism) Restrictive and Repetitive Behaviours and Interests
sacrament	in the Church, a ritual enactment of a spiritual truth, e.g., baptism, marriage; The Sacrament usually meaning the Eucharist
sacred profane	Thomas Altizer's term indicating the assertion that all is sacred and all is profane (i.e., secular)
savantism	uncanny abilities of observation possessed by autists
Scotism	the teaching of John Duns Scotus
second naïveté	see naïveté, second
self-subverting	that which undoes itself; two terms used together to negate each other, e.g., brilliant darkness
Sensory Connoisseur	autistic person who has a fine appreciation of sensory detail

signified	something which is indicated by another thing eg, roses (signified) are red (signifier)
signifier	something which indicates another thing, eg, magnolias (signified) are white (signifier)
simile	poetic statement which indicates that one thing is similar to another, e.g., dry leaves are like paper
skandalon	(Greek) a stone which people stumble over; an obstacle
Sorge	literally "Care" (German); in Heidegger's thought, an awareness of our finitude
Soteriology	study or doctrine of the nature of Christ as saviour
sprung rhythm	archaic form of poetic rhythm which is complex and irregular; used by Gerard Manley Hopkins
stigmatic	person whose body mysteriously displays the wounds Christ suffered on the Cross
stimming	repeated body movements, often appearing eccentric, as a means to relieve stress
subjective	from one's own individual point of view
syndrome	medical term for a collection of symptoms which frequently occur together

GLOSSARY

synthesis	in Hegel, the process of opposites meeting and a new thing arising from them
systematic theology	theological thinking expressed in a coherent and logical system
Tantalus	mythical Greek figure destined to be forever hungry and thirsty despite being ("tantalisingly") close to food and water
telos	(Greek) end or purpose for which something is made
teleological	concerning the end or purpose of something
textual-historical	method of studying ancient documents where differences of style and content can be inferred to mean different authors or historical periods when the document was written (see also Redaction History)
thatness	identity of an object as specified by its characteristics (see *quidditas*)
Theatre of the Absurd	See Absurd, Theatre of the
Theism	belief in one supreme God alone
theodicy	argument to explain why evil and suffering exist in a world created by a loving God
theonomy	the rule of God in the sense of a rationale or natural law, rather than a despotic or judicial rule

Theory of Mind Mechanism	Baron-Cohen's concept of a brain mechanism where one is able to understand (theorise) another person's feelings and intentions intuitively, by tone of voice, body language etc.
thisness	the identity of an object characterised simply by the fact of its existence (see *haecceitas*)
Thomism	The teaching of St. Thomas Aquinas
thrash metal	musical genre with heavy bass and aggressive sound
threatenedness	feeling of existential vulnerability
TOMM	see Theory of Mind Mechanism
Transcendental Signified	the ultimate object which cannot describe or indicate anything else because it is the origin of all; Gxd/the Absolute
troubadour	poet mainly writing Courtly Love poetry, in Medieval Europe
Übermensch	literally "Overmen" (German); Nietzsche's concept of a superior form of humanity which would be able to rise above fear and inauthentic moralities of submission
unconditioned	what is beyond and above the chain of cause and effect
undifferentiated	purely One, and not composed of different parts or elements

universal autism	see autism, universal
universal sacrament	Hugh de Victor's Medieval concept of all creation as the body of Christ, and therefore charged with sacred significance
Univocal Language/ Univocity	language where analogy is not used to compare things, but where there is an identity; eg, "roses are red"
Very Light	absolute light (archaic English)
vocative	grammatical formula of words which is addressed to someone in the second person, eg. "Come here."
WCC	see Weak Central Coherence
Weak Central Coherence	brain processing pattern where there is great attention to detail, but an impaired ability to make wider connections in order to grasp the bigger picture

Bibliography

LITERATURE AND THEOLOGY

Books and Articles

Altizer, Thomas J. J. *The Descent into Hell: A Study of the Radical Reversal of the Christian Consciousness*. New York: Seabury, 1979.

———. *Godhead and the Nothing*. Albany: State University of New York Press, 2003.

———. *The Gospel of Christian Atheism*. Philadelphia, PA: Westminster, 1966.

———. *Living the Death of God: A Theological Memoir*. New York: SUNY Press, 2006.

———. *The New Apocalypse: The Radical Christian Vision of William Blake*. Aurora, CO: Davies Group, 1967.

———. *Oriental Mysticism and Biblical Eschatology*. Philadelphia: Westminster, 1961.

———. *The Self-Embodiment of God*. New York: Harper Row, 1977.

Altizer, Thomas J. J., and John Warwick Montgomery. *The Altizer-Montgomery Dialogue: A Chapter in the God Is Dead Controversy*. Downers Grove, IL: InterVarsity, 1967.

Altizer, Thomas J. J., and William Hamilton. *Radical Theology and the Death of God*. London: Pelican, 1968.

Aristotle. *Complete Works*. Buffalo, NY: Prometheus Classics, 2017.

Auden, W. H. *Collected Shorter Poems 1927–1957.* London: Faber and Faber, 1966.

BIBLIOGRAPHY

Auerbach, Erich. *Mimesis: The Representation of Reality in Western Literature*. Translated by W. Trask. Edited by W. Said. Princeton: Princeton University Press, 2013.

Augustine of Hippo. *The Confessions of Saint Augustine*. Translated by E. M. Blaiklock. London: Hodder and Stoughton, 1983.

Barth, Karl. *The Epistle to the Romans* (Der Römerbrief). Translated by Edwyn C. Hoskyns. Oxford: Oxford University Press, 1968.

Barthes, Roland. *Image, Music, Text*. Translated by Stephen Heath. London: Fontana, 1977.

———. *Roland Barthes by Roland Barthes*. Translated by Richard Howard. New York: Hill & Wang, 2010.

Bassnett-McGuire, Susan. *Luigi Pirandello*. London: McMillan, 1983.

Bevis, Matthew, ed. *The Oxford Handbook of Victorian Poetry*. Oxford: Oxford University Press, 2013.

Bini, Daniela, "Pirandello's Philosophy and Philosophers," in DiGaetani, John, ed., A Companion to Pirandello Studies, Santa Barbara, CA; Greenwood, 1991.

Birch, Jonathan. "Gospel Narratives, Miracles, and the 'Critical' Reader: The Eclipse of the Supernatural—Case Studies in Eighteenth and Nineteenth Century Biblical Hermeneutics." *Relegere: Studies in Religion and Reception* 5.1 (2016) 61–93.

Blake, William. *Complete Poetry and Prose*. Edited by David Erdman, Harold Bloom, and William Golding. New York: Anchor, 1982.

Blanchot, Maurice. *The Space of Literature* (L'espace littéraire). Translated by Ann Smock. Lincoln: University of Nebraska Press, 1982.

Bonhoeffer, Dietrich. *The Cost of Discipleship*. New York: Simon & Schuster, 2018.

———. *Letters from Prison*. London: Macmillan, 1967.

Borges, Jorge Luis. *Labyrinths: Selected Stories and Other Writings*. Translated by Donald A. Yates and James E. Irby. London: Penguin, 1964.

Bradbury, Malcolm, and James McFarlane, eds. *Modernism: A Guide to European Literature 1890–1930*. London: Penguin, 1991.

Büdel, Oscar. *Pirandello*. London: Bowes and Bowes, 1969.

Bultmann, Rudolf. *Jesus Christ and Mythology*. London, UK: SCM Press, 2012.

Calvino, Italo. "I Livelli della Realtà." In *Una Pietra Sopra*, by Italo Calvino. Milan: Mondadori, 1995.

———. *Invisible Cities*. San Diego: Harcourt Brace Jovanovich, 1974.

Caputi, Anthony. *Pirandello and the Crisis of Modern Consciousness*. Chicago: University of Illinois Press, 1988.

Chadwick, Henry. *The Early Church*. London: Penguin, 1982.

Chesterton, G. K. *Saint Francis of Assisi*. Nashville: Sam Torode Book Arts, 2011.

Christ, Carol T. *Victorian and Modern Poetics*. Chicago: University of Chicago Press, 1984.

Christensen, Darrel E. *The Search for Concreteness: Reflections on Hegel and Whitehead: A Treatise on Self-Evidence and Critical Method in Philosophy*. New York: Associated University Presses, 1986.

Church of Scotland et. al. *The Church Hymnary, Revised Edition*. London: Oxford University Press, 1927.

Clark, Timothy. *Heidegger*. Oxford: Routledge, 2002.

Coleridge, S. T. *Biographia Literaria, Collected Works*. Vol. 7. Edited by James Engell and W. Jackson Bate. Princeton: Princeton University Press, 1983.

Cotter, James F. *Inscape: the Christology and Poetry of Gerard Manley Hopkins*. Pittsburgh: University of Pittsburgh Press, 1972.

Cox, Harvey. *The Secular City*. 2nd ed. New York: Macmillan, 1990.

D'Amico, Sandro, ed. *Pirandello, Ieri e Oggi*. Milan: Il Piccolo Teatro della Città di Milano, 1961.

De Certeau, Michel. *The Mystic Fable*. Chicago: University of Chicago Press, 1995.

Derrida, Jacques. "How to Avoid Speaking: Denials." Translated by Ken Frieden. In *Languages of the Unsayable: The Play of Negativity in Literature and Literary Theory*, edited by Sanford Budick and Wolfgang Iser. New York: Columba University Press, 1989.

———. *Memoires for Paul de Man*. Edited by Avital Ronell and Eduardo Cadava. New York: Columbia University Press, 1989.

———. *Of Grammatology*. Translated by Gayatri Chakravorty Spivak. London: Johns Hopkins Press, 1997.

———. *Positions*. Translated by Alan Bass. Chicago: University of Chicago Press, 1981.

———. *Writing and Difference*. Translated by Alan Bass. London: Routledge, 2001.

Detweiler, Robert. *Breaking the Fall: Religious Readings of Contemporary Fiction*. San Francisco: Harper & Row, 1989.

DiGaetani, John, ed. *A Companion to Pirandello Studies*, Santa Barbara, CA: Greenwood, 1991.

Dionysius the Areopagite. *The Mystical Theology and the Divine Names*. Translated by C. E. Rolt. New York: Dover, 2004.

Dostoevsky, Fyodor. *The Brothers Karamazov*. Translated by David McDuff. London: Penguin, 2003.

Dubois, Martin. "Hopkins' Beauty." In *The Oxford Handbook of Victorian Poetry*, edited by Matthew Bevis. Oxford: Oxford University Press, 2013.

Dunster, Ruth M. "The Abyss of Calvino's Deconstructive Writing: An Apology for Non-Foundational Theology." Mth thesis, University of Glasgow, 2010. https://theses.gla.ac.uk/1961/1/2010dunstermth.pdf.

———. "Garden Swing." In *Nomad* 9. Glasgow, UK: Survivors Press Scotland, 2000.

Eliade, Mircea. *Myths, Dreams and Mysteries*. Translated by Philip Mairet. New York: Harper Row, 1967.

Eliot, George. *Felix Holt the Radical*. Ware, Herts, UK: Wordsworth Classics, 1997.

———. *Middlemarch*. London: Penguin Classics, 1994.

Eliot, T. S. *The Complete Poems and Plays of T. S. Eliot*. London: Faber & Faber, 1973.

Ellsberg, Margaret. *Created to Praise: The Language of Gerard Manley Hopkins*. Oxford: Oxford University Press, 1987.

Esslin, Martin. *Reflections: Essays on Modern Theatre*. New York: Doubleday, 1971.

Fabbri, Diego. "Pirandello poeta drammatico" (Pirandello dramatic poet). In *Atti del congresso internazionale di studi pirandelliani* (1961) 37–49.

Fish, Stanley. *Doing What Comes Naturally: Change, Rhetoric, and the Practice of Theory in Literary and Legal Studies*. Durham: Duke University Press, 1989.

Ford, David F., and Rachel Muers. *The Modern Theologians: An Introduction to Christian Theology Since 1918*. Cambridge, MA: Blackwell, 2005.

Gadamer, Hans-Georg. *Truth and Method*. Translated by Len-Doepel. London: Sheed & Ward, 1979.

Giudice, Gaspare. *Pirandello: A Biography*. Translated by Alastair Hamilton. Oxford: Oxford University Press, 1975.

Greene, Graham. *Monsignor Quixote*. London: Bodley, 1982.

Haddon, Mark. *The Curious Incident of the Dog in the Night-Time*. London: Vintage, 2004.

Hansen, Ron. *Mariette in Ecstasy*. London: Harper Perennial, 1992.

Happé, Peter. "Staging Folly." In *Fools and Folly*, edited by Clifford Davidson. Kalamazoo, MI: Medieval Institute Publications, Western Michigan University,1996.

Heaney, Seamus. *Collected Poems*. Edited by Padraic Fallon and Brian Fallon. Oldcastle, Ireland: Gallery Press, 1990.

Heidegger, Martin. *Elucidations of Hölderlin's Poetry*. Translated by Keith Hoeller. New York: Humanity/Prometheus, 2000.

———. *Hölderlin and the Essence of Poetry*. Translated by Douglas Scott and Werner Brock. Chicago: Henry Regnery, 1949.

———. *The Principle of Reason.* Translated by Reginald Lilly. Bloomington: Indiana University Press, 1991.

———. *What Is Called Thinking?* Translated by J. Glenn Gray and F Wieck. New York: Harper & Row, 1968.

Hölderlin, Friederich. *Hölderlin, Selected Verse.* Translated by Michael Hamburger. Vancouver, Canada: Anvil, 1986.

Hopkins, Gerard Manley. *The Journals and Papers of Gerard Manley Hopkins.* Edited by Humphry House. London: Oxford University Press, 1959.

———. "Letters." In *Gerard Manley Hopkins: Poems and Prose,* edited by Humphry House, 151–216. London: Penguin, 1985.

———. *Poems of Gerard Manley Hopkins.* Edited by Robert Bridges. London: Oxford University Press, 1930.

———. *The Poems of Gerard Manley Hopkin.* Edited by W. H. Gardner and N. H. Mackenzie. London: Oxford University Press, 1967.

———. *The Sermons and Devotional Writings of Gerard Manley Hopkins.* Edited by Christopher J. Devlin. London: Oxford University Press, 1959.

———. *The Works of Gerard Manley Hopkins.* Ware, Herts, UK: Wordsworth, 1994.

Houlgate, Stephen. *Freedom, Truth and History: An Introduction to Hegel's Philosophy.* London: Routledge, 1991.

———. *The Opening of Hegel's Logic: From Being to Infinity*. West Lafayette: Purdue University Press, 2006.

Hulbert, Steve, and Jeanyne Slettom. "Poetics, Post-Structuralism, and Process." *Process Perspectives* 29.1 (Summer 2006) 9–10.

Humphrey, N. *Consciousness Regained.* Oxford: Oxford University Press, 1984.

Ingham, Mary Beth. *Scotus for Dunces: An Introduction to the Subtle Doctor*. St. Bonaventure, NY: Franciscan Institute, St. Bonaventure University, 2003.

Inwood, Michael. *Heidegger.* Oxford: Oxford University Press, 1997.

Iser, Wolfgang. *The Implied Reader: Patterns of Communication in Prose Fiction from Bunyan to Beckett.* Baltimore: Johns Hopkins University Press, 1978.

Jasper, David. *The Sacred Community.* Waco: Baylor University Press, 2012.

———. *The Sacred Desert: Religion, Literature, Art, and Culture.* Cambridge, MA: Blackwell, 2004.

———. *A Short Introduction to Hermeneutics.* Louisville: Westminster John Knox, 2004.

———. *The Study of Literature and Religion*. London: Palgrave McMillan, 1992.
Jeanrond, Werner G. *Theological Hermeneutics: Development and Significance*. London: SCM, 1994.
John of the Cross. *The Ascent of Mount Carmel*. Translated by E. Allison Peers. Vancouver, Canada: Wilder, 2008.
———. *The Dark Night of the Soul*. Translated by E. Allison Peers. Westminster, MD: Newman, 1953.
Joyce, James. *Finnegan's Wake*. London: Penguin, 1999.
Judaken, Jonathan, and Robert Bernasconi, eds. *Situating Existentialism: Key Texts in Context*. New York: Columbia University Press, 2012.
Kelly, Anthony. *Medieval Philosophy*. Oxford: Clarendon, 2007.
Kelsey, David H. *The Fabric of Paul Tillich's Theology*. Eugene, OR: Wipf & Stock, 2011.
Kerr, Fergus. *Theology After Wittgenstein*. Oxford: Blackwell, 1986.
Languilli, Nino, ed. *European Existentialism*. Piscataway, NJ: Transaction, 1997.
Leavis, F. R. *The Common Pursuit*. London: Penguin, 1969.
Lewis, C. S. *The Four Loves*. London: Geoffrey Bles, 1960.
Llewellyn, John. *Gerard Manley Hopkins and the Spell of Duns Scotus*. Edinburgh: Edinburgh University Press, 2015.
Lucas, George R., and Hans-Christian Lucas. "Spinoza, Hegel, Whitehead: Substance, Subject and Superject." In *Hegel and Whitehead: Contemporary Perspectives on Systematic Philosophy*. Albany: State University of New York Press, 1986.
MacCulloch, Diarmaid. *Groundwork of Christian History*. London: Epworth, 1994.
Marion, Jean-Luc. *God Without Being: Hors-Texte* (Dieu Sans l'être: Horstexte). Translated by Thomas A Carlson. Chicago: University of Chicago Press, 1991.
McCullough, Lisa, and Brian Schroeder, eds. *Thinking through the Death of God: A Critical Companion to Thomas J. J. Altizer*. New York: State University of New York Press, 2004.
McDonagh, Enda. "Prayer, Poetry and Politics." In *Language, Meaning and God: Essays in Honour of Herbert McCabe OP*, edited by Brian Davies OP, 228–60. London: Geoffrey Chapman, 1987.
McEwan, Ian. *Atonement*. London: Vintage, 2007.
McFarland, Ian, Karen Kilby, and Iain Torrance, eds. *Cambridge Dictionary of Christian Theology*. Cambridge: Cambridge University Press, 2010.
McGinn, Bernard. *The Foundations of Mysticism*. Vol. 1, *The Presence of God: A History of Western Christian Mysticism*. London: SCM, 1991.

McGrath, Alistair E. *Historical Theology: An Introduction to the History of Christian Thought*. Oxford: Blackwell, 1998.

Meister Eckhart. *Selected Writings.* Translated and edited by Oliver Davies. London: Penguin, 1994.

Merton, Thomas. *New Seeds of Contemplation*. New York: New Directions, 1972.

Methodist Publishing, *Singing the Faith*. Canterbury, UK: Canterbury Press, 2011

Mueller-Vollmer, Kurt, ed. *The Hermeneutics Reader: Texts of the German Tradition from the Enlightenment to the Present*. Oxford: Blackwell, 1986.

Musser, Donald W., and Joseph L. Price, eds. *A New Handbook of Christian Theologians*. Nashville: Abingdon, 1996.

Nicholas of Cusa. *Of Learned Ignorance* (De Docta Ignorantia). Translated by Fr. Germain Heron. London: Routledge and Kegan Paul, 1954.

Nietzsche, Friedrich. *Joyful Wisdom (The Gay Science)*. Translated by Thomas Common. New York: Ungar, 1973.

———. *A Nietzsche Reader*. Translated by R. J. Hollingdale. London: Penguin, 1977.

———. *On Truth and Lies in a Non-Moral Sense*. CreateSpace Independent Publishing Platform, 2015.

———. *On Truth and Untruth: Selected Writings*. Translated and Edited by Carman Taylor. London: Harper Collins, 2021.

———. *Twilight of the Idols/The Antichrist*. Translated by R. J. Hollingdale. London: Penguin, 1990.

Norris, Christopher. *Deconstruction: Theory and Practice*. London: Routledge, 1991.

Otto, Rudolf. *The Idea of the Holy*. Eastford, CT: Martino Fine Books, 2010.

Pattison, George. "Fear and Trembling and the Paradox of Christian Existentialism." In *Situating Existentialism: Key Texts in Context*, edited by Jonathan Judaken and Robert Bernasconi, 211–36. New York: Columbia University Press, 2012.

Pears, David. *Wittgenstein*. Glasgow: Fontana/Collins, 1975.

Pirandello, Luigi. *Il Fu Mattia Pascal*. Florence: R. and F. Bemporad, 1927.

———. *The Late Mattia Pascal*. Translated by William Weaver. New York: New York Review Books, 2005.

———. *Naked Masks: Five Plays by Luigi Pirandello*. Edited by Eric Bentley. London: Meridian/Penguin, 1952.

———. *One, No-One, One Hundred Thousand*. Translated by William Weaver. New York: Marsilio, 1992.

———. *Pirandello: Three Plays.* Translated by Robert Rietty, Julian Mitchell, and John Linstrum. London: Methuen, 1985.

———. *Saggi e Interventi.* Edited by F. Taviani. Milan: Mondadori, 2006.

———. *Uno, Nessuno e Centomila.* Milan: Mondadori, 1984.

Plato. *The Republic.* Translated by Desmond Lee. London: Penguin, 1979.

Raine, Kathleen Hopkins. *Nature and Supernature.* Third Annual Lecture, The Hopkins Society, 1972.

Ramsey, Ian. *Religious Language: An Empirical Placing of Theological Phrases.* London: SCM, 1957.

Rancière, Jacques. *The Flesh of Words: The Politics of Writing.* Translated by Charlotte Mandell. Redwood City: Stanford University Press, 2004.

Raschke, Carl. *Theological Thinking: An Inquiry.* Atlanta, GA: American Academy of Religion/Scholars Press, 1988.

Ribatti, Domenico. *Omaggio a Italo Calvino - Autobiografia di uno scrittore.* Manduria-Bari-Roma: Piero Lacaita Editore, 1995.

Ricœur, Paul. *The Rule of Metaphor: The Creation of Meaning in Language,* (La métaphore vive). Translated by Robert Czerny, Kathleen McLaughlin, and John Costello, SJ. London: Routledge, 2003.

———. *The Symbolism of Evil.* Translated by Emerson Buchanan. Boston: Beacon, 1969.

Robinson, John A. T. *Honest to God.* London: SCM, 1963.

Rossetti, Christina. *Selected Poems of Christina Rossetti.* Edited by Katharine McGowan. London: Wordsworth Poetry Library, 1995.

Rushdie, Salman, *The Satanic Verses.* London, UK: Viking Penguin, 1988.

Saxon, Wolfgang. *The Secular Meaning of the Gospel: Based on an Analysis of Its Language.* London: Macmillan, 1963.

Scharlemann, Robert P. *Inscriptions and Reflections: Essays in Philosophical Theology.* Charlottesville: University Press of Virginia, 1989.

Scotus, Duns. "Ordinatio." In *Five Texts on the Medieval Problem of Universals: Porphyry, Duns Scotus, Ockham,* translated and edited by Paul Vincent Spade. Indianapolis: Hackett, 1994.

Smart, Ninian. *The Religious Experience of Mankind.* Glasgow, UK: Fount, 1980.

Stafford, William. *The Darkness Around Us Is Deep: Selected Poems of William Stafford.* Edited by Robert Bly. New York: HarperCollins, 1993.

Super, R. H., ed. *English Literature and Irish Politics.* Ann Arbor: University of Michigan Press, 1973.

Sweeney, Jon. *Almost Catholic: An Appreciation of the History, Practice, and Mystery of Ancient Faith.* San Francisco: Jossey-Bass Wiley, 2008.

Swinton, John. *Building a Church for Strangers.* Edinburgh: Contact Pastoral Trust, 1999.

Taylor, Mark C. *After God*. Chicago: University of Chicago Press, 2007.
———. *Erring: A Postmodern A/theology*. Chicago: University of Chicago Press, 1984.
———. *Refiguring the Spiritual: Religion, Culture and Public Life*. New York: Columbia University Press, 2012.
———. *Tears*. Albany: State University of New York Press, 1990.
Teresa of Àvila. *The Interior Castle.* Translated by Mirabai Starr. New York: Riverhead Books, 2003.
———. *Life of Teresa by Herself.* Translated by J. M. Cohen. London: Penguin, 1957.
Tillich, Paul. *Morality and Beyond*. London: Routledge, 1964.
———. *The Shaking of the Foundations*. London: Penguin, 1963.
TIME magazine. April 8, 1966. Time Inc., New York.
Trevett, Christine. "Asperger's Syndrome and the Holy Fool: The Case of Brother Juniper." *Journal of Religion, Disability & Health* 13 (2009) 129–50.
Turner, Denys. *The Darkness of God: Negativity in Christian Mysticism*. Cambridge: Cambridge University Press, 1999.
Tyler, Peter. *Teresa of Àvila, Doctor of the Soul*. London: Bloomsbury, 2013.
University of Glasgow. "Literature, Theology, and the Arts at Glasgow." https://www.gla.ac.uk/schools/critical/research/researchcentresandnetworks/literaturetheologyandtheartsatglasgow//.
Vahanian, Gabriel. *The Death of God: The Culture of Our Post-Christian Era*. Eugene, OR: Wipf & Stock, 1961.
Vattimo, Gianni. *La Fine della Modernità*. Milan: Garzanti, 1985.
Voltaire, Candide. *Or Optimism*. Translated by Theo Cuffe. London: Penguin, 2005.
Wallace-Hadrill, D. S. *Christian Antioch: A Study of Early Christian Thought in the East*. Cambridge: Cambridge University Press, 1982.
Walton, Heather, ed. *Literature and Theology: New Interdisciplinary Spaces*. Farnham, Surrey, UK: Ashgate, 2011.
Wesley, Charles. "Let Earth and Heaven Combine (1745)." In *Singing the Faith*, by Trustees for Methodist Church Purposes, no. 208. London: Hymns Ancient and Modern, 2011.
Williams, Charles. "Introduction." In *Poems of Gerard Manley Hopkins,* by edited by Robert Bridges. Oxford: Oxford University Press, 1930.
Williams, Rowan. *Dostoevsky: Language, Faith and Fiction.* London: Continuum, 2011.
———. *The Edge of Words: God and the Habits of Language*. London: Bloomsbury, 2014.
———. *Teresa of Ávila*. London: Geoffrey Chapman, 1991.

Williams, Thomas, ed. *The Cambridge Companion to Duns Scotus*. Cambridge: Cambridge University Press, 2003.
Wittgenstein, Ludwig. *The Blue and Brown Books*. Oxford: Blackwell, 1958.
———. *Notebooks 1914–1916*. Edited by G. H. von Wright and G. E. M. Anscombe. Oxford: Blackwell, 1961.
———. *Tractatus Logico-Philosophicus*. Friburg, Sweden: Wisehouse/Chiron Academic, 2016 (1921).
———. *Wittgenstein's Lectures Cambridge 1932–1935*. Edited by Alice Ambrose. Oxford: Blackwell, 1979.
Wordsworth, William. *The Works of William Wordsworth*. Ware, UK: The Wordsworth Poetry Library, Wordsworth Editions Ltd, 1994.

Film, Video, TV, Music

Ashby, Hal, dir. *Being There*. Lorimar Productions, 1979.
Bowen, Bob, dir. Acts of God, *Family Guy* Season 12 Episode 13
Brand, Russell. "Is There a God? YES! Stephen Fry Proves It." YouTube, February 2, 2015. https://www.youtube.com/watch?v=1Run1jpZvS4.
De Long, Ate, dir. *Drop Dead Fred*. Polygram and Working Title Films, 1991.
Elwood, Reid, dir. *The Bridge*. FX Productions and Shine America, 2013.
Fry, Stephen, in Gay Byrne interview. *The Meaning of Life*, aired February 1, 2015, on RTÉ. https://www.youtube.com/watch?v=2-d4otHE-YI. Interview transcript: http://www.age-of-the-sage.org/quotations/quotes/stephen_fry_irish_tv_interview.htm.
Knight, Travis, dir. *Kubo and the Two Strings*. Hillsboro, Oregon; Laika, 2016
Levinson, Barry, dir. *Rain Man*. United Artists and The Guber-Peters Company, 1988.
McGinn, Bernard. "Mystical Language in Meister Eckhart and His Disciples." Lecture, Smith College, Northampton, MA, October 20, 2011. https://www.youtube.com/watch?v=Uxh2MHzEc3g.
Sackur, Stephen. "Victims of a Down: Serj Tankian Talks Music and Politics on BBC (HardTalk Podcast, 2021)." YouTube, April 14, 2021. https://www.youtube.com/watch?v=htv4puVhFA8.
Saks, Gene, dir. *Barefoot in the Park*. Paramount Pictures, 1967.
System of a Down. "Chop Suey!" *Toxicity*, Sony Records, 2001. https://www.youtube.com/watch?v=MlcJQYON2Go.
Winterbottom, Michael, dir. *A Cock and Bull Story*. BBC Films et al., 2005.

Websites, E-books, and Online Access Journals

Altizer, Thomas J. J. *Living the Death of God: A Theological Memoir*. New York: SUNY Press, 2006. http://www.altizer.narod.ru/memoir/memoir.html.

Ashworth, Jennifer E. "Medieval Theories of Analogy." In *The Stanford Encyclopedia of Philosophy* (Winter 2013 Edition). Edited by Edward N. Zalta. http://plato.stanford.edu/archives/win2013/entries/analogy-medieval/.

Baldick, C. "Metaphor." In *The Oxford Dictionary of Literary Terms*. Oxford: Oxford University Press, 2008. http://www.oxfordreference.com/view/10.1093/acref/9780199208272.001.0001/acref-9780199208272-e-712.

Batalvi, Shiv Kumar. *Separation, You Are King* (Birha Tu Sultan). Translated by Suman Kashyap. http://www.apnaorg.com/suman/batalvi_poems.html.

Bergman, Paul, and Sibylle K. Escalona. "Unusual Sensitivities in Very Young Children." *The Psychoanalytic Study of the Child* 3.1 (1947) 333–52.

Blake, William. "The Garden of Love." *Songs of Experience*. http://www.poetryfoundation.org/poem/175220.

———. "A Memorable Fancy." Plate 12, *The Marriage of Heaven and Hell*, 1790. http://www.gailgastfield.com/mhh/mhh.html.

British Province of Carmelite Friars. http://www.carmelite.org/index.php?nuc=content&id=236.

Burgess, Michael. "Gerard Manley Hopkins and Priest-Poets." Talk delivered at St Beuno's Jesuit Spirituality Centre, Denbighshire, Wales. June 13th 2015. https://www.newman.org.uk/files/upload/Newman%20Journal%20Sept%202015.pdf.

Cox, Harvey. "The Secular City 25 Years Later." *The Christian Century*, November 7, 1990. https://www.religion-online.org/article/the-secular-city-25-years-later/.

Curiel, Erik, and Peter Bokulich. "Singularities and Black Holes." *The Stanford Encyclopedia of Philosophy* (Fall 2012 Edition), June 29, 2009. http://plato.stanford.edu/archives/fall2012/entries/spacetime-singularities/.

Derrida, Jacques. "White Mythology: Metaphor in the Text of Philosophy." Translated by F. C. T. Moore. *New Literary History* 6.1 (1974) 5–74. http://www.jstor.org/stable/468341.

Gorski, Philip. "Holy Fools in Russian Literature." In Communion: Website of the Orthodox Peace Fellowship, February 2, 2007. https://incommunion.org/2007/02/02/holy-fools-in-russian-literature/.

Hass, Andrew, David Jasper, and Elizabeth Jay, eds. *The Oxford Handbook of Literature and Theology*, 2009. http://www.oxfordhandbooks.com/.

Hearing Voices Network. www.hearing-voices.org.

Hilgevoord, Jan, and Jos Uffink. "The Uncertainty Principle." *The Stanford Encyclopedia of Philosophy* (Fall 2016 Edition), July 12, 2016. http://plato.stanford.edu/archives/fall2016/entries/qt-uncertainty/.

"Inuktitut Words for Snow and Ice." *The Canadian Encyclopedia*, July 8, 2015. http://www.thecanadianencyclopedia.ca/en/article/inuktitut-words-for-snow-and-ice/.

Knox, T. Malcolm. "Hegel." *Encyclopedia Britannica Online*. http://www.britannica.com/EBchecked/topic/259378/Georg-Wilhelm-Friedrich-Hegel/41239/At-Heidelberg.

Kreps, Daniel. "Serj Tankian Thanks President Biden for Recognizing Armenian Genocide." Rolling Stone, April 24, 2021. https://www.rollingstone.com/music/music-news/serj-tankian-president-biden-armenian-genocide-1160770/.

Lentz, Robert, OFM. "St. Francis, Jongleur de Dieu." Trinity Stores: Religious Artwork & Icons. https://www.trinitystores.com/artwork/st-francis-jongleur-de-dieu.

Monbiot, George. "Aspirational Parents Condemn Their Children to a Desperate, Joyless Life." *The Guardian*, June 9, 2015. http://www.theguardian.com/commentisfree/2015/jun/09/aspirational-parents-children-elite?CMP=fb_gu.

Morgan, D. "Mindfulness-based Cognitive Therapy for Depression: A New Approach to Preventing Relapse." *Psychotherapy Research* 13.1 (2003) 123–25. http://www.tandfonline.com/doi/abs/10.1080/713869628?journalCode=tpsr20.

Nietzsche, Friederich. *Thus Spake Zarathustra*. http://www.philosophy-index.com/nietzsche/thus-spake-zarathurstra/xxv.php.

O'Meara, Thomas F. "Thomism." *Encyclopaedia Britannica*. https://www.britannica.com/topic/Thomism.

Origen. *The Song of Songs: Commentary and Homilies*. Issue 26. New York: Paulist, 1957. https://books.google.co.uk/books?id=Mjxy0Fl7VMsC&q=love#v=snippet&q=love&f=false.

Saxon, Wolfgang. "Paul van Buren, 74, 'Death of God' Exponent." *New York Times*, July 1, 1998. http://www.nytimes.com/1998/07/01/us/paul-van-buren-74-death-of-god-exponent.html.

Searle, Joshua T. "The Divine Imagination: William Blake's Vision of Theosis and the Theology of Hope." *Luvah: Journal of the Creative Imagination* (Summer 2013) 1–14. https://www.academia.edu/8358853/The_Divine-Human_Imagination_William_Blake_s_Vision_of_Theosis_and_the_

Theology_of_Hope_pp._1–14_Link_Luvah_Journal_of_the_Creative_Imagination.

Strong's Lexicon of New Testament Greek. "Kata. http://www.biblestudytools.com/search/?q=kata&rc=LEX&rc2=LEX+GRK&ps=10&s=References.

Swinton, John. "Reflections on Autistic Love: What Does Love Look Like?" *Practical Theology* 5.3 (2012) 259–78. http://www.tandfonline.com/doi/abs/10.1558/prth.v5i3.259.

The Poetry Foundation. http://www.poetryfoundation.org.

The Thomas Merton Center at Bellarmie University. http://merton.org/chrono.aspx.

Victoria and Albert Museum. "British Watercolours 1750–1900: J. M. W. Turner and John Ruskin: Turner's 'Golden Visions.'" http://www.vam.ac.uk/content/articles/b/british-watercolours-turner-and-ruskin/.

Westminster Shorter Catechism. http://www.reformed.org/documents/wsc/index.html.

White, Norman. "Poet and Priest: Gerard Manley Hopkins, Myth and Reality." *Studies: An Irish Quarterly Review* 79 (Summer 1990) 140–49. http://www.jstor.org/stable/30091944.

Music

Nick Cave and the Bad Seeds. "Today's Lesson." *Dig, Lazarus, Dig.* Mute Records, 2008.

System of a Down. "Chop Suey!" *Toxicity*. Columbia Records, 2001. https://www.youtube.com/watch?v=MlcJQYON2Go.

AUTISM

Books and Articles

Ariel, Cindy N., and Robert A. Naseef, eds. *Voices from the Spectrum: Parents, Grandparents, Siblings, People with Autism, and Professionals Share their Wisdom*. London: Jessica Kingsley, 2006.

Attwood, Tony. *Asperger's Syndrome: A Guide for Parents and Professionals*. London: Jessica Kingsley, 1998.

Baron-Cohen, Simon. *Mindblindness: An Essay on Autism and Theory of Mind*. Cambridge: MIT Press, 1995.

———. *Zero Degrees of Empathy: A New Theory of Human Cruelty and Kindness*. London: Penguin, 2011.

Baron-Cohen, Simon, and Jaime Craig. "Creativity and Imagination in Autism and Asperger Syndrome." *Journal of Autism and Developmental Disorders* 29.4 (1999) 319–26.

Baron-Cohen, Simon, et al. "Attenuation of Typical Sex Differences in 800 Adults with Autism versus 3,900 Controls." *PLOS One* 9.7 (July 2014). doi: e102251.

Baron-Cohen, Simon, et al. "The Autism Spectrum Quotient (AQ): Evidence from Asperger Syndrome/High-Functioning Autism, Males and Females, Scientists and Mathematicians." *Journal of Autism and Developmental Disorders* 31 (2001) 5–17.

Bogdashina, Olga. *Autism and Spirituality: Psyche, Self and Spirit in People on the Autism Spectrum*. London: Jessica Kingsley, 2013.

Bovell, Virginia. "Autism and Severe Learning Difficulties: Implications for a Good Autistic Life." Talk presented at British Academy/Kings College London Conference, *Autism, Ethics and the Good Life*. London, April 2, 2012.

Bregman, Joel. "Definitions and Characteristics of the Spectrum." In *Autism Spectrum Disorders: Identification, Education and Treatment*, edited by Dianne Zager, 1–23. London: Lawrence Erlbaum, 2005.

Buckle, Leneh K. "Is Increasing Functionality Always Good?" Talk presented at British Academy/Kings College London Conference, *Autism, Ethics and the Good Life*. London, April 2, 2012.

Clarkson, Alastair. "The Sensory Connoisseur." MSc diss., University of Strathclyde, Scotland, 2013.

Coleman, M., and C. Gillberg. *The Autisms*. New York: Oxford University Press, 2012.

Eiesland, Nancy. *The Disabled God: Towards a Liberatory Theology of Disability*. Nashville: Abingdon, 1994.

Fitzgerald, Michael. *The Genesis of Artistic Creativity*. London: Jessica Kingsley, 2015.

———. *The Link between Asperger Syndrome and Scientific, Artistic and Political Creativity: Eleven Case Studies*. New York: Edwin Mellen, 2014.

Fitzgerald, Michael, and A. Walker. *Unstoppable Brilliance: Irish Geniuses and Asperger's Syndrome*. Dublin: Liberties, 2014.

Frith, Uta. *Autism: Explaining the Enigma*. Medford, MA: Blackwell, 2003.

———, ed. *Autism and Asperger Syndrome*. Cambridge: Cambridge University Press, 1999.

Gerland, Gunilla. *A Real Person: Life On the Outside*. London: Souvenir, 1997.

Gil, Eyal, et al. *The Autism Matrix: The Social Origins of the Autism Epidemic*. Cambridge: Polity, 2010.

Gillberg, Christopher. "Reflections on Autism and on What Scotland Needs in Research." Paper delivered at Conference on Action on Autism Research in Scotland, *What Does Scotland Need?* Glasgow, Scotland, November 2014.

Grainger, Roger. *Strangers in the Pews: The Pastoral Care of Psychiatric Patients within the Christian Congregation.* London: Epworth, 1993.

Happé, Francesca G. E. "Communicative Competence and Theory of Mind in Autism: A Test of Relevance Theory." *Cognition* 48 (1993) 101–19.

Happé, Francesca, and Uta Frith, eds. *Autism and Talent.* Philosophical Transactions of the Royal Society. London: The Royal Society/Oxford University Press, 2010.

Hermelin, Beate. *Bright Splinters of the Mind: A Personal Story of Research with Autistic Savants.* London: Jessica Kingsley, 2001.

Hobson, Peter. *The Cradle of Thought: Exploring the Origins of Thinking.* Reigate, Surrey: Pan, 2004.

Howell, Paul. "From Rain Man to Sherlock: Theological Reflections on Metaphor." *Practical Theology* 8.2 (2015) 143–53.

Jackson, Luke. *Geeks, Freaks and Asperger's Syndrome: A User's Guide to Adolescence.* London: Jessica Kingsley, 2002.

Lawson, Wendy. *Life Behind Glass: A Personal Account of Autism Spectrum Disorder.* London: Jessica Kingsley, 1998.

Lyons, V., and M. Fitzgerald. *Asperger's Syndrome: A Gift or a Curse?* New York: Nova Science, 2005.

Markram, Henry, Tania Rinaldi, and Kamilia Markram. "The Intense World Syndrome: An Alternative Hypothesis for Autism." *Frontiers in Human Neuroscience* 1.1 (2007) 77–96.

Markram, Kamila, and Henry Markram. "The Intense World Theory—A Unifying Theory of the Neurobiology of Autism." *Frontiers in Human Neuroscience* 4.224 (2010) 1–29. doi: 10.3389/fnhum.2010.00224.

O'Brien, B., and M. Fitzgerald. *Genius Genes.* Shawnee, KS: Autism Asperger Publishing, 2007.

Ritvo, Edward R. *Autism: Diagnosis, Current Research and Management.* Richmond, Victoria: Spectrum, 1976.

Silberman, Steve. *Neurotribes: The Legacy of Autism, and How to Think Smarter about People Who Think Differently.* London: Allen & Unwin, 2015.

Simpson, Amy. *Troubled Minds: Mental Illness and the Church's Mission.* Downers Grove, IL: InterVarsity, 2013.

Stillmann, William. *Autism and the God Connection: Redefining the Autistic Experience through Extraordinary Accounts of Spiritual Giftedness.* Naperville, IL: Sourcebooks, 2006.

———. *The Soul of Autism: Looking Beyond Labels to Unveil Spiritual Secrets of the Heart Savants*. Newburyport, MA: Career, 2008.

Swinton, John. "Reflections on Autistic Love: What Does Love Look Like?" *Practical Theology* 5.3 (2012) 259–78. http://www.tandfonline.com/doi/abs/10.1558/prth.v5i3.259.

Szatmari, Georgiades, et al. "Investigating the Structure of the Restricted, r\ Repetitive Behaviours and Interests Domain of Autism." *Journal of Child Psychology and Psychiatry* 47.6 (2006) 582–90.

Tataryn, Miroslaw, and Maria Truchan-Tataryn. *Discovering Trinity in Disability: A Theology for Embracing Difference*. New York: Orbis, 2013.

Tustin, Frances. *Autistic States in Children*. London: Routledge, 1992.

Williams, Donna. *Autism—An Inside-Out Approach: An Innovative Look at the Mechanics of "Autism" and Its Developmental "Cousins."* London: Jessica Kingsley, 2004.

———. *Autism and Sensing: The Unlost Instinct*. London: Jessica Kingsley, 2001.

Wing, Lorna. *The Autistic Spectrum*. London: Constable, 1996.

———. "The Relationship between Asperger's Syndrome and Kanner's Autism." In *Autism and Asperger's Syndrome,* edited by Uta Frith, 93–122. Cambridge: Cambridge University Press, 1991.

Zager, Dianne, et al., eds. *Autism Spectrum Disorders: Identification, Education and Treatment*. London: Lawrence Erlbaum, 2005.

Websites, E-books, and Online Access Articles

American Psychiatric Association. "Autism Spectrum Disorder." DSM-5 Autism Spectrum Disorder Fact Sheet. Arlington, TX: American Psychiatric Association, 2013. https://www.psychiatry.org/File%20Library/Psychiatrists/Practice/DSM/APA_DSM-5-Autism-Spectrum-Disorder.pdf.

———. *Desk Reference to the Diagnostic Criteria from DSM-5 (R)*. Arlington, TX: American Psychiatric Association, 2013. http://www.dsm5.org/about/pages/faq.aspx.

Asperger, Hans. "'Autistic Psychopathy' in Childhood." In *Autism and Asperger Syndrome*, edited by Uta Frith, 37–92. Cambridge: Cambridge University Press, 1991. https://doi.org/10.1017/CBO9780511526770.

"Autism/Asperger Syndrome." Irlen: Where the Science of Color Transforms Lives. https://irlen.com/autism-asperger-syndrome-the-irlen-method/.

"Autism Spectrum Disorder in Adults: Diagnosis and Management." National Institute for Health and Care Excellence, June 27, 2012. https://www.

nice.org.uk/guidance/cg142/chapter/Introduction#identification-and-assessment.

Baron-Cohen, Simon, ed. "Current Perspectives and Future Directions in Autism, Dyslexia and Conduct Disorder: A Celebration for Uta Frith." Uta Frith Festschrift. *The Psychologist* 20 (August 2007) https://thepsychologist.bps.org.uk/volume-20/edition-8/online-only-article-uta-frith-festschrift.

Gould, Judith. "The Triad of Impairments, Past, Present and Future." The NAS Lorna Wing Centre for Autism: PowerPoint presentation. https://slideum.com/doc/2983474/the-triad-of-impairments-past--present-and-future.

Grandin, Temple. "The World Needs All Kinds of Minds." TED Talk, 2010. https://www.ted.com/talks/temple_grandin_the_world_needs_all_kinds_of_minds?language=en.

Kanner, Leo. "Autistic Disturbances of Affective Contact, 1949." *Nervous Child* 2 (1943) 217–50.

Rundblad, Gabriella, and Dagmara Annaz. "The Atypical Development of Metaphor and Metonymy Comprehension in Children with Autism." *Autism* 14.29 (2010). https://www.researchgate.net/profile/Dagmara_Dimitriou/publication/41399590_The_atypical_development_of_metaphor_and_metonymy_comprehension_in_children_with_autism/links/0fcfd50de1d32c131e000000.pdf.

Strochlic, Nina. "This Incredible British Artist Can Draw a Whole City From Memory." National Geographic, November 3, 2017. https://www.nationalgeographic.co.uk/travel-and-adventure/2017/11/incredible-british-artist-can-draw-whole-city-memory.

Szalavitz, Maia. "Autism—It's Different in Girls." *Scientific American*, March 1, 2016. https://www.scientificamerican.com/article/autism-it-s-different-in-girls/.

"What Is Autism?" National Autistic Society UK. https://www.autism.org.uk/advice-and-guidance/what-is-autism.

Wilson, Deirdre, and Dan Sperber. *Relevance Theory*. UCL Papers, 249–87. http://www.phon.ucl.ac.uk/publications/WPL/02papers/wilson_sperber.pdf.

Wing, Lorna. "Language, Social, and Cognitive Impairments in Autism and Severe Mental Retardation." *Journal of Autism and Developmental Disorders* 11.1 (1981) 31–44. https://www.ncbi.nlm.nih.gov/pubmed/6927697.

Autism Blogs

Alli, Renee A. "What Does the Word 'Autism' Mean?" WebMD, September 28, 2021. www.webmd.com/brain/autism/history-of-autism.

"The Beautiful and Dangerous Innocence of the Autistic Mind." *Autistic Bean,* May 12, 2014. https://autisticbean.wordpress.com/the-beautiful-and-dangerous-innocence-of-the-autistic-mind/.

Bridges, Katie. "Special Interests." Thinking Person's Guide to Autism (blog), July 27, 2011. https://thinkingautismguide.com/2011/07/special-interests.html.

Carly's Voice. https://www.carlysvoice.com/.

"CNN, CBC and the Amanda Baggs Controversy Site." Facing Autism in New Brunswick (blog), July 15, 2009. www.autisminnb.blogspot.co.uk/2009/07/cnn-cbc-and-amanda-baggs-controversy.html.

Wing, Lorna. "Asperger Syndrome: A Clinical Account." Mugsy (blog), n.d. http://www.mugsy.org/wing2.htm.

Film

Autism Speaks. "I Am Autism Commercial by Autism Speaks." YouTube, April 20, 2016. https://www.youtube.com/watch?v=9UgLnWJFGHQ.

Baggs, Amanda. "In My Language." YouTube, Jan 15, 2007. https://www.youtube.com/watch?v=JnylM1hI2jc.

Schaber, Amythest. "Ask an Autistic n. 6 — What's Wrong with Autism Speaks?" YouTube, March 14, 2014. https://www.youtube.com/watch?v=ez936r2F35U.

ScottishAutism. "Peter Howson - Scottish Autism." YouTube, May 26, 2014. https://www.youtube.com/watch?v=wAJdJu3lZi8.

Index

Absent Presence, 57–59, 67, 194, 250
Absolute Autism, 47, 77, 83–84, 90–91, 104, 106–7, 115, 123, 133, 155, 178–79, 191, 193, 207–8, 220–21, 244–46, 250–55, 259–62, 267, 281, 297, 300, 324, 331–32, 348–49
Absolute Other. *See* Other, Absolute
Abyss, 53–55, 234–36, 305, 310, 321, 355
Alienation, 255, 263, 278
Aloneness, 303, 305, 342, 359
Altizer, Thomas J. J., 4, 6–7, 24–26, 49–50, 57, 94, 210–29, 233–58, 261, 264–67, 269, 297
American Psychiatric Association, 1, 29–30
Analogy, 10–11, 22–23, 176, 275, 277–78
Apophasis, 151–52, 156, 175–77, 183, 207–8
Apopathic Fiction, 144–208, 216–18, 234, 260, 266, 337, 341–43

Apopathic Theology, 19–24, 53, 94, 216–18, 234, 243–44, 330
Aporia, 132–33, 142
Aquinas, Thomas, 22–23, 273–78, 284–85
Archetype, 2, 38, 41, 61, 67–68, 81–82, 84, 91, 181, 220, 247, 262, 294, 312, 334
Aristotle, 22–23, 99–100, 176, 274–75, 277–78, 340, 352
Ascent of Mount Carmel, the, 177, 180–85
Ashby, Hal, 90
Asperger/Asperger's Syndrome, 28–33, 36–37, 41–44, 76, 96, 219
Asperger, Hans, 28–30, 37, 81–82, 85, 87
Atheism, Honest, 16–17, 224, 350, 356, 359
Atheism, Christian. *See* Christian Atheism

INDEX

Atheology, 16–17, 24–26, 48–50, 67, 128–30, 143, 153, 187, 196, 200, 212–14, 216, 223, 236–37, 244–46, 327, 350
Attwood, Tony, 32–33, 36, 96
Auerbach, Eric, 262–63
Augustine of Hippo, Saint, 127, 161–62, 165–66, 168
Autism
   Absolute (*see* Absolute Autism)
   Conscious (*see* Conscious Autism)
   of Gxd, 1–2, 26–27, 45, 57, 93, 186, 209–67, 270, 273, 297, 302, 332–33
   history of, 28–30
   mythical (*see* Mythical Autism)
   relative (*see* Relative Autism)
   universal (*see* Universal Autism)
Autism Speaks, 46
Autistic Bean, 72–73
Autistic Metaphor. *See* Metaphor, Autistic
Autistic Spectrum. *See* Spectrum, Autistic
Autism Spectrum Disorders, 1, 30, 140, 354
Autistic Empathy, 41–44, 47–48, 73, 77, 91, 102, 140, 178, 293
Autistic Fascination, 34–37, 39–41, 58–59, 74–76, 84–89, 91, 102, 107–11, 124–26, 133, 138, 140, 142, 154–55, 178–79, 191, 193, 206–7, 218–23, 237, 244, 249–50, 252, 258–62, 264, 273, 276, 279, 281–82, 290–96, 310, 320, 324, 326, 343
Autistic Hermeneutic, definition of, 65–67, 72–73, 83, 90, 96, 104–9
Autistic Trinity, the, 60–94, 102–3, 155–56, 244–45
Autos, 29–30, 60, 85, 105, 177, 255, 258, 264

Baldick, C., 98–99, 113
Barefoot in the Park, 199
Baron Cohen, Simon, 30–31, 33, 41–44, 47, 61, 77, 84, 91, 105, 117, 123, 207, 262, 338
Barth, Karl, 12–16, 26, 50, 93, 227–28, 233, 345–46, 351
Barthes, Roland, 140–43, 304, 329
Bassnett-McGuire, Susan, 302, 347
Batalvi, Shiv Kumar, 62, 254
Beatitudes, 116, 197, 237, 252, 264, 351
Becoming (Hegelian), 178, 238–42, 245, 250–52
Being There, 90
Betrayal, 199–206, 229–33
Bini, Daniela, 307–9, 311–12

INDEX   411

Blake, William, 25, 40, 224–29, 233, 261, 321
Blanchot, Maurice, 54, 112, 117, 142, 185–89, 191–94, 196–99, 201–5, 263, 352
Blasphemy, 2, 15, 79, 212, 223–24, 226–29, 232–38, 322
Bleuler, Eugene, 28
Bogdashina, Olga, 40, 78, 89, 259, 325
Bonhoeffer, Dietrich, 14–16, 25, 195, 211–12, 246, 248
Bregman, Joel, 35, 37, 40, 140, 219
Bridges, Katie, 36–37, 259–60
British Province of Carmelite Friars, 198
Brother Juniper, 71, 225
Buckle, Leneh, 30, 75, 85, 193, 260
Büdel, Oscar, 302, 305, 307, 311–13, 326, 328, 346
Bultmann, Rudolf, 26–27, 81, 179, 212

Calvino, Italo, 110, 164–65, 167, 173, 177, 355, 358
Carmelite Friars. *See* British Province of Carmelite Friars
Cartesian. *See* Descartes, René
Cataphatic Theology. *See* Kataphatic Theology
Chesterton, G. K., 70–71, 320
Christ, Carol T., 283

Christendom, 17, 24–25, 49, 54, 223–27, 229, 233, 235–36, 274
Christian Atheism/Atheology, definition of. *See* Atheology
Clarkson, Alistair, 39, 74, 86, 107, 273, 279–80
Clinical Narrative, 34, 40, 56, 83, 92, 101, 112, 114
Cock and Bull Story, A, 173
Coincidentia Oppositorum, 58, 155, 240, 252, 256–57, 263
Cognitive Empathy, 33, 42–43, 47, 91, 155, 179–80, 186, 206, 231, 249, 345
Coleridge, Samuel Taylor, 55–56, 176, 294
Conscious Autism, 73, 83–84, 124, 142, 253, 258, 300, 313, 317, 320–21, 345, 358
Courtly Love, 148, 160, 163, 174
Cox, Harvey, 211–12
Craig, Jaime, 117, 262
Creation, 24, 65, 90, 168, 227, 238, 240–42, 245, 251, 253, 278, 281, 283

Dark Night, 181, 184–85, 198, 203–5, 234, 247, 250, 282, 342
Dasein, 11, 109–10, 117

Death of God, 6, 18, 24, 48–49, 57, 141, 210–49, 253, 256–57, 261, 264–66, 275, 299, 322, 331
De Certeau, Michel, 148, 154, 160
Deconstruction, 122, 127–43, 187, 195–96, 200, 229, 233, 241, 266, 307, 309–11, 315–16, 318, 329, 334
Deconstructive Atheology, 128–43, 187, 200
Deism, 9–11
Demonic, the, 18, 214, 226–29, 233, 271
Demythologization, 26–27, 81
Derrida, Jacques, 90, 128–43, 187–88, 194–96, 205, 309–10, 329–31
Descartes, René, 122, 127, 192, 266
Dialectic, 11, 236, 238–43, 245, 250–51, 261
DiGaetani, John, 308
Dionysius the Areopagite, 20–21, 51, 147, 149–54, 166- 171, 175–79, 183, 194–97, 205, 207, 309, 323, 330, 342
Disability Theology, 41, 64
Distress, 32, 34–35, 43, 58, 92, 107, 184, 200, 202–6, 220, 251, 321–22, 359
Dostoyevsky, Fyodor, 12–13, 17, 224, 344
Doxological Language, 119–21, 130, 223, 260, 266

DSM-5, 29–30, 74
Dubois, Martin, 283
Duns Scotus, 21–24, 270, 273–85, 288, 290

Ecceitas, 218, 222, 281, 287, 291, 331–32, 359
Echolalia, 108
Eckhart, Meister, 167, 201, 206, 274, 323
Eiesland, Nancy, 65, 249, 262
Eliade, Mircea, 24–25, 49, 78–79, 212–19
Eliot, George
  Middlemarch, 80, 303
  Felix Holt, the Radical, 225–26
Eliot, T. S., 73, 351
Ellsberg, Margaret, 292, 298
Empathy Bell Curve, 42
Empathy
  Affective, 42–43, 47–48, 77, 91, 107, 131, 179, 186, 206–7, 225, 231–32, 245, 249–50, 324, 338
  Autistic, 41–44, 47–48, 73, 77, 91, 102, 140, 178, 293
  Cognitive, 33, 42–43, 47, 91, 155, 178, 180, 186, 206, 231, 249, 345
  Zero Negative, 42–43, 178
  Zero Positive, 42, 47, 178, 207
Emperor's New Clothes, the, 136, 138–39, 199, 232, 237, 356, 358
Etiology, 82
Eucharist, 264, 266–67, 269

Existentialism, 12–18, 49–51, 81–83, 93, 132, 139, 177, 210, 213–16, 228, 240, 243
Exodus, 150–51, 217, 245, 246, 253

Failure, 43–44, 80, 100, 102, 109, 112, 115, 151, 155, 175, 332–33, 337, 340, 346–49
Fairy Stories, 60–61
Fall, 13, 93, 238, 240–42, 245–47, 251, 253–57
Family Guy, 2
Fitzgerald, Michael, 87, 123, 262
Ford, David F., 215, 227
Francis of Assisi, Saint, 24, 69–71, 89, 274, 276–78, 292–93, 320
Frith, Uta, 31–32, 34–35, 37–39, 56, 60–61, 68, 71, 76, 86, 107, 117, 280
Fundamentalism, 90, 297,

Gadamer, Hans-Georg, 103–4, 253
'Geek', 76, 138, 193, 294–95
Geist, 11, 238–44, 257, 261
Genocide, 229
Giudice, Gaspare, 306, 308, 314, 326, 346
Glossolalia, 118
Gould, Judith, 29–30
Grandin, Temple, 87–88
Greene, Graham, 172–74

Gxd as Absence, 4, 14, 16, 20, 50, 57, 94, 188–89, 194, 204, 229, 252–53, 256, 259, 263, 265–67, 276
Gxd, riddle of, 1,

Haddon, Mark
  The Curious Incident of the Dog in the Night-Time, 34, 260
Haecceitas, 23–24, 139, 218, 270, 272–90, 299, 341, 349
Hansen, Ron, 200, 205
Happé, Francesca, 38–39, 58, 72, 76, 86, 100–101, 113, 117, 280
Hearing Voices Network, 200
Hegel, Georg Wilhelm Friedrich, 11, 224, 238–62, 308–9
Heidegger, Martin, 11, 90, 103, 109–10, 132, 187–96, 201, 220, 232, 243, 259, 279, 312
Hell, 50, 224, 246–48, 255, 264–65, 356
Heresy, 2, 49, 54, 148, 161, 199, 212, 224, 233, 253

Hermeneutics, 7–9, 24–26, 46, 65–67, 72–73, 81, 83–84, 90, 92, 96–109, 111–18, 121–25, 130, 132–35, 144–46, 154, 157, 164, 170, 173, 177, 188, 207, 212, 216–19, 222, 225–32, 237, 244, 249, 254, 279, 282, 294, 299–303, 310, 317, 319–20, 332–33, 339–41, 348
Hölderlin, Friedrich, 201, 203–5
Holy Fool, the, 67–73, 89–90, 111, 116, 136, 140, 166, 180, 186, 199, 225, 232, 291, 302, 311, 316, 322, 331
Hopkins, Gerard Manley, 58–59, 116, 279, 281–98, 357
  As Kingfishers Catch Fire, 116, 288
  Carrion Comfort, 282
  Dun Scotus' Oxford, 284
  Inversnaid, 295–96
  Journals and Notes, 285–88, 295
  May Magnificat, The, 293–94
  No Worst, There is None, 282
  Windhover, The, 290–93,
  Wreck of the Deutschland, The, 281–82
Hyperessentiality, 188, 191, 194–96, 207

Incarnational Metaphor. *See* Metaphor, Incarnational
Ingham, Mary Beth, 276, 278
Inscape, 283, 285–86, 296, 298
Instress, 283, 285–86, 288
Intense World Syndrome, 39–41
Irony, 196, 307–16, 324, 330, 334, 347
Iser, Wolfgang, 140–43
Islets of Ability, 38
Isolation, 32, 60, 84, 179, 254–55, 258, 262, 276, 320

Jackson, Luke, 76, 294
James, William, 49
Jasper, David, xi-xiv, 52, 54, 56, 176, 199, 230–32, 355
Jeanrond, Werner, 8, 97, 103
Jesus, 5–6, 14, 24–27, 48–50, 53, 65, 73, 81, 92–93, 116, 128, 132, 158, 167, 170, 172, 224–28, 230–31, 236–37, 241, 246, 248–49, 252, 255–58, 261, 263–66, 269, 277, 323, 329, 336, 351, 357–58
John of the Cross, Saint, 20, 147, 149, 158, 164, 180–86, 197–201, 203–6, 234, 247
Jongleur, 69–70
Jouissance, 130, 135, 142
Joyce, James, 216–17, 224, 264, 301, 352

Kairos, 81

INDEX

Kanner, Leo, 29–30, 85
Kataphatic Theology, 19–20, 145–47, 150, 152, 168–69, 175–76, 182, 201, 218, 358
Kelsey, David H., 17–18, 213–14, 227
Kenosis, 55, 91, 93, 117, 130, 133, 142–43, 188, 220, 241, 245–46, 248–49, 251–53, 258, 261, 267, 332, 350–51, 157
Kenotic Incarnational Metaphor, 117, 142–43, 241, 245–49, 251–53, 261, 267
Kenotic Sacrifice, 93, 133, 188, 241, 245–49, 251
Kerr, Fergus, 121–28
Kerygmatic Language, 119–20, 246
Kierkegaard, Søren, 12–13, 17
Knox, T. Malcolm, 239
Krisis, 13, 26, 50, 93, 227, 233, 346
Kubo and the Two Strings, 136

Lawson, Wendy, 88
Leavis, F. R., 283
Levinson, Barry, 38, 124
Liberal Theology, 9–13, 26
Literal-mindedness, 32–33, 68, 73–75, 90, 108, 114, 117, 266
Llewellyn, John, 289–90
Logocentrism, 128–29, 132, 240
Logos, 6–7, 24, 128, 132–34, 139, 144–45, 240–43

Love, 23, 41, 44, 45, 47–48, 59, 61–62, 64, 74, 77, 84–85, 89, 91–92, 94, 102, 109 104, 148, 154–55, 159–60, 163, 174, 177, 179–80, 182, 185, 186, 191, 193, 197–98, 200, 223, 225, 232, 244–46, 248, 251–54, 259, 261, 264–65, 269, 278, 281, 293, 297, 314, 343, 350–51, 359
LTA (Literature, Theology and the Arts), 52–53, 55, 56, 144, 177, 350, 355
Lucas, George R., 239
Lucas, Hans-Christian, 239

McDonagh, Enda, 143
McFarlane, James, 301, 304
McGinn, Bernard, 274
Madness, 173–74, 201, 203, 302, 315–16, 322–24, 343, 348
Markram, H & K., 40
Marion, Jean Luc, 153, 167, 186, 323–24
Meister Eckhart. *See* Eckhart, Meister
Merton, Thomas, 18–19, 144–45, 268–70, 279
Metaphor
  Autistic, 85, 101, 139–40, 206–7, 331
  Dead, 113–14, 131, 136, 139, 145–46, 309, 331

Incarnational, 95, 97, 107, 112–13, 115, 117, 126–43, 145, 147, 155–57, 176–79, 185, 187–88, 191, 194, 199, 202, 207–8, 217–23, 237, 244–45, 249–53, 260, 264–67, 293, 299–300, 310, 312, 324, 331–33, 341, 345, 350

Literal, 84, 89–91, 95–97, 100–104, 109, 111, 114–17, 120–22, 127, 131, 136, 141, 146–47, 154–56, 173, 176–78, 207, 218–19, 222, 312, 331

Ostensive, 98, 100–102, 111–12, 114, 155, 199, 219, 221, 281, 291, 293

Resurrected, 113–14, 133, 136, 141, 331

Self-negating, 153, 188

Metaphore Vive, 113, 133, 138

Metaphysics, 110, 119, 126–27, 129, 131–35, 137, 140–41, 187, 190–92, 220, 228, 240, 277–79, 309–11, 315, 326, 334–37, 344, 347–48

Miller, Hugh, 10

Mindblindness, 30–33, 73–75, 84–85, 91, 105–6, 124, 154, 206, 232, 303, 319–20, 354, 356, 358

Mindfulness of Separation, 61, 85–86, 91, 93–94, 102–7, 122, 131, 133, 138–39, 142, 154–55, 177–79, 185–86, 191, 193, 202, 206–7, 219, 223, 237, 244, 249–50, 252–53, 258–59, 264, 301, 306, 310–12, 337, 340–42, 349–50

Mindreading, 105, 123, 303, 315–19, 338, 348, 358

Monsignor Quixote, 171–74

Muers, Rachel, 215, 227

Mute Language, 185–94, 207

Mysticism, 7, 14, 20–21, 50–51, 53, 57, 67, 74, 77–78, 91–92, 94, 104, 122, 135, 146–60, 166–70, 181, 187–88, 194, 196, 200, 208, 212, 218, 243, 248, 250, 254, 258, 265–66, 269, 274, 287, 294, 313, 323–24, 326–27, 343, 349, 350

Mythical Autism, 16, 38, 46, 56, 59, 66–67, 75, 83–85, 89, 97, 102–4, 109, 111–16, 121–23, 128, 140, 154–56, 178–86, 193–94, 207, 237, 244, 249, 252, 270, 279, 281–82, 293–94, 299, 303, 315

Mythical Hermeneutic, 25, 67, 97

INDEX 417

Myth/mythology, 3–4, 7–8, 18, 22, 25–27, 45–49, 56–62, 66, 78–83, 85, 92–94, 96, 111, 117, 134–39, 150, 154, 182, 212, 214, 216–17, 227, 231, 235, 238, 240–42, 245, 247, 253, 257, 264, 275, 279, 301. *See also* Demythologisation, Mythical Autism, Mythical Hermeneutic, Remythologisation, White Mythology

Naïveté, second, 73, 281, 332, 351
Natural Theology, 9–11
Negation, 21, 149–56, 183, 188, 199–206, 234, 238, 243, 251, 253
Neurodiversity, 63–64
Neurotribe, 39, 63, 65, 92, 97, 138, 210, 244, 294, 297
Neurotypicality, 2, 30, 37, 39, 41, 57, 75, 77, 99–100, 102–3, 105–8, 112, 117–18, 123, 125, 141, 169, 223, 225, 260–61, 280–81, 300, 306, 317–19, 323, 332–33, 342, 345–46, 348, 353, 355, 361
  Absolute, 123
Nicholas of Cusa, 177,
Nietzsche, Friedrich, 25, 50, 137, 224, 226–29, 233, 246–47, 249, 253, 261, 305, 310, 314

Nonbeing, 215, 245, 247, 250–54, 260, 324
Nonsense, 16, 231, 297, 354

O'Brien, B., 262
O'Meara, Thomas F., 285
Ontological Difference, 186, 191, 220, 259, 275, 279, 324
Onto-theology, 134
Optimism, Franciscan, 276, 278, 292
Orestes, 348
Other, Absolute, 275
Otto, Rudolf, 219

Paley, William, 10
Panentheism, 313
Pantheism, 248, 312–13, 328
Pattison, George, 215
Perichoresis, 74, 91–92, 144, 244
Phenomenology, 11, 78–79
Pirandello, Luigi, 59, 140, 299–349, 350, 352
  Art e Conscienza d'Oggi [Art and Consciousness Today], 306–7, 314
  Enrico IV [Henry IV], 303–5
  Il Fu Mattia Pascal [The Late Mattia Pascal], 300, 322, 332–46, 347–49
  Sei Caratteri in Cerca D'Autore [Six Characters in Search of an Author], 303–4, 346–47

Uno, Nessuno e Centimila [One, No-one and One Hundred Thousand], 140, 300, 305–6, 315–32, 333–34, 337, 340, 341–44, 347, 352
Pitch, 287–90
Plato, 22, 149–51, 154, 182, 207, 274, 348
Plenum, 159, 251, 254, 257
Poetics, 216, 240, 283
Post-Cartesian Theology, 122, 266
Profane, 79–80, 212, 216–24, 234, 237, 240, 261, 264. *See also* Sacred Profane, the
Psychopathy, 28–29, 42–44, 47, 77, 87, 91, 338–39, 345

Quidditas, 23, 277–79, 281, 287

Rain Man, 38, 124
Ramsey, Ian, 90, 118–21, 127, 130, 223, 266
Rancière, Jacques, 257
Raschke, Carl, 351
Reader Response Theory, 170
Relativism, 307–13
Relevance Theory, 100
Remythologization, 27
Restricted and Repetitive Behaviors and Interests (RRBIs), 30, 36–39, 58, 74, 76, 84, 86, 89, 107, 219, 280, 354

Resurrection, 65, 112–15, 141, 175, 236, 238, 241, 246, 253, 323, 331, 335, 341–42
Resurrected Metaphor. *See* Metaphor, Resurrected
Ricœur, Paul, 73, 113, 133–34, 281, 311
Rinaldi, Tania, 39–40
Robinson, Bishop John A. T., 17, 211
Rolt, C. E., 20, 149
Rousseau, Jean-Jacques, 129
RRBIs. *See* Restricted and Repetitive Behaviors and Interests
Rushdie, Salman, 101

Sacrament, 115, 158–59, 175, 220, 257, 269, 275–76, 279, 293–94, 335. *See also* Universal Sacrament
Sacred Profane, the, 216–24, 237, 240, 264
Sally-Anne Test, the, 30–31
Salvation History, 241, 245–46, 251, 256–57
Satan, 50, 233–36
Savantism, 38, 117, 124, 126–27
Scharlemann, Robert P., 62
Second Naïveté. *See* Naïveté, second
Secularisation, 9, 17, 212, 216, 237
Self-Embodiment of God, the, 238–49, 256–58, 264–66

Self-Righteous Suicide, 230–35, 246
Sensory Connoisseur, 39, 74, 86, 107, 219, 259, 273, 279–81, 332
Sensory Delight, 58, 220
Sensory Sensitivity, 34–35, 39, 41, 58, 74, 76, 86, 295–96
Silberman, Steve, 63, 65, 67, 92, 138, 294
Silence, 53–54, 64, 103, 122, 126–27, 152, 154, 186–87, 191–94, 208, 215, 235, 240–45, 251–52, 256–60, 262–67, 276
Smart, Ninian, 79
Sorge, 189
Soteriology, 13–14
Space of Literature, the, 54, 112, 117, 142, 145, 177, 187–89, 192–94, 198–206, 263
Special Interests, 4, 35–38, 74, 219, 260, 353
Spectrum, Autism, 28–44
Speech, 19, 98, 100, 131–32, 151, 175, 186, 192–93, 241–44, 251–54, 256, 258–59, 262–65, 321
Sperber, Dan, 100
Spivak, Gayatri Chakravorty, 129, 196
Starr, Mirabai, 156–58, 161, 163, 170, 199
Stewart, Catriona, 153
Stillmann, William, 78
Stimming, 38, 86

Suspension of Disbelief, 56, 176, 294, 329, 348
SWAN, 353
Sweeney, Jon, 172
Swinton, John, 41, 63–65, 67, 78, 91, 94, 351, 356
System of a Down, 229–38, 246
Szalavitz, Maia, 353

Taylor, Mark C., 48, 53–55, 130, 132, 140, 187–88, 195–96, 198, 200, 205, 355
Teresa of Ávila, 20–21, 146–49, 156–80, 181–83, 185, 197–207, 282, 289, 342, 349
 Interior Castle, the, 147–49, 156–80, 197–200, 202, 204–7
 Life of Saint Teresa by Herself, 157–59, 161, 163, 166, 171, 176, 197–98, 200–207
Theatre of the Absurd, 59, 300–301, 311, 347
Theonomy, 215, 242
Theory of Mind Mechanism (TOMM), 31, 43, 72–73, 105, 123, 338
Thatness. See *Quidditas*
'Thin' Places, 271–72
Thisness. See *Haecceitas*
Tillich, Paul, 16–18, 24–25, 49, 51, 153, 201, 211–17, 223–24, 227, 242–43, 251, 259

TIME Magazine, 210–11
Trevett, Christine, 68, 71
Turner, Denys, 14, 21, 50, 150–53, 158–60, 162, 165–66, 175, 184–85, 187, 194, 200, 204, 206, 275–76
Tustin, Frances, 86
Tyler, Peter, 161, 199

Universal Sacrament, 220, 238, 240–41, 292–93
Univocity, 22–23, 275–77, 279
Uselessness, 117
  Apophatic, 197–99

Vahanian, Gabriel, 211
Vattimo, Gianni, 309–12
de Victor, Hugh, 275–76

Walton, Heather, 54–55, 352, 355
Weak Central Coherence (WCC), 37, 124
Weak Thought, 309, 311–12
White Mythology, 133–40
Williams, Charles, 286–87, 292
Williams, Donna, 33, 88
Williams, Rowan, 130, 161–62, 346, 351
Williams, Thomas, 275, 278
Wilson, Deirdre, 100
Wing, Lorna, 29, 34–35, 41–42, 60–61
Winterbottom, Michael, 173
Wittgenstein, Ludwig, 90, 122–28, 132, 138, 188

Zager, Dianne, 140

Lightning Source UK Ltd.
Milton Keynes UK
UKHW051820060123
414863UK00012B/154